The Theatre of the French Revolution

The final scene in Marie-Joseph Chénier's *Charles IX* as produced at the Théâtre-Français, November 4, 1789.

The Theatre of the French Revolution

BY MARVIN CARLSON

Cornell University Press

ITHACA, NEW YORK

CORNELL UNIVERSITY PRESS

First published 1966

Library of Congress Catalog Card Number: 66-16740

PRINTED AND BOUND IN THE UNITED STATES OF AMERICA

BY THE MAPLE PRESS COMPANY

Preface

THE theatre, the most public of the arts, was affected tremendously by the social turbulence of the decade of the French Revolution. It was a period of frantic dramatic activity—new dramas numbered in the thousands and new theatres in the hundreds—and the disorder of the time was clearly reflected in the careers of dramatic artists and in the productions of theatrical companies in Paris. As shifts in political opinion and power grew more frequent and violent, the milieu in which plays were presented altered from week to week, even from day to day. For those in the public eye, survival became a matter of choosing obscurity or adaptability. The theatres had not even this choice. Obscurity for men whose only means of livelihood was public performance simply meant death in a different form, so adaptability was their only recourse. Each character, each word of every play, was subject to the rule of the changing governments, and of the fickle and violent mob. "The actors became weathercocks," says the actor Abraham-Joseph Fleury in his memoirs, but so likewise did the author and the producers, if they wished to survive. Every major upheaval, indeed every significant shift in political opinion, was reflected with remarkable alacrity in the theatres of Paris—in their audiences, actors, producers, authors, and the theatre organizations themselves.

The Comédie Française, the first theatre of France, naturally holds the center of interest, and its day-to-day history alone is an excellent index to the progress of the Revolution. Yet its story must share attention with the "thousand and one" theatres that sprang up in this decade to challenge the old monopoly, with colorful entrepreneurs such as Mlle. Montansier, Claude Ruggieri, and the ambitious Sageret, all of whom made adaptability an art. Part of the story also must be devoted to the great crowd of lesser figures, actors and other artists, who added significant pieces to the complex, fascinating, and terrible mosaic of the times.

This was a decade which saw the meteoric rise of the great actor François Joseph Talma, of the Revolutionary playwright Marie-Joseph

Chénier, who helped launch the actor on his career, and of the neoclassic artist Jacques Louis David, who helped Talma in his campaign for authentic costumes on the Parisian stage. It saw the Comédie almost destroyed by the loss of its century-old monopoly, by schism, and finally by the imprisonment and threatened execution of its actors. It saw a tremendous increase in theatrical production, much of it clearly inspired by the stirring events of the hour. The Revolution left its mark everywhere on the theatre, and from time to time it is not surprising to find that the theatre left its mark on the Revolution. So we find, for example, a troupe of actors setting off to war in stage chariots and presenting battle re-creations on fields where the blood was scarcely dry. Or again, we see the leaders of the Revolution concerning themselves with great theatrical festivals, offering to the masses entertainments such as only monarchs had previously enjoyed.

The theatres themselves remain the focal points of this history, and the material within individual chapters of the book is organized as far as possible around the separate houses. Hopefully, this will help clarify developments in an era when theatres opened, closed, and changed names and directors with bewildering rapidity. A chart in the Appendix will provide further orientation. Since the history does focus on the theatre as an active art rather than on drama as a literary form, the plays, their literary antecedents, and their place in the development of the dramatic genres are discussed only when such concerns help to illuminate the interaction between theatrical production and Revolutionary activity.

The great number of plays of the period which have been preserved have provided much useful detail, but far more valuable have been reports on the stories behind the plays, how and why they were presented and how they were received. Here diaries and journals of the period, especially those of actors such as Louise Fusil and Abraham-Joseph Fleury, have been of particular help. The contemporary history of the Comédie Française by Charles Guillaume Etienne and Alphonse Martainville, if sometimes biased, is still invaluable as a day-by-day record of Revolutionary incidents. In the early years of our own century, detailed studies of lesser theatres have appeared, such as L. Henry Lecomte's history of the Variétés Amusantes and Louis Pericaud's study of the Beaujolais. Thanks to such studies, one may now trace the fortunes not only of the major houses, as Frederick Hawkins does in his *The French Stage in the Eighteenth Century* (surely the most complete work on the subject now in English), but also of many minor theatres, which were a tremendously significant part of the Revolutionary theatre. In the chapters that follow, the contribution of the smaller houses will be indicated by selected examples, chosen for both interest and representativeness. General trends in stage scenery and costume at major and minor theatres are also noted, although detailed analysis of production techniques lies outside the scope of this volume.

To understand the theatre of the Revolution, the reader will of course need a general historical orientation. Hence the major shifts in political climate are described, but further details are added only where they seem most helpful, since data on the period are so rich that the primary study could easily be submerged by its background.

The illustrations in this book have been selected to represent many aspects of the Revolutionary theatre—actors, authors, costumes, scenes from plays, theatre exteriors, interiors, and floor plans—plus festivals and other related material. These illustrations have been made available through the generosity of the Yale Theatre Collection, the Ohio State University Library, the Cornell University Library, the Bibliothèque de l'Arsenal, and the publishers Firmin Didot et Cie, and Ernest Flammarion et Cie.

Many friends and colleagues have provided me with help and inspiration in the course of my investigation, but I should like to express particular gratitude to Professor Anthony Caputi for his early encouragement and later reading and criticism of my manuscript. The many hours of work contributed by my wife, Patricia, toward the preparation of the final manuscript also merit special notice.

Although the research for this study has been done at a number of institutions, I must particularly cite my debt to the Andrew Dickson White collection of materials on the French Revolution at the Cornell University Library. This fine collection, including hundreds of plays and scores of studies of the drama or related subjects, allowed me to do much of my basic research in Ithaca.

Finally, I wish to express thanks to those publishers and institutions who have granted permission to reproduce illustrations; acknowledgment is given with each illustration.

M. C.

Ithaca, New York
November 1965

Contents

	Preface	v
	Prologue: *Le Mariage de Figaro*	1
I	Talma and *Charles IX* July–December, 1789	7
II	Schism in the Comédie January–December, 1790	34
III	The Theatres Set Free January–June, 1791	73
IV	The Nation in Danger July, 1791–August, 1792	94
V	The Fall of the Comédie August, 1792–September, 1793	129
VI	The Theatres under the Terror September, 1793–July, 1794	169
VII	The Reaction August, 1794–November, 1795	207
VIII	Three Comédies November, 1795–October, 1797	236
IX	The Comédie Reunited October, 1797–June, 1799	259
	Epilogue: The End of Liberty	280
	Chart of Major Theatres of the Revolution	288
	Notes	293
	Selected Bibliography	309
	Index	313

Illustrations

PLATES

	The final scene in Marie-Joseph Chénier's *Charles IX*	*frontispiece*
I	The closing of the Opéra, July, 1789 *facing page*	50
II	Jean-François Ducis	51
III	Marie-Joseph Chénier	51
IV	Interior of the Richelieu	82
V	View from the stage of the Richelieu	82
VI	Fair theatres of the late eighteenth century	83
VII	The Théâtre-Français, Rue de Richelieu	83
VIII	The Festival of Federation, July 14, 1790	114
IX	The arrival of Voltaire's remains at the Panthéon	115
X	The Théâtre de la Nation	146
XI	The Salle Favart	146
XII	François-Joseph Talma	147
XIII	The Festival of the Supreme Being, June, 1794	178
XIV	A member of the gilded youth	179
XV	Plaster bust of Marat	179
XVI	The foyer of the Théâtre Montansier	210
XVII	The Théâtre du Marais	210
XVIII	The Tivoli Gardens	211
XIX	Caroline Petit-Vanhove	211

FIGURES

1	The actor Beauvisage	11
2	The dinner of the King's Guards, Versailles, 1789	25

3 Plan and elevation of the Théâtre-Français Comique et Lyrique 63
4 Exterior of the Théâtre de Monsieur, Rue Feydeau 86
5 Interior of the Théâtre Molière 91
6 Plan and interior of the Vaudeville 118
7 An entr'acte at Nicolet's theatre 167
8 Théâtre National de la Rue de la Loi 173
9 Plans of the Gaîté and the Ambigu-Comique 226
10 The Théâtre-Français 242
11 Map of central Paris during the Revolutionary period, showing the location of the principal theatres 268

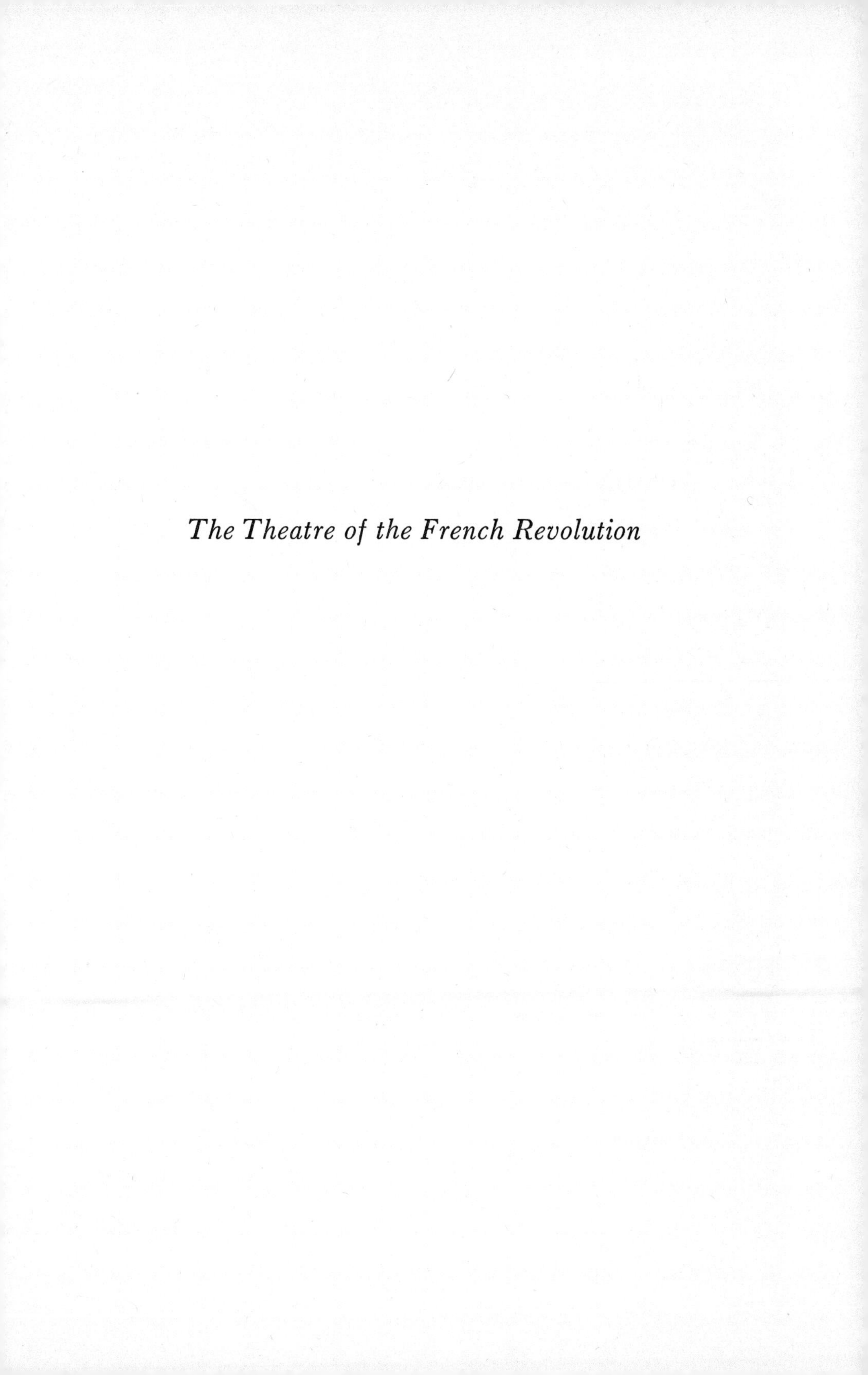

The Theatre of the French Revolution

PROLOGUE

Le Mariage de Figaro

IN 1782 the King's Players, the Comédie Française, first performed in a new theatre erected for them near the Luxembourg Palace. The architects, Marie-Joseph Peyre and Charles de Wailly, were widely praised for their work, and especially for the lavish interior, but many felt that the plays the company brought to this new home were by no means equally deserving of unqualified praise. The active repertoire, dominated by serious works, was badly unbalanced. It is true that Molière and Lesage were revived with some frequency, interspersed with elegantly phrased commentaries on contemporary social customs, but the public of the time found Molière too boisterous and unrefined and the comedies of their contemporaries cold and sterile. As a result, a number of years had passed without the production of any comedy of lasting interest.

At this point Pierre Augustin Caron de Beaumarchais, whose *Barbier de Seville* had been a great success in 1775, came forward with a new play which seemed destined to infuse the theatre anew with comic spirit. *Le Mariage de Figaro*, a continuation of the adventures of the characters introduced in Beaumarchais' earlier play, was readily accepted by the Comédie and passed on to Jean-Pierre Lenoir, the lieutenant general of police, for official approval. Lenoir hesitated. The work unquestionably had merit, but it fairly bristled with references to inflammatory contemporary issues—the powers of the police, freedom of discussion, and the privileges of the aristocracy. The intent of the piece in spite of this did not appear to be revolutionary, and its author had even been of great service to the nation on various confidential missions in the past. On the other hand, these were unstable times, and such sentiments, publicly expressed in the national theatre, might have serious repercussions. At last Lenoir put the problem before Louis XVI himself. Jeanne Louise de Campan, who read the manuscript to him, describes his reaction in her *Mémoires:* "Detestable!" he cried. "This play must never be given. The man mocks everything that should be respected in the government. The Bastille would have to be torn down before the presentation of this play could be anything but a dangerous folly."[1]

As a bourgeois who had made himself noticed at court, Beaumarchais had gained the suspicion of his own class and the scorn of the nobility. He had therefore learned how to thrive on opposition, and he did not shrink even from engaging his sovereign. He went about repeating, "The King does not want *Le Mariage de Figaro* to be performed—therefore, it shall be performed."[2] Well aware of the growing resistance to authority among the populace, Beaumarchais did not find it at all difficult to represent himself to them as the victim of arbitrary and tyrannical suppression. Yet he knew well enough, of course, that he could count on much more than the support of the general public. Marie Antoinette and her friends were known to favor the play, as did the Comte d'Artois, the King's second brother. Moreover, the shrewd author began to enlist support even among the very group most directly threatened by the play—the aristocracy. His work had by this time gained a certain notoriety as a piece of dangerous and subversive tendencies. It thus became forbidden fruit, most attractive to the leaders of the capital's literary salons. Soon Beaumarchais was deluged with requests for private readings. He feigned reluctance, explaining that he did not want to give too much currency to a drama forbidden by the King himself, but he let slip no opportunity to read his play. Mme. de Campan informs us that almost daily the leaders of fashion were heard to say that they were going or had been to hear Beaumarchais' play. As the author expected, the demand to see the comedy staged soon came from all quarters.

The increased pressures for the play culminated in an invitation from the Grand Duke of Russia for Beaumarchais to premiere his work in St. Petersburg. Beaumarchais declined, for the honor of France, he explained, but he took care to see that the offer was heard of at Versailles. Not to be outdone by the Russians, the Queen then arranged for a "private performance" for herself and her party at the Menus-Plaisirs in Paris, with actors from the Comédie. It was generally hoped that the announcement of this venture as private and its open endorsement by the Queen would free the performance from the King's veto.

The plan seemed to work. Rehearsals were openly begun and the play announced for June 13, 1783. The day arrived with no word from the sovereign, and a triumphant throng descended upon the theatre. Five or six hundred coaches filled the streets near-by. Then, half an hour before the curtain, a special messenger from the King arrived backstage with word that if the play were presented, it would be "under pain of incurring His Majesty's indignation." The actors had no choice but to cancel the performance. Mme. de Campan assures us that the words "oppression" and "tyranny" were never shouted more bitterly than at the news of this development, and rioting crowds surrounded the theatre for the remainder of the night.

This setback only whetted the desire of most of the court to see the notorious play, and the Comte de Vaudreuil organized another production, on a much smaller scale, at his château. This project succeeded, and in September of 1783 most of the court at last witnessed *Le Mariage de Figaro*. The ballroom of the Château de Gennevilliers was so crowded that many ladies of the court felt faint, and one of them, Elisabeth Vigée-Lebrun, recounts that Beaumarchais himself knocked out several windows with his cane to aid the ventilation, giving one of the court wits occasion to remark, "He has broken the windows in more ways than one."[3]

This production at Gennevilliers might have been expected to lessen pressures on the King to permit the play, but on the contrary, it gained new adherents to Beaumarchais' cause. Louis called in a series of five censors to read the play, but instead of requiring changes, they joined in its praise. The King, feeling himself betrayed on all sides, finally consented to a public performance, having no hope left but the rather faint one that the piece might fail. The Comédie Française announced that the long-suppressed play would be performed on April 27, 1784, and a crowd such as Paris had rarely seen assembled in front of their new theatre on that date. "Many hours before the opening of the ticket office," the actor Abraham-Joseph Fleury recounts, "I really believe that half the population of Paris was at the doors."[4] Even princes of the blood besieged the author for tickets. As always, great crowds of valets were present early to obtain seats for their masters, but now these were almost lost in the mass of commoners who sought admittance to a play which was rumored to be so suited to their sympathies. Ordinarily the box office opened at three o'clock, two and one half hours before the performance, but well before that hour the eager crowd overcame all restraint. The guards at the entrances were pushed aside, the iron bars which blocked the entrances broken down, and the doors of the theatre forced open. Most of the crowd was unable to procure tickets in the rush, and many simply threw their money at ushers as they passed.

For those who could push their way inside, the interior presented a scene of the greatest confusion. The huge circular house was already crowded with people. No less than three hundred persons were dining in the boxes, having procured their tickets privately and entered by the stage door. "Our theatre," Fleury noted, "might have been taken for a tavern."[5] The nation's proudest aristocracy had begged invitations from various players and filled their private loges. The pit was a sea of people, and so great was the press of bodies that few indeed were able to sit on the benches which were the new theatre's major innovation. These merely provided a higher place to stand.

The huge audience greeted Beaumarchais' work with delight from the very first scene. The allusions which had so disturbed the King were hailed with sustained applause. No efforts had been spared to make the production a success, and the first players of the Comédie filled its parts. Marie Sainval, the tragic actress then most in vogue, had at Beaumarchais' request accepted the role of the Countess Almaviva, wherein she showed a surprising mastery in another genre. The great Jean Larive, apparently not wishing tragedy to be represented on this important occasion by Mlle. Sainval alone, asked for the minor part of Grippe-Soleil. François René Molé, versatile, polished, and one of the pillars of the society, played the Count. The popular Joseph Jean Dazincourt was Figaro. Jean-Henri Dugazon, now building a reputation as the wit of the Comédie, played Brid'oison. Denis Desessarts, grown tremendously fat in his advanced years but still master of a rich comic sense, portrayed Bartholo. Chérubin was portrayed by Jeanne Adelaide Olivier, a young and very pretty actress whose death shortly after, at the age of eighteen, was a great loss to the company. Ernest Vanhove and Jean-Baptiste Bellemont filled the secondary roles of Bazile annd Antonio. Yet amid this impressive array of talent, it was a comparative unknown who took the first honors. Louise Contat, for whom the part of Suzanne had been written, justified the hopes of Beaumarchais and of old Pierre-Louis Préville, her tutor, and emerged from the premiere as one of the great actresses of the Comédie.

The play, contrary to the King's hopes, ran for a triumphant seventy-five nights, and people came from distant parts of the country to applaud its revolutionary sentiments. In a time when public defiance of authority was steadily increasing, the play's popularity was most embarrasing, but the King realized that any action to remove its more inflammatory passages would now only give new weapons to the malcontents. It is likely, however, that some royal encouragement was behind the various attacks on Beaumarchais' character and personal life which now began to appear in the *Journal de Paris*. The author remained silent for a time, but finally was goaded into printing an imprudent reply which his enemies used to arouse the King to action. Beaumarchais was arrested and imprisoned, not in the Bastille, as might be expected, but in Saint-Lazare, a detention house for juvenile offenders.

As Louis apparently planned, this action made the author look ridiculous, rather than martyred. Even so, within a few days enough sympathy had been stimulated for him that Louis ordered his release. As if to prove once and for all that he bore no grudge, Louis even permitted *Figaro*'s performance at Versailles, with the Queen herself and the Comte d'Artois in the cast. After this victory, Beaumarchais attempted, unsuccessfully as it turned out, to retire from the public eye. On March 8, 1786, he married and soon after retired, having amassed a comfortable fortune. He now devoted himself to planning a sumptuous home in which to pass his last years. In June of 1787 he purchased a lot almost two acres in size in the Saint-Antoine district and engaged the noted architect Lemoyne to draw up grandiose plans for a structure which eventually cost over a million and a half francs. No one has ever explained why Beaumarchais chose for his pleasure dome this strange location, on the edge of one of Paris' worst slums and a few hundred yards from the Bastille. Perhaps his recent experiences had turned him toward the people (all of the profits from *Le Mariage de Figaro* were given to charity), yet it seems odd that he would demonstrate such feeling by constructing in a blighted area a rich home that could only emphasize the poverty around it, acting as an insult and a challenge to the populace of that restless district.

The house was about half completed in 1789 when the States-General convened. Beaumarchais witnessed the event with joy, for, more optimistic than most of his friends, he felt certain that a peaceful settlement of the abuses he had helped to expose was imminent. After his imprisonment at Saint-Lazare, Beaumarchais' public image was never quite the same, and he did not seek to become a deputy, but kept at a distance, observing events and occupying himself with his new home. For all his experience with court caprices, he was surprised by the reckless actions of the aristocracy in the face of popular demands, and the sudden onrush of events that swept Paris in July, 1789, came as a brutal if not totally unexpected shock to him.

After the tempestuous night of July 14, which Beaumarchais spent in his still-unfinished new home, watching his neighbors of the Saint-Antoine quarter storm the near-by Bastille, the dramatist realized that the peaceful last years he had planned would never be his. He launched himself into the whirl of activity that would last until his death by taking part in the demolition of the former prison and the clearing of the ground on which it had stood.[6] As he moved about among the workmen engaged in this task during the weeks that followed, there must surely have echoed in his mind a phrase spoken only a few years before by a monarch now seated precariously on a tottering throne: "The Bastille would have to be torn down before the presentation of this play could be anything but a dangerous folly."

I

Talma and *Charles IX*

July–December, 1789

ALTHOUGH indications of the calamities to come had appeared in the theatres, as they had appeared in many aspects of French life, before 1789, the eve of the Revolution found the world of the theatre in a period of relative calm and stability. For over a century Paris had consistently enjoyed theatrical excellence unknown elsewhere on the continent. Only there could one find daily dramatic performances and troupes of seasoned actors organized, protected, and supported by the government, since Louis XIV had made the theatre, like everything else, an instrument of policy. He encouraged it, as he encouraged all the arts, as a means not only of glorifying his own reign but also of soothing and settling the turbulent spirits of a nation still seething from the upheavals of the Fronde.

Thus it happened that toward the end of the seventeenth century scattered performers and small companies were drawn together, organized, and given both official support and a national status. The first theatre so honored was the Opéra. In 1669, Louis XIV granted a certain René Perrin, author of the first French opera, permission to establish the Académie Royale de Musique, a home for that genre in Paris. Perrin soon discovered that the production of operas was more expensive than he had expected, and he ended in debtors' prison, but his successor, Jean Baptiste Lully, proved a more astute man of business. His reorganized Académie Royale de Musique, also called the Opéra, replaced Perrin's foundering venture after only three years. During the confusion in Molière's company following the master's death in 1673, Lully gained that theatre for the opera, and although the expenses of this first national theatre remained tremendous, it had by 1789 already survived two terrible fires and produced the works of Jean-Philippe Rameau and Christoph Willibald Gluck, Lully's major successors.

Molière's dispossessed troupe, in the meantime, rallied behind Charles Varlet de La Grange and merged with the Théâtre du Marais to assume undisputed primacy in the spoken drama. Louis XIV officially adopted this company in 1680, calling it the Comédie Française, granting pensions, and guaranteeing it a certain financial stability. For the next century this theatre enjoyed a virtual monopoly in the production of comedy and tragedy. The greatest treasures of the French repertoire were its undisputed property and the most brilliant actors in France made up its company. The Comédie, the most significant and influential of the Parisian theatres, was naturally one of those most severely affected by the vicissitudes of Revolutionary production; the fortunes of this theatre—its actors, directors, and playwrights—are central to the history of the Revolutionary theatre.

Only one other theatre had gained official governmental protection by the latter part of the eighteenth century—the Comédie Italienne, a venture with a history as long, but not so respectable, as that of the Opéra or the Comédie Française. Italian comedians had toured regularly in France since the late sixteenth century, but no troupe settled in Paris until 1660, when a company began alternating with Molière's troupe in the Palais-Royal, expanding to daily presentations only after La Grange merged with the Marais company. During the years which followed, the Italians retained their name, but began introducing French into their repertoire—first lines, then scenes, finally whole plays. The old Italian farcical and satiric tradition was not deserted, however, and traditional improvised comedies alternated with modern works by such writers as Pierre Marivaux, Charles Favart, and Louis-Sébastien Mercier until 1780, when the Italian comedies were finally abandoned. In 1762 the Comédie Italienne had merged with the Opéra-Comique and been granted government support, whereupon it began purging its repertoire, improving its company, and generally making itself worthy of its place as the last of the triumvirate of governmental theatres which dominated French drama in the years before the outbreak of the Revolution.

Since the Comédie Française possessed exclusive rights to all plays by authors no longer living, and in fact to almost all spoken drama, and since the Opéra and Comédie Italienne controlled musical theatre, it would seem that so crushing a monopoly would preclude new theatrical ventures. Such, however, was not the case. Pantomimes, acrobatic demonstrations, and animal acts continued at the fairs; many wealthy Parisians followed the example of their sovereign and installed private theatres in their homes; and, rather more surprising, public theatres were built even in the face of the monopoly.

A few examples will indicate the ingenuity and tenacity employed by these small public theatres to remain alive in such stifling circumstances. Since the end of the sixteenth century, certain minor dramatic efforts had appeared among the rope-dancers, jugglers, magicians, and animal acts at the annual Parisian fairs, especially at the fairs of Saint-Germain and Saint-Laurent, and actors and authors of some talent did not refuse association with them.[1] Such minor theatre entered a new phase in 1759, when Jean-Baptiste Nicolet, a successful actor in and producer of farces at both the famous fairs, obtained permission to rent a permanent location in the Temple district of Paris. His example opened the Boulevard du Temple and near-by streets to similar ventures and established some acts from the hitherto seasonal fairs as regular competition for the national theatres. Nicolet's official permit was granted on his avowed intention to present only acrobats and rope-dancers, so that his performers were barred from singing or even speaking before the public. The fair theatres had been seeking ways to circumvent such restrictions for half a century, however, and Nicolet followed their time-honored procedure of gradually infringing on the regulations without ever making so serious a change as to attract the attention of the authorities. Bits of dialogue slowly crept into the acts, until in five years Nicolet was openly offering farces, comedies, and harlequinades. The official theatres protested, and the director, despite his pleas, was required to return to the terms of his original contract. How seriously he was affected by this reprimand may be seen from the fact that in 1767, when he was again formally ordered to decrease his program, he boasted thirty actors, sixty dancers, twenty musicians, and a repertoire of 250 plays.

In this same year, 1767, a musician and comic actor named Nicolas Médard Audinot left the Comédie Italienne after a bitter quarrel with his directors and fellow actors. His revenge took the form of a small puppet theatre called Les Comédiens de Bois, established near Nicolet, in which the wooden figures performed in caricature the works of

Audinot's former associates. This novelty attracted large audiences at first, but when attendance slackened, Audinot, like Nicolet, began to expand his venture. The puppets gave way to a company of child actors, aged eight to ten, and by 1771 he was presenting opera. The Académie de Musique protested and Audinot, again like Nicolet, was reprimanded; he was forbidden to present singing and dancing on his stage and his orchestra was reduced to four musicians. Audinot accepted the restrictions for a respectable period; then the ages of his actors gradually increased and their presentations slowly enlarged in scope. Within a few years the Ambigu-Comique, as the theatre was named when its wooden actors first disappeared, was again a full-blown rival for the major houses.

Another competing company was the Théâtre des Associés. The "associates" were Jean Baptiste Sallé, a former actor in Nicolet's theatre, and Vienne, popularly known as Beauvisage and Grimacier because of his facial contortions. The Associés was established on the premise that Sallé would provide puppet shows and Beauvisage would grimace during the intermissions, but the now familiar pattern was repeated —the puppets gave way to live actors and the classics were ruthlessly pillaged for their productions. The authorities closed the theatre once, but in 1778 it reopened, soon again offering comedies, tragedies, and dramas as if no restrictions existed. By the beginning of the Revolution, its success was posing a serious threat to Audinot and Nicolet.[2]

Two other so-called puppet theatres deserve mention, located not on the boulevard but in the Palais-Royal, home of the Duc d'Orléans. In 1784 a M. Delomel was given permission to establish a puppet theatre in the palace in honor of the Comte de Beaujolais. The little theatre was given the grandiose title of Les Petits Comédiens de Son Altesse Sérénissime Monseigneur le Comte de Beaujolais, but it was soon understandably nicknamed the Beaujolais. This little venture was at first very popular, but it suffered heavily when a few months after its opening the Duke rented another part of his palace to the entrepreneurs Antoine Gaillard and Poupart Dorfeuille, who opened the Variétés Amusantes, another "puppet" theatre where the puppets appeared only in the announcements. To meet this new competition, the Beaujolais followed the example of others and introduced child actors. Since his permit forbade speaking on his stage, Delomel hit upon the idea of having the children mime the parts with adult actors giving their lines offstage in the wings. This peculiar compromise delighted the public by its novelty, and such crowds were attracted that the Comédie Française once again complained. The police thereupon ruled that

1. The actor Beauvisage. This cofounder of the Théâtre des Associés is shown entertaining with one of the grimaces which were his specialty. (Arthur Pougin, *Dictionnaire du théâtre*. Reproduced by courtesy of Imprimerie Firmin-Didot et Cie.)

Delomel could employ only one actor per role, and could have no singing or speaking, even in the wings. The fickle public went elsewhere, so that Delomel was facing bankruptcy when the Revolution broke out.[3] The Variétés, on the other hand, by dint of performing only three-act plays and avoiding open theft from the Comédie repertoire, managed to keep both its audiences and its good relations with its powerful rival.[4]

Such was the theatrical situation in the years just before the Revolution—three firmly entrenched national theatres, possessing among themselves an almost complete monopoly of all dramatic material, yet increasingly challenged by smaller theatres forced to every sort of subterfuge to present plays. These minor theatres survived and on occasion even prospered, hedged in by a ludicrously complex set of police rulings. Some could let their characters faint or bleed, but not die. Some could let their performers do only acrobatics or pantomime. Two small establishments, the Délassements-Comiques and the Bluettes, were forced to hang a gauze curtain between actors and audience. One amateur theatre in the Rue Saint-Antoine could open only at seven, over an hour after the others, and so on.[5] Still, the police were generally sympathetic to the troubles of the smaller houses, and would wink at infractions of these regulations until the subsidized houses made specific complaints. Thus in each small theatre the chronicle of the pre-Revolutionary years is much the same—a pushing out from the restrictions, police action, a pause, and then a cautious new pushing out. Even with the protection of official authority, the national theatres were hard pressed by these little rivals, and they were not to enjoy that protection much longer.

In early 1789 a new theatre opened which proved the most serious threat to date for the Comédie. Léonard Autié, whose brother was coiffeur to the Queen, obtained permission from Monsieur, the King's brother, to open a new theatre and to present in it Italian operas and "other authorized plays"—a phrase vague enough to give Autié carte blanche. The actors at the Comédie feared this venture, knowing that Paris had long desired a rival first theatre, and appealed to the First Gentlemen of the Chamber, the governmental body in charge of theatrical matters. The First Gentlemen decreed that the new Théâtre de Monsieur could present only comedies of one and two acts, and for a time the danger seemed over.

Autié, checked in one direction, decided to emphasize Italian opera, the nonspoken part of his program. To gain funds for this project, he sold a partnership to Mlle. Montansier, later to become a major figure in Parisian theatre, but at this time directress of the royal theatre at Versailles. No sooner was the partnership formed than quarrels arose. Autié wanted to stage French and Italian opera, vaudeville, and spectacles of all kinds. Montansier felt this program too ambitious to succeed and relinquished her share to Giovanni Battista Viotti, a noted violinist. In the meantime, Autié went to Italy to assemble a company. He brought back some of that country's most highly praised actors and singers, and the theatre had a brilliant opening. The company was presented a contract allowing them to perform in the Tuileries for the next thirty years.[6]

These early months of 1789 were months of tension, excitement, and expectancy in Paris. The opening of the States-General at Versailles, the creation of the National Assembly, and the Tennis Court Oath had raised the populace to a high pitch of political involvement by summer. Despite such diversions, business at the theatres was good, although the national houses continued the familiar complaints about their unsanctioned competitors. Theatre interest among Parisians ran deep, and as we shall see, remained constant even during the dark years to come.

A mysterious gathering of royalist troops around Paris during the first week of July added new tension; but the action which convinced the people of Paris that the aristocrats had betrayed them was the dismissal of the popular minister Jacques Necker on July 11. The King was well aware that the disappearance of this man, generally considered responsible for the present strength of the third estate, would not be well received, but other pressures made this dismissal seem unavoidable. He therefore requested Necker to leave, but to keep his departure a total secret. The King's confidence was justified, for the obliging minister set out without speaking to either friends or family and was soon far from the court. Versailles is only a few miles from Paris, however, and the distance could easily be covered several times in one day. In an atmosphere so charged with suspicion, so volatile a secret could not long be kept. By noon of Saturday, July 12, rumors of the dismissal had appeared in Paris, and the very secrecy of the act encouraged the rumors. Soon it was said that a whole host of ministers had been removed and replaced by men known for their opposition to the popular cause.

The people of Paris thronged that afternoon to the courtyard of the Palais-Royal, long a center for political agitation. There Camille Desmoulins, an unemployed actor, spurred them to action by leaping on a table and shouting: "Citizens, you know that the nation demanded that Necker be kept and that he has been driven away. Can you be so insolently dared? After this, they will dare anything, and perhaps this very night they are plotting a St. Bartholomew's Day for patriots." He urged them to take up arms against the foreign troops that surrounded the city, and took a leaf from one of the garden trees as a sign of identification. Soon the trees were stripped. One of Desmoulins' audience was a certain Maret, a playwright for the near-by Beaujolais, who shouted, "Let all entertainments stop until the soil of France has been purged of the foreign soldiers who threaten us. Let us close the balls, the spectacles, the theatres." With cries of "To arms," the crowd dispersed, while Maret himself went to the Beaujolais to see that his proposal was carried out there.[7]

The letters of Edward Rigby, a visiting Englishman, describe this momentous evening in the theatres. Dr. Rigby had spent the morning at Versailles and gone in the evening to the Comédie Française. Shortly after five, just as the signal was given for the curtain to rise, a disturbance began in the street outside. The curtain remained lowered, and soon a player announced that no play would be given that evening. The audience demanded an explanation, but the actor said only that a people's deputation had arrived to declare that no theatre should open that night. The crowds, pouring from the theatres, joined those already milling about on the boulevards.[8] The mob invaded a wax museum near the Comédie, the Salon de Curtius, and carried off busts of Necker and the Duc d'Orléans, whom rumor threatened with exile. These, draped in black, were then paraded through the streets.

On the morning of July 13, Paris seemed calm once more, and theatre managers, believing that the worst was over, hopefully posted announcements of productions for that evening, but the crisis continued and the theatres remained closed. On July 14, the managers tried again, with less hope. After that, no posters appeared at all.[9] What diversion could attract a public participating in the opening of a new era? Even so, the closure was not a protracted one. On July 15, the King announced to the National Assembly that he was withdrawing his troops from the city. The Marquis de Lafayette, who brought the news, was received with transports of joy. Bailly, president of the Assembly, was appointed mayor of Paris, an action warmly approved by the populace, and on July 17 the King visited the quieted capital, accompanied only by deputies from the three estates and a small retinue. Among those who accompanied him were three actors from the Comédie—Dugazon, Julien Naudet, and Jean Saint-Prix. At the gates of the city, Bailly met his sovereign with the keys to Paris, and the King was cheered wherever he went.

The following day this decree was posted throughout the city:

> Free movement is hereby re-established within Paris and on all highways, so that all public, private, and hired vehicles cannot be stopped by any patrol.
>
> Carriages, of whatever kind, can suffer no constraint within Paris except in the matter of speed.
>
> The theatres will be opened and public promenades frequented as usual.[10]

Despite the decree, it was not until Tuesday, July 21, that the theatres of Paris reopened. The directors and actors of the city met and decided that all proceeds of that opening day in all theatres would be given to the mayor of Paris for distribution among the unfortunates who had suffered the most in "the events of recent days." A number of the theatres gave further benefit performances during the following week.[11]

The influence of the Revolution on the French theatre was profound and entered every aspect of theatrical presentation. An immediate result of the events in July was that the Comédie, which relied so heavily on royal support in struggling against its potential rivals, found that its position was weakened with the weakening of the throne. The burgeoning of new producing groups, one of the most striking effects of the Revolution on the theatre, did not really get under way for some time, but with the eclipse of the aristocracy and the growing power of the lower classes, the position of the Comédie grew more insecure almost daily. Only three days before the fall of the Bastille, the Comédie had finally triumphed in a three-year legal battle with a small society theatre in the Saint-Antoine district which had been usurping the treasures of the national theatre by presenting them as declamation exercises.[12] The Comédiens feared, with some justification, that the new freedom in society would bring new demands for freedom in the theatre, and they gathered their forces for a bitter struggle.

In the boulevard theatres, on the other hand, the new age was greeted with understandable delight. Plancher Valcour, the director of the Délassements-Comiques, represented the directors of all such oppressed little theatres in his reaction to the news of the fall of the

Bastille. Tearing down the curtain of gauze the police had required on his stage, he threw himself onto the forestage, shouting, "Long live Liberty!" The battle for freedom was launched.

The Comédie soon found its plays being flagrantly presented by the Variétés, the Beaujolais, Audinot, Nicolet, the Associés, the Délassements-Comiques, even the Ombres Chinoises. The success of these competitors seriously reduced the receipts at the national theatre, and to add insult to this injury, the quality of the successful competition was generally frightfully low. To be threatened by worthy competition would be unpleasant, but the infuriated Comédiens found themselves losing favor to a host of licentious, uncontrolled, and unmannerly upstarts.

Obviously, complaints should be made, but to whom? In the political upheaval, it was difficult to decide whether to appeal to the King, the Commune, or the people, so the Comédiens appealed to all three. First a letter to Versailles threatened to close the theatre every day but one. "Despite the great lessons of patriotism and virtue that they teach," ran the complaint, "our masterpieces no longer please; we no longer attract the public; and if this scorn continues, we will soon be able to open only on Sundays."[13]

In all fairness, it should be observed that the Comédie was not entirely without blame for this decline, as the more honest of its members admitted. Even Françoise Marie Raucourt, a domineering, masculine actress whose virtual monopoly of major tragic roles made her an unlikely champion for the rights of the young, complained of the small number of debuts each year, these generally limited to students of declamation rather than acting. Rose Pétronille Bellecour complained of the high admission prices, costing the good bourgeois who supported Corneille almost a louis to bring his wife and a child or two to the theatre. The parterre price of 48 sols kept away the stimulating audience of workers, students, and professors, and greatly restricted the clientele. Mlle. Jeanne Devienne and Abraham-Joseph Fleury pointed out the difficulties placed in the path of new authors, discouraging these from bringing fresh life to the theatre.[14]

These reservations did not diminish the ardor of the Comédie's campaign against its smaller rivals, however. The letter to the King receiving no immediate response, the Comédiens launched a broader attack on the boulevard theatres through a petition to the Commune and a series of brochures and public papers. These widely circulated statements complained that comedy was being presented everywhere, and presented badly. Up until now, tragedy was safe, but that domain might be invaded at any time. Patriotic arguments seemed most suited to the situation, and were widely employed. How, the pamphlets asked, could France hold up her head to foreigners, who could see Molière and Corneille so ill performed, or worse yet, abandoned for shameful and obscene presentations?

Two theatres presented so serious a threat to the Comédie that the national theatre demanded their immediate closing; these were the Variétés and the Associés, which were suddenly expanding. The Variétés had recently had the good fortune to acquire one of the outstanding theatres in Paris as a result of a dispute over the future home of the Opéra. In 1781, after the Opéra burned, the Duc d'Orléans conceived the idea of making that national theatre an adjunct of his blossoming Palais-Royal. Accordingly, he employed the architect Victor Louis, who had just won great renown for his design of the Grand-Théâtre at Bordeaux, to create a home worthy of France's most opulent theatre. The architect followed much the same plan he had employed in the provincial house, but rectified his greatest error there—a superabundance of columns which hampered sight lines. He left only four, a pair on either side of the stage where side boxes changed to facing boxes. Between these was located the so-called *loge d'entre-colonnes.* He also departed from the conventional semicircular house, straightening the sides to give a wider proscenium opening. His new arrangement was widely copied, most notably in the present Opéra.[15]

The Duke's apparent plan to make the Opéra his private possession aroused the jealousy of other members of the court. These led the King to pass a decree keeping the theatre in its temporary home, a wooden building rather hastily constructed in the Boulevard Saint-Martin. Nicolas Lenoir, its architect, required only eighty-six days for its construction and guaranteed it to last for thirty years—a guarantee which was more than fulfilled, for although the Opéra finally did leave the building, as we shall see, in 1794, Lenoir's theatre remained in use until 1871, when it was deliberately burned.

The ruling which kept the Opéra in the Boulevard Saint-Martin thus left the Duc d'Orleans with a magnificent theatre, worth more than three million louis, and no company to put in it. He therefore turned to Gaillard and Dorfeuille, the directors of the Variétés, and offered them the house for 24,000 louis rent annually. The directors accepted and began plans for a magnificent opening in the spring of 1790. Public and authors alike had been for some time calling for a second Comédie Française, and Gaillard and Dorfeuille aspired to become nothing less than that. They paid high prices for new plays, purified their old repertoire, sought out better actors, and provided a varied and well-chosen program. The protection of the Duke gave them the precious privilege of presenting plays without first submitting them to the censorship of the national theatres. In 1788, two years before the theatre actually opened, it was agreed that the board of censors for the new venture would have three members: one picked by the directors themselves, one by the Duke, and one by the lieutenant of police. Since none of them represented the vested interests, the theatre was thus promised virtual freedom of action.[16]

The Associés seemed a smaller threat with its two-sol seats, its handwritten notices, and its undistinguished productions. Spectators in the 1780's reported that the acting was unbelievably gauche; typical was the performer who in his awkwardness broke a glass and played the rest of the scene drinking out of the hollow of his hand. The theatre was, moreover, a rendezvous for prostitutes and the dregs of society. As the decade wore on, however, and the directors Sallé and Beauvisage gradually improved their offerings, a better clientele began to appear. Plays were then taken straight out of the classic repertoire, and with minor changes and new names, openly presented in defiance of the Comédie; thus *Zaïre* became *Le Grand Turc mis à mort* and *Père de famille*, *Embarras du ménage*. By 1789 the theatre was fast becoming one of the most elegant in Paris, and while the Variétés threatened to become a second Comédie Française, the Associés was quietly usurping the domain of the first.[17]

The Comédie's pleas to the King, the Commune, and the public went unheeded. The events of the day left little time for the King or Commune to consider a problem so relatively minor as declining receipts at the box office of the national theatre, and the public had little sympathy for an aristocratic monopoly which felt its prerogatives endangered by the new order. The Comédiens soon realized that to compete successfully with its new rivals the old theatre must reckon with the spirit of the times, as the new were doing. As soon as the theatres reopened on July 21, many of the minor houses assured themselves an audience by presenting occasional pieces glorifying the French people and celebrating the recent events. The Comédie was understandably less enthusiastic about an upheaval which threatened the monopoly it had defended so long, but the times seemed to demand some compromise. The theatre therefore reopened with a more patriotic title, the Théâtre de la Nation, even though the actors still designated themselves the "*comédiens français ordinaires du roi.*" Such fence-straddling did not pass unnoticed, as a contemporary poem indicates:

> How cautious the Comédiens became
> In choosing, as good citizens, the name
> Théâtre de la Nation.
> The title their well-known ambition meets
> By guaranteeing plentiful receipts,
> But they remain "King's actors" all the same
> To guarantee their pension.

As further proof of their devotion to the cause of liberty, the actors of the Comédie served several nights during July in the National Guard and sent 23,000 livres to the Assembly to aid the nation. On July 23, a performance of Pierre du Belloy's *Gaston et Bayard* and Charles Collé's *Partie de chasse de Henri IV* was given for the benefit of the National Guard—a tribute to the popularity this corps enjoyed as a result of their conduct during the taking of the Bastille. The Guard refused the money.

During his tour of Paris on July 17, the King had promised the return of Necker, who had taken refuge in Basel. Within a week, word came to the capital that the Minister was returning, making a triumphal journey across France. On July 29, he appeared at the Town Hall in Paris, covered with adulation, and pleading for conciliation and amnesty for those who had replaced him. The Comédie saw in these events a further opportunity to demonstrate its sympathy with the common cause, and on the evening after Necker's return, the national theatre presented a revival of Philippe-Néricaut Destouches' *L'Ambitieux et l'indiscrète*, an insignificant work which had lain unperformed in the repertory since 1717. The public, however, realized the contemporary significance of the story of an honest minister who sacrificed his interests and his pride to his duty and his king, and the play was an enormous success. Hearty applause greeted verses in honor of Don Philippe, the faithful minister. Molé and Louise Contat played the principal roles.[18] The success of this effort inspired a revival of *Le Souper de Henri IV* by Maximilien Bouthellier and Desprez-Valmont. Full of similar sentiments about the monarchy, it achieved a similar success. Thus, at the very outset of the Revolution, theatre audiences began to turn the drama to their own ends. In 1789 the theatre became a tool; a few years more, and it became a weapon.

Despite the great success of these revivals, the Comédie, unlike many of the boulevard theatres, was not prepared to embark upon a series of plays designed to cater to the enthusiasms of the hour. A sense of obligation to the traditional repertoire made the Comédie naturally conservative, but, even more important, its older and more influential members tended to view with concern the path the country was taking. Bound to the court by century-old ties and long dependent upon the support of the royal family for advancement, for pensions, and for the protection of their now seriously threatened primacy, the Comédiens could hardly be expected to favor a popular uprising which seemed to threaten the entire old order. Yet because the younger members of the company generally had little sympathy for such misgivings, the Comédiens found themselves divided into opposing factions—one side favoring the Revolution, the other opposed to it. These groups came into sharper and sharper disagreement as summer gave way to fall.

On August 12 the Comédie attempted a new work, Robert's *Les Fausses Présomptions*, but this romantic and ridiculous play proved completely unacceptable to its audience and was not repeated. Two days after, the Théâtre de Monsieur, on the other hand, premiered the highly successful *Retour de Camille à Rome* by Joseph Aude. This work showed a generous military hero, the savior of his country, clearly modeled on Lafayette, whose recent campaigns in America had made him, like Necker, a great hero to the general public. The Théâtre de Monsieur added further to the woes of the Comédie, now that the Revolution was underway, by following an openly patriotic course in accord with Monsieur's expressed sympathy toward the popular cause. The Comédie, less willing to align itself with the new forces and powerless against the Théâtre de Monsieur because of its protection by the King's brother, naturally declined as its opportunistic rival rose in popularity.[19]

Unable to agree politically, but strongly aware that conventional drama would continue to be unprofitable in the supercharged atmosphere of a Paris in which the Assembly was now discussing its Declaration of the Rights of Man, the Comédie company at length agreed to attack a part of the feudal system for which few of them had any particularly warm feelings—the Church. Many of the Comédiens had known the favor of the court and regretted its passing, but the Church was a common enemy, having constantly persecuted the profession for nearly two hundred and fifty years.

Drama incorporating sentiments opposing the Church was not difficult to find, for even while the old regime was in power, the writings of the mid-century philosophers had encouraged widespread questioning of religious tenets, even among the third estate. As early as 1768, the Comédie had accepted Jean-Gaspard de Fontanelle's *Ericie,* a play so openly antagonistic to the Catholic monastic system that it was immediately banned. Although the play had subsequently been published at Lyons, it had never been staged. Now, with the rights and procedures of much of the old regime under attack, the Comédiens no longer feared governmental interference, and the work was produced. The story concerned a Roman maiden (played by Marie-Rose Vestris), forced to become a Vestal, who allows the sacred flame to expire and is condemned to be burned, with the result that she and her lover stab themselves. The classical setting did not at all disguise the fact that the monastic system was the real villain of the piece, and its sentiments should have guaranteed the play a success at this moment, whatever it lacked in literary excellence. Fate, however, decreed otherwise. At its opening, it was overshadowed by a similar drama, Jean François Laharpe's *Mélanie,* which had opened the night before at another theatre; and on the unfortunate *Ericie's* second night a disturbance broke out which introduced a struggle that was to tear asunder the Comédie. The curtain had just descended on Fontanelle's tragedy and was about to rise on the evening's second production, Molière's *Ecole des maris,* when the orchestra was showered with handbills demanding the immediate performance of a "national tragedy" entitled *Charles IX* written by a certain M. de Chénier.[20]

Although Marie-Joseph Chénier was to become a major theatrical figure in the following years, both play and author were probably unfamiliar to the surprised patrons of the Comédie that evening. Theatre demonstrations were not new, and actors were often called upon to repeat favorite lines or scenes, but this demand for an almost unknown play took both actors and audience by surprise. Chénier had had two plays produced earlier, neither of them successful. *Edgar ou Le Page supposé* had been given at the Comédie on November 14, 1785. It was hissed from start to finish and never heard of again. *Azémire* fared only slightly better. First given at Fontainebleau, it was there hissed by the entire court, and it was barely tolerated at a later performance in Paris. The experience at Fontainebleau turned Chénier against the nobility. He dropped his aristocratic coat of arms and in 1787 began writing *Charles IX*, a play which showed the monarch of its title largely responsible, through his weakness in being led by machiavellian ministers, for the St. Bartholomew's Day massacre. The play, according to custom, was approved by an examiner and read before the assembled actors of the Comédie. On September 2, 1788, they unanimously accepted it. Next the play went to J. B. Antoine Suard, the royal censor, who considered its attacks on church and state excessive and banned it.

Chénier was not discouraged by this check. On the contrary, it seems only to have strengthened his patriotic inclinations. He followed Beaumarchais' example, taking his play about to read at various salons, and in January of 1789 even read it before the Duc d'Orléans. Unlike *Le Mariage de Figaro*, however, *Charles IX* aroused mixed feelings of fear and boredom.[21] Months passed, and Chénier failed utterly to build any of the groundswell of opinion which had carried Beaumarchais to success. The upheavals of July encouraged the author to publish articles condemning censorship, and his own struggle attracted the attention of the popular leaders, who saw in his play's references to St. Bartholomew's Day a means for stimulating Revolutionary opinion. A group of patriots headed by Georges Jacques Danton, Fabre d'Eglantine, and Collot d'Herbois espoused Chénier's cause and vowed to force a presentation of the banned play, choosing the second night of *Ericie*, August 19, to open their campaign.

The evening was well chosen. The audience was charged with the liberal enthusiasm engendered by the events of the last two months. Nobles were daily renouncing their feudal rights and the National Assembly was abolishing feudal privileges. Moreover, the audience had been drawn to the Comédie by a play attacking the entire monastic system under the most transparent disguise. When the curtain rose on the Molière play, Danton, seated in the orchestra, called out for *Charles IX*. Others supported him, and the play was stopped. At last Fleury came out alone and explained that the theatre had not received permission to present the play. "No more permissions," cried the aroused audience. Fleury, unable to quiet the demonstration and equally unable to accede to the demand, promised to appeal to the municipality the following day for permission to present the play. The demonstrators, appeased, departed and the play was allowed to continue.[22]

This demonstration was particularly significant in that it was the first time within memory that a play had been demanded by a political rather than a literary faction. It meant that the new popular leaders considered tragedy as a legitimate form of political propaganda, thus opening the way to Revolutionary drama. Chénier had abandoned literary goals to seek the support of a political group, and Danton's ready acceptance of his proposal brought the attention of the political world to the potential power of literature. The pattern for Revolutionary artistic expression was thereby set within a month after the Bastille fell, and Chénier launched on his career as the first poet laureate of the new order.

The shifts in power in mid-July had given the mayor of Paris, Bailly, definitive control over the city's theatres; and although Suard retained his post as censor, he was now answerable to the municipality instead of the monarchy. It was therefore to Bailly that Fleury and his delegation of actors appealed on August 20. Bailly, a Constitutional Royalist and a prudent man, saw clearly that the demand was really the demand of a minority less interested in the play itself than in stirring up the populace. He postponed a decision, pleading that he would have to refer the matter to the National Assembly. This delay encouraged opposition to the play, and on August 27 Suard published an anonymous article in the *Journal de Paris* upholding censorship. Chénier, perfectly aware, as many were, of the article's authorship, then himself published a pamphlet under Suard's name. This publication praised *Charles IX*, refuted the anonymous article, and called its author an ass. It was now early September. The Assembly appointed a committee to study the controversial play. The committee approved its presentation, but new opposition arose; a deputation of bishops and representatives from the Sorbonne went to court to demand its suppression. In the meantime, Chénier set out to gain the support of the Comédie actors.

While the controversy over *Charles IX* continued, the Comédie sought to attract a large audience with another new play, Barthélemy Imbert's *Marie de Brabant*, the first new tragedy of the Revolution. It resembled *Charles IX* without the inflammatory passages, but its success was not great. Later in September, Jean-Michel Sédaine's *Ray-*

mond V was hissed from the stage. The Comédie audience was growing impatient.[23]

On October 3, the attention of all of Paris turned to the theatre at Versailles, but not because of any play given there. The preceding evening the King's guards had taken over the theatre for a dinner in honor of the officers of the garrison. The boxes were filled with members of the court and officers of the national guard. It was an occasion of great revelry and wine flowed freely. The company, with swords drawn, drank to the health of the royal family, while a toast to the nation—the ordinary concomitant in these days—was pointedly omitted. The trumpets sounded a charge and the troops scaled the boxes, much to the delight of the spectators. The troops vowed to die for the King, as if he had been in the most imminent danger. Black and white cockades were distributed, and, rumor had it, the national colors were trodden under foot, in the presence of the King and Queen. The news of such prodigality, such effrontery, and such display of military force soon reached Paris, and shouts of "To Versailles" were heard all over the city. Within a few days a great multitude descended on Versailles and forced the King to consent to come to Paris, a virtual prisoner. He and his family arrived at the Tuileries on October 6, amid so great a popular demonstration that most of the theatres of the city were forced to close for want of customers. The records of the Comédie Italienne note that admissions were refunded to the two persons present there.[24]

All through September, Chénier had continued to press for the production of *Charles IX*, complaining of the hostility of certain actors who refused to espouse his cause, and threatening to withdraw all his plays from the repertoire—a gesture hardly likely to cause the Comédie serious inconvenience. The forced return of the royal family to Paris strengthened the Revolutionary party, however, and, later in October, Chénier was able to appeal directly to the sixty Parisian districts. The enemies of the play continued to protest, but Chénier's supporters had grown too strong to be denied, and *Charles IX* was approved for presentation on November 4. Many noted, with a touch of irony, that this was also the Catholic St. Charles' Day.[25]

It would be well at this point to summarize the action of this drama which, even before its opening, was so warmly supported by the patriots and so feared by the partisans of the old order. The weak and vacillating King Charles IX of Chénier's drama is held in check when the drama opens by the noble advice of Coligny, who represents the Protestants. Soon, however, the fanatic Cardinal of Lorraine, the Duc de Guise, and Catherine de Médici gain the upper hand and influence Charles to give the order which unleashes the St. Bartholomew's Day massacre. The Cardinal blesses the deed and promises a martyr's reward to the murderers who fall at their task. As the tocsin sounds,

2. The dinner of the King's Guards, Versailles, 1789. Reports of this banquet, held on the stage of the Royal Theatre, helped stimulate the march on Versailles early in October. Several architectural details of the stage can be seen, particularly the "intercolumn" boxes, which later in the Revolutionary period were replaced in many theatres by heroic statuary. (Alexandre de Laborde, *Versailles, ancien et moderne.*)

Henry of Navarre comes to reproach the King, who collapses crushed by remorse and cursing his counselors. The set speeches and declamatory nature of the writing give the play a slow and ponderous quality for the modern reader, but the characters are powerfully drawn, and the material was sufficiently inflammatory to guarantee the play a striking effect. Absolute monarchy is attacked not only in the person of the weak King, but by descriptions of the tyrannies of Louis XI and Philip II of Spain. The heroes of the play condemn the papacy and clergy, and the hypocritical Cardinal is one of the drama's darker villains. Little better is the Duke, who represents the privileged aristocracy. The Chanceler de l'Hôpital speaks for the author, calling for popular sovereignty, freedom of thought and expression, and progress through general enlightenment.

Once the play was approved, the Comédiens set about casting it. The forced return of the King had deepened the gulf within the society between the patriots, called the "reds," and those suspicious of the Revolution's ultimate good, called the "blacks." The "blacks" were not at all pleased to receive a drama they felt convinced would only add fuel to the Revolutionary fire, but public opinion was now running so high that further postponement was impossible. Accordingly, Naudet was chosen for the virtuous Coligny, Saint-Prix for the rabid cardinal, Vanhove for l'Hôpital, and Mme. Vestris for the scheming Catherine. "Really," she observed to Chénier, "I am running some risk on your account. This queen mother is so hateful that I am certain to be shot at." The part of Charles IX was offered to Etienne-Maynier Saint-Fal, but he refused. Being among the "blacks," he resented this defamation of a King of France, especially since the Comte de Mirabeau a few days previously had levied an apostrophe against the same king in the National Assembly. "I can see from this tribunal," the orator had proclaimed, "the window from whence the infamous Charles IX fired on his subjects, whose only crime had been to love God instead of him." Saint-Fal requested the part of Henry of Navarre instead, and the part of Charles IX was assigned to a young tragedien who had not yet appeared in a major role at the Comédie—François Joseph Talma.[26]

This young man, who was to become one of the greatest tragedians of the French stage, came to his first major role with a rather unusual background. Although born in Paris, in 1766, Talma had been taken to London when he was four. His father, a successful dentist, undertook the move at the request of a grateful English patient. The elder Talma was an enthusiast of the Enlightenment, and young Talma learned to read from Voltaire and Rousseau. Sent back to Paris to school, he became fascinated by the theatre and regularly attended the Comédie until his schooldays were abruptly terminated when the headmaster overheard him teaching atheism to his classmates. Talma returned to London, considering himself a martyr to philosophy, and entered his father's profession.

His interest in theatre continued, however, and he went to see Mrs. George Anne Bellamy, Charles Macklin, and John Philip Kemble, much impressed by the strength of their delivery and by their interest in authentic costume. He joined a group of young Frenchmen who were producing plays in French for the English aristocracy, and eventually the Earl of Harcourt, his father's patron, introduced him to Molé, who had just achieved great success in *Le Mariage de Figaro* in Paris. Molé, convinced that the youth showed real promise, gained him admission to the Comédie School of Declamation, and the young actor made his debut in 1787 as Seide in *Mahomet.* Although he created only four new roles in the following two years, by April 1, 1789, he was considered ready to join the company. Since it was a time of few new plays, and the older actors were jealous of their prerogatives, Talma, like most new members, was placed in tertiary roles with the prospect of eventually inheriting the better ones. Such was the long-standing practice, willingly accepted by generations of Comédiens. The impetuous young Talma, however, chafed under this restraint. Even in small roles, he began to attract attention, and not always merely by the force of his delivery. Cast in the minor roles of the tribune Proculus in Voltaire's *Brutus,* he appealed to his friend Jacques Louis David for a sketch of the sort of authentic costume he had seen worn by Macklin in London. The artist obliged, and Talma appeared backstage with his hair cut short and in an unadorned cloth mantle. His fellow actors, all in traditional wigs and rich silks, were aghast. "Good heavens," said Louise Contat. "He looks like a statue!" Others tried to dissuade him from going on stage, but Talma persisted. The audience was at first stunned, but then applauded the innovation.[27] After several such incidents, it is hardly surprising that the older actors tended to view whatever Talma did with apprehension, if not irritation. Surely they must have assigned him the role of Charles IX with some misgivings, but none of the older generation would take it.

Internal dissension and threats of demonstrations from outside led almost everyone to anticipate trouble on the evening of November 4. Chénier was warned that his play would be hissed and his person subjected to ridicule. The actors received anonymous warnings. As late as fifteen minutes before the curtain an unknown person appeared in Mme. Vestris' dressing room, and as if in fulfillment of her jesting prophecy to Chénier, warned her of a plot to assassinate her on stage.[28] Swords and pistols were plainly in evidence as the audience gathered, but before the curtain rose, a speaker in the orchestra proposed that the first person to disturb the performance be delivered over to the justice of the people. Charles Palissot, an older dramatist who had become Chénier's friend and mentor, seconded this motion, and the terrible cry for an impromptu hanging, "To the lamp-post," came from several parts of the house. Would-be demonstrators were apparently cowed into submission, for the performance proceeded peacefully.

The notoriety of the play guaranteed a huge attendance. Orchestra seats, ordinarily 48 sous, sold for a louis apiece, and the income for a single evening was prodigious. Mirabeau brought a delegation from the National Assembly and led applause from his box. Danton, Desmoulins, and the future nucleus of the Cordelier Club added to the approving chorus.[29] It was an hour of triumph for the forces which had guided the Revolution thus far. None could suspect that even while they cheered, a body was being formed which would in four tempestuous years destroy these moderate Revolutionists as coolly as they were now destroying the aristocracy. On November 6, the society called the Friends of the Constitution, later the Jacobins, was organized.

Talma's attention to costume led him to appear in *Charles IX* in black hair, unpowdered, dressed simply but strikingly in a black velvet coat decorated in gold, stockings of white silk, and a white gauze ruff. Mme. Vestris was dressed to match, with a black satin cap, simply crimped hair, a ruff of white gauze, and a cloak and dress of black velvet decorated with golden buttons.[30] Talma, at last given scope for his talents, overwhelmed his audience. His fellow actor Fleury, won over in spite of himself by Talma's rendition of the closing scene, records in his *Mémoires:*

> It must be confessed that we did not expect him to produce the effect he did here. When, after being crushed by remorse, his face hidden in the folds of his royal mantle, he suddenly raised himself at the curse hurled upon him, and, shuddering under the look of the man who pronounced it, shrank back convulsively as if to shake off the drops of blood which had fallen on him from his victims—the sublimity of his conception filled us with amazement.[31]

The curtain fell amid thunderous applause, and Chénier rushed backstage to congratulate Talma. Both were carried off in triumph by republican friends to a near-by café. Danton there predicted, "If

Figaro killed the aristocracy, *Charles IX* will kill the royalty," and Desmoulins observed, "This play will do more for our cause than all the events of October."[32]

In 1764 Voltaire had written, "Some day we shall introduce popes on the stage, as the Greeks represented their Atreus and Thyestes, to render them odious. The time will come when the massacre of Saint Bartholomew's Day will be made the subject of a tragedy."[33] The second part of this striking prophecy was now fulfilled, the first would follow soon after.

The popular enthusiasm which greeted *Charles IX* on its opening night did not diminish with subsequent performances. The second night, during the fourth act, a Parisian lawyer cried out that the play should be subtitled "The School for Kings." Chénier agreed, and that title was added to later announcements. All over the capital the new play was read and discussed. A popular song of the time was devoted to it, of which I translate several representative verses:

The latest play I've been to see
Sacristans hate above all things
Because this play, the "School for Kings"
Has rapped their knuckles heartily.

The author is a Socrates
Who dislikes aristocracy
And turns his battery of wit
Upon the noble hypocrite.

But all the common folk have blessed
His struggle to uphold their rights.
The "School for Kings" was given twice
To aid the poor, at his request.

But he's done yet a greater thing
By heaping praise on our good King.
In light of this, who can gainsay
What a good fellow is Chénier.[34]

There were powerful persons in Paris who did not subscribe to these sentiments, however, and the popularity of the play spurred them to ever greater efforts to close it. The clergy of the city, fearing that the drama was deepening popular feeling against the Church, appealed to the King. Louis was only too happy to seize the opportunity offered by this complaint to forbid the play. He passed the recommendation on to the First Gentlemen of the Chamber, the group traditionally charged with the administration of the Comédie, and they passed on the interdict to the company. The conservative older actors, such as Fleury, Molé, Dazincourt, and Naudet, were much relieved to table a play with which they were so little in sympathy, although by now it had been given thirty-two times, always to good houses. The liberals, led by Talma, Dugazon, and Mlles. Vestris and Desgarcins, considered the ban a defeat for Revolutionary ideas. Talma, forced to return to such parts as Proculus in *Brutus*, was particularly angry, insisting that he was being made a victim of the "theatrical feudalism" of his elders.[35]

As this inner strife continued, and audiences still called for *Charles IX*, the Comédie attempted to distract attention from the dilemma by presenting two new works. On November 19, Palmézeaux Cubière's *La Mort de Molière* was given. The play had been a great success in the provinces, but it offered little of interest to the capital audiences and failed. Rather more successful was *Le Paysan Magistrat*, offered December 7, an adaptation by Collot d'Herbois from Calderon's *Alcalde de Zalomea*. The drama flattered the contemporary passion for equality by showing a well-born man, Don Alvare, brought to trial before the man whose daughter he carried off, a rustic now elevated to the magistry. The author, a provincial actor still smarting from being hissed from the stage in Lyons, played the judge.[36]

The pressure from competing theatres increased once the Comédie was deprived of the certain drawing power *Charles IX* offered, and the Comédiens demanded again that the Variétés and Associés be closed. They further requested that the Beaujolais company should be restricted to musical presentations, Audinot to pantomime, and Nicolet to acrobatics, and that a clear line of demarcation appear on general notices between the major theatres and the rest.[37]

Although this campaign gained no more success than those of a few months before, certain of the Comédie's small rivals were running into difficulties on their own. The Théâtre de Monsieur had, since October 6, been forced to share the Tuileries palace with the returned royal family. The idea of living under the same roof with actors, protected by Monsieur or not, offended many members of the court, and royal ears were occasionally assaulted by orchestral outbursts. At last Marie Antoinette, already furious at her husband's conceding to live in the Tuileries, demanded that he evict the players. On December 12, therefore, the directors of the Monsieur were told to close the theatre on December 24, the locale being needed for the King's aunts.

The distraught directors, Autié and Viotti, faced the grim prospect of being literally turned out into the snow with a troupe of 250 persons, a full orchestra, and a theatre full of scenery, properties, furniture, machinery, and manuscripts. They appealed to the municipality and got no satisfaction. The Comédie Italienne, then crippled by debts and on the point of closing, suggested a merger, but its demands were impossibly high. Nothing remained but to build a totally new theatre, and Autié and Viotti purchased a suitable plot of ground in the Rue Feydeau and asked the architects Jacques-Guillaume Legrand and Jacques Molinos to plan a building for them.[38]

Another theatre which found itself in serious trouble as 1789 drew to a close was the Beaujolais. With the fall of the Bastille, it had abandoned its policy of featuring child actors, only to discover, too late, that that novelty had been its chief drawing card. Only by continuous borrowing and increasing indebtedness was the unhappy director, Delomel, able to keep his doors open. On December 23, the theatre world was amused by the opening of a comic opera at the Beaujolais entitled *Le Directeur dans l'embarras*. Many wondered why Delomel had not asked for the title to be changed, but actually he had wryly chosen the work for its title, so grimly applicable to his present situation.[39]

At this point a new figure appeared at the Beaujolais, a person who was destined to play so important a part in the Revolutionary theatre that she deserves a few lines of introduction. Marguerite Brunet, as she was christened, was born in Bayonne in 1730. When her mother died, she went to live with an aunt in Paris, adopting her name, Montansier. There she fell in love with Bourdon de Neuville, a young leading man in a minor theatre, who introduced her to that world. The charming young girl attracted a host of powerful admirers, whose support gained her the position of directress of the theatre at Rouen. Her talent in this field showed at once, and within a few years she had successfully guided the fortunes of theatres all over France, often managing several at once. She had a theatre built at Le Havre, then moved on to Nantes and to Versailles. The faithful Neuville served as secretary, administrator, and general supervisor, hurrying to carry her directives from one theatre to another.

It was at Versailles that Montansier met and was befriended by

Marie Antoinette. According to one story, the Queen went incognito to a performance of Favart's *Les Moissonneurs.* During one scene, the odor of the cabbage soup the actors were eating penetrated to the stage box where the Queen sat, and Marie Antoinette found it so appetizing that she sent to the directress to ask if she might share in the repast. It is the sort of whim one might expect from the mistress of the Petit Hameau. Before long, Mlle. Montansier was so far in the Queen's good graces that she was admitted to the *petits levers* and encouraged to perform before the court.

Soon the little theatre on the Rue de Satory in Versailles was too small for Mlle. Montansier, and she built a larger one, the scene of many important debuts. She was given the directorship of various royal theatres: Saint-Cloud, Marly, Fontainebleau, Compiègne. After 1785 artists ready to debut at the Comédie were regularly brought first to Montansier's theatre at Versailles, a custom which was not officially abolished until 1801. As we have seen, Autié thought first of this successful directress when seeking a partner with both capital and theatrical acumen for the new Théâtre de Monsieur. By the outbreak of the Revolution, in any event, Mlle. Montansier had made herself one of the most influential figures in the French theatre. The shrewdness, adaptability, and bravado she had demonstrated so far were outstanding, but the following years would call upon her to exercise these qualities even more. On October 6, when the royal family returned to Paris, Montansier saw her whole empire dissolving before her eyes, but she was never content to look back. If the theatre world moved to Paris, she would conquer Paris. She rode into the city with her Queen.[40]

Montansier's first thought upon her arrival in the capital was naturally to obtain a theatre. The logical choice seemed to be the Beaujolais, which was by now in such serious financial difficulties that almost everyone wondered how Delomel could keep running. Through the intervention of Marie Antoinette, therefore, Montansier gained control of this expiring venture, paid off its debts, and began planning for a reopening under her direction in 1790. All this was done without any consideration of Delomel, who protested in vain against such high-handed action. The deposed director continued to put on plays, but on the side he began looking for a new home for his troupe.[41]

In the closing days of 1789 the thoughts of many of the actors of Paris turned toward the National Assembly, where a debate was in progress on the rights of citizens. Deprived of all such rights by their profession, the men and women of the theatre looked hopefully to the new order to grant them equality. They were not disappointed. The deputy Pierre Louis, comte de Roederer, first spoke in their behalf, then Stanislas Clermont Tonnerre proposed a bill giving the rights of citizenship to all, regardless of profession or faith. On December 23, Maximilian Robespierre added his voice to the support of the actors. When the Abbé Jean Siffrein Maury dissented, insisting that actors were unfit for citizenship, the Comédiens wrote a letter appealing to the president of the Assembly, an action which Maury denounced as impudent and highhanded. A tempestuous discussion followed with certain prominent churchmen on one side and the more liberal Revolutionaries on the other. But Mirabeau called for equal rights for "Jew, Protestant, and actor," and at last a decree was passed allowing non-Catholic Frenchmen to join their countrymen in all civil and military rights and offices.[42]

So the first eventful year of the Revolution drew to a close. To the theatre it had brought greater freedom of action and a new respectability, but with these boons had come a weakening of the tradition, *inter se* quarrels, the first of those audience demonstrations that were to plague the theatres all during this period, and little indication that the new freedoms would improve the quality of dramatic fare in the capital. Even so, the actors and authors of Paris shared in the general atmosphere of hope and satisfaction which dominated France at the end of 1789. No sudden upheavals had taken place since the sixth of October; the National Assembly was steadily improving the common lot; the King was separated from his evil counselors and surrounded by his faithful children, the people of Paris. *Le Menuisier de Bagdad*, produced by the struggling Beaujolais on December 22, gave an indication of the feeling of the times. In it, a pasha advises his wives to go to France, where they are assured of a happy future. One of them, Fatmé, sings:

> A fierce and evil tyrant
> Assures eternal discord—
> But a monarch filled with goodness
> Will calm his faithful people.
> That gentle King's good subjects
> Will follow his example,
> And soon it will be said of all
> "The child is like the father."

II

Schism in the Comédie January–December, 1790

THE second year of the Revolution was a stimulating one for Parisian theatres. It brought new challenges and conflicting enthusiasms, but as yet no real dangers, and it saw a growing rift in the Comédie between the "reds" and the "blacks" as the popularity of Talma and Chénier increased and as Revolutionary pressures on the theatre and its repertoire became more insistent. The rise of the Théâtre de Monsieur, the great success of the new Variétés-Palais-Royal, and the blossoming of the boulevard theatres made it an exciting year for theatregoers, who increasingly dictated the subject matter of the plays they were offered. Yet, while the Revolution entered the theatre, affecting audience, actors, and repertoires, theatrical manifestations now also entered the Revolution, and when the nation celebrated the anniversary of the fall of the Bastille with a grandiose Festival of Federation, theartrical people were not surprisingly among the leading contributors to the occasion.

The Comédie Française opened the new year fittingly with its first play dealing directly with the Revolution—*Le Réveil d'Epiménide à Paris,* by Carbon de Flins des Oliviers. The author had been removed from a governmental position by the Revolution, but he apparently retained no ill feelings. His play is full of the optimistic feeling of the day, exalting the new order and praising the King for his help in bringing it about.

The subject of the play is particularly well adapted to such a purpose—a legend, already treated in dramatic form in 1735 by Philippe

Poisson and in 1755 by Charles Hénault, of a man who never dies, but who sleeps for a hundred years between awakenings.[1] This Epiménide, according to Flins' play, last awoke at the peak of Louis XIV's power and now reawakens in the Paris of 1789. He visits the Tuileries and heartily approves of the new king's democratic tendencies and of the destruction of the Bastille. He is overjoyed at the changes in France: the present monarch prefers Paris to Versailles, does not surround himself with a foreign guard, chooses honest men for counselors, disdains an ostentatious court. Moreover, censorship has disappeared, philosophers are respected, and the peasants are no longer abused. Epiménide reads with delight the Rights of Man and scoffs at an abbot who weeps over his lost benefices. He meets a tailor, a lawyer, and a notary who have joined the National Guard, and he is informed by their leader d'Harcourt (played by Talma):

> We all are warriors, for the King of France
> May count as soldiers all he counts as subjects.

Eulogies of the king fill the play, and the public warmly applauded such stanzas as:

> Our monarch, whom we all revere,
> Has come to live among us here.
> Our troubles and our strife have passed;
> His calming influence at last
> Brings to his happy subjects peace.
> Employ of foreign guards can cease,
> For midst his children, what need father fear?
> The more we see him, more we hold him dear.

Flins' play proved most successful and enjoyed several revivals. Yet an even more brilliant success followed: *L'Honnête Criminel* by Fenouillot de Falbaire, whose work had the double advantage of having been banned under a less liberal regime in 1767 and of dealing with religious freedom, a topic of great popular interest. Audiences cheered the story of Jean Fabre, a young Protestant in Nîmes who volunteers to go to the galleys in place of his father, whom the authorities have arrested at a forbidden religious meeting. Saint-Fal played the young hero, supported by Molé and Mlle. Contat.[2]

Despite these successes, however, internal strife continued to plague the Comédie as the public maintained its demand for a revival of

Charles IX. Finally, on January 13, Chénier's play was given its twenty-fourth showing. Many persons were turned away, and the receipts were unusually high—4,200 livres. Then, rather surprisingly, the play was repeated the night immediately following, as a benefit for the poor. It brought in a scant 1,700 livres. Chénier's enemies seized the occasion for ridicule, asking how so controversial a play could do so little for charity. The *Spectator national* noted:

Wednesday evening the twenty-fifth presentation of *Charles IX* was given for the benefit of the poor. One would have expected that this tragedy, which once attracted so many spectators out of curiosity alone, would be even more successful in a charitable cause. The expectation was disappointed, and the national masterpiece which made so much money, raised so many tempers, caused so many quarrels and charges of antipatriotism, produced a receipt for charity of a little over 1,200 livres. There was little enthusiasm or humanity in this.

Chénier felt he had been personally shamed by the incident and lashed out angrily, saying, with some justification, that the actors were responsible for the meagerness of the receipts, since they had only posted notice of the play the morning it was given. He exercised his power as author to withdraw the play, vowing that he would not release it again until the actors agreed to give a second benefit, announced several days in advance. "I am quite sure," he concluded in an open letter to the Comédie, "that there have been efforts to compromise me and to cast doubt on my zeal for the interests of the public. I hope that this letter will answer all such charges, and I dare to promise that my conduct will always be in accord with the principles which I have stated in all my writings."[3]

Those Comédiens who were hostile to Chénier were doubtless relieved by his action. It was the rule that a play, once withdrawn, had to wait its turn before again entering the active repertoire, so the problem presented by *Charles IX* was, if not solved, at least indefinitely postponed. The theatre was thereby free to turn from contemporary concerns, and on January 19 it presented Jean Louis Laya's *Les Dangers de l'opinion*, which, despite its title, avoided all topical questions. It was a highly romanticized story of two young lovers whose match is about to be broken off by a stigma on the young man's name. Just as they are about to commit suicide, however, the dishonor is suddenly removed and they are reunited. Mme. Petit-Vanhove, who had been growing steadily in popularity since her brilliant debut as a tragic actress in 1785, at the age of 14, further distinguished herself as the heroine and guaranteed success for the play.

Yet a month of discouragement followed this success, while the Comédie tried vainly to generate public enthusiasm with new works, comic operas, and even reworkings of previously successful scripts. Most ambitious of these reworkings was Pierre Nicolas Murville's *Le Souper magique*, obviously inspired by *Le Réveil d'Epiménide*. In *Le Souper*, Cagliostro conjures up figures from the past to elicit their reactions to the Revolution. The theory that if one Epiménide were good, half-a-dozen would be better was, not surprisingly, proven false. On February 12, Charles-Philippe Ronsin's *Louis XII, père du peuple* was given. Its object was to capitalize on the current adulation of Louis XVI as the restorer of French liberty. A preliminary statement praising the King for his decision to come to Paris was well received, but the play proper was so poorly conceived and so loosely constructed that the audience did not even permit it to finish. Ronsin retired to work on other dramas.

On February 22, the Comédie announced *Le Philinte de Molière*, which its author, Fabre d'Eglantine, proposed as a sequel to Molière's *Misanthrope*. A large crowd came prepared to hiss an author who dared compare himself to the master, but they were won over in spite of themselves. D'Eglantine continued the story of Alceste, but only indirectly, centering rather on Alceste's young friend Philinte. With Molé playing the misanthrope, the comedy proved one of the year's greatest successes, and d'Eglantine was everywhere hailed as a major new comic writer. To add to the jubilation of the Comédiens, the following night's offering, although less substantial, was another gratifying success. This, *Les Trois Noces*, was a sort of pastoral with songs and dances, featuring military defiles, a happy nobility, and a simple and lovable king surrounded by childlike subjects.[4]

By March the Comédiens felt that *Charles IX* could not be postponed much longer and at last acceded to the continuing public demand for the play. As Chénier had requested, the performance was well publicized and attendance was good. The play was then repeated several times more before the regular Easter closing. At this time, all theatres in Paris were required to close during the Easter holidays, and it was customary for one of the actors to give a speech at the final performance before the closing and at the first performance upon reopening.

These speeches were devoted for the most part to thanking the audience for their support and promising to continue to serve them in the future. Frequently comments would be made on the season just passed or on plans for the future, so that such speeches served as a sort of crystallization of current theatre policy. The closing address for the Easter of 1790 at the Comédie was given on March 27 by Dazincourt. The issues raised by *Charles IX* were naturally uppermost in the Comédiens' minds, and the address considered these issues. Dazincourt did not mention *Charles IX* by name, however; instead he pictured the Comédie as under daily persecution and reminded the audience that the house had an obligation to many plays and that it should present them in order even if certain ones were especially popular. The implication was clear, and Talma and Chénier at once began making plans to refute this position.[5]

The Comédiens had good reason to fear for their freedom to choose their presentations, since the success of popular demands for *Charles IX* had encouraged audiences in other theatres to demand unannounced productions. In mid-March the Comédie Italienne presented *Le District de village*, a typical play of the times, showing a marquis and marquise renouncing their feudal rights amid the cheers of the villagers, who conclude the play by crowning a bust of the king and singing a hymn in his praise. On March 18 the curtain had no sooner fallen on this exemplary and generally applauded drama than the audience began to shout for a play called *Les Religieuses danoises*. Antireligious plays would soon appear in many theatres, but as yet official sanctions were laid upon dramas which presumed to attack the Church directly instead of, like *Ericie*, under classical trappings. The director protested that he had orders not to present *Les Religieuses danoises;* the author appeared and assured the house that the play had been submitted to the municipality for consideration. "No more censorship," the audience cried, and only a promise of immediate appeal to Bailly, the mayor, prevented a riot. On this occasion the delay was successful and the play was not demanded again, but the experience served as a warning that the demand for *Charles IX* was not an isolated phenomenon, and that more such demands could be expected in the future. The mob was beginning to rule the theatres.

Talma, of course, could hardly be expected to share his more conservative companions' misgivings about the public which so strongly supported his own efforts. As a recently elected member of the company, he was the logical candidate to deliver the customary opening address after Easter. Well aware of this, Talma asked Chénier to write a speech for him and took the extra precaution of having it approved by Bailly before showing it to his comrades. The address was a paean of praise for *Charles IX*, with an implicit condemnation of the actors who were attempting to keep it from the stage. It was, in short, a rebuttal to the speech Dazincourt had given at the closing in March. The "blacks"—Fleury, Naudet, Dazincourt, and others—naturally refused to allow Talma to give such a speech and selected Naudet in his place.

This might have closed the incident had not unknown persons distributed Talma's undelivered speech at the door on opening night. The address seems tame enough when read today, but its appeal to Revolutionary spirit was clearly designed to guarantee a popular outburst. A few sentences will show the tone and, incidentally, provide a suggestion of the developing esthetic of Revolutionary drama:

> The way is now open for truly national plays. Now the most important genre, tragedy, can combine esthetic charm with the seriousness of history, blending the highest moral and political ideals with lofty poetical expression. . . . And the stage, freed forever from arbitrary limitations, will become what it should always have been: a school for morality and liberty.[6]

The excited public, convinced that an important freedom was at stake, demanded that Talma's speech be read. Naudet refused. Certain of the Comédie actors wrote later that Talma had to be forcibly restrained from going on stage to answer the public demand. Talma denied this, but the action is so much in his character that his opponents' statements carry more conviction. Whatever the true story, the public demand was refused, and Talma did not appear.

The incident heightened the impression held by much of the Parisian theatre public that the older members of the Comédie were openly opposing the work of the Revolution and that only a few younger members, headed of course by Talma, were valiantly struggling for the new cause. Even leaving aside the important matter of Talma's personal ambition, *Charles IX* still being his only major role, there was enough truth in this impression to give the Comédiens some uneasiness. Naudet, who had been personally attacked for his refusal to read Talma's speech, resolved to carry the battle into the enemy camp, charging Talma himself with betraying the Revolution.

Naudet had been in charge of a Revolutionary company on July 14, 1789, and he charged that on that date, while a corps of Hussars was attacking the company, Talma, who was under his command, had been discovered hiding in an attic. Talma hotly denied this, and he was supported by Saint-Prix, a member of the same company, who claimed that Naudet dispatched a unit to fortify the Hôtel de Tours. Saint-Prix, in charge of this unit, left twenty of his twenty-five men there, returning when the Hussars had passed. He found Talma in a window recess, not an attic, ready to fire if the building were attacked. When both sides of the dispute had been widely circulated, the public sided with Talma, and the open altercation served only to widen the breach in the now seriously divided company.[7]

The first new play presented at the Comédie after the holidays, Pierre Laujon's *Le Couvent*, demonstrated how much censorship had diminished in less than a year. Although the nation had abolished monastic vows, suppressed religious orders, and confiscated ecclesiastical property early in 1790, and although plays had previously been approved which indirectly considered the monastic system (even quite unfavorably, as did *Ericie*), until this date the theatres had respected the old ban against portrayal of Church costume or ceremony on the stage. *Le Couvent* flew in the face of such restrictions: religious garb, cloisters, confessionals, all the grills and galleries of a convent were reproduced at the Comédie. The play itself was as inoffensive as its subtitle, "the fruits of character and education." A certain marquise comes to a convent to judge at first hand a young lady there proposed as a wife for her son. The girl is proud and overbearing and is disliked by the entire convent. A complete contrast is offered by another young novice, who, though poor, has been carefully raised and whose gentle ways are the delight of all. The marquise, disguised as a teacher of painting and music, soon discovers the unfitness of the young de Fierville and the laudable qualities of the poor Sister Saint-Ange. When she finds that Saint-Ange has met her son and preserves the tenderest memories of him, she hesitates no longer, but arranges a marriage with this poor but deserving novice. Aside from the democratic arguments implied in its theme, the play had little Revolutionary spirit about it, and few later convent plays possessed so gentle a tone. The author, Laujon, was a quiet little gentleman whose sympathies were, if anything, with the aristocracy.[8]

Even so, the Church remained sensitive on the subject of actors, especially the actors of the Comédie. It was scarcely surprising that Talma and Louise-Julie Careau were refused when on April 30 they asked the curate of Saint-Sulpiceto to publish their bans. Talma appealed as a citizen, according to the new freedoms granted in December of 1789, to the National Assembly, but that body was already experienced in the ways of bureaucracy. His request was referred to a committee and never heard of again. Actually, actors had for some time been married in the Church. Talma was apparently refused marriage not so much for being an actor, but for being the actor of *Charles IX*, just as Molière had been refused burial, not so much for being an actor and playwright, but for being the author of *Tartuffe*. The curate suggested that Talma renounce his profession for the purposes of the ceremony, clearly a *pro forma* request, but Talma, rarely one to compromise, refused. There, for a time, the matter rested.[9]

Le Couvent successfully attracted audiences away from the ever more numerous boulevard theatres, but its attractiveness was soon exhausted. The Comédiens' next tactic to win attention was to call Larive out of retirement. This noted tragedian had left the stage in 1788 in a fit of pique after being hissed, and he was not eager to return. Finally, however, he was convinced by an indirect appeal through his friend the Abbé Gouttes, now president of the National Assembly, and he consented to appear in *Oedipus*, the first important classical revival in several years. Although 1788 was not far in the past, the intervening events made it seem almost that an actor of another era had been summoned up, and curiosity alone brought huge crowds to the theatre. Gouttes watched his friend's triumph from a private box. After *Oedipus*, Larive went on to play Brutus in *La Mort de César* and Spartacus in the play of that name, but his audiences dwindled rapidly. After the impassioned delivery of Talma, Larive's pre-Revolutionary acting seemed now too cold and studied. Within two years Larive's style, once so widely praised, had become obsolete.[10]

After the mixed success of Larive's reappearance, the Comédie attempted to repeat the formula of *Le Couvent*, offering on May 14 *Les Amans malheureux ou Le Comte de Comminges* by François Baculard d'Arnauld. Like *Ericie*, it had been written in the 1760's, but its setting in an abbey kept it from the stage during the old regime. Unusual care was lavished on the production, and the severity of costumes and settings focused attention on the interpretation, which received much praise. Saint-Fal and Magdaleine-Marie Desgarcins played the hero and heroine, while the third major role, of the abbot, was given to Naudet.

Talma, as usual, was cast in a minor role, but his lack of preferment at the Comédie did not prevent him from demonstrating his talents elsewhere. A letter written by Louise Fusil notes that he was much in demand during this spring and rarely refused a request to perform outside the Comédie. He appeared often at suburban theatres, at Versailles and Saint-Germain, in casts of amateurs and unemployed actors. Indeed, his growing crowd of admirers came down from Paris to see him in roles he was not allowed at the national theatre. A large, or at least highly demonstrative, element of the Comédie audience supported his struggle for recognition, as an incident related by Mlle. Fusil demonstrates. When Talma appeared in a small role in *L'Impromptu de campagne*, another actor addressed to him the line:

> You have great talent; it is clear to me,
> You'll be accepted at the Comédie.

The audience applauded warmly and demanded three repetitions of the couplet. It is surprising that the Comédiens were so imperceptive as to allow such a line, for even before the Revolution audiences seized upon such references as pretexts for demonstrations. In any case, this manifestation of popular support gained nothing for Talma. His position at the Comédie did not improve, and he continued to chafe in minor parts, even though Mlle. Fusil comments that many young authors requested in vain that he be allowed to play important roles in their offerings.[11]

On June 5, the Comédie successfully revived *Le Présomptueux*, which had been given once in January, 1789, and immediately withdrawn, its author, Fabre d'Eglantine, going on to establish his reputation with *Le Philinte de Molière. Le Présomptueux* had on its first appearance suffered from too close a resemblance in plot, incident, and character to *Les Châteaux en Espagne*, a contemporary comedy by Colin d'Harleville. D'Harleville accused his rival of plagiarism; and when d'Eglantine pointed out that his play had appeared for the Comédie's consideration a month earlier, d'Harleville answered that he had read his manuscript earlier still before a society of which d'Eglantine was a member. The arguments were well balanced, but the inferior structure of *Le Présomptueux* convinced the public that d'Harleville was in the right and d'Eglantine's play failed.

Both of these dramas were good-natured satires on the false security of the court and the aristocracy, full of thinly disguised advice to the royal family, a theme popular enough to assure the success of both, once the heat of competition was past. On its second offering, therefore, *Le Présomptueux* was much better received. The Comédie's only other new presentation that June, Antoine Marin Lemierre's tragedy *Barneveldt*, did not prove so attractive, even though it was another of the plays written in the 1760's which the Revolution had freed for production. Its pleas for tolerance and equality and its implied criticism of recent political events had seemed dangerous under the old regime, but they were apparently not extreme enough to interest the audiences of 1790—so much had the world changed in those few years.[12]

The first anniversary of July 14, that momentous day which all now considered as the beginning of a new era, was fast approaching, and the citizens of Paris began planning to celebrate it. Many cities, and even entire provinces, had already confederated to resist the enemies of the Revolution. The municipality of Paris therefore proposed a general federation of the entire nation, to be celebrated in the capital on July 14 with deputies of the National Guard and all the corps of the army. The idea was enthusiastically received almost everywhere, and grandiose plans were soon under way.

The place chosen for the ceremony was the Champ de Mars, a vast parade ground in the heart of Paris, and to convert it into an amphitheatre capable of accommodating the anticipated multitude, a vast army of workers—some twelve thousand according to Thiers—set to work day and night to remove the earth from the center of the area and heap it on the sides. The project was so huge that even this force was found to be inadequate, and a general appeal went out to all the citizens of Paris. The population swarmed to the Champ de Mars to participate in the great effort; soldiers, priests, beggars, and women of the highest social rank worked side by side. Different sections rallied to the sound of drums and marched to work together, banners flying, then spread out at the field until nightfall, when they would rejoin to march triumphantly home. The theatres of Paris greeted this project with great delight and their companies came in large numbers to help. Each actor chose a partner, to whom he offered a delicate little spade decorated with ribbons and bouquets. Both sexes adopted a special dust-resistant costume made of gray muslin, and the actresses wore also little gray boots and silk stockings, a tricolor scarf, and a large straw hat. The orchestras from the various theatres accompanied the other artists, so that they could work to music. The quality of work produced by these enthusiastic volunteers was not so exemplary as their spirits, however, and despite their reluctance, the actors and orchestras were soon dismissed from the project.[13]

The Comédiens, most of whom had been willing enough to labor in the Champ de Mars for the glory of the nation, greeted more coolly a request for a rather more personal demonstration of patriotism. The famous orator Mirabeau came one evening to the green room to personally appeal to the Comédiens to present *Charles IX* for a delegation of deputies from the provinces on the evening after the ceremonies in the Champ de Mars. The actors were still smarting from the recent publication of *La Critique de Charles IX*, a vituperative defense of the play by Chénier's close friend Palissot, and they refused. Several pointed out, with some justification, that the play might provoke an outburst of partisan feeling on what was intended to be a day of brotherly understanding. "Do you think," queried the angry orator, "that you have the right to refuse?" "M. le Comte," Dazincourt replied, "that right is recognized by your coming here on the matter." Mirabeau, routed, left the theatre.[14] Chénier likewise applied, but accomplished no more. Finally, on the day before the festival, the deputies themselves petitioned the actors, and Chénier's cabal, its present means of appeal exhausted, anxiously awaited the Comédie's decision.

The evening, July 13, the festival was launched at Notre Dame cathedral by a strange ceremony. Actors and musicians from the Comédie Française, the Comédie Italienne, the Théâtre de Monsieur, the Opéra, the Variétés Montansier, and even the small theatres, such as those of Audinot and Nicolet, gathered to celebrate an immense and solemn introduction to the festivities of the following day. Artists of the Opéra sang solos, and a "religious drama, drawn from the Holy Scriptures" and entitled *The Fall of the Bastille* [!] was presented by artists from various theatres. Its author, Marc-Antoine Désaugiers, had performed the interesting feat of composing a topical patriotic drama with scraps of biblical text; rarely were the Scriptures put to stranger use. A few interchanges, referring to the dismissal of Necker, will give an idea of the style and technique:

CITIZEN: Shall not the land tremble for this, and every one mourn that dwelleth therein?
THE PEOPLE: Why?
CITIZEN: Our protector is taken away.

. . . . .

A citizen announces the exile of "a minister in whom they trust."
THE PEOPLE: Woe unto us! (*The Tocsin is heard*).
THE WOMEN: Oh Lord, have mercy upon us and upon our children.
ALL: Help us, O Lord.

After a series of such interchanges, the soloists sang a military phrase, which was repeated in chorus, the orchestra struck up a march, cannons fired, trumpets sounded a charge, a huge explosion came from the orchestra, and the chorus burst forth with a passage from the Book of Judith:

Woe be unto the nation that riseth up against my people; for the Lord almighty will take revenge on them. In the day of judgment he will visit them.

This was followed by a universal *Te Deum.*[15]

Surely no stranger spectacle had ever been seen within the ancient walls of that great cathedral. Whatever startled spirits were stirred into wakefulness by this ebullient intrusion from the secular world would find little rest in the next few years, however, and they would look down upon ceremonies stranger still. "If you will not let me give my *Mariage de Figaro* in the Comédie," Beaumarchais had once observed, "it shall be given in Notre Dame." Suddenly, the threat no longer seemed so absurd.

The long-awaited Festival of Federation began early the following morning. A magnificent procession of federal deputies from the provinces and federal troops departed from the site of the Bastille and marched to the Tuileries. There they were joined by the Assembly and the municipal officers. The procession continued through streets jammed with cheering throngs, across a bridge built over the Seine especially for this occasion, and into the great amphitheatre. Four hundred thousand spectators filled the ramparts, and at the far end sat the King, the President of the Assembly, ministers and deputies. The procession was three hours late in arriving, and the rain fell in torrents, but the enthusiasm of the throng remained unabated. At last the ceremony began, just as the skies happily cleared. A company of three hundred priests in white surplices and tricolored scarves opened the ceremony with a mass held at the altar of the country—raised on a platform twenty-five feet high in the center of the field. The King's oath was the high point of the observance; his hand stretched toward the altar, he swore to uphold the Constitution, while all over France, representatives gathered in the principal towns and swore to love the King as he loved them.[16]

After the ceremony, the procession returned and the populace of Paris devoted itself to several days of celebration. The site of the Bastille was converted into a huge open-air dance pavilion, and the Champs Elysées was filled with crowds of happy celebrants, all classes intermingling, as they had on the Champ de Mars, without rivalry or rancor. For a brief moment, all the promises of the Revolution—liberty, happiness, prosperity, brotherhood—seemed fulfilled.

The theatres, of course, shared in this enthusiasm and excitement and selected presentations especially to suit the occasion. The Théâtre de Monsieur revived *Le Souper de Henri IV* and *L'Epiménide français* to much acclaim. The Comédie Italienne offered *Le Chêne patriotique*. Mlle. Montansier's Variétés showed Ronsin's *La Fête de la liberté ou Le Dîner des patriotes*, wherein a duke gives a dinner for proven Revolutionaries, and despite his wife's misgivings, appears with a cockade in his hat and drinks to liberty, explaining, "My action is natural enough/I have taken my heart as guide and my King as model." Another theatre offered a revival of a spectacular pantomime by the fireworks artist Ruggieri called *La Prise de la Bastille*, featuring as extras French guards who had actually participated in its storming.[17]

The Comédie Française also contributed to the celebration, but it ignored the requests of Mirabeau, Chénier, and the visiting deputies for *Charles IX*. Presented instead was Aude's *Le Journaliste des ombres ou Momus aux Champs-Elysées*, which portrayed Momus, the god of gaiety, taking refuge in France after having been expelled from Olympus because of his jokes. He is impressed by the Revolution but finds no source of humor in it and at last descends to Hades. There he sets up a paper to inform the shades about the work of the National Assembly and delights the spirits of Voltaire, Rousseau, and Franklin with reports on the progress of their ideas. Talma's interpretation of the shade of Rousseau won praise from the Chénier faction, but the deputies were hardly pleased by the substitution of this play for *Charles IX*.

The following day, July 15, the Comédiens announced to them, as they had earlier announced to the citizens of Paris, that Chénier's play would be given, but only in its turn. The deputies, fearing that they would have to return to their homes before they could see this famous play, continued to protest. The political powers behind the July 14 celebration were embarrassed by this contretemps and the unfortunate impression it was making on the delegates. On July 17, therefore, Mirabeau led a committee to plead again with the Comédiens, and on the same day Danton applied in the name of his district, the Cordeliers. Still the national theatre remained firm in its refusal to be swayed by the force of popular, or even political, opinion.[18]

On July 21, during the intermission between *Alzire* and its afterpiece, *Le Réveil d'Epiménide*, the clerk at the box office came backstage to warn the actors that one of Chénier's servants had come three times during the day, buying a total of ninety-six parterre tickets for a "wedding party." The actors held a hasty consultation and commissioned Naudet to inform the audience, in case of a disturbance, that *Charles IX* could not be presented because Saint-Prix and Mme. Vestris were ill.

In the meantime, Chénier's "wedding party" had arrived. Chénier himself came among a group of friends whom he had just treated to dinner at the home of one Beauvillier. One wonders how deeply Talma was involved in Chénier's plans for the evening, though Mirabeau eventually claimed all responsibility, and Talma, as shall be seen, denied any knowledge of his friend's plans. The actor had been working so closely with Chénier that it seems almost impossible that he was not informed of the impending demonstration. One historian even insists that Talma was present at Chénier's dinner that evening, along with Palissot, Camille Desmoulins, and a number of National Guards. If so, the actor must have left the conspirators early in order to prepare for his performance, smiling inwardly later as his fellow actors realized the threat and made plans to forestall it.

When the curtain rose on Carbon de Flins' play, Talma, Naudet, and Anne Françoise Lange were on stage, and the theatre was in such an uproar that none of the opening words was heard. Then M. Sarrazin, one of the deputies, called for silence to read a demand for *Charles IX*. Naudet stepped to the footlights and pleaded, as Fleury had done in 1789, that the play was still officially under ban, and added that in any case the illness of Saint-Prix and Mme. Vestris would make its performance impossible. Here Talma took the step that he must have known would mean his certain expulsion from the Comédie. He openly contradicted Naudet's explanation—the explanation agreed upon backstage by the rest of the company. He announced that the play could be given, that Mme. Vestris (who, like Talma, was among the "reds") would give the play despite her illness as evidence of her patriotism, and the Saint-Prix's part could be read. When Palissot arose in the audience and volunteered to read the role if no actor would do so, the audience cheered triumphantly. The infuriated Naudet challenged Talma to a duel on the spot, but the audience, less interested in watching this clash of personalities than in seeing the forbidden play, slowly subsided and allowed the company to finish the scheduled production.[19]

The following morning Talma and Naudet exchanged shots which wounded neither and did nothing to relieve the intense animosity between the two men. That same afternoon a delegation of actors appealed to Bailly to forbid the play as a potential source of disturbance. The prudent mayor had no wish to incur the displeasure of the federal deputies who now filled his city, however, and once again the actors were forced to capitulate. *Charles IX* was presented on July 23. Mme. Vestris appeared from her sickbed and Palissot was released from his promise by Jean-Baptiste Grammont, who read the cardinal's lines. This time, opponents of the play made certain that their faction was well represented in the audience, and the uproar throughout was great. One center of disturbance was Danton, who wore his hat throughout the play in open defiance of general custom, and who was at last arrested for disturbing the peace. Troops finally had to be called out to disperse the audience with bayonets.

Talma was naturally accused of being largely responsible for this riot, and to clear himself of such charges, the actor wrote an open letter to Mirabeau:

I appeal to your good nature, sir, to defend me against the calumnious imputation that my enemies are spreading. According to them, it was not you who requested *Charles IX;* I was the one who organized a cabal to force my companions to give the play. They have paid journalists to spread such lies among the public. If you will permit me to tell the truth, I will be cleared of an accusation which they are trying to turn to their advantage. I therefore beg you, sir, to allow me to enlighten the public, who are being aroused against me by a hundred mouths.

Mirabeau's answer was also made public:

Certainly, my dear sir, you may say that it was I who asked for *Charles IX* for the federalists from the provinces, even that I demanded it. It is the truth, and I am proud of it. The repugnance that certain actors showed about this (if rumor can be believed) was ungracious to the public and based on motives completely unrelated to their calling (as if they should be the ones to judge whether a work approved by the authorities is inflammatory or not). The importance which they attached to the request and their refusal were extraordinary and impolitic. Finally, they haughtily told me that they would yield only to public demand. The demand was made, and, I must say, ill received. It is all simple enough, and I don't see why anyone should be confused by it. That they are now trying to make you or others responsible for all this shows a sort of childish rancor which you should not allow to disturb you. Still, I gladly attest that this is the truth.[20]

Talma assumed that this statement cleared him of any responsibility for the riot, but his enemies were not convinced. His Revolutionary sentiments were well known, and Mirabeau himself was living at that time in a house belonging to Talma's wife (a civil ceremony had been performed even though the Church still refused to bless the union).[21] It seems unlikely that Talma's friends would plan a project in which he was so intimately concerned without telling him.

The open letters from Talma and Mirabeau were only part of a campaign which developed in August. *Revolutions de France et de Brabant*, a new paper published by Desmoulins, printed an article accusing Naudet of interfering with the liberty of the stage by suppressing his young colleague. Naudet replied, and in the ensuing controversy Talma fanned the flames by submitting to Desmoulins charges against Naudet based on happenings behind the scenes at the Comédie some six months before. This breach of company etiquette shocked the Comédiens, and Fleury proposed that Talma be expelled from the company. The rest agreed, with only Dugazon, Talma's former tutor, casting a negative vote.[22]

In the midst of all this uproar, Larive attracted a large crowd to the theatre for his debut in comedy, in perhaps the most difficult role in the repertoire, Alceste in *Le Misanthrope*. He was well received, although his best scenes seemed to be those in which he could unleash his passions, as he had learned to do in tragedy. On the last day of August another important debut took place—Grandménil appeared as Arnolphe in *L'Ecole des femmes*.

These successful debuts were a blessing for the hard-pressed Comédie. Aside from its internal troubles, the theatre was threatened ever more seriously by its boulevard rivals, by the government, even by its presumed allies, the dramatists themselves. A large number of playwrights, unsure of presentation in the major theatres, made common cause with those houses which could guarantee them production, and organized a committee of thirty representatives to meet on the subject of freedom in the theatre. Most of the important dramatists of the time were included—Beaumarchais, Laharpe, Chénier, Sédaine, Louis Sébastien Mercier, Jean François Ducis, Palissot, Fabre d'Eglantine, Lemierre, Collot d'Herbois, and Jean-François Cailhava headed the list. This group saw an opportunity to promote its own interests by taking advantage of the present weakness of the Comédie, and a petition was drawn up which Laharpe, the oldest member, presented to the National Assembly. As a preface, he pointed out the important part played by drama in the present emancipation of humanity, citing his own *Warwick*, *Jeanne de Naples*, and *Coriolan* as pleas for freedom. He called for an abolition of special privileges, for an unlimited number of theatres, for all classic works to enter the public domain, and for all living authors to have the right to make their own terms with actors and directors. The Comédie naturally protested, pleading that its legal rights were not being considered and expressing concern that the classics would be degraded in the hands of inexperienced actors. These arguments were passed over, however, and a committee was appointed to study Laharpe's recommendations. The proposals made by the dramatists were accepted almost *in toto* and passed into law on January 13, 1791. Nothing in the course of the Revolution was to have more effect on the theatrical world than the adoption of this legislation.[23]

Leaving the dramatists to pursue this legislation, the boulevard theatres returned to their own strategy of arousing both popular and official distrust in the national theatre. Somewhat surprisingly, they even attacked the obscenity of the Comédie, a charge generally reserved in the past for the boulevard theatres themselves. The small houses now pointed out, however, that their own plays had to pass a censor who did not review the offerings of any of the national theatres, and

I. The closing of the Opéra, July, 1789. The aristocratic Opéra was among the first theatres which the populace forced to close during the July uprisings. The building shown here later housed the Théâtre de la Porte-Saint-Martin. (Armand Dayot, *La Révolution française*. Reproduced by courtesy of Librairie Ernest Flammarion.)

II. Jean-François Ducis (1733–1816). Adaptor of Shakespeare's major tragedies for the French stage. (Paul Lacroix, *Directoire, Consulat et Empire*. Reproduced by courtesy of Imprimerie Firmin-Didot et Cie.)

III. Marie-Joseph Chénier (1764–1811). The first dramatist of the Revolution. (Paul Lacroix, *Directoire, Consulat et Empire*. Reproduced by courtesy of Imprimerie Firmin-Didot et Cie.)

they insisted that this allowed the Comédie to offer such "licentious" pieces as *Le Mariage de Figaro* and Molière's *Georges Dandin*.[24]

The charge most frequently repeated against the Comédie, however, remained that of aristocratic sympathies and practices, since this was most likely to arouse popular indignation. The papers lent their support to the cause of equality; they abandoned the practice of speaking of the "three theatres" of Paris and treated all theatres as equals, as all members of society were now considered equals. The National Assembly testified to the government's interest in discouraging a privileged theatre by dropping from the public treasury (beginning the following year) the pensions of actors at the Comédie and the Comédie Italienne.[25]

In taverns and coffeehouses, popular condemnation of the national theatre grew. The expulsion of Talma was widely viewed as the work of aristocratic and reactionary elements in the Comédie, and on September 16 an overflow crowd halted a production of *Spartacus* with cries of "Talma! Talma!" The actors, in order to get on with the play, promised to give the reasons for the actor's dismissal on the following evening.

The play announced for that night was Molière's *L'Ecole des maris*. Both sides sent their supporters, and the house was filled. Fleury, impeccably dressed in a black suit with gloves, appeared to make the promised announcement. When silence at length descended on the packed and turbulent house, he calmly stated, "Messieurs, the *sociétaires*, convinced that M. Talma has injured their interests and compromised public tranquillity, have unanimously resolved to sever their association with him until the question can be resolved by the proper authorities." But once again the Comédiens' plan for a display of unanimity in public was embarrassingly disrupted. As an angry murmur arose from the house in response to Fleury's curt announcement, Dugazon rushed onstage and shouted: "Messieurs, the Comédie is going to take the same action against me as against M. Talma, but I denounce them all. It is not true that M. Talma betrayed his companions and compromised public tranquillity. His whole crime is having said that *Charles IX* could be given—that is all." The actor then rushed from the stage and disappeared as the house erupted in fury. The Comédiens were powerless to calm the tempest, especially since they could not even begin the announced play because the vanished Dugazon had the leading role. Women hurried out of the theatre, and men in the pit began to tear up their seats to throw them at the players on stage who were vainly trying to restore order. Only the arrival of military forces saved the theatre from extensive damage.[26]

Spurred to action by the seriousness of this riot, Bailly sent the players a request the following morning that they readmit Talma. The actors met, with Dugazon still absent, and agreed that Talma's reinstatement could only lead to more trouble in the future. They refused the mayor's request and ignored a summons to appear before him. "I will never submit to a municipal official's orders," observed the aristocratic Louise Contat. "He might be my candlemaker or my cloth merchant." Bailly then ordered the actors to appear before the City Council, and two representatives, Bellemont and Vanhove, answered the summons. Neither the mayor nor the actors were prepared to compromise, however, and the meeting was fruitless. While Bailly threatened, the players coolly informed him they would submit their case only to the judgment of the King.

In the meantime, Dugazon had sent to several papers a public apology for deserting *L'Ecole des maris*, and Bailly took advantage of the actor's repentant mood to fine Dugazon and confine him for a week to his home. The Comédie as a whole was not so easily disciplined, however, and Bailly, fearful of further destructive popular demonstrations in Talma's favor, grew increasingly alarmed. On September 24, he sent a new decree to the theatre repeating his demand and had copies of it posted all over Paris.[27] Such publicity, despite whatever pressure it may have exerted on the recalcitrant actors, was ill advised, for it made the defiance of the Comédie generally known and resulted inevitably in the very sort of demonstrations the mayor was trying to avoid. The *Chronique de Paris* of September 25 denounced the theatre as a "hotbed of rebellion and aristocracy," and all over the city the story was repeated of a patriot named Déchosal who had interrupted a play at the Comédie by demanding that the actors obey Bailly's order only to be beaten out of the theatre by almost a hundred (or according to him, two hundred) young men with canes.[28]

On September 26, an angry crowd converged on the theatre, and only the personal appearance of the highly respected Bailly prevented a serious riot. The actors were undismayed, however, and calmly announced a new week of plays with no presentation of *Charles IX* and no indication of Talma's reappearance. The aroused citizenry began to demand reform in the Comédie or a new national theatre, and the harassed Bailly finally took the only course left open to him. On September 27, he declared the Comédie closed.[29]

Faced with the triple threat of popular indignation, municipal impatience, and an indefinite suspension of performances, the Comédiens at last capitulated. Bailly closed the theatre on a Monday. On Tuesday morning posters appeared announcing a performance of *Charles IX* for that evening. Bailly immediately sent a letter to Lafayette, now chief of the Parisian National Guard, asking him to station enough troops at the theatre to handle any disorder which Talma's reappearance might cause, but the evening passed quietly. Dugazon and Talma were warmly applauded, and the relieved mayor and a group of municipal officers watched the performance from the King's box. The common people once again turned out in great numbers to support the play, leading more than one journal to comment scornfully on the rabble infiltrating the theatres.[30] The play was less successful when repeated on Thursday, but nonetheless was announced for the following Sunday when Chénier suddenly withdrew it. According to the laws of the time, the author of a play lost all rights to it once it had been presented three consecutive times with receipts below a certain figure (12,000 livres in winter, 8,000 in summer). The small attendance at this revival of his play aroused Chénier's concern lest he lose control of it. The petition he and the other dramatists had submitted to the National Assembly was pending, and once it passed into law, he would be free to do as he wished with *Charles IX*.[31]

Talma was not seen again at the theatre for several weeks. It was reported that no one in the company would speak to him, to Dugazon, or even to Mme. Vestris and Mlle. Desgarcins, who were willing to reaccept him. As fall gave way to winter, no new plays were given, the theatre and the cashbox remained almost empty, and the troupe began to fall apart. Talma and Naudet carried on their war of letters, published in various papers. Mlles. Contat and Raucourt left, refusing to work with Talma; Mlle. Sainval the Younger departed after a quarrel with Mme. Vestris.[32] It began to look as though the citizens of Paris, who so recently had been clamoring for two Comédies, would soon have no Comédie at all. In a desperate attempt to attract audiences, Marie-Elisabeth Joly, the company soubrette, appeared as Athalie. The novelty of so obviously miscasting Racine's tragic queen did indeed bring crowds to the theatre, but the performance suffered from all the ills of the Revolutionary theatre, full blown. Popular figures in the boxes were hailed and applauded during the performance; verses with Revolutionary application set off prolonged demonstrations; Talma was plagued whenever he was on stage by a whistle in the audience that could not be traced, and the play was virtually drowned in the uproar.

In mid-November, an audience demanded to know the reason for the disappearance of Mlles. Contat and Raucourt, and in response, Fleury read a letter from the former in which she stated that she found it impossible to accept Talma as a companion—that his presence at the Comédie disturbed all the rest, and that his friends disturbed public tranquillity and wished to reduce the actors to miserable slaves without even the basic right of choosing their own programs for their own best interests.[33] This outspoken letter aroused new rumors of anti-Revolutionary bias in the theatre, and drove the Comédie to demonstrate its patriotism by a presentation of Voltaire's *Brutus* on November 17. The play had been promptly forgotten when first presented, but its subject matter was now better suited to the times, and the public had for some months been requesting its revival. Bailly, fearing that the evening might be a stormy one, again warned Lafayette to send out patrols to prevent trouble.[34]

The mayor's fears were more than justified, for the performance was one of the most turbulent since the beginning of the Revolution. Even before the play began, Mirabeau was sighted in the fourth box and heartily cheered; he stepped forward to acknowledge the tribute to a new burst of applause. This Revolutionary fervor carried over into the performance, moreover, as verse after verse was followed by extended applause. At last came the lines: "I will die like you, avenging the Roman name, still free and without a king." An uneasy silence followed, broken by a few tentative hisses and a smattering of equally tentative applause. Then a man shouted, "What, is monarchy no longer desired in France? Has 'Long live the King' lost its meaning?" In a moment, everyone was standing and hats and handkerchiefs filled the air. A great shout of "Long live the King" arose, followed by a small but determined "Long live the nation" from a minority in the pit. The opposing shouts continued until a compromise was reached with "Long live Voltaire." While cheers for the dramatist arose, two grenadiers carried in his bust from the lobby and brought it onto the stage to receive homage. There they held it until the demonstration subsided, since they were unable to set it down on the inclined floor. For the second performance this problem was remedied by the installation of niches for busts of Voltaire and Brutus on either side of the stage.

Opposing sides continued to send representatives to later performances of the play, and the clash of enthusiastic patriots and angry aristocrats became a standard evening feature at the theatre. Within a week the municipality was forced to take action, and the mayor required a note appended to all announcements of *Brutus:* "According to the orders of the municipality, the public is warned that no canes, sticks, swords, or offensive weapons will be allowed in the theatre." The next offering, a revival of *La Mort de César*, inspired further demonstrations; Anthony was hissed throughout for his "aristocratic sentiments."[35]

On December 2, the Comédie turned to a dramatization of a contemporary incident, the sort of incident which soon became a staple of Revolutionary drama. George François Desfontaines' *Le Tombeau de Desilles* was based on the story of a young officer who was killed on August 30, 1790, while suppressing a revolt of the soldiers in the garrison at Nancy. Doubtless the Comédiens were attracted to the script as a glorification of the victory of order over anarchy, but the general public viewed it only as an illustration of love for the fatherland. The piece was so successful that imitations of it soon appeared at several other theatres. The Italienne presented Jean Claude Dejaure's *Le Nouveau d'Assas*, and Olympe de Gouges, an eccentric old lady who possessed an uncanny ability for writing unsuccessful plays on apparently foolproof subjects, produced an unpopular *Henry IV et le jeune Desilles.*[36]

The last new play of the year at the Comédie turned again to an attack on the Church. *Jean Calas*, by Laya, told the story of the Dreyfus affair of the eighteenth century. Calas, a Protestant, had been judicially murdered in 1762, but his name was cleared in 1765, largely through the efforts of Voltaire. Given the philosopher's present popularity and the anticlerical possibilities of the subject, the play was extremely well suited to the times. Indeed, the Comédie had to compete with *Calas ou Le Fanatisme*, by Lemierre d'Argy, which opened at the Palais-Royal the preceding day. Chénier too had begun work on a drama about the Protestant martyr, but his play did not appear until 1791. Palissot, Chénier's professional apologist, claimed that both earlier Calas plays were stolen from Chénier through actors who had betrayed the dramatist's confidence, but there is no proof of this.[37]

Turning now for a look at the capital's other theatres, we find that the Comédie's sister theatres, the Opéra and Comédie Italienne, were far less seriously affected by the changes of this first year of the Revolution. On April 8, during the Easter closing, the King turned the administration of the Opéra over to the city of Paris, pleading that the venture had become too expensive for him to maintain. An administrative committee was formed with delegates representing playwrights, singers, dancers, and orchestras, and with three officers selected by the municipality. The most immediate change observed was that cases of artistic temperament and the squabbles traditionally associated with operatic performances were sharply reduced, but otherwise the programs continued with little change. The way was now open for the opera to become a Revolutionary force, though for the time being nothing of the sort occurred. The patriotic commoner who had begun to exercise his influence in other theatres left the Opéra to its upper-class audiences and the repertoire to which they were accustomed.

Indications of change were rather more evident on the Rue Favart at the Comédie Italienne. The standard repertoire still predominated, but several plays with clearly Revolutionary sentiment had already appeared, probably less because of any patriotic feeling in the company than because patriotic plays and reviews would almost certainly attract audiences. This became an ever more serious concern at the Italienne as controls over the smaller houses disappeared and their competition increased. Thus we find the Italienne offering *Le Chêne patriotique* in observance of July 14 and shortly after, on August 23, presenting the first of what was to become a most popular form of anticlerical drama, a convent play.

Early in August all of Paris was shocked and filled with pity by the story of an unfortunate girl who had been shut up against her wishes in the convent of Argenteuil. She asked that her vows be annulled and, upon the recommendation of the Council General, Herault de Séchelles, her request was granted. The monastic system, already the object of widespread suspicion, came under heavy attack, and the Comédie Italienne hastened to make dramatic capital of the situation. The result was Joseph Fiévée and Henri Berton's *Les Rigueurs du cloître*. In it a young orphan, Lucile, takes monastic vows to save her menaced lover, but she is unable to bring herself to renounce him. For her obstinacy she is confined on bread and water, to be subsequently rescued by her lover and the National Guard. The latter proclaim the release of all those taken from society by indiscreet or forced vows and lead the young people out of the cloisters, singing "Long live liberty, the nation, and the King." The play was so tremendous a success that convent plays soon filled the Parisian theatres. The Associés gave *Les Religieuses;* the Délassements-Comiques, *Les Religieuses délivrées* and *La Sortie du couvent;* the Ambigu, *Les Soeurs du pot.* Scorn for the organized Church was apparent in all such plays, even in so seemingly harmless a trifle as *Vert Vert,* the next offering at the Italienne, which showed a parrot taken from a convent and later returned, fully debauched, to mix gross comments with the sacred chants. The Comédie Française remained almost alone in its refusal to stoop to such antireligious sensationalism, a scruple which was roundly condemned as aristocratic by the enemies of the theatre.

The Italienne's final production of the year capitalized on the current glorification of the *philosophes* as the fathers of the new liberty. Jean-Nicolas Bouilly's *Jean Jacques Rousseau à ses derniers moments* was primarily a sentimental piece, but the presumed dying words of the philosopher show the spirit in which the play was conceived: "Let the French follow my principles, let them support my writings, and soon they will break all the chains which degrade them and become the first people of the world." At the second performance the audience, doubtless recalling the honor shown Voltaire at the Comédie after the production of *Brutus,* had the bust of Rousseau carried onto the stage and crowned.[38]

The relatively heavy demands of comic opera seem to have protected the Italienne during this first year of the Revolution from serious competitors in this genre, but this monopoly was soon threatened. The Théâtre de Monsieur, as we have seen, was so successful in 1789 at the Tuileries that upon its eviction the Italienne suggested a merger. When the demands of the Italienne proved unacceptably high, the Monsieur troupe announced, on January 4, 1790, that it would open in a little theatre in the Saint-Germain fair which had housed Nicolet's Variétés before prosperity allowed him to move to the boulevard. On January 10 a large crowd attended the opening of this theatre in a section of Paris where such entertainment had been absent for years. The opening offering was Giovanni Paisiello's *Il Barbieri di Siviglia,* and most of the company's repertoire was repeated in the days which followed. The first new play in the new theatre was given on January 25—*L'Epiménide français,* by a M. de Riouf, a successful attempt to capitalize on the success of Carbon de Flins' play, *Le Réveil d'Epiménide à Paris*, which had opened a few days before at the Comédie.

In the meantime, planning continued for the new theatre which Autié and Viotti, the directors of the Monsieur, had decided to build in the Rue Feydeau. When work actually began on this building, impressively large and uncomfortably near the Italienne, the directors of the latter theatre finally recognized their danger and demanded that Bailly, the mayor, stop the project. Since the wishes of the national theatres still commanded some respect, Bailly sent a letter to the directors of the Monsieur informing them that for reasons of "policy and administration" he could not allow several theatres to cluster too closely together in the capital. Autié and Viotti chose to ignore this decree and ordered work on the theatre to continue, hoping that Bailly, when presented with a *fait accompli*, would back down. Such indeed proved to be the case.

The remainder of the winter in the Saint-Germain fair was not encouraging. Several weeks went by with only a single new offering, Nicolas Pariseau's comedy *Rosalie*, given February 13. The production was hissed throughout, and the author unleashed a tempest by dashing onto the stage at the end and shouting, "You deserve not roses, but thistles!" A turbulent crowd awaited him afterward at the stage door, but Pariseau prudently declined this demonstration and left by another way. The *Almanach général* dismissed the evening by noting, "The work proves that however accustomed an author may be to gathering roses, he may sometimes encounter thorns."[39]

It was not until July 17, during the festivities following the Festival of Federation, that the Monsieur mounted a truly successful play in its temporary quarters. Collot d'Herbois' *La Famille patriote ou La Fédération* drew heavily on the enthusiasm generated by July 14, placing its action on that glorious day. In it, M. Gaspard embraces his servant as an equal and friend and tells his daughter, who is about to wed, "You will be proud to say: I was married on July 14, the day of the great Federation." Friends and Gaspard's employees arrive to share their joy and accompany the family to church. During the intermission, while the wedding was presumably taking place, the orchestra played both marriage airs and songs from the Champ de Mars ceremony, and when the action resumes, the characters comment on the day's events. The servant describes the Federation service:

And then the King, the good King, in the midst of the federalists like a father among his children, seemed to show all along from the depths of his heart that feeling which he at last expressed: 'Liberty—I shall preserve it.' And then the altar where the priest mounted, raising his hands as if to say to God: 'Lord, come to take your place among a free people!' And then the respectful silence when the priest turned to bless us, and the cry of joy that followed—I was overwhelmed. You can't imagine how beautiful it was.

Yet, it is not only the common folk in the drama who feel so inspired. Gaspard's brother-in-law, an aristocrat, cries, "I forswear my prejudices forever. I have become a citizen. All other titles are chimerical. I renounce them—I sacrifice them on the altar of the country." He then sang a song which many members of the audience already knew and which received thunderous applause. It was repeated five times, with the house joining in with delight on the frequent refrains. This melody, the "Ça ira," was to become so important a Revolutionary symbol that a few lines of the version sung that night appear below. They are simple enough, and the tremendous appeal of the song is perhaps difficult to understand unless we remember the supercharged atmosphere of patriotism into which it was released:

Ah ça ira, ça ira, ça ira
Drum beating, fuses always lighted,
Ah ça ira, ça ira, ça ira
All good Frenchmen march forward.
Liberty will never die.
They will fight for her with ardor.
Ah ça ira, ça ira, ça ira
Drum beating, fuses always lighted,
Ah ça ira, ça ira, ça ira
All good Frenchmen march forward
When the law requires it
When our land approves it
Then the oldest soldier
Grows youthful at her call.
Ah ça ira, ça ira, ça ira
etc. etc.

La Famille patriote proved so attractive that Autié and Viotti urged d'Herbois to write another patriotic piece for them. His *Le Procès de Socrate ou Le Régime des anciens temps,* presented on November

7, achieved another substantial success. Through the dramatization of the trial of Socrates, the author claimed:

I wanted to portray in dramatic form all the defenders of the popular cause, all those who have suffered and been persecuted for it. Athens was governed by aristocrats, and these aristocrats, justly called tyrants, were much more dangerous in full power than during a counter-revolution, for they had already deprived a nation of its rights and massacred all the friends of liberty.

A critic of the time noted:

The play is popular and deserves to be; great truths boldly expressed, striking allusions to contemporary events, touching interchanges, a courageous philosophy, and the honest interpretation of M. Paillardelle, who is always marvelous but who is particularly so in the role of Socrates—all assure M. Collot d'Herbois' play a great success, despite any cabal of egoists who may wish to keep such truth from the stage.[40]

Apparently there was indeed an unfavorable reaction to d'Herbois after *La Famille patriote*, and a number of persons who disagreed with his philosophy gathered to hiss the new work. When Camille Desmoulins started a fight with one of this group, a challenge resulted and tempers ran high. Ironically, the account of the accusation and trial of the Greek philosopher as given by d'Herbois now suggest much more strongly the methods of the impending Revolutionary Tribunal than those of the "tyrannical" regime which had just disappeared. The settings, as usual, were detailed and spectacular, but with little regard for period. The German dramatist Augustus von Kotzebue, visiting the theatre, noted, "The Greek soldiers were in long Turkish trousers, with their hair well powdered and pomatumed in the true French style. But the most curious thing of all was a painted chimney in Socrates' prison, with the tongs and fire-shovel, and some tobacco-pipes lying upon the chimney-piece."[41]

On December 31, the Théâtre de Monsieur gave its last production in the Saint-Germain fair and looked forward to becoming one of the major theatres of the capital in the almost completed building in the Rue Feydeau. A return to the center of the city would surely add to the core of faithful audience members who had followed the Monsieur troupe to this remote suburb. This final evening ended with a song written by the popular dramatist Cousin Jacques and delivered by the actor Nicolas Lesage, promising that the actors would redouble their efforts in their new home.[42]

The Revolution brought a flood of new playhouses to Paris, a number of which had already appeared before the new Monsieur opened its doors. The Easter vacation was the logical time to launch such ventures, and many small theatres appeared in the spring of 1790. Alexandre Tuetey quotes a letter to Bailly dated April 8 praising his efforts in preventing the installation of rude stages and theatres in the major intersections of the Champs Elysées, but minor houses elsewhere successfully avoided municipal sanction.[43]

Certainly the most significant opening during this spring was that of the Variétés-Palais-Royal in the sumptuous theatre the Duc d'Orléans had hoped would house the Opéra. The directors, Gaillard and Dorfeuille, had for six years kept the Variétés among the most popular of the minor houses, but the acquisition of the Duke's theatre encouraged them to aspire to elevate the Variétés to the first rank. They were well aware that the sort of offerings accepted in a wooden theatre with pasteboard decorations would never suffice in this vast stone edifice. They purged their troupe of the gross comedians who had formed its nucleus and sought more subtle and versatile artists to replace them. Among these new actors were Antoine Michot, Mme. Fiat, M. and Mme. Saint-Clair, and at least one first-rate talent—Jacques de Monvel.[44]

Monvel was already well known to Parisian audiences, having made his debut at the Comédie in 1770 and joined that company two years later. He generally served as understudy to Molé, playing tragic roles with style and spirit. He had neither the talent nor the reputation to step into Lekain's place when that artist died, however, and his attempt to do so was met with general disapproval. The disheartened Monvel left the country to become official reader for the King of Sweden. He returned to Paris in 1786, but the Comédie would not reaccept him, and he remained at loose ends until he joined Gaillard and Dorfeuille's project. Before the opening in the Rue de Richelieu, he had allied himself with the Variétés, playing leading roles in *Louis XII* and *Le Pessimiste*.

The new theatre also conducted an intensive search for promising authors; and if it discovered only minor figures, they were still many of the best dramatists the period produced; Cailhava, Laya, Guillaume

Pigault-Lebrun, and Collot d'Herbois had all presented works on the new stage before it was a year old. The theatre suffered heavily from the restriction which still prevented it from presenting the classic repertoire, but even so, it almost immediately established itself, as its directors had hoped, as one of the major playhouses of Paris.

Another successful new theatre was launched in June, two weeks after the opening of the Variétés-Palais-Royal; this was the Théâtre-Français Comique et Lyrique, which boldly established itself in the Rue de Bondy, directly opposite the Opéra. It was on this site that Gaillard and Dorfeuille had begun their upward climb, as codirectors of a small and uncomfortable marionette theatre. Here, too, Audinot's troupe had played for two years after Gaillard and Dorfeuille had moved to more prosperous quarters. This little wooden theatre had been torn down in 1787, however, and replaced by a paper mill.

In 1790 a certain Charles-Louis Desnoyer bought the mill and destroyed it to make way for a new theatre, larger than the old one and built of stone. On June 21, this new theatre opened with a comedy, *Le Danger des conseils* and a comic opera, *Les Trois Mages*. Vaudeville, comedy, drama, and comic opera were the staples of the house, but as time passed, occasional plays became more and more important. Although, as we shall see, the theatre produced no major success for six months (until Cousin Jacques' *Nicodème dans la lune* in November), it was popular from the very beginning.[45]

The Revolution by no means guaranteed such popularity to boulevard theatres. Rather more typical was the Bleuettes-Comiques, founded before 1789 but unable to survive amid the increased competition the Revolution encouraged. Early in 1790 its director, Clément de Lornaison, gave up the struggle, closed his theatre, and joined forces with Desnoyer at the Comique et Lyrique. It is difficult to determine precisely why Desnoyer's venture succeeded when so many failed—perhaps its proximity to the Opéra actually worked to its advantage, perhaps the public was attracted by fond memories of the old Variétés, perhaps the appeal was in the theatre itself, small, but considered by at least one writer of the time "one of the loveliest in France."[46] Whatever the reasons, for over a year the Théâtre-Français Comique et Lyrique was one of the most frequented theatres in Paris, a new source of competition and irritation for the struggling major playhouses.

The spring of 1790 saw also the long-awaited opening of Mlle.

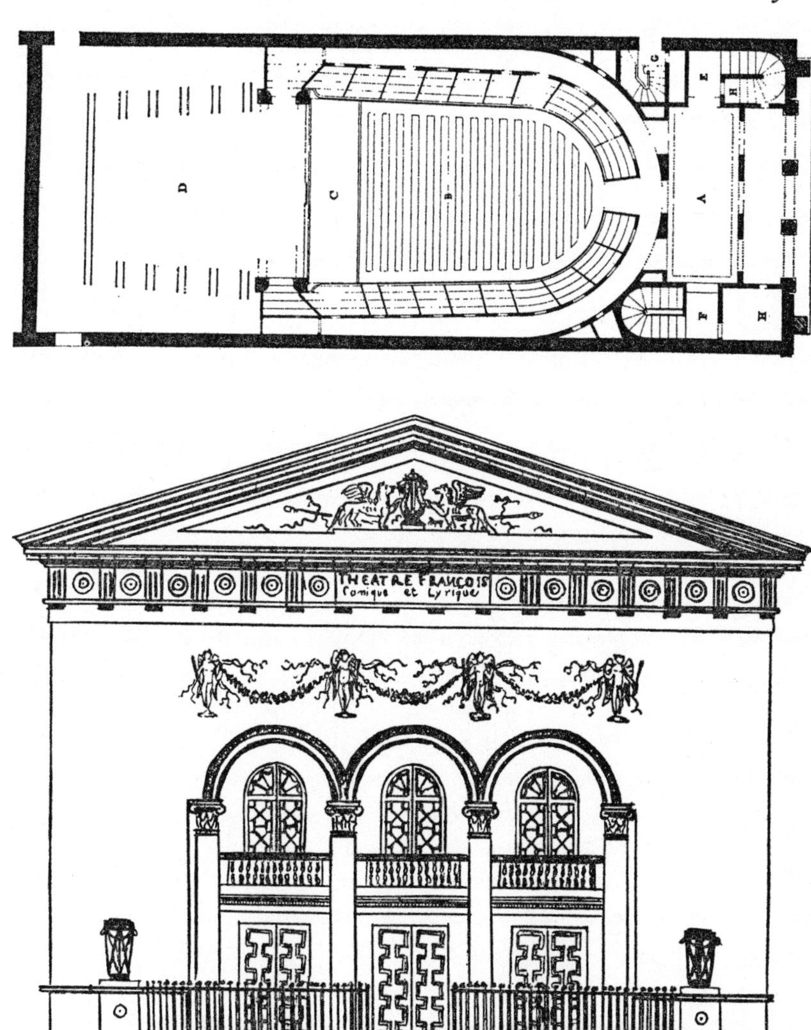

3. Plan and elevation of the Théâtre-Français Comique et Lyrique, built 1790. One of the first new theatres of the Revolution, the Comique et Lyrique recalls theatres of an earlier period in its elongated horseshoe auditorium, at this time rarely seen in Paris. The classic trimmings on the façade, however, clearly reflect contemporary taste. (Reproduced by courtesy of the Harvard Theatre Collection.)

Montansier's new theatre in the former home of the dispossessed Beaujolais. Perhaps again under pressure from the national theatres, Bailly had delayed the opening all winter, but Montansier's many friends at court were still an advantage rather than a liability and at last the Council General commanded Bailly to allow the theatre to open at the end of the holidays. Of the staff who had worked with her at Versailles, Montansier kept only the prompter, who had worked under her twenty years before in Rouen. Her faithful friend Neuville shared the new directorship with her, and another of her admirers, the Abbé de Bouyon, helped finance the venture. The opening evening featured the usual opening address, written by the popular Cousin Jacques, Paul Ulric Dubuisson and Storace's comic opera *Les Epoux mécontents*, and P. J. B. Desforges' comedy *Le Sourd ou L'Auberge pleine*. The latter proved one of the theatre's greatest successes and established the reputation of Baptiste the Younger, who played the leading role.

This theatre too was popular from the very outset, though the *Almanach des spectacles* reports that many patrons found "the theatre too small and the actors too large." The stage, after all, had been designed for puppets, and full-grown actors on it were forced to play uncomfortably close to their audience. Mlle. Sainval the Elder, who had rather hard and severe features, was often quite frightening for spectators seated within a few feet of her, and Grammont, whose less than handsome physiognomy had caused no problem at Versailles, found these intimate audiences less willing to accept him in romantic leads.[47] Mlle. Montansier had gained her immediate goals, however. She had obtained a theatre in the very heart of Paris and had attracted a public. The physical improvements could come later. A further boon came when the younger Sainval sister left the Comédie in October amid the ill feeling generated by Talma's forced return. Montansier hastened to hire the disaffected actress to join her older sister and Grammont. Anne Mars and MM. Dufresse and Lacane, actors with less impressive backgrounds but with considerable promise, were signed to supplement the three top performers.[48]

Five other minor theatres survived the vicissitudes of this first year of the Revolution, all located near the Boulevard du Temple, the section of Paris which had now largely replaced the fairs as the center of popular entertainment. These were the Beaujolais, the Délassements-Comiques, Nicolet's Grands Danseurs du Roi, Audinot's

Ambigu-Comique, and Sallé's Théâtre des Associés. A stroll down the boulevard was an exciting excursion in these days. At every step one was assailed by the shrill cries of barkers and doormen for the tiny dramatic shows called "parades" which lined the street. The shouts and laughter of the festive crowds were punctuated with drums, trumpet calls, and bursts of music from the host of little restaurants clustered among the fair booths and tiny theatres. These, the first *café-concerts,* featured popular singers as a means of attracting the holiday crowds. An atmosphere we would associate today only with the ephemeral splendor of a carnival midway could be found here every evening more or less permanently established in the heart of Paris. Theatre was now very much in vogue, with some thirteen periodicals regularly running dramatic reviews,[49] but the public was fickle, and box-office receipts, especially along the boulevard, were highly erratic. Long-run successes were rare indeed; the average minor theatre, plagued by police restrictions, often a victim of fire, tightly hemmed in by competition, led a most uncertain existence. Only constant variety in the programs offered could assure continuing audiences, and most of these little houses indulged in a frantic shuffling of musicians, variety acts, pantomimes—anything that came their way.

The unpredictable and ephemeral nature of such presentations caused many journals to refuse to carry notices for the minor theatres. The editors complained, with justification, that if other theatres were sometimes reproached for a lack of novelty, the opposite was the case here. "When will theatre directors understand," one such asked, "that a striking play is worth more, even if they must play a hundred louis for it, than thirty ephemeral bagatelles which cost 12 francs apiece?"[50] With ruin so often threatening, however, none of these little theatres could hope to aspire to a hundred-louis production. Many could not even afford to repair their roofs, and Fleury describes a *Roméo et Juliette* given at one where the death scene was ruined by rain dripping on Juliette's upturned face.[51] Chief among the offenders in constant program changing was the Délassements-Comiques, whose director, Plancher Valcour, may be remembered as the demonstrative gentleman who greeted the Revolution by tearing down the gauze curtain required by law in his theatre. Valcour's zeal for the republican cause led him to write a whole series of plays burning with hatred of curates and aristocrats. Other dramatists, such as d'Eglantine and Fabre d'Olivet, supplemented this patriotic fare with dramatizations of contemporary events, reproducing events of the day almost immediately on Valcour's stage. Toward the end of 1790, the director turned his enterprise over to M. and Mme. Coulon, who were less successful and found themselves within a few months on the verge of bankruptcy.[52]

The old rivals Audinot and Nicolet had in the course of 1790 both put together troupes of homogeneity and polish. Neither had actors of the first rank, but all of their performers were adequate and many were quite good. After the first full year of the Revolution, these two oldest boulevard theatres were still the most secure. The Théâtre des Associés also prospered, despite the low caliber of both actors and audience. Upon the death of Vienne, the remaining "associate," Sallé, changed the theatre's name to the Théâtre Patriotique, replacing all the comedies, vaudevilles, and dramas in his repertoire with political pieces. He kept the tragedies, however, most of them openly stolen from the classic repertoire. In the midst of its own troubles, the Comédie still found time to protest this plagiarism, especially in light of the popularity Sallé was gaining from it. The director, facing an official injunction, made a surprising defense. He wrote a letter to the Comédie, saying, "Sirs, on Sunday I will give a presentation of *Zaïre;* I pray you to be good enough to send a delegation from your illustrious company, and if you recognize Voltaire's play after you see it performed by my actors, I will accept your protest and never again present it on my stage." Two members of the Comédie obligingly went and found Voltaire's drama so disfigured that their anger dissolved in laughter. The following day, the Comédie approved all of Sallé's repertoire.[53]

The Associés stood in the very heart of the boulevard carnival, a bit of fortune not shared by all of the minor theatres. At the very end of the boulevard, the last bright refuge before the oppressive gloom of a blighted residential district, stood the Café Goddet. Intrepid souls venturing past this point and down the Boulevard Mesnil-Montant would find, just before the gay sounds of that last boulevard pleasure-dome faded behind them, the new home of Delomel's Théâtre Beaujolais.

Delomel had not willingly come to this pass. He had resented and resisted the highhanded manner in which Mlle. Montansier had arrived from Versailles and appropriated his theatre. During the first weeks of 1790, the director had sent his troupe out all over Paris to post placards bearing the names of the company and the notice:

In the face of the unjustifiable persecutions which the director of the Théâtre de Beaujolais is suffering, he notifies the public that nothing will diminish his courage, nor that of his actors. On the contrary, they will redouble their activity and talent to continue to merit the favors which the people of Paris have always heaped upon them and by which they hope to be honored again.

The productions of the Beaujolais will therefore continue in the theatre which they occupy at the septentrional corner of the Beaujolais gallery of the Palais-Royal.

Signed: Delomel.[54]

The protest was in vain, as Delomel himself must have recognized it would be. Mlle. Montansier had on her side the royal favor of Marie Antoinette, still a powerful force, the protection of the police, and sufficient monetary reserves to fight the case out in court if necessary. Delomel had nothing but the courage of his despair. Despite the claims of his posted notice, his theatre could not even claim a faithful public who would protest its closing.

Tuetey reproduces a letter dated January 15 from Bailly to de Gourion, major general of the National Guard, asking him to reinforce the guard at the Palais-Royal to stem any disorder which might arise from the eviction of the Beaujolais actors.[55] Apparently, in the face of this threat, Delomel left quietly. For a week thereafter, the *Chronique de Paris* carried promises of a reopening, while the director continued his frantic search for a building to house his company. To keep alive, the troupe began playing in the suburbs, in Saint-Denis, Corbeil, and Palaiseau, until at last, late in February, Delomel located the shelter in the stygian darkness of the Boulevard Mesnil-Montant. The little house had been erected in 1779 to house a group of students from the Opéra who wished to demonstrate their talents. Unable to make ends meet despite the introduction of popular pastoral dramas, harlequinades, and light comedies, the Théâtre des Elèves de l'Opéra, as it was called, closed in 1780. In 1787 it reopened under the title Feux Physiques, and despite its unfavorable location, managed to remain open until the Revolution with showings of firework displays.[56] The location of the theatre made large audiences rare, but Delomel managed to keep going, with the aid of his devoted troupe, his own dramatists, and above all, with the help of Cousin Jacques.

In the course of this history we have already encountered Cousin Jacques' name several times, and not surprisingly, for his prolific pen supported from time to time in the early years of the Revolution almost every Parisian theatre except the Comédie and the Opéra. Cousin Jacques was the pen name assumed by Beffroy de Reigny, a former college professor who sought to follow the example of Voltaire, first by writing extravagant poetry, then by editing *Les Lunes*, an early comic review. Turning to drama, he tried to enter the Comédie, but had not yet gained enough of a reputation to be considered by that body. Later, his great success in the minor theatres barred this door against him even more firmly, but his work was by then in such demand elsewhere that his disappointment could not have been great. His early triumphs were all at the Comédie Italienne, but in 1790 he was produced and applauded in a great number of other theatres. His specialty was light topical plays, just the sort of thing the audiences of the Revolution were seeking. His early works, such as *La Couronne des fleurs* and *Sans Adieux*, were light muscial fancies of only moderate popular appeal, but the tremendous success of Collot d'Herbois' *La Famille patriote* at the Théâtre de Monsieur in July inspired him to turn to patriotic revues. A rapid series of these, with titles such as *La Prise de la Bastille*, *La Fête de la Fédération* and *La Fédération du Parnasse* soon brought him to the position in the minor theatres which Chénier filled at the Comédie—the acknowledged playwright of the Revolution. Caps and bustles based on the costume of one of his characters enjoyed a great vogue. A crockery maker grew rich selling crystal goblets in the "Cousin Jacques" style. His bust appeared in the library of Lyons, and he sent his portrait, completely packed, to whoever requested it, for twelve livres. He inspired a host of imitators, but no serious rivals.[57]

It was one of Cousin Jacques' patriotic revues, *Le Retour du Champ-du-Mars*, which saved the Beaujolais from bankruptcy in 1790, for it was the only success in this disastrous year. The play was insubstantial enough, but its subject matter appealed strongly in 1790 to audiences. Soldiers were shown carrying in triumph a bust of Louis XVI, which was given into the hands of Apollo, who in turn confided it to the Muses to place in the "Temple of Memory." Each transfer was accompanied by songs honoring the "Good King," all greeted with cheers from the audience. The actors apparently recognized upon first reading that the play would be a success, for they wasted no time in presenting it. Cousin Jacques submitted the script to them in early October, and it was read, rehearsed, and given in five days.

The custom of the day was that the author of a new play was introduced only if the play pleased the audience sufficiently for them to demand him after the presentation. Otherwise his name, which did not appear on the posters, would be mercifully lost unless the author insisted on wooing posterity by committing the work to print. *Le Retour du Champ-du-Mars* delighted its audience so much that the curtain fell amid enthusiastic shouts for the author, but the actors looked about for him in vain. Furious over the speed with which his play had been mounted, and over the resulting hesitations and forgotten lines, Cousin Jacques refused to face his public, and chose instead to take refuge in the flies of the theatre, where he hid behind a bank of pulleys. The actor Dumily announced the author's name, and cries of "Cousin Jacques! Cousin Jacques!" shook the walls of the theatre. Delomel, his manager, and his actors frantically searched the backstage area, realizing that a catastrophic riot might break out at any moment. At last Cousin Jacques was discovered in his retreat by a stagehand who sounded the alarm, and a body of actors carried the struggling author, pale with anger, onto the stage. As the house cheered, he freed himself and stalked to the footlights. A silence fell, during which Cousin Jacques stammered with rage for a few moments, then sputtered, "The villains didn't know a word of it! They ruined it!" Dumily hastened to cut off the author's tirade, crying, "Ah well, what of it? It didn't go well today, and that makes you angry? Calm yourself; tomorrow, *ça ira!* Right, comrades?" and plunged into the popular song, which the actors immediately joined. It was a brilliant stroke. The audience took up the refrain with delight, redoubling their applause, and the curtain fell with the enraged author shouting ineffectually into the tumult. Cousin Jacques swore, not surprisingly, never to return to the Beaujolais, but Delomel was too pleased by his windfall to be concerned. With the spectre of financial failure driven off for a time, he was even able to give some wages to those few actors who had faithfully remained with him.[58]

Cousin Jacques' next produced work went far toward soothing the author's ruffled feelings. *Nicodème dans la lune*, presented at the Théâtre-Français Comique et Lyrique on November 7, was the first major success for that theatre, and one of the most popular pieces produced in Paris in 1790. It also marked a somewhat new direction in Cousin Jacques's style. Perhaps the experience with *Le Retour du Champ-du-Mars* at the Beaujolais in October had soured the playwright on such loosely organized patriotic revues, for *Nicodème* presented its Revolutionary ideas in a much more cohesive dramatic form, reminiscent of the successful *Epiménide* at the Comédie. *Nicodème dans la lune* was thus one of the first boulevard plays to succeed both as entertainment and propaganda, for the traditional drama in these popular houses—fast moving, comic, full of song, spectacle, and farce—was not easily adapted to propagandistic ends.

All the spectacle beloved by boulevard audiences was present: the opening scene showed vine-covered hillsides and high up in the rear a hut, where a hermit was following with a telescope a balloon floating in the air. At the foot of the hill, peasants worked in the fields; and downstage in a small wood, a young man sat in a tree he was pruning, singing and chatting with two old ladies who sat knitting below. The two other settings—a gilded reception room in an imperial palace and an ornamented classic garden—were equally detailed and splendid.[59]

The story concerns Nicodème, a rough, naïve, good-hearted French peasant apprenticed to an old inventor. Nicodème's master, afraid of the consequences of the Revolution, plans to escape in a balloon; but while he sleeps, Nicodème steals the device and flies off. This choice of locomotion reflected a popular concern of the day, for although balloons had been flown by the Montgolfiers in 1783, they did not attract wide interest until 1790, when André Garnerin launched a hydrogen balloon as part of the festival of July 14. Nicodème experienced the same problems of control common to most early balloonists, but with more spectacular results: he ended at last on the moon.

In this faraway place, the apprentice finds a situation much like the popular picture of the old regime; here is an oppressed peasantry, evil lords, and a well-meaning but uninformed monarch surrounded by unscrupulous advisers. After a few scenes depicting Nicodème's romantic intrigues with ladies of the court, the major plot line is again taken up. Aided by a brave curate, Nicodème manages to gain an audience with the ruler to inform him of the sufferings of his subjects. The good king, anxious to improve the situation, asks Nicodème's advice. Nothing easier, says the clever peasant; merely follow the example of France and insist that everyone give up his selfish demands. The simple words convert the court on the spot, and minister, prelates, and courtesans all embrace the peaceful revolution Nicodème proposes. The moon thus enters the happy condition already existing in Nicodème's native land.

Despite the moderate tone of the piece, the director of the theatre feared that it might arouse partisan debate and inserted a notice in the papers announcing that his projected presentation had been lawfully approved by all authorities. He added that he understood that a cabal was being formed against him, but bravely affirmed that "the walls of this theatre will not fall at the sound of hisses as did those of Jericho at the sound of trumpets."[60] His fears proved groundless. A large audience (all seats were sold in advance and even places in the orchestra corners and corridors went for high prices) accepted the play with delight, and within the next year it was repeated almost two hundred times, providing the foundation stone of the theatre's repertoire. By late 1793, when the theatre was forced to close due to mismanagement, *Nicodème dan la lune* had been presented a total of 363 times.[61]

As for Cousin Jacques, his success encouraged him to write a whole series of plays in the same vein. The Théâtre-Français Comique et Lyrique itself presented two of them, *Les Trois Voyageurs* and *Arlequin cherchant un logement.* All of these works had the same moderate tone; since Cousin Jacques wanted to avoid the extremes of both sides in the Revolutionary struggle, he pleaded always for a liberal monarchy without abuses and special privileges. In 1790 this was a popular philosophy, though as time passed it became less so. In 1791 the Jacobins accused Cousin Jacques of being a reactionary, bribed by aristocrats to preach monarchy. In 1793 he was arrested, but managed to escape the Revolutionary Tribunal. By that time the author of *Nicodème dans la lune* must have looked back ruefully on its optimistic subtitle—"the peaceful Revolution."[62]

As the year drew to a close, theatre owners, actors, playwrights, and public all looked forward to the impending legislation on freedom of the theatres and speculated on its possible results. Yet even before the decree was passed, forces were in motion which would bring tighter controls to the theatre than it had ever experienced under the old regime. Ironically, it was old Laharpe, who had represented the dramatists in their initial plea for freedom, who helped launch the countermovement. In a speech entitled "A Discourse on the Liberty of the Theatre" given before the Society of the Friends of the Constitution (the club that would become the Jacobins), he denounced the Comédie and accused the theatre of espousing the cause of the enemies of the Revolution. He called for more patriotic plays and censorship

III

The Theatres Set Free

January–June, 1791

DURING the next six months the spreading effects of the Revolution brought threats to several long-established institutions. The monarchy, so lately in popular favor, became increasingly suspect with Louis' flight to Varennes; the Church became the object of violent attack, an attack pursued vigorously on the stages of Paris. Yet theatrical institutions suffered as well. The Comédie experienced a double loss: the government deprived it of its long-held monopoly of French plays, and Talma and half its troupe left to join another theatre.

The Comédie's first offering in 1791 was in sharp contrast to the almost royalistic *Tombeau de Desilles* of the previous month. *Liberté conquise ou Le Despotisme renversé*, by Harny de Guerville and Favart, was a series of Revolutionary tableaux glorifying the spirit which led the guards of the Bastille to mutiny. The action is simple, and although it occurs in an imaginary locale, the events described are clearly Parisian. When a local governor arouses the suspicion of the populace by mustering foreign troops, a popular leader is chosen who rallies the citizens. The governor then takes refuge in a Bastille-like fortress; but as the tocsin sounds, the guards of the fortress join the people in its destruction. The fate of the governor is not disclosed.

Public reaction to the play was enormous. Between the third and fourth acts, the orchestra raised the house to a pitch of delirium by playing the "Ça ira"; and when the insurgents took the civic oath before attacking the fortress, the spectators arose, waving hats and handkerchiefs, with cries of "Long live the nation" and "Long live the King." On the opening night, an actress in the play not only named the authors, according to custom, but also crowned them on stage, to the great joy of the audience. At the third performance one Arné, a guard who had mutinied at the Bastille, was recognized in the audience and carried to the stage to be crowned as well. Although the author's crown was not handy, the bonnet of one of the extras was used as a symbol of liberty, and the aptness of this gesture brought the audience to new heights of enthusiasm. The play was often repeated afterward, always to great acclaim, and on at least one occasion the crowd rushed onto the stage, determined to tear the governor to pieces.[1]

On January 7, Dugazon and Talma offered to make peace with Naudet, then playing one of the leading parts in *Liberté conquise*, and the schism in the company seemed healed. The following day Mlles. Contat, Raucourt, and Sainval the Younger, all absent since the quarrels of the previous October, returned to the theatre and were warmly applauded that evening in Harny and Favart's play.[2] As for Harny himself, the author of the popular libretto, the success of *Liberté conquise* after a series of failures turned his interest to political matters, and he eventually found himself a judge on the Revolutionary Tribunal, a position which he loathed but could not escape. He often, it is reported, shed tears over the unfortunates he was forced to condemn to the guillotine.[3]

Early January saw also the report of the committee which, it will be remembered, had been appointed by the National Assembly in July, 1790, to study the proposal advanced by Laharpe and other dramatists for greater freedom in the theatre. The Comédie, realizing at last the menace this offered to the *status quo*, offered to allow the establishment of a rival theatre in the capital, which would have rights over the present Comédie repertoire with the exception of Corneille, Racine, Molière, Crébillon, and a few others. This major concession, if made a year earlier, might have prevented the disastrous legislation now under discussion, but the time for half measures had passed. On January 13, the delegate Chapelier condemned the proposed compromise in the National Assembly, arguing that it would divide privileges and not destroy them. He insisted that all theatres be freed and all authors given control of their own works. Only in this way, he asserted, could the theatre "become a school of virtue and patriotism."

Chapelier's ideas were put into a concrete eight-point proposal by Mirabeau, and this proposal was passed the same day. Some of its more influential articles decreed:

> Any citizen can establish a public theatre and present in it plays of any kind, by making a declaration to the municipality before its opening.
>
> The works of authors dead more than five years are public property and can, former privileges notwithstanding, now be presented in all theatres indiscriminately.
>
> The works of living authors cannot be presented in any public theatre without the formal consent in writing of the authors, under penalty of confiscation of the total receipts for the benefit of the author.
>
> The directors or members of the different theatres will be, by reason of their position, subject to the inspection of the municipality. They will receive orders only from the municipality, which cannot stop or forbid the presentation of any play except at the request of author or actor, and which can require nothing except that which conforms to the laws and to police regulations.[4]

Authors and directors of the minor theatres naturally hailed this decree, and the national houses naturally resented and attempted to circumvent it. They argued that the new law was not retroactive and that they could therefore retain plays written before its proclamation. The authors again petitioned the Assembly, and soon after, a further decree was passed extending the law of January 13. The two new articles stated:

> I. In respect to the disposition of article III of the decree of January 13 concerning plays: The works of living authors, even those works given before that date, printed or not, cannot be presented on any public stage anywhere in the kingdom without the formal consent in writing of the authors, or, if the authors have been dead for less than five years, of their heirs or beneficiaries. The penalty for failure to obtain consent will be forfeiture of the total profit of the presentation to the author, his heirs, or his beneficiaries.
>
> II. The agreement between authors and theatre directors will be perfectly free, and the aforementioned works cannot be taxed by municipal officers or any other public functionaries to increase or to decrease the agreed price. The author's payment, agreed upon between him or his representative and the director, cannot be seized or stopped by the creditors of the director.[5]

The major houses complained once again that these laws had been passed without their consultation, but they were forced to accept them. No manifestation of the Revolution affected the theatre as much as did this legislation.

A host of new theatres sprang up under the stimulus of the January 13 decree, but such organizations, however ephemeral, required time for preparation, and the first did not open its doors for several weeks. A more immediate result was that certain popular plays were suddenly offered all over Paris. A rash of productions of *Charles IX* appeared, especially along the boulevard. The office of censor was abolished, and Joly, who had replaced Suard, found himself without a post. Now that inflammatory plays had one less check, disorder in the theatres increased sharply, and many houses became virtual clubs, where the most innocuous passage might set off a violent patriotic demonstration. The triumphant dramatists, meanwhile, lost no time in organizing to protect their new privileges. They met at the home of Delange-Savalette to discuss how the new law was to be enforced, since the National Assembly, content with its work, had passed on to other matters. One of the dramatists, Nicolas-Etienne Framery, was elected to direct a central office in Paris to correspond with theatres throughout the kingdom and arrange for permission to produce their plays.[6]

In February, anticlerical drama entered a new phase with the Comédie's presentation of Carbon de Flins' *Le Mari directeur ou Le Déménagement du couvent*, a drama depicting the "liberation" of a convent by the Revolution. The national commissioner who brings the good news decides for a lark to dress himself in the habit of the director of the order. Thus disguised, he hears the confessions of his wife and daughter, and thus discovering that the latter is in love with a monk, gives her to him in marriage. All then repair to the refectory to join in bawdy songs and dances.

Dramas attacking monasticism had of course appeared earlier, but *Le Mari directeur* brought to such drama a vitriolic and licentious character hitherto quite unknown. Indeed, only a year before, Suard had banned Bertin d'Antilly's *La Communauté de Copenhague* at the Italienne for its subject matter, which concerned the affair of a bishop with a superior, a gardener with a novice, and the director with a nun. The censor's letter to the author is worth quoting in full:

> I can hardly believe, Monsieur, that you seriously thought that it would be possible to stage a licentious scene in which the actors portray a bishop, a monk, and nuns. I do not think the freedom of the theatre will ever

go that far. However, if you persist in your demands, I will write out the motives for my ban and will send them to you before sending them to the police. You may dispute them however you think best, and I shall leave the matter to the mayor to decide.[7]

The words "I do not think the freedom of the theatre will ever go that far" stand as testimony to the speed with which society was changing in these turbulent years. Less than a year had passed, but Suard was gone, his post outlawed, and the first of a series of plays had appeared which made *La Communauté de Copenhague* seem almost inoffensive by comparison.

Other theatres attempted to capitalize on the success of *Le Mari directeur*. The Théâtre de Monsieur presented *Les Capucins* and *Amélie ou Le Couvent;* the boulevard houses followed suit. Religious settings appeared everywhere. Says Fleury:

The performers at every one of the theatres, great and small, soon found it necessary to include among the articles of their wardrobe the chasuble, the surplice, the coif and the girdle of St. Francis. The chanting of vespers was heard on every stage, and no theatre could dispense with its different orders of clergy. For our part, we had a cardinal in *Charles IX*, a cardinal in *Louis XII*, some Chartreux monks in the *Comte de Comminges*, and a group of pretty nuns in *Le Couvent ou Les Fruits de l'éducation.*[8]

Monvel's *Les Victimes cloîtrées*, presented at the Comédie on March 29, proved the most successful of such dramas, drawing large crowds to the theatre week after week by its attractive mixture of anticlericism and licentiousness. Father Laurent, the villain of the piece, is attracted to the lovely young Eugénie Saint-Alban. He manages to get her into his power and entomb her in his monastery. Then, greedy as well as lustful, he goes to Eugénie's rich lover, Dorval, tells him she is dead, and convinces the stricken young man to enter the monastery and leave his goods to the Church. Once Dorval is at his mercy, Father Laurent has him thrown into the dungeon adjoining Eugénie's. In the climactic scene, the cells are shown side by side on the stage (Eugénie on the queen's side and Dorval on the king's—a remnant of aristocratic nomenclature that was soon to be replaced by the republican terms "court" and "garden" side). Attempting to escape, Dorval breaks into his love's cell, and after a poignant reunion, they are rescued by the National Guard, which arrives to destroy the monastery and release the prisoners entombed within it.

Fleury was outstanding in the leading role, and was ably supported by Naudet, Saint-Fal, Dazincourt, Barthélémy Larochelle, and Mlle. Contat. None of these actors proved so effective on opening night, however, as a spectator who interrupted the action just as Dorval was being shut away with a shout of "Exterminate those rascals!" All eyes turned toward the speaker, who, trembling with passion, explained in a loud voice, "Your pardon, sirs, but I was formerly a monk. Like Dorval I was thrown into a cell, and in Father Laurent I thought I recognized my own superior." This testimony contributed greatly to the success of the play, and there is little doubt that the "monk" in question was a friend of Monvel, who as actor and author knew well how to appeal to an audience. He was summoned and loudly applauded after the production.[9]

The Easter closing of 1791 brought an air of expectancy to theatregoers, for several of the major houses hinted at important changes for their reopenings. The Variétés-Palais-Royal, which had proved popular but not a serious rival for the Comédie despite its favorable location and impressive building, created much speculation by promising important new artists, not named, to join their troupe for the coming year.

During the closing, which lasted between two and three weeks, tension in the capital concerning the King's future sharply increased. Mirabeau, in his final illness, disappeared as a political force. This loss seriously weakened the royalist party, and the apprehensive King decided to leave Paris temporarily. On April 18, Louis departed for Saint-Cloud, but his carriage was stopped by an angry mob, aroused by rumors that the King was seeking a priest for Holy Week who had not taken the civic oath or, worse yet, that he was attempting to flee the capital for good. When the King returned and complained of the treatment he had received, the National Assembly promised him satisfaction and future freedom of movement. But the citizens of Paris were already beyond the control of that body, and Louis must have realized that he could now escape the capital only by stealth.

Tension was still high in Paris when the theatres reopened, but even so, a huge audience attended the April 27 reopening of the Palais-Royal, brought by the rumors of significant new attractions. They were not disappointed. Gaillard and Dorfeuille had finally realized their goal of becoming a second national theatre, as their new name proudly proclaimed—the Théâtre-Français, Rue de Richelieu. The decree of January 13 had opened the classic repertoire to their use, but far more important, the directors had profited by the schism in the Comédie to enrich their own acting resources. Almost all of the "reds" appeared in triumph at the new theatre—Talma, Mme. Vestris, Dugazon, Mlle. Desgarcins, Grandménil, Mlle. Simon, and Mlle. Lange—and to complete the grand opening, a new play by Chénier, *Henry VIII*, was presented.

Henry VIII had been written before the first production of *Charles IX* and had been accepted by the Comédie on February 14, 1789. Suard refused to approve it, however, because a prelate appeared in the cast. A few months later this would not have been a serious objection, but by then, because Chénier was embroiled in a dispute with the majority of the Comédiens over *Charles IX*, the later play was withdrawn. When Talma began to disagree with his fellow Comédiens, several of his influential friends—Chénier, David, and Dugazon—urged the actor to quit the Comédie for good. Chénier was of course delighted when this finally occurred, and he hastened to put *Henry VIII* at the disposal of the new company. The opening-night audience was demonstrative but sharply divided. Many strongly applauded the new company, while others condemned the "reds" for deserting the Comédie and fatally weakening the old tradition. The play, concerned with the events leading up to the death of Anne Boleyn and full of Chénier's usual ponderous rhetoric, seemed under the circumstances rather more spirited than it actually was. Even Chénier's partisans lost some enthusiasm during the tedious fourth act when a ridiculously untalented child cast as the young Elizabeth drew general hisses. But the acting was brilliant among the leading parts; Talma's interpretation of the king added much to his reputation, and he was well supported by Mme. Vestris as Anne, Mlle. Desgarcins as Jane Seymour, and Monvel as Cranmer. Even when the script fell short, these actors commanded respect.[10]

The afterpiece, a one-act play called *L'Epreuve nouvelle* and featuring Dugazon and Grandménil, was so vigorously hissed that the actors were unable to finish, and the evening ended with a hostile demonstration. Palissot quickly published a letter blaming the "blacks" of the Comédie for organizing this unpleasantness, and though there is no evidence of it, they surely might have done so.[11] The opening of the Comédie was a week away, the Comédiens were unoccupied at the moment, and they could hardly have viewed with equanimity the founding of so powerful a rival. Indeed, but for the imagination of

Dugazon, all of Talma's costumes would have been kept by the angry Comédiens. When the actor announced his intention of leaving the company, the wardrobe upon which he had lavished such care was immediately confiscated. For a time it seemed as though Talma would be forced to appear in traditional garb at his new location. Then, during a meeting between the opposing parties at the Comédie, Dugazon and eight extras slipped off to the wardrobe. There Dugazon dressed himself as Achilles and loaded himself and the extras with other costumes. He then descended and marched, visor lowered, through the astonished company. By the time the actors recovered, he was gone and Talma's costumes were his own again.[12]

During this same momentous Easter closing, Talma performed a most astonishing action. He officially renounced his profession and registered with the city as a simple bourgeois. With his wife now in her last month of pregnancy, the actor finally decided to make the gesture demanded by the Church before his union could be sanctified. Although it must have been apparent to all that Talma could remain a common bourgeois only for the length of the Easter closing, the Church was satisfied, and on April 19, the marriage was blessed by M. Lepipe, vicar of Notre-Dame-de-Lorette. Three days after the opening of *Henry VIII*, with Talma openly resuming his trade, and eleven days after the wedding ceremony, Julie gave birth to twins. On May 1, the morning after Talma opened as Rodrigue in *Le Cid*, M. Lepipe baptized the infant sons, apparently considering the Easter recantation sufficient penance for the actor's sins. The priest, at any rate, seems to have taken no offense at the names Talma chose, although these were indicative of the depth of the artist's conversion. Both names were hyphenated—a common custom at the time—with part of each derived from Chénier's dramas and the other from pagan mythology. Dugazon was godfather and Mlle. Desgarcins godmother to the new Talmas—Henry-Castor and Charles-Pollux.[13]

The Comédie, stunned by the defection of half its members and the sudden appearance of a major rival, was one of the last theatres to reopen after Easter. Although the public referred to both the old and new companies as the Comédie, the national theatre was now too seriously divided by personal grievances and political issues to be reunited at any time in the foreseeable future. Gradually, even the name Comédie Française tended to disappear. The old Comédie became known by a name which it had first employed the previous year—the

Théâtre de la Nation—and the theatre in the Palais-Royal was called the Richelieu, from the street on which it was located.

The Nation immediately felt the consequences of sharing the first place among Parisian theatres. The reopening was traditionally an important occasion, and a full house could usually be expected. By May 2, however, Montansier's new theatre was drawing large crowds, and the Richelieu had already staged two major tragedies. The attendance at the Nation's opening presentation of *L'Ecole des maris* and *Iphigénie en Aulide*, accordingly, was dishearteningly small. The "blacks" knew that they would have to outdo their past efforts to hold their own in the new circumstances. The first new play after the reopening reflected this realization. Considering that the company had split largely along political lines, it was a bit surprising that the split was also reflected in the genre specialties of the actors involved. The actors who had made their reputation in comedy were, for the most part, the ones who remained at the Nation, while it was the tragedians who left. The following months saw each theatre stressing its particular genre, with occasional forays into enemy territory.

The Nation, aroused to a competitive situation, opened with such a foray. The choice of Antoine Vincent Arnault's tragedy *Marius à Minturnes* was an open challenge to the Richelieu. The story, drawn from Plutarch, dealt with the struggle between Marius and an evil governor Germinius, who is eventually killed in a popular uprising. Despite the Revolutionary turn of the plot, the general tone of the play was one of political conservatism, well suited to the opinions of the remaining actors. The Nation's experiment succeeded; Vanhove was warmly applauded as Marius, and Saint-Fal, Saint-Prix, Naudet, and Dupont were commended in secondary roles. The twenty-one-year-old Arnault was cheered with enthusiasm and welcomed as an important new dramatist. The only unsuccessful aspect of the production was its costumes and physical setting. When Talma was a member of the company, he had encouraged Jules-Armand Boucher, a painter, to work with him and David for minute exactitude in historical dress. These had worked together so closely that Boucher had accompanied his mentor to the Richelieu, a loss keenly felt at the Nation, which had to fall back on the old illogical stock settings and costumes that many in the audience were no longer willing to accept.[14]

The Richelieu, on the other hand, staged a very successful production of *Brutus* just two days after the opening of *Marius*, and no small part of the success was due to the completely new settings and costumes, all of the most painstaking authenticity. The public, which had already begun to associate costumes of silk with the old regime, were delighted to see Talma portray Brutus and Monvel play Titus in the more austere authentic classic costumes.[15]

Partisans of the Richelieu generally felt, after the success of *Marius à Minturnes* at the Nation, that the rival theatre should answer the challenge with a major new comedy. At last, on June 15, the Richelieu obliged with *L'Intrigue épistolaire,* by Fabre d'Eglantine. Dugazon exhibited a rare comic skill, but the evening's great surprise was Talma, who appeared as a comic young lover, showing a range in his talents previously unsuspected. The play itself impressed the audience by its craftsmanship, for d'Eglantine managed to keep a complicated intrigue going for five acts without the use of aides or confidants, but solely by the device of letters.[16]

After *L'Intrigue épistolaire*, the Richelieu returned to tragedy with Jean François Ducis' *Jean Sans-Terre ou La Mort d'Arthur.* Ducis, passionately devoted to Shakespeare although he unfortunately did not understand a word of English, had set himself the task of acclimating the foreign master to the French stage. Guided only by his zeal, a general knowledge of the dramas, a vision of fitting Shakespeare into a classic mold, and engravings of the master and of Garrick playing Hamlet as inspiration, he plunged into his task. *Jean Sans-Terre* was Ducis' fifth Shakespearian adaptation, preceded by *Hamlet* in 1769, *Roméo* in 1772, *Léar* in 1783, and *Macbeth* in 1784. In all of these efforts confidants swarm, action is replaced by narrative, and as if to atone for the lack of onstage horrors, those offstage are heavily increased in number.[17]

The Comédie had produced Ducis' previous adaptations, but Ducis, like Chénier, was a close friend of Talma and submitted his later works to the new theatre. Talma was to become Ducis's greatest interpretor, although his John was not nearly so successful as his Hamlet, his Macbeth, or his Othello. The plot of this play is worth outlining, if only to show the extent of his originality. In *Jean Sans-Terre*, John has locked young Arthur in a tower and unjustly assumed the crown. He fears Arthur, however, and sends Hubert to sound out the prince without revealing his claim to the throne. Hubert, in tears, reveals that Arthur has thrown from his cell a gold cross, a gift from Constance,

IV. Interior of the Richelieu, 1790. Many of the details of this interior, designed by Victor Louis, disappeared in 1794, when the *fleurs-de-lis* and other aristocratic emblems which made up the decoration were removed. (Reproduced by courtesy of the Bibliothèque de l'Arsenal.)

V. View from the stage of the Richelieu, 1790. This actor's view of the theatre gives an impression of the seating arrangements, the huge dome, much admired by specialists in iron construction, and the handling of scenery. (Reproduced by courtesy of the Bibliothèque de l'Arsenal.)

VI. Fair theatres of the late eighteenth century. The Saint-Ovid fair, shown here, never achieved the importance of the Saint-Germain and Saint-Laurent fairs, but it was host to the same sort of dramatic entertainments, including one directed by the ubiquitous Nicolet. The little outdoor stages for short scenes to attract customers remained a feature of many smaller boulevard theatres on into the next century. (Arthur Pougin, *Dictionnaire du théâtre*. Reproduced by courtesy of Imprimerie Firmin-Didot et Cie.)

VII. The Théâtre-Français, Rue de Richelieu. This theatre, opened in 1785 under the title of Variétés Amusantes, became a second Comédie when Talma and others left the national theatre to perform here. After the re-union of 1799, it was this building that became the permanent home of the reorganized Théâtre-Français. (Paul Lacroix, *Directoire, Consulat et Empire*. Reproduced by courtesy of Imprimerie Firmin-Didot et Cie.)

his mother, on which he has written the words "Englishmen, save Arthur." John suppresses a revolt aroused in Arthur's behalf and orders Hubert to spread word that Arthur has become blind. He then orders Hubert to make the rumor truth, and when Hubert refuses, John himself oversees the deed. Hubert reports the blinding to Constance, who seeks out her son and consoles him, despite the King's precautions. John then orders mother and son locked in separate dungeons and sends poison to them. Constance expresses her willingness to die, but insists that it must be with her son. The King agrees and watches as mother and son take the poison together. Hubert arrives at the head of a liberating army, but too late to save the victims. John, deposed and contrite, begs for death, but Hubert condemns him to live on in remorse. Monvel played the part of Hubert, and Mlle. Simon, a newcomer, won much praise as Arthur. The young actress had until recently played only child parts at the Nation, but on June 14 she made her debut at the Richelieu in a last-minute substitution for Mlle. Desgarcins, playing Chiméne in *Le Cid* so well as to establish her reputation at one sweep.[18]

While the two rival theatres competed for audiences with major new productions, they carried on a subsidiary struggle through public letters of accusation against each other. Palissot continued to complain of the general lack of respect in Parisian theatre audiences and accused the actors of the Nation of taking advantage of this disrespect by creating a disturbance at the opening of *Henry VIII*. The accused actors were not long in replying. In an open letter of their own, they called Palissot an imposter, denied all his charges, and challenged him to name any of their number seen at the opening. Palissot wilted under this direct attack, but Chénier himself took up the gauntlet, repeating all of Palissot's charges and accusing the charming Mlle. Contat of disporting herself "most indecently" at the premiere of his play. The actors of the Nation then shifted the attack to Chénier, accusing him of plagiarism and a general lack of artistic integrity. So the dispute continued all that spring and into the summer.[19]

The freeing of the classic repertoire and the general loosening of restrictions had, of course, tremendous effects on the minor theatres. Now that they could produce plays by such writers as Molière, the boulevard theatres found the classics not nearly so scandalous or indecent as these had appeared to them six months previously. On the contrary, Molière was now recognized as a playwright as advanced and Revolutionary in spirit as Fabre d'Eglantine or Cousin Jacques. A commentator of the time explained how his comedies should be viewed:

> Requested, even forced to remain silent in a period of slavery, he exuded liberty from every pore. When forced to praise Louis XIV, he wantonly wrote bad, even detestable prologues. He even broke the rules of versification and consciously employed platitudes and the most vulgar commonplaces, as if to show posterity his position, his distaste and horror at the task imposed upon him by fate, and his desire to give expression to his talent and his philosophic mind.[20]

Nicolet, at the Grands Danseurs du Roi, brought Molière to the boulevards with *Georges Dandin*, the play most condemned there a year before, and followed this program with offerings by Corneille and Racine, mixed in with the skits and harlequinades which composed his regular repertoire. *Horace*, *Le Cid*, and *Brutus* captivated the boulevards, but Molière, more easily interpreted by troupes accustomed to light farce and comic opera, remained the favorite. Only Nicolet, however, produced the master with some degree of faithfulness, for his rivals were forced to mask the inferiority of their interpretations with interpolated scenes, ballets, and even fireworks.[21]

In all fairness, it must be admitted that the traffic in appropriated plays was hardly all one way; the established houses also pillaged boulevard drama. Repertoires became completely confused. The Comédie gave not only straight plays like *Les Fausses Confidences*, but even comic opera—*Paulin et Clairette ou Les Deux Espiègles*. The Comédie Italienne deserted its own repertoire almost entirely and began presenting spectacular historical dramas confiscated from Nicolet—*Jeanne d'Arc*, *Pierre le Grand*, and *Le Combat de Nancy*. While *Horace* and *Le Cid* appeared on the boulevards, *Robert, chef de brigands* trod the boards of the Palais-Royal.

An even more marked result of the decree of January 13, however, was a proliferation of new theatres in Paris. The new Théâtre de Monsieur, feared and fought by the Comédie Italienne as a potential rival, had been planned long before the decree was even considered and opened before its promulgation. The directors, Léonard Autié and Viotti, gave their last performance in their temporary home in the Saint-Germain fair on December 31, 1790, and hoped to open in their new home the following evening. A thousand details delayed this opening, however, and January 1 found the building still full of carpenters and painters. The workmen insisted that they would need at least two weeks more to finish the building, but the directors had been put off long enough. The theatre opened on January 6 with *Nozzi di Dorina*, an Italian opera by Guiseppe Sarti. A capacity crowd picked its way to seats amid scaffolding, rope-lines, and buckets of paint, but still pronounced the evening a success.

The new theatre's design was strongly influenced by the theatres of Viotti's native Italy, and its antique form and decor foreshadowed the "classic" trends of the end of the century. White columns and Etruscan friezes abounded, and all the experimental forms of the intervening centuries—pear-shaped, oval, and square auditoriums—were forsaken for a frank return to the semicircle of the Romans. There were eight rows of boxes, with three galleries, and above the audience rose a huge cupola designed by Legrand and Molinos with a chandelier that critics agreed was the most beautiful in Paris. As an added convenience for spectators, the auditorium began on the second floor, and the ground floor was made accessible from the street by three large archways, which allowed carriages to enter the theatre and deposit their passengers on rainy evenings in dryness and comfort.

Despite its splendor, the new edifice was not totally successful as a theatre. The auditorium was really too short for the number of seats it contained, and it had an uncomfortably steep slope. The huge dome, though impressive, was acoustically unsatisfactory, and actors' voices were often lost in the vast interior. Perhaps most irritating was a huge wall, which extended some fifteen feet into the house on either side to support the proscenium arch, thus seriously restricting the view of some four hundred spectators. Many patrons apparently agreed with the critic who wrote, "No theatre ever presented a more delightful spectacle to the eye. There is beauty in every part, and the spectator in an orchestra seat can imagine himself in the center of a majestic bouquet of flowers,"[22] but even this decoration was not to the taste of some, who were not so impressed by a welter of gargantuan painted figures, headless classical statuary, and papier-mâché griffons and other mythological beasts.[23]

The first new theatre to open after the January 15 decree was the Variétés Comiques et Lyriques (not to be confused with Desnoyer's Théâtre-Français Comique et Lyrique, which opened in 1790), where performances were given on Thursdays and Sundays in Audinot's old theatre in the Saint-Germain fair. This was shortly followed by the Théâtre de la Liberté and the Petits Comédiens du Palais-Royal, the latter directed by a certain Moreau, formerly a harlequin at Audinot's Ambigu-Comique. Theatres then began to spring up everywhere—in ballrooms, in empty houses, even in churches, for recent decrees of the National Assembly suppressing religious edifices had closed down

4. Exterior of the Théâtre de Monsieur, Rue Feydeau, built 1791. This contemporary sketch shows clearly one of the interesting architectural features of this important theatre—ground-floor access for carriages so that patrons need not step outside. (Reproduced by courtesy of the Harvard Theatre Collection.)

a number of choice buildings on the Ile de la Cité. Spring saw the opening of the Vauxhall d'Eté, the Théâtre de la Rue Saint-Antoine, the Théâtre de la Concorde, and several others.[24]

For the theatres in financial difficulties even before January of 1791, this sudden increase in competition created a desperate situation. The Délassements-Comiques managed to keep open only by presenting on alternate days M. Perrin, "noted physicist," who, according to the advertisements, gave such demonstrations as "the completely isolated ink bottle which furnishes red, green, or lilac ink at will," "the famous lemon trick," and "the experiment of the watch ground in a mortar and brought back perfect as before."[25]

The Beaujolais, in its unfavorable location in the boulevard Mesnil-Montant, suffered even more in these new circumstances. The ominous word "*Relâche*," announcing a temporary closure, appeared so often on the Beaujolais posters that the *Almanach général* reports that a joke about it became almost proverbial: "What are they giving this evening at the Beaujolais?" "They're giving *Relâche*." Cousin Jacques, despite his vow, gave the theatre a new play, *Toute la famille*, in December, 1790, but it did not enjoy the success of his earlier work. Again Cousin Jacques blamed the actors, and again he swore never to return to the theatre. A good troupe or an outstanding play might have compensated for the remoteness of the Beaujolais, but Delomel lacked both. It was clearly only a matter of months before the theatre would have to close permanently.

The impending legislation of January 13 encouraged Delomel to plan for a new theatre, more favorably situated, in the Rue de Louvois. He turned the directorship of the declining Beaujolais over to a M. Briois, who resorted to a spectacular expedient for attracting audiences to the theatre. On February 4, he posted a notice of *Mahomet* "for the benefit of an unfortunate family, given by M. de Larive and several other actors of the Comédie." When the directors of that theatre informed M. Briois that M. de Larive and any other actors he might have in mind were committed to the Comédie and would not be available, Briois, apparently prepared for this eventuality, produced posters immediately at the Beaujolais: "Closed!—the directors of the Comédie refuse to come to the aid of an unfortunate family." That evening a crowd gathered at the theatre to hear M. Briois complain, "They are heartless aristocrats! Because I refused to bow before them, they would not come to the aid of wretches dying of cold and hunger!" Soon a crowd of fifty or sixty persons was marching on the Comédie with shouts of "Down with the aristocrats," and "To the lantern with the actors!" By the time this crowd reached the Comédie, it had grown to four or five hundred persons, and only police action prevented a siege of the building. The following morning, the Comédiens prevented further action from M. Briois by a public announcement that M. de Larive and his fellow actors had privately seen to the needs of the "unfortunate family."

Still the lot of the Beaujolais actors grew steadily worse, and when one of them, Hugot, committed suicide, the other boulevard theatres were finally driven to take up a collection for their distressed comrades. The money was sent to Briois, who promptly disappeared, leaving his company in worse straits than ever. Creditors began carrying off the theatre's goods, with the result that production became almost impossible even for the few patrons who still came. The troupe fought bravely—Tuetey lists a complaint to the police from one Jacques Marguerit, who came to the theatre to remove machinery and settings and could not get past the actors—but they were finally forced to capitulate. On March 6, the theatre gave its final production. The homeless actors appealed to Delomel to help them find new quarters, and he introduced them to Philip Astley, who rented them the building which housed his circus. On March 20, this reconverted hall opened with the enigmatic name Théâtre des Comédiens sans Titre. This venture proved no more successful than its predecessors, however, and shortly after, the Beaujolais troupe disbanded for good.[26]

The Comédie Italienne, which had protested in vain against the new location of the Théâtre de Monsieur and which now had to deal with a host of smaller rivals as well, weathered this difficult period with surprising good fortune. Indeed, a series of successes seemed to promise an immediate future far brighter for the theatre than the immediate past. *Griselidis,* an opera by Desforges and Mereaux, successfully opened the year, and was followed by Edmond-Guillaume de Favières and Rodolphe Kreutzer's *Paul et Virginie,* which was so popular that when the Parisian paper *Petits affiches* gave it insufficient praise, patrons brought copies of the paper to the second performance demanding that they be publicly burned on stage. This small auto-da-fé was so popular that it was attempted again on succeeding evenings, but was halted by a municipal officer. The *Petits affiches* did not escape, however, for copies were burned after the performance in front of the theatre.[27] Later in January, Laroche's *Les Deux Voisins* was well received, and shortly afterward, Fabre d'Eglantine scored his first major success with *Le Convalescent de qualité ou L'Aristocrate.* The theme again echoed Epiménide, for the protagonist of *Le Convalescent* is a marquis who knows nothing of the Revolution because he has been kept at home two years by gout. Suddenly manifestations of the new order burst upon him: his lackey addresses him as an equal, a creditor menaces him with process servers, a rural tenant suggests his son—a commander in the National Guard—as a match for the marquis' daughter. The convalescent swears, rages, and threatens until his doctor reveals what has happened:

> The whole state is changed. Men are equal;
> There are no more lords, no more vassals.
> Parliaments are dead, the high clergy too,
> The army has sided with the highest law,
> The King, agreeing with all, is honored in our hearts,
> And is moreover the father we have chosen.

The stunned marquis accepts this new system and consents to his daughter's marriage.

On April 2, the theatres of Paris were deserted, and an immense crowd gathered around a house in the Rue Chaussée-d'Antin belonging to Louise-Julie Careau, Talma's wife. The crowd was silent except for hastily passed whispers from those nearest the house, for inside, the great Mirabeau was dying. When word came at last of the orator's death, the entire city went into mourning. The Assembly suspended its proceedings, all theatres were officially closed, and a magnificent funeral ceremony was prepared. Mirabeau was the first contemporary judged worthy of entombment in the recently completed church of St. Geneviève, which, rechristened the Panthéon, had been dedicated as a perpetual shrine to the departed great men of the nation. An enormous procession accompanied the body from the Rue Chaussée-d'Antin to the church, with officers of the National Guard bearing the coffin, preceded by a full orchestra dressed in black and playing funeral music. Torchbearers accompanied the late evening procession, and its slow progress through the narrow streets of the Latin Quarter was a striking and memorable spectacle. Chénier was asked to write an epitaph to be placed on his friend's tomb. He wrote:

> Mirabeau's soul breathes in this place;
> Free men, weep. Tyrants, bow your heads.

The street where the orator died was renamed the Rue Mirabeau, but fame was unstable in those swiftly moving times, and within two years the original name was quietly restored and Chénier's verse was expunged from the Panthéon.[28]

As might be expected, the theatres of Paris followed the obsequies with a rash of Mirabeau plays. Olympe de Gouges managed to get her *Mirabeau aux Champs-Elysées* onto the stage of the Comédie Italienne a mere thirteen days after the orator's death. The allegorical figure of Destiny introduces the play, informing the audience that the hands of the Fates trembled for the first time in ending Mirabeau's life. Rousseau, Voltaire, Montesquieu, Henri IV, and Louis XIV welcome the newcomer to the Elysian Fields, and he readily answers their inquiries about the recent events in France, ending with an observation less suited to the speaker than to the author, a militant royalist: "May France never forget that the only form of government suited to her is a wisely limited monarchy." Like all of Olympe de Gouge's efforts, *Mirabeau aux Champs-Elysées* had little to recommend it but its timeliness, and on May 21, after the annual Easter closing, it was replaced by Dejaure's *L'Ombre de Mirabeau*, a considerably more polished work on exactly the same theme. Here Voltaire meets Mirabeau in the Elysian Fields and extends to him the civic crown, while Cicero, Demosthenes, Rousseau, Franklin, and Brutus offer their felicitations. A more down-to-earth note was struck at the rival Théâtre de Monsieur, where the anonymous *Mirabeau à son lit* showed the dying orator anguishing over the future of the nation.[29]

The Variétés Montansier, like the Variétés-Palais-Royal, appeared greatly strengthened after the Easter closing of 1791. Mlle. Montansier, as we have seen, had long been irritated by the restricting size of the former Beaujolais theatre, designed originally for marionettes. Having assembled a respectable company, therefore, she turned her attention to the theatre itself. She hired the architect Victor Louis to remodel the house, and during the two-week closing he worked such wonders that returning spectators could hardly believe the theatre was the same. The capacity of the house was increased to seat 1,300 spectators, the stage area had been doubled in height and depth, and Montansier could stage tragedy and spectacle dramas, even opera, without embarrassment.[30] The directress' dreams were by no means fulfilled, but she could now present her Variétés as one of the major houses of Paris, and a new source of concern for the divided Comédie.

Late in June, another powerful rival appeared to complicate the theatrical situation still further. Jean-François Boursault-Malherbe, a successful businessman and a member of the National Assembly, like many others saw in the decree of January 13 an opportunity for extending his interests, and he began plans for a new theatre. Unlike many less successful entrepreneurs, however, he recognized the value of selecting a repertoire which would set his theatre apart from both old rivals and new and give it a distinctive character. He and a delegation of actors requested permission from the government to open a theatre which would produce only patriotic plays. Permission was granted and Boursault-Malherbe faithfully adhered to his promise. The new theatre was christened the Théâtre National Moliére, but its namesake was

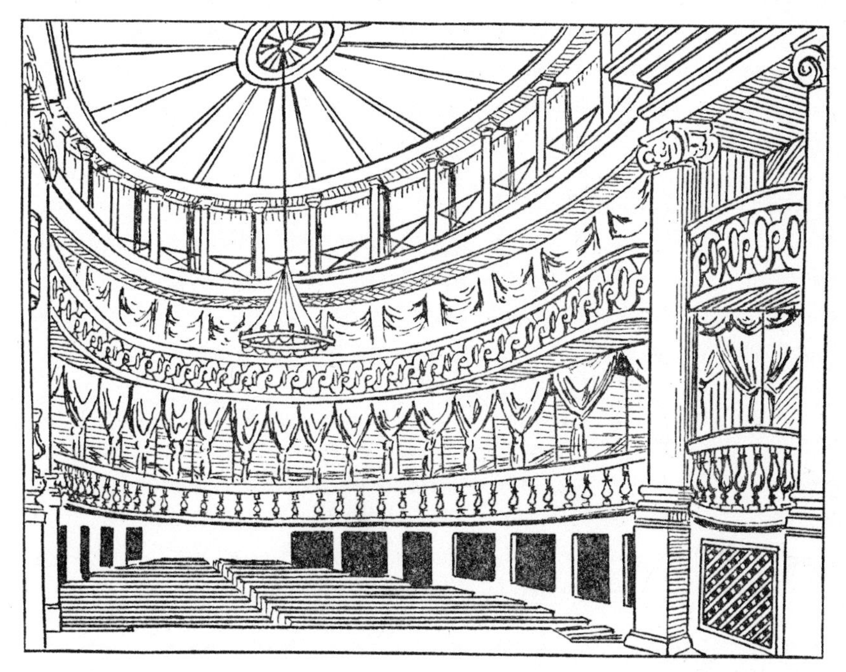

5. Interior of the Théâtre Molière, built 1791. Though somewhat larger than the average "boulevard" theatre, the Molière possessed a fairly typical interior. The orchestra is composed of backless benches, there are three tiers of boxes and at the top, a gallery. (Alexis Donnet and Jacques-Auguste Kaufmann, *Architectonographie des théâtres.*)

conspicuous by his absence from its programs. He was too easygoing, too indulgent for this company, which exhibited from its opening so virulent a patriotism that the journals from time to time refused even to comment on its plays.[31] *La Ligue des fanatiques et des tyrans*, by Ronsin, was the opening production, and a typical one. In it, a deputy from the National Assembly arrives to arouse patriotism in a town on the frontier. Priests, royalists, and reactionaries, drawn in the darkest colors, band together against him, but they are expelled by an aroused populace.

Only two days after the opening of Ronsin's play, every theatre in Paris was closed in the wake of a royal action of tremendous implications. On the evening of June 21, the King and his family slipped from the palace in disguise, and after a series of tense delays, departed by coach for Montmedy, near the Luxembourg border, where the monarch need no longer fear the whims of the Parisian populace. Simultaneously Monsieur, who had taken a vow in February never to leave France, headed for Flanders by a different route. The King's brother escaped, but Louis was recognized and his carriage stopped at Varennes. Under a heavy guard, the family began a slow return to the capital. This precipitous flight turned Parisian sentiment against the royal family; and as the reluctant fugitives were brought back to Paris, the police took every possible precaution to prevent an anti-royalist uprising. Everywhere posters appeared: "Whoever applauds the King shall be flogged; whoever insults him shall be hanged."

The theatres offered a special problem to the keeping of the peace, since the decree of January 13 made censorship extremely difficult, and the King's flight was a subject certain to attract audiences. All along the boulevard potentially inflammatory plays were hastily written and put into rehearsal—plays like *La Journée de Varennes ou Le Maître de poste de Sainte Menehould* at the Ambigu-Comique and *La Journée de Varennes* at the Molière. For *La Ligue des fanatiques et des tyrans,* then playing at the Molière, Ronsin, the author, wrote new lines for his hero Sélymars in which he condemned the Queen as a source of internal and external trouble and spoke of Louis XVI in terms like these:

> When nations north and south have joined
> To reimpose the yoke we've broken,
> Our King, the one all Europe saw
> Abjure the bloody league of tyrants
> Betrays us, and far from leading us forward
> Has run to support those who would destroy us.

Such lines show an interesting change of heart in an author who a year before had written the warmly royalistic *Louis XII, père du peuple.* His conversion seems to have been sincere, however, for Ronsin soon after enlisted in the army and fought faithfully for the republican cause. Sincerity was of little interest, unfortunately, to the Paris police, who were anxious only to prevent further disturbance of the populace.

Unable to censor his play directly, they applied moral pressure to the director of the Molière, suggesting that the new sentiments in Ronsin's play were not really in the spirit of patriotism which Boursault-Malberbe had pledged for his theatre. The director was convinced, and the lines disappeared from the stage, although they reappeared later in the printed version. Ronsin had only to wait for more "propitious" circumstances.[32]

The King arrived back in Paris in eight days, and thanks to the precautions of the police, was received by enormous but quiet and orderly crowds. The theatres of Paris voluntarily closed the day of the return simply because all of Paris was in the streets hoping to catch a glimpse of the fateful carriage returning to the Tuileries. The Comédie Italienne was almost alone in opening its doors, but no play was presented because, as the doorkeeper's record notes, only four persons appeared in the orchestra and three in the balcony.[33]

IV

The Nation in Danger

July, 1791–August, 1792

THE year between the flight to Varennes and the gathering of the National Convention brought new and graver threats to the young Revolution. The anger and suspicion aroused by Varennes were somewhat soothed by the King's ready acceptance of a new Constitution, but the period of conciliation which followed was bitterly brief. The threat of war with Austria brought new internal strife with it, and as various parties struggled for power the theatres were drawn into this strife. All too often dramatic offerings were supplanted by political demonstrations and riots. Various parties espoused different theatres and had much control over their repertoires. It was a difficult and uncertain period for the theatres of Paris, made more complex still by the host of new small houses springing up as a result of the decree of January, 1791. After the flight to Varennes, republicanism became more appealing, and except for one brief Indian summer of popularity, royalty joined aristocracy on the roster of discarded social institutions.

By the time the King returned to Paris, the Assembly had formally suspended him from his functions and mounted a guard over his family. For all practical purposes, he returned dethroned. The theatres reacted immediately to this change, not only in the plays offered, but even by divorcing themselves, wherever possible, from any hints of a previous connection with the court. The Théâtre de la Nation dropped its subtitle "Comédiens Ordinaires du Roi," even though the majority of the former Comédie Française still held sympathetic feelings for the court. The Académie Royale de Musique officially changed its name to the appellation already generally accorded it—the Opéra.[1] At the Monsieur, the directors, Léonard Autié and Viotti, quarrelled. Autié was unwilling to change the name of the theatre he had founded, but Viotti feared that keeping it would arouse hostility in their public. Autié was soon forced to resign, however, when the public confused him with his brother, hairdresser to the Queen. The triumphant Viotti announced immediately that the Monsieur would henceforth be entitled the Théâtre Français et Italien de la Rue Feydeau, a name which the public soon shortened to the Feydeau.[2]

Both the Richelieu and the Nation passed rather unsuccessful summers after their impressive series of openings in the late spring. *Pauline ou La Fille naturelle*, at the Nation, was an uninspired anonymous adaptation of a German drama. Next came the Richelieu's only new offering in all of July—Chénier's new play, *Calas ou L'Ecole des juges*. His third major play was clearly his weakest, a pale reworking of the material presented in the rival Calas plays at the Palais-Royal and Comédie six months before. Talma brought warmth and energy to the role of Lasalle, the magistrate, and Monvel and Mme. Vestris put much effort into the roles of the wronged Protestant and his wife, but the play was sadly lacking in literary values or even sufficient contemporary allusions to conceal temporarily its other weaknesses. The dispute with the actors of the Nation engendered by the opening of *Henry VIII* still continued, and the failure of Chénier's new work added even more bitterness to the quarrel. Chénier's enemies accused him of copying Laya's earlier work, explaining the weakness of Chénier's drama by its derivative nature. Laya too entered the dispute, which with this new fuel went on through the summer.[3]

The Théâtre de la Nation, in the meantime, attempted to refute the charges of aristocratic leanings frequently brought against it by presenting, on July 13, Billardon de Sauvigny's *Washington ou La Liberté du Nouveau-Monde*. The play, set in Washington's camp near Philadelphia, sought to point out parallels between the French and American revolutions. The author's own feelings were expressed by the French ambassador in the play, who near the end signs a treaty with the victorious Washington and praises him for gaining freedom without hatred. The play was not successful and was not repeated, but the author was called for, and when the audience found that it was Sauvigny, a former royal censor, they warmly applauded his patriotism, if not his talent. Shortly after this failure, the Nation provided the only bright spot of the summer with the debut of Marie Mézeray, who showed herself immediately as a most accomplished performer. At the end of July, a new play by Louis-Benoît Picard, *Le Passé, le présent, et l'avenir*, was put into rehearsal but then suddenly abandoned. The problem was apparently that after the flight to Varennes this play, although Revolutionary in tone, was too moderate for the turn events had taken. The disappointed author took his work to other theatres during August, but it was refused everywhere as being "too constitutional."[4]

One of the most brilliant festivals of the Revolution took place this summer, completely overshadowing the mediocre fare offered in the major theatres. The occasion was the transportation of Voltaire's remains to the Panthéon. The idea of so honoring the philosopher seems to have been first expressed at the third presentation of *Brutus* at the Comédie in 1790. The Marquis de Villette, Voltaire's nephew, proposed that the author of the play should join Descartes in the recently dedicated Panthéon, an idea warmly applauded and rapidly circulated. Circumstances favored the Marquis' plan, for the Abbey de Seillières, where Voltaire was buried, had been emptied by Revolutionary decree, and in mid-1791 the building came up for sale. The Marquis informed the city of Paris that the remains of the great philosopher were about to be expropriated, and on May 30, the National Assembly decreed that Voltaire was to be admitted to the "number of great men" in the Panthéon.

The memory of the Festival of Federation the previous summer inspired the organizers of this event to make it a "festival of philosophy," to which artists, authors, and musicians would contribute their talents. Chénier headed the planning committee. François Joseph Gossec, who had distinguished himself in the ceremonies following Mirabeau's death, was to compose the music, and David, only beginning to build his reputation as a classicist, was to design the decorations. Although such artists as David were to raise it to new heights, interest in Greek and Roman antiquity had been steadily growing all during the century, fed by translators, collectors of artifacts, travelers to the Mediterranean, and, most particularly, by the widely publicized excavations at Pompeii and Herculaneum in the 1730's and 1740's. In the theatre, Voltaire himself reflected this interest in the classic settings of his later works. Later, Ducis and Laharpe produced dramas modeled much more closely on Greek originals, thereby encouraging the 1785–1789 publication of Pierre Brumoy's *Théâtre des Grecs*, a translation of all Greek drama known, running to thirteen volumes. This in turn provided, on the very eve of the Revolution, a new stimulus for neoclassic theatre. Thus, with the scholars of the day engaged in translations and commentaries on the classics, and artists like David producing volumes depicting classic objects from earthen lamps to statuary, it is not surprising that this ceremony, and many of those which followed, took on a decided Greco-Roman air. The triumvirate assembled for this "*pompe vraiment antique,*" Chénier, Gossec, and David, were to become the standard organizers of such festivities.[5]

Voltaire's body was exhumed, and the coffin, after a triumphant journey across France to the capital, arrived in Paris to be placed amid flowers and wreaths on the ruins of the Bastille. Special presentations were given in many theatres on July 9, the evening of its arrival. The Richelieu, as we have seen, premiered Chénier's *Calas*, while the Molière presented Charles d'Abancourt's *Voltaire à Romilly*, fairly bristling with contemporary references. One of the high points in the latter drama was the speech made by Favreau, the mayor of Romilly, over the sarcophagus of Voltaire before sending it on to Paris:

> Favreau: Hear me my friends. Not content with spreading the practice of philosophy, Voltaire wanted himself to practice those great lessons which he was giving the human race. His only desire was to destroy fanaticism, but those who found fanaticism useful banded together to slander him. Voltaire died rich in years and glory, but fanaticism triumphed. Reason remained silent and the criminal priests refused burial to the man whom the Greeks would have elevated to the ranks of the gods.
>
> The Peasants (moved): The monsters!
>
> Favreau: Happily, the legislators have avenged his memory by decreeing that his ashes will be transferred to the Panthéon.

Nature rarely smiled on Revolutionary festivals. On July 10, the funeral procession assembled at the Bastille at eight o'clock, but the same sort of driving rain which had plagued the opening of the Festival of Federation prevented it from departing until two in the afternoon. Representatives of letters and the arts occupied the places of honor in the center of the cortege, immediately preceding the sarcophagus. First came the deputation from Paris' theatres, then a statue of Voltaire by Houdon, carried by four men and surrounded by Beaux Arts students in classic costume carrying banners bearing the names of the master's principal works. Then came the Academicians, accompanying a golden casket containing a complete edition of Voltaire's works, a gift from Beaumarchais. Beaumarchais himself headed the delegation of authors, carrying a banner which said "Voltaire's family, the men of letters." The sarcophagus was supported by wheels of bronze and drawn by twelve white horses. Above it rose a statue of Immortality symbolically placing a crown of stars on the author's head. On the four sides of the coffin were carved grieving spirits, with torches held downward, and classic theatrical masks decorated the corners; all these decorations were of bronze and were connected by laurel boughs.

The procession, accompanied by three full orchestras with classic instruments and by innumerable drummers and trumpeters, moved down the boulevards to the Opéra. The façade of that building was hung with draperies and foliage, and a bust of Voltaire had been set up before the theatre. Two medallions bore the names of the operas the author had written for music by Rameau: *Samson* and *Le Temple de la gloire*. The former work seemed especially suited to the occasion since its biblical subject matter had caused it to be banned by the royal censor. Moreover, it had passages of Revolutionary sentiment which Gossec had set to choral music and which the singers in the procession delivered when they reached the Opéra:

> People, awake, break your chains!
> Regain your ancient grandeur.
> Liberty calls you,
> Proud people, you were born to this.
> People, awake, break your chains!

Amid cheers, the bust was crowned, and, with the bands striking up a march, the procession, now more triumphal than funereal, moved on to its next station, the home of the Marquis de Villette, where Voltaire had died. Here an amphitheatre covered with foliage had been erected, and the sarcophagus was placed under a triumphal arch, where it was saluted by Mme. de Villette and the daughters of Calas, dressed in mourning. These were accompanied by a great number of young people in classic robes and rose garlands, bearing palm branches.

As night was falling, the procession moved on to the Théâtre de la Nation, which had been temporarily rechristened the Temple de Melpomène for the occasion. The façade, like that of the Opéra, was hung with draperies, and a huge banner stretched across it bearing the legend "At eighty-three he created Irène." When the procession halted, a curtain parted to reveal the lobby, and in it an illuminated statue of the philosopher. The orchestra once again struck up "People, awake," and certain actors from the theatre, dressed as Voltaire's characters, appeared to do him homage. Brutus offered him a bundle of laurel branches, Orosome perfumes of Arabia, Alzire treasures from the New World, and Nanine a bouquet of roses. Unhappily, the rain resumed in the midst of this ceremony, and the crowd had to rush in disorder into the theatre for shelter. There the orchestra continued to play the chorus from *Samson* until the rain abated somewhat. At last, near midnight, the procession moved on to the Panthéon, now not far off, and Voltaire's remains were finally put to rest.[6]

During August and September, while the National Assembly worked on a new Constitution, the Richelieu catered to the widespread anti-royalist feeling with a series of uninspired productions. *L'Hôtellerie de Worms,* a flat farce presented on August 11, was a new comment on the flight to Varennes. A group of drunken emigrants—aristocrats who have fled Paris—are shown in the German city. All are penniless but convinced that an unnamed savior is coming to pay their bills. This stranger, the King, is stopped at Varennes, and they must face the future without his aid.

On August 25, the theatre gave *La Prise de la Bastille,* whose author, Pierre-Mathieu Parcin, explained his inspiration: "After having fought under the walls of that formidable fortress, I considered that I could do nothing better than to recreate that great event on the stage." The subject still attracted audiences, despite a mediocre treatment, and Parcin's play drew patrons from *Despotisme renversé,* a drama on a similar theme offered at the Nation. Doigny du Ponceau's *Virginie ou la Destruction des Décemvirs,* a weak tragedy dealing with freedom from oppression, did not fare nearly so well.[7]

On September 3, Talma sought to capitalize on post-Varennes sentiment by reviving *Charles IX,* but response to the play was surprisingly small. The times had passed it by. Far more feeling was demonstrated at the Nation two days later during a production of Collé's *La Partie de chasse de Henri IV.* A strong faction in Paris still supported the King despite his attempt to desert the capital, and representatives of this group clashed bitterly with partisans of the Revolution over the royalist sentiments in Collé's play. Only armed intervention by the authorities prevented bloodshed.[8]

On September 14, the King accepted the completed Constitution and swore to uphold it. "The Revolution is over," Louis hopefully declared. "Let the nation resume its happy character." In celebration of the new accord, the King requested a *Te Deum* for September 22 at Notre Dame, organized dances for the populace, and distributed money to the city's poor. On Sunday, September 18, Bailly, followed by a cortege of municipal authorities and a military orchestra, publicly read the document in several places in Paris, ending in the Champ de Mars, as crowded as it had been for the Festival of Federation. After reading the Constitution, Bailly, on the summit of the altar, raised the book over his head to show it to the assembly. "At this august moment," says a report of the times, "one almost seemed to see Moses receiving the tablets of the law from the Master of the universe, and offering them to the awed Hebrews." After the ceremony, the audience sang Gossec's version of Voltaire's hymn, "People, awake!"[9]

In the upsurge of good feeling that followed the acceptance of the Constitution, only the most unyielding patriots still talked of deposing the King. The people rallied behind Louis again, and partisan disputes in the theatres declined sharply. On September 16, Dazincourt interrupted his role in *La Partie de chasse de Henri IV* to say to Mlle. Mézeray: "Before leaving you, Mlle. Catau, I am going to sing you a few lines which a friend has written about our good King." He then sang such lines as:

> These scurvy rogues will never tell
> Our good King wishes naught but well.
> This causes me great pain.

These were the sort of sentiments which two weeks before had aroused such violent dispute, but now the house received them with undivided enthusiasm.[10]

Perhaps no play presented in these weeks more clearly expressed the prevailing public spirit than Charles Demoustier's *Le Conciliateur*, offered at the Nation on September 19. In it, a young man, played by Fleury, enters his love's home under an assumed name because of a family feud. His warmth and gentleness not only dissolves the feud, but also overcomes two rivals, mellows two irascible old aunts, and reconciles a quarreling husband and wife. Audiences warmly applauded this demonstration of the powers of moderation.[11]

After the ratification of the Constitution, the royal family were seen more often about Paris and were cheered almost everywhere. On September 26, Louis requested Pierre La Chaussée's *La Gouvernante* at the former Comédie and went there with his family. Applause followed them from the palace to the theatre and doubled when they entered the house. The play contained no political allusions, but the orchestra supplied them by playing melodies during the intermissions calculated to encourage royalist sentiment. Shortly after, the royal family visited the Opéra, with even more favorable results, to see *Castor et Pollux*, which abounded in favorable allusions to royalty. The audience warmly applauded the orchestra's choice of the melody "What happier place than in the bosom of one's family"; and when Castor said to Pollux, "Reign over a faithful people," the crowd arose with shouts of "Long live the King!" and "Long live the Queen!"[12]

A popular offering at the Richelieu in October was *Abdélazis et Zuléima*, a highly romantic tragedy set in Granada. Talma and Desgarcins appeared in the title roles, with Monvel in a major supporting role. When a sudden illness struck Monvel and the play was withdrawn, the author, Murville, was so disconsolate that he volunteered to play Monvel's part himself, though he had never appeared on any stage. His offer was accepted, and this novelty continued to attract audiences to the Richelieu despite the rather uneven quality of the author's interpretation.[13]

The Richelieu was winning renown for its authenticity of costume in *Abdélazis et Zuléima* and in other plays, and other theatres tried to follow its example. By the end of 1791, most of the major theatres of Paris had at least experimented with authentic costume, and an unprecedented interest in the study of dress of other ages and nations arose. At the Opéra, in the second act of *Oedipe à Thèbes*, Adrien appeared in a wool tunic, breaking a long-standing tradition by leaving his neck, arms, and legs bare. Although the actor had only a single line, the audience warmly applauded him for his daring. The situation was, in fact, almost an exact repetition of Talma's similarly unexpected appearance in Roman garb in *Brutus* at the old Comédie; the exposed limbs too recall an anecdote of that earlier evening told by Emile Deschanel. When Talma appeared on stage, Mme. Vestris reputedly regarded him from head to toe and exchanged with him these whispered comments:

"But Talma, your arms are bare!"
"Roman arms were bare."
"But, Talma, you have no breeches!"
"The Romans wore none."
"Swine!"

Whatever Mme. Vestris and her companions at the Nation may have thought of Talma's reforms, however, the success of these reforms at the Richelieu forced the older theatre to make some concessions to the change in taste. "Fine progress," grumbled old Vanhove, as he was fitted for a classic robe to wear in *Agamemnon.* "Not even a pocket at the side of your thigh to carry your housekey!"[14] Since David, who had made a specialty of research in classic costume, was committed to the Richelieu, the Nation appealed to François Vincent, head of a rival school. Delighted at the offer, he set to work designing a totally new stock of costumes, for the actors discovered that there was not a single authentic costume in the vast stores of the Comédie. Even the presumably realistic costumes of Henri Lekain and Hippolyte Clairon were grotesquely inaccurate.[15]

Despite such innovations and great efforts by an outstanding company, the situation of the former Comédie gradually worsened as 1791 drew toward its close. Two months passed without a new play, and the changes in settings and costume, though they were both extensive and costly, appeared only as weak imitations of the methods employed at the more energetic Richelieu. After its early attempts, the Nation made no further challenges to its rival's superiority in tragedy, while the Richelieu could, and did, continue to produce comedies which, if not superior to those at the Nation, still provided serious competition. Typical was Fabre d'Eglantine's *L'Héritière ou Les Champs et la ville*, given November 11, in which Talma gave new evidence of his versatility by appearing as a delightfully foppish marquis.

The retirement of Mlle. Sainval the Younger after a career of twenty years was a heavy loss to the Nation, and their worsening circumstances led its actors to appeal to the great comic actor Préville, living in retirement at Senlis since 1786, to help them recover their disappearing audiences. Since he had become almost a tradition after a reign of thirty years, his reappearance would draw great crowds even if his talents had declined. Préville consented to Fleury's personal request, and he appeared with his wife on November 26 in *La Partie de chasse de Henri IV*, with an overflowing house adjudging the master as great as ever. The Richelieu's competing program, on the other hand, a new tragedy in a Spanish setting called *La Vengeance,* was a total failure, displeasing even the small audience which came. Préville remained at the Nation for a dozen more performances, adding further honor to his name with his interpretations of *Amphytrion, Le Philosophe sans le savoir*, *La Surprise de l'amour*, and *Le Mercure galant*. Then he returned in glory to Senlis, leaving the company revitalized and ready to carry on the battle.[16]

The month of December, however, added little to the luster of either theatre. The Richelieu offered Laharpe's *Mélanie*, another play which censorship had kept from the stage twenty years before. The play had been printed, and its appearance was widely anticipated;[17] but once on stage, its dramatic weaknesses became evident. The Nation fared no better with its *J. J. Rousseau dans l'Ile de Saint-Pierre*, which attempted to extend the honors given to Voltaire to his brother philosopher. The play was a stale retelling of the ideas expressed in *Emile* and elsewhere and well deserved its failure. A charming but insubstantial piece entitled *Minuit ou L'Heure propice* ended the year.

The year 1792 opened with France under threat of war. The aristocratic emigrants whom the Revolution had driven to the courts of neighboring kingdoms were calling for an invasion, and the sovereigns of Europe—motivated either by a sincere wish to relieve their unhappy brother Louis XVI, or a less altruistic desire to capitalize on French weakness—lent a sympathetic ear to such pleas. In the face of this external threat, the men brought to power by the Revolution turned from the problems of codifying their gains to the challenge of defending them. The King supported the Assembly and gave every indication of standing with this new governmental body, but many of his subjects wondered if this position would last during a war in which the King's own brothers and former political allies were ranged on the other side. Such doubts naturally added to the anxiety of the time.

Belligerent patriotic revues appeared in many theatres, but January's most successful productions, at the Nation and the Richelieu, were nonpolitical in nature. Apparently on this occasion at least, an appreciable number of Parisians sought for a time to escape the preoccupations of the hour. On January 5, the Nation gave *Paulin et Clairette ou Les Deux Espiègles*, a light comic opera which, by invading the traditional genre of the Italienne, caused some concern at that theatre, although the freedom of the theatres prevented any protest. Two days later the Richelieu gained a similar success in *La Jeune Hôtesse* by Carbon de Flins des Oliviers, whose *Réveil d'Epiménide* had been one of the first great successes of the Revolution. The new comedy, based on Carlo Goldoni's *Mistress of the Inn*, lacked some of the appeal of the old, but the charm of Mlle. Marie Candeille, who made her debut in the title role, assured the play a good reception.[18]

Near the end of January, word spread through Paris that a new play by Chénier was about to appear and that all who had read it declared it a masterpiece. *Caïus Gracchus* opened at the Richelieu, already sarcastically referred to in some quarters as the Théâtre-Chénier,[19] on February 9. It was a time of great public excitement; two days before, Austria and Prussia had joined forces against France, and on the very day of the premiere, a decree was passed confiscating the property of the *émigrés*. Partisan feeling was running higher than it had at any time since the beginning of the Revolution. The premiere of *Caïus Gracchus*, accordingly, was viewed by many as a new opportunity to test the strength of the rival parties whose representatives had clashed so violently during *Charles IX*. Both aristocrats and patriots supplemented their forces with organized claques and hired sympathizers, and there is some evidence that the Queen herself, remembering unfavorable references to her person in *Charles IX*, helped to finance the aristocratic faction. This latter group, as usual, gathered in the boxes, while the patriots filled the pit.

The patriots scored the first victory by obliging the orchestra to play the "Ça ira" even before the curtain went up and by drowning out all protests with hearty applause. As the play progressed, however, the patriots were surprised to find the aristocrats applauding certain passages too. The plot (which showed the increasing influence of Greek and Roman themes on artists and men of letters) tells of Caius, a tribune who swears to restore to the people of Rome the rights usurped by the Senate. Having aroused the populace, however, Caius pleads with them to be just and tolerant. The Senate brands him a traitor and Caius' followers desert him. Pursued and betrayed, he finally kills himself. Despite its classic setting, the play abounded in contemporary references. The second act, a debate in the Senate, had all the characteristics of a Revolutionary club meeting, and rancorous allusions to Varennes, concern over the King's recent actions, and condemnation of foreign invaders filled the work. Yet for all that, the moderate expressions of the hero won the sympathy of the royalist party. The Revolution was taking an ominous turn, and even the despised Chénier could be applauded by conservatives when his hero advised the populace to deal in "laws and not blood" and warned them that "liberty does not mean license." As a result, the play achieved the almost impossible feat of being approved by both sides, with only a few extremists demurring. Monvel played the title role, and Talma, his friend Fulvius. They were supported by Mme. Vestris, Mlle. Desgarcins, and Valois.[20]

On February 24, the Nation, which preferred to avoid contemporary concerns, countered with one of the best plays of the period, a highly successful comedy with hardly a trace of politics. This was Colin d'Harleville's *Le Vieux Célibataire*. The quiet and retiring d'Harleville had established himself just before the Revolution as one of the foremost comic dramatists in France by producing three important successes in as many years. During the summer of 1789 he finished the rough draft of a fourth work, eagerly awaited by the public, but he spent the rest of the year reworking and polishing, and the play did not appear. A new delay came in 1790, when France established National Guard units in every village and d'Harleville was placed at the head of the unit in Mévoisins, his native town. He took this appointment seriously and organized a local police force which worked so effectively that throughout the most violent period of the Revolution Mévoisins remained peaceful and untroubled. Since the town was not affluent, he designed and paid for his own uniform, which was one of the richest on display at the Festival of Federation in 1790.[21]

All these civic duties prevented d'Harleville from writing; and, though he managed to produce a popular one-act farce in 1791 called *M. de Crac dans son petit castel*, his major new comedy was not ready for presentation until a year later. The plot concerns a M. Dubriage, an impressionable old bachelor whose servants have come to run his life for their own benefit. The housekeeper, Mme. Evrard, a masterfully drawn villainess, already controls the house and is maneuvering herself into a marriage with her employer. The old bachelor's only relative, a nephew named Armand, is kept out of the house; and when he marries a poor but honest girl, the uncle is informed that she is a common prostitute. At last, in an attempt to rescue the misguided Dubriage, Armand and his wife disguise themselves as servants and enter Mme. Evrard's retinue. After a series of narrow escapes, they save the old man and drive the unscrupulous Mme. Evrard from the house. The audience, notes a contemporary critic, always breathed an audible sigh of relief. Molé, who had introduced d'Harleville's earlier comedies to the public before the Revolution, continued a sequence of fine interpretations as Dubriage, but Mlle. Contat as Mme. Evrard carried the honors of the production. The play was frequently revived in following years, and by the beginning of the next century was generally considered the finest French comedy since Molière. After d'Harleville's death in 1806, his plays no longer received such lavish praise, but *Le Vieux Célibataire* continued to be revived for another sixty years until at last its pleasant humor and naïveté proved too light to support further interest. This popular comedy was followed by Gabriel Legouvé's *La Mort d'Abel*, a tragedy which proved almost as great a success. This first produced work by a dramatist who was to become a figure of some importance featured Saint-Prix as Cain and Dupont as Abel.

Two such triumphs in a row by their rival spurred the Richelieu company to action. The play which Talma's company selected to compete with *Le Vieux Célibataire* was Palissot's *Les Courtisans*, which, as the work of Chénier's close friend, won the support of the patriots, but not of the general public. The Richelieu then turned to Fabre d'Eglantine, who had been an enemy of Colin d'Harleville since 1789, when d'Harleville's *Châteaux en Espagne* had succeeded a few weeks after d'Eglantine's *Le Présomptueux*, on a similar theme, had failed. Delighted to write a new competitive piece, d'Eglantine produced *Le Sot orgueilleux ou L'Ecole des élections*, hoping that its many contemporary references would make it more attractive than the politically neutral *Vieux Célibataire*. D'Eglantine misjudged his audiences, however, by making the "fool" of his title the president of a club. Parisians, who spent much of their time in such clubs, were not amused, and the play failed. The theatres closed for Easter with the Nation clearly dominating its more patriotic rival.[22]

It was now mid-April, and though war had not yet been declared, clashes between French and Austrian troops had already begun. Tension in the capital increased daily, and with it the bitterness between opposing parties. The Champ de Mars, scene of the unifying Festival of Federation, now witnessed smaller but equally enthusiastic demonstrations of partisan feeling. On April 15, the *sans-culottes* presented a Festival of Liberty in honor of the mutinous soldiers of the Châteauvieux regiment, who, according to the fluctuations of the Revolution, had been condemned in 1790, pardoned in 1791, and hailed as martyrs to liberty in 1792. Chénier and Gossec wrote two new hymns for the occasion; and while the orchestra played on the steps of the altar to the fatherland, the public danced about it to the strains of the "Ça ira" and a recently composed "Ronde national."[23]

Within a few weeks, the moderate forces in Paris organized a rival festival, taking as a pretext the death of Jacques Simoneau, the mayor of Etampes who had been killed in a Revolutionary uprising. The funeral march played for Voltaire and Mirabeau was repeated at this Festival of Law, as were several hymns. At the height of the ceremony, with the orchestra again on the steps of the huge altar and the funeral cortege passing below, the inevitable spring rain began and the crowd broke to head for shelter. To rally the departing populace, the orchestra struck up the "Ça ira," to the great joy of many in the audience, who began dancing in the rain. Shortly after, the storm passed over, and the funeral services were solemnly resumed.[24]

As the Austrian situation rapidly deteriorated, the King was forced to appear before the National Assembly to open debate on a possible declaration of war. After several days of heated debate, the Assembly voted for war by an immense majority on April 20. That same night the Nation opened after its Easter closing with *Lovelace*. With a major European war impending, only an outstanding offering could attract patrons to the theatres, and several weeks passed before any Parisian theatre mounted such an offering. The failures were varied. On May 4, Arnault, the author of *Marius à Minturnes*, was represented at the Nation by a new version of the legend of Lucretia starring Naudet, Saint-Fal, Saint-Prix, and Mlle. Raucourt, but despite these talents and painstakingly accurate costumes by David's rival Vincent, the play was coolly received. The following evening the Richelieu offered *L'Amour et l'interêt*, an undistinguished comedy by Fabre d'Eglantine. Some applause was given to Baptiste the Younger, who had left Montansier's theatre to appear in this production, but the play itself inspired no such enthusiasm. Three days later the theatre presented *L'Exigéante*, one of the most complete failures in its history. Not a word could be heard above the hissing.

Finally, on May 9, the Richelieu was blessed with a successful play—Laharpe's *Virginie*. The author, another deserter from the Comédie, prepared the way for his offering with an open letter in which he explained that while a number of plays had been written on this subject, his was the first, having been presented as early as 1786. It was then given anonymously, he explained, because the leading actress had sworn never to appear in one of his plays. Such a testimonial seems rather ill suited to inspiring audience interest in a forthcoming production, but either Laharpe's name or his statement did prove attractive, for the opening of *Virginie* was well attended, and the play, featuring Monvel and Talma in leading parts, was warmly received.[25]

Virginie was the last bright moment at either the Nation or the Richelieu for several months. These were difficult days in Paris. The war with Austria was going badly; French armies had been routed and the capital was in panic. The frightened Assembly declared itself in permanent session and passed three major pieces of legislation: disbanding the King's household troops, who were largely foreign and therefore suspect; banishing refractory priests, who might preach invidious doctrines; and bringing several thousand provincial troops to Paris to protect the city. Louis, knowing that most of the threatened clergy supported his regime and fearing the Revolutionary influence of the provincial troops, vetoed the last two measures. This action temporarily paralyzed the Assembly and was immediately seized upon by patriot extremists as a pretext for further arousing the terrified populace.

On June 20, great crowds gathered to celebrate the anniversary of the Tennis Court Oath, but this peaceful demonstration soon grew out of control. Mobs bearing banners inscribed "Down with the veto" and "The Constitution or death" surrounded the Assembly building and demanded that that body ignore the King's veto. The lower-class citizens who made up the bulk of these mobs had early been derisively nicknamed the *sans-culottes*—that is, those without breeches—by the aristocrats, who considered the fashionable tight knee breeches of the time the *sine qua non* of their station. The people, who had no use for such affectation, had embraced this originally derogatory epithet, and ragged breeches on poles were hoisted aloft as banners by the mob. After a time, the *sans-culottes* deserted the Assembly and descended on the Tuileries palace itself. The doors were forced and Louis found himself surrounded by screaming rabble. The King greeted them calmly, promising to uphold the Constitution, which somewhat mollified them. Even so, the Tuileries was overrun for a tense two hours until Jerôme Pétion arrived with troops to support the monarch.

This eventful day caused all parties to reassess their position. The moderates realized at last the dangers of arousing the populace and initiated measures to prevent the recurrence of such an uprising and to punish the instigators of this one. The patriot extremists, on the other hand, saw in the incident an untapped source of power and began planning to use the unstable populace for their own ends. The citizens who composed the mob were for their own part impressed by the King's calmness and dignity in a dangerous situation, and for a time the majority of the violent and fickle public rallied to his support.

The third anniversary of July 14 thus approached amid general apprehension. The jubilation and good will which had marked earlier festivals could hardly be expected now, with the capital divided into bitterly opposed parties, with foreign armies at the frontiers, with the King under suspicion of encouraging these armies, and with the Assembly in permanent session to meet the crisis. Nowhere was the change more evident than upon the great field of the Champ de Mars. Few traces of the celebration of 1790 were to be seen in the festival on July 14, 1792. The magnificent altar and its three hundred priests were gone. The huge grandstands and the intoxicated multitudes were nowhere to be found. The seats of honor for the royal family were understandably absent.

Instead, new structures filled the field. The emphasis of the festival was changed from a manifestation of solidarity to a manifestation of preparedness for war. Eighty-three tents, representing the eighty-three departments, were erected on the field, and by each stood a poplar with a tri-colored flag at its top. The King had his own tent, as did the Assembly, and the whole gave a most appropriate impression of all France encamped in the presence of the enemy. A truncated column stood on the site of the altar of the fatherland, with a supplementary monument on either side. One of these was a memorial to those who had died, or who were about to die, on the frontiers. The other was an immense tree, called the "tree of feudalism," arising from a huge pile of discarded feudal trappings and bearing on its branches crowns, ribbons, cardinals' hats, titles of nobility, coats of arms, and so on.

Because the sympathy for the King engendered by the events of June 20 was already fading, Louis was brought to the Champ de Mars under a strong guard and along a circuitous route to avoid possible insults by the mobs. During the afternoon's ceremonies, he ascended a platform erected on the site of the altar, and many later commented on his resemblance to a victim led to sacrifice. After the ceremony, which passed without incident, the populace called for Louis to set fire to the tree of feudalism. He refused, saying that feudalism was already dead and that such a ceremony would be inappropriate. This reply satisfied the crowds, and he retired with the troops amid shouts of "Long live the King." It was the last time the people of Paris were to see their King before he went to the scaffold.[26]

During the summer, other nations joined Austria against the French, and at last the Assembly appointed a number of committees to study all phases of the country's military situation. These committees were unanimous in their report that the country was in the gravest peril, and the Assembly issued a solemn declaration: "The nation is in danger." These formal words set off a frenzy of military activity all over the country; municipal, district, and departmental councils joined the National Assembly in permanent session, and the National Guard went on twenty-four-hour alert. On Sunday, July 22, drums were sounded all over Paris at daybreak to alert the populace to the Assembly's pronouncement. At six, cannons began to sound, and they continued all day. The Army of Paris gathered and paraded solemnly through the streets, preceded by trumpets and drums. An enormous tricolored banner accompanied this procession, bearing the somber words: "Citizens, the nation is in danger." The cortege stopped in squares, in the streets, on the bridges, while a spokesman read the Assembly's proclamation to the city. Fifteen thousand volunteers reportedly enrolled themselves in a single day for the defense of the city at amphitheatres hastily erected in all the squares of Paris. Patriotic music was performed at these amphitheatres almost continuously to encourage and inspire the volunteers. The "Ça ira" was, of course, especially favored; the "Marseillaise," Rouget de Lisle's stirring melody, was unfortunately not known in Paris until a few weeks after, when the first troops arrived from that southern city. A host of hastily constructed playhouses aroused enthusiasm for enlistment by such dialogues and pantomimes as *Les Racoleurs*, *L'Enrôlement du bûcheron*, and *L'Enrôlement d'Arlequin*.[27] The smaller regular theatres, especially those which depended on occasional pieces for their offerings, did a brisk business, but during these days of turmoil all the major theatres of Paris remained closed.

Having reached this hiatus in the stories of the Nation and the Richelieu, we may now pause to catch up on the fortunes of their fellow ventures, large and small. The theatrical scene steadily increased in complexity as more and more new houses opened and attempted to establish themselves. Private theatres abounded, the most noted of them being the Théâtre de la Rue Renard Saint-Méry, the Théâtre de Montparnasse, and the Théâtre du Sieur Doyen, which for a brief and catastrophic period tried its fortunes as a public theatre as well.[28] Every section of Paris saw the opening of new public theatres—in the east were the Théâtre de la Rue Saint-Antoine and the Vauxhall d'Eté; in the Saint-Germain area another Variétés opened; a M. de Saint-Pierre built a theatre in the Cirque du Palais-Royal; and on the Cité appeared the Théâtre de Henri IV. The boulevard area, already packed with fair booths and cafés, was naturally the scene of the most intense of this theatrical activity. A host of new attractions appeared there in 1791, among them the Lycée Dramatique, the Elèves de Thalie, the Petits Comédiens Français, the Théâtre Minerve, and the Variétés Lyriques. Certain café theatres, where ten sols spent for a glass of beer entitled one to dramatic presentations, also attained some importance: the Café Yon, the Café Godet, and the Café de la Victoire. A statistician of the times calculated that twenty-three such theatres opened in Paris within a year after the decree of January 13, 1791, and that their total seating capacity added to the others required 60,000 persons daily to attend the theatre for all to support themselves. The population of Paris in 1791 was about 65,000. "If this goes on," one critic complained, "Paris will have a theatre in every street, an actor in every house, a musician in every basement, and an author in every garret."[29]

Many of these little houses managed to survive for only the briefest periods in the frenzied competition; the Concert Spirituel, the Théâtre de la Liberté, the Montparnasse, the Estrapade, the Théâtre des Muses were but a few of those whose existence lasted only a few weeks, or even a few days. A brief description of one of these ephemeral ventures will serve for all. The Théâtre des Petits Comédiens Français featured plays written primarily by actors at the neighboring Délassements-Comiques and performed by children from seven to twelve years of age. It was said that the theatre was so small that spectators in the right and left boxes could shake hands. The stage was, in fact, less than ten feet square and was filled when seven or eight of its diminutive actors appeared on it. Nonetheless, competition with other attractions forced the theatre to introduce a staggering amount of spectacle, and this minuscule stage featured sunrises, clouds, descending goddesses, and choirs of nymphs, all naturally somewhat reduced in size. If such ventures failed, it was rarely for want of either will or ingenuity.[30]

During the next few years, even the better established minor houses opened, closed, and changed titles and directors with dizzying frequency. Only the fortunes of the few most important need be traced here, for their stories are all much alike—a continual struggle for patrons and income, importations of novelties to remain open, an occasional successful play for a few prosperous months, then the inevitable decline, as director after director attempted to salvage something from the ruin.

All of the older boulevard theatres except the Beaujolais survived this first period of liberty with its greatly increased competition, but all were forced to adapt their programs rather seriously to suit the new circumstances. Audinot resigned the Ambigu to one Picardeaux, who soon passed that declining theatre into other hands. Nicolet remained at the Grands Danseurs du Roi, but prudently changed the title of his venture to the Théâtre de la Gaîté. Sallé continued to offer all genres, even opera, at the former Associés, now called the Théâtre Patriotique. The Délassements-Comiques remained open by offering a constant variety of programs supplemented by the popular magician Perrin. The Théâtre-Français Comique et Lyrique continued to present its single success, *Nicodème dans la lune*, but to dwindling audiences, for this plea for constitutional monarchy already sounded a bit dated to patriotic ears. The theatre managed to survive for three more years, but with never another success.[31]

The similarly named Variétés Comiques et Lyriques, the first new house to open after the January decree, shortly clarified matters somewhat by dropping the "et Lyriques" from its title, but this new name was equally short lived. On April 29, 1792, during the Easter closing, the theatre hired Ange Lazzari, a noted Italian pantomimist. Pantomime had been presented at the theatre before, scattered amid the parodies, the opera, the ballets, and the patriotic dramas, but after Lazzari's first offering, *L'Amour puni par Vénus*, ran for an extraordinary sixty-two consecutive performances, this became the establishment's predominant genre. As performer and playwright Lazzari made the theatre's fortune; it seemed only a matter of giving official recognition to an already existing state of affairs later in the year when the Italian assumed directorship of the theatre and changed its name to the Théâtre du Citoyen Lazzari.[32]

Summer of 1791 saw the opening of the Théâtre Marais, less a new venture than an offshoot of the Italienne, whose financial situation had steadily worsened during the Revolution. In 1791 the company decided to cut its number to twenty and to establish another theatre with the actors thus freed, in the hope that a two-pronged venture would be more remunerative. Beaumarchais apparently helped subsidize the new theatre, which was built near his home in the Marais district.[33] Courcelles, the director of the theatre, was not interested in the current classic revival, and although he retained the half-circle form of other recently constructed playhouses, he insisted upon gothic rather than classic *décor*, which gave the interior of the Théâtre Marais a vaguely ecclesiastic air.[34]

Laharpe stated in a letter written somewhat later that the Théâtre Marais was the only one of the playhouses to spring up after the January 13 decree which showed any real ability.[35] The actors from the Italienne were skilled performers, and Courcelles was fortunate to find three good new actors to supplement them—Desforges and the Baptiste brothers. As a result, this was one of the few theatres in Paris to end this theatrical season with a balanced budget. The theatre was located in an area inhabited primarily by the well-to-do bourgeoisie, and this opulent public heartily supported its efforts. The Marais responded by avoiding the strong Revolutionary fare favored by citizens in less prosperous circumstances. Dramas, comedies, and tragedies were offered, including every work Beaumarchais had written, even down to the quite unpopular ones.

Beaumarchais became so closely associated with the Marais that he took there *La Mère coupable*, his latest play. Since the outbreak of the Revolution, the dramatist had involved himself in a number of nonliterary projects—working on the demolition of the Bastille; struggling to save his new home, located at the entrance of the most turbulent district in Paris, from the growing threat of mob violence; designing an immense monument to be erected on the Champ de Mars; lending his services to the great festivals. Even so, by January of 1791 he had completed a new full-length play and submitted it to the Comédie. It was accepted, but Beaumarchais' impassioned defense of the rights of authors caused a break between him and the national theatre, and he was forced to withdraw the play. *La Mère coupable* was thus premiered at the relatively insignificant Marais on June 6, 1792. The event, now long awaited, was of great interest to the Parisian world of letters, but the play failed. It not only lacked the strength and interest of Beaumarchais' earlier works, but had not even the dubious virtue of contemporary allusions to attract audiences, for its emphasis was not on patriotism, but on that more general eighteenth-century concern—sensitivity. Said the author:

> If you find some pleasure in mixing your tears with the griefs and pious repentance of this unfortunate woman, if her tears call forth yours, let them flow freely. *La Mère coupable* is a portrait of the internal agonies which sunder families, agonies which divorce never remedies, whatever else it may remedy. Any action aggravates such wounds instead of healing them, and the only cures are the sentiments of paternity, goodness of heart, and forgiveness. That is what my play attempts to demonstrate.[36]

At one time these introspective agonies would surely have found a public, but now, with patriotic and nationalistic concerns in every heart and war with Austria on every mind, such a play from the author of *Le Mariage de Figaro* seemed disappointingly trivial.

The Marais' parent theatre, the Italienne, joined many others in changing its title this season, becoming the Salle Favart, from the street on which it was located. The Favart made few other concessions to the Revolution, however, for, like the other former national theatres, it still felt a strong sympathy with the departed order. All three of these theatres—the Nation, the Favart, and the Opéra—were visited by the royal family during the conciliatory weeks which followed the adoption of the Constitution in September, 1791. The Favart welcomed the King on October 8 for a production of *L'Amant jaloux*. The intermissions were filled with songs in his honor and the theatre resounded with cries of "Long live the King!" "Long live the Queen!" and "Long live the Constitution!"[37]

A somewhat less unanimous demonstration took place at the theatre shortly after when an actor in the tragedy *Richard* substituted Louis' name for Richard's in a speech which became:

> Oh Louis, oh my King!
> Our love surrounds you.
> It is the law of our hearts
> To be faithful to your person.
> With the universe as witness
> We will break your bonds
> And return to you your crown.

The boxes applauded and betrayed considerable advance planning by showering the house with papers on which these verses were printed. The patrons below responded furiously with cries of "Down with the

VIII. The Festival of Federation, July 14, 1790. This view, from the grandstands near the royal seats, was drawn by Monnet, painter to the King. The triumphal arch beyond the great altar led to a temporary bridge over the Seine. (Armand Dayot, *La Révolution française*. Reproduced by courtesy of Librairie Ernest Flammarion.)

IX. The arrival of Voltaire's remains at the Panthéon, July 11, 1791. Although the background has been given an unauthentic, if appropriate, "classic" look by the painter Lagrenée the Younger, Voltaire's funeral cortege itself is here accurately portrayed, with its antique dress, musical instruments, and standards. (Armand Dayot, *La Révolution française*. Reproduced by courtesy of Librairie Ernest Flammarion.)

verse! Burn it!" The theatre orchestra struck up the "Ça ira" in an effort to restore order, but the riot did not subside until the police arrived.[38]

Although the majority of the Favart company remained favorably disposed toward royalty, the months which followed changed the opinions of their audiences, and royal visits to the theatre soon ceased. The following June, friends of the Queen, whose Austrian background made her particularly suspect, advised her to appear in public, hoping that she would receive some approbation during the brief period of good feelings which followed the storming of the Tuileries. Marie Antoinette therefore went with Mme. Elizabeth and the Dauphin to see *Les Evénements imprévus* at the Favart. In the course of the second act, Louise-Rosalie Dugazon, playing Lisette, turned toward the royal box to deliver the lines, "I love my master dearly. Ah, how I love my mistress," while placing her hand on her heart. This open homage to royalty and the applause which followed it aroused the patriots in the house. A number of them leaped onto the stage to chastise the actress, but she was spirited away by her fellows, and the overzealous demonstrators were forced by the outraged majority to quit the stage. Marie Antoinette did not attend the theatre again, and Mme. Dugazon received such threats about reappearing that she did not return to the stage until December, 1794, after the Jacobin menace had passed.[39]

After this incident, the Favart avoided political involvement for the remainder of the summer, relying upon spectacle rather than timeliness to attract audiences. In early July, *Tout pour l'amour*, a version of the Romeo and Juliet story with heavy emphasis on staging, drew good houses and even inspired a burlesque at the Montansier called *Tout par l'opium.* Even more ambitious was the opera *Lodoiska,* presented the first week in August. The *Almanach des spectacles* credited the great popularity of this work almost entirely to its overwhelming stage fires, with explosions, collapsing buildings, and similar effects. A lady leaving the theatre was overheard to say, "I sensed much pathos in that play," to which a wit replied, "Heavens, I sensed nothing but smoke." Several journals imprudently contradicted public opinion and noted the shallowness of the work. As a result, at the second performance, a pile of the *Petits affiches,* one of the most caustic, was thrown onto the stage to add to the conflagration.[40]

By 1792 the Opéra was the only major theatre in the capital which had not presented Revolutionary *pièces de circonstance.* The disturbances and demonstrations which had destroyed the tranquillity of other houses had never erupted here, where the audience was homogeneous and royalist in sentiment. Now at last this theatre too was brought into the political maelstrom through its production of François Hoffman and Etienne-Nicolas Méhul's *Adrien.* The plot of the opera was innocuous enough, but a scene which showed a Roman emperor entering in triumph offended republican sensibilities, especially since the four white horses which drew the royal chariot had previously belonged to Marie Antoinette, now widely suspected of encouraging foreign armies to invade the nation. Although the work was quite peacefully received, complaints were made to the Council of the Commune. That body pointed out to the directors of the Opéra, who were now answerable to the municipality, that a play depicting a triumphant emperor could hardly be tolerated at the very moment when the Emperor of Austria was reported headed toward Paris with an invading army. The directors, who had invested heavily in the production, tried to get Hoffman, the librettist, to modify his work, but he refused. In desperation, the directors turned to David, as a known patriot and friend of the arts, hoping to gain his approval of the disputed scene. The artist coldly replied that he would rather set fire to the Opéra than see an Emperor in triumph there. *Adrien* was therefore withdrawn, appearing at last in 1799.

Hoffman's refusal to modify his work was remembered during the Reign of Terror, and only the intervention of his friend Gabriel, a member of the Revolutionary committee of Hoffman's district, saved the author from imprisonment and perhaps death. Even so, Hoffman was obliged to give evidence of his patriotism by writing in 1794 an opera entitled *Callias ou Amour et patrie*, which laid strong stress on the latter. The fall of Robespierre allowed the author to revert to his former opinions, and his later opera, *Brigand*, made clear his feelings about his persecutors.[41]

On January 12, 1792, a major new theatre, the Vaudeville, opened near the Louvre. For ten years prior to the beginning of the Revolution a writer and a composer, Augustus, Chevalier de Piis and Pierre-Yves Barré, had worked to revivify the old genre of vaudeville, a native French form developed by Charles Panard and Favart which the Comédie Italiennne had gradually discarded in favor of Italian opera. Although the Italienne had denied Piis a pension in 1790, other writers, among them Cousin Jacques, encouraged Piis and Barré to persevere, and when the freedom of theatres was declared, they petitioned the city for permission to form a Théâtre du Vaudeville. Here they would present works of their own which they had written originally for the Italienne, selected vaudevilles of an earlier day rejuvenated with new songs, new vaudevilles, and anecdotes of the day in vaudeville form. This form—a lighthearted mixture of dialogue and song in a generally satiric vein—did not seem particularly suited to the Revolutionary temperament, but the municipality denied few requests for new theatres, and Piis and Barré were authorized in March to establish their venture.

They rented an abandoned dance hall called the Vauxhall d'Hiver and hired the architect Lenoir to convert it into a theatre for their troupe, fortunately enlarged by several rejected members of the Italienne who had not found work at the newly formed Marais. The theatre opened with a play by Piis called *Les Deux Panthéons* (Le Petit-Panthéon was one of the dance hall's earlier names). The opening program, hastily mounted with unsure actors, was mercilessly hissed, but the directors continued undaunted, and later productions steadily improved. Within a few months, the theatre had become one of the most popular gathering places in Paris. It lasted for forty-six years, building a fine company and an excellent reputation, and had the rare distinction of never changing its name throughout the Revolution.[42]

The career of the Vaudeville was a stormy one, especially in its early years, for Barré had a brother in the Queen's guard, and it was suspected that the court hoped to use this new theatre to turn public opinion against the patriots by means of ridicule.[43] The allegation has never been proven, but trouble was inevitable as the Revolutionary powers grew more sensitive to criticism and the theatre continued its tradition of satire. Within weeks after its opening, the Vaudeville was hurling barbs at a variety of persons annd institutions. On February 14, for example, Barré's playlet *Les Mille et un théâtres* ridiculed the Committee of Dramatic Authors for upholding authors' property rights and for favoring so many competing stages. Since this Committee's work had made Barré's own theatre possible, his choice of satiric subject seems somewhat questionable, but apparently his efforts were taken in the right spirit and no objections were raised.[44]

A new work presented the following week, however, did not fare so well. The play was *L'Auteur d'un moment*, by Pierre Léger, an actor of the theatre, and it satirized Chénier and his mentor Palissot under the conventional sobriquets of Damis and Baliveau. Chénier's

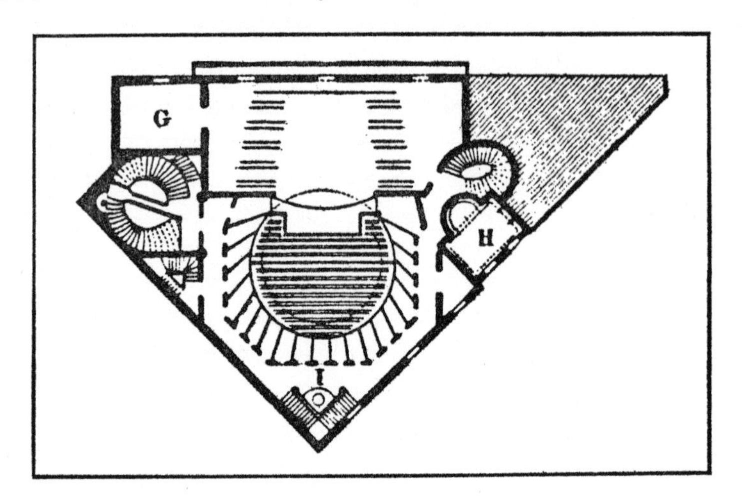

6. Plan and interior of the Vaudeville, built 1792. This proved ultimately the most successful new theatre of the Revolution. Its interior is typical, with the usual oval shape, three tiers of boxes, orchestra benches, and ornate chandelier. (Alexis Donnet and Jacques-Auguste Kaufmann, *Architectonographie des théâtres.*)

recent popularity, following the success of *Caïus Gracchus* at the Richelieu, made him a natural subject for comic attack, so his patriot supporters let the Vaudeville continue unchallenged until a defiant manifesto by Léger and the announcement of a new one-act attack by Barré entitled *La Revanche* spurred them to action. On the night of the fourth performance of *L'Auteur d'un moment*, before an audience composed primarily of royalists who, though somewhat mollified by *Caïus Gracchus*, were still delighted by a comic attack on the author of *Charles IX*, the first dissenting voice was heard. Just before the curtain rose, a member of the audience arose to attack the play, identifying himself only as a member of the extremist patriot society, the Jacobins. He was hustled to the door amid general applause, and though a few other patriots in the audience attempted to protest, Prestat, the police officer assigned to the theatre, restored order. All went smoothly until the lines:

> Though he claims to be tutor of Kings,
> We don't care for the song that he sings.
> He must be sent back to his school.

The royalists greeted this sentiment with applause, bravos, and shouts of "Down with the Jacobins!" Several voices in the pit responded with hisses, and in the ensuing tumult an infantryman stood on his chair to speak. Taken for another Jacobin, he was knocked down, dragged about, pushed out of the theatre, and thrown against a wall. The police arrested him for creating a disturbance and the unhappy soldier was taken to jail, where he expired shortly after from his wounds.

This brutality further aroused the patriots in the theatre, and although they were greatly outnumbered, they lashed out with swords and canes at all about them. As the riot grew worse, pistol shots were heard. The frantic Prestat ordered the doors closed, fearing that the rioters inside would leave to call others to their support, but his action served only to heighten the fury of the patriots in the theatre, who now became convinced that they had been led into a trap. In spite of the closed doors, news of the riot spread immediately all over the city. Pétion, Danton, and others hurried from their clubs to alert the National Guard, and troops arrived at the theatre just in time to prevent a growing mob from beseiging the barricaded doors. Frustrated in this, the Jacobins outside the Vaudeville forced the waiting coachmen to move their carriages some distance from the building. When the patrons were finally released, under the protection of the National Guard, they were forced to walk in their elegant attire through the unpaved and filthy streets to reach their carriages. Those who did not cry "Long live the nation!" upon emerging risked pelting with mud and snow from the angry crowd. One old gendarme announced that he would make no such cry, since the nation was immortal, but that he would cry "Long live the King," since the King was mortal, and yet should be preserved. His bravery was respected, and he passed unmolested, but not all royalists were so fortunate. Two of the Queen's pages, conspicuous for their brutality in the theatre, were seized by the crowd despite the efforts of the Guard and so savagely beaten that one of them died a few days later. The following morning Henri Larivière, a conservative member of the Assembly belonging to the Girondist party, reflected the concern of the authorities by denouncing actors and managers whose unpatriotic plays caused violence and disorder. At his proposal, the Assembly quickly voted to empower the Committee of Public Instruction to enforce a ban on these plays. So ended the theatre's emancipation from censorship, a scant thirteen months after it began.[45]

Many patriots considered even this insufficient reparation, however, and that same evening they appeared at the Vaudeville in such numbers as to reduce the aristocrats to silence. When a guardsman rose and demanded that Barré apologize and promise not to repeat Léger's play, Barré hastened to comply. The audience then called for a public burning of the script, and Léger fled from a rear door, apparently fearing that he might share its fate. Someone pointed out that burning the play would violate the author's property rights, assured by the Revolution, so in a curious mixture of vengeance and deference to legality, the crowd burned a printed copy, to the singing of "Ça ira." The commissioner Prestat arrived in the midst of this ceremony, having heard that the patriots were about to burn down the theatre. Finding their goal more modest, he allowed the demonstration to continue.[46]

The aristocratic faction nevertheless hailed the Vaudeville riots as a triumph for their party, and articles in the royalist papers *Feuille du jour* and *Journal général de la cour et de la ville* reported delightedly on February 24 that royalist cabals were holding their own in Parisian theatres:

> The Jacobins, having lost Monday's skirmish at the Théâtre Italien, tried to avenge their defeat the next day at the Théâtre Feydeau, and on the day after that at the Théâtre de la Nation and at the Vaudeville. They were vanquished everywhere; indeed, their present position in Paris is that of a significant minority. . . . The Jacobins met with another setback the day before yesterday. They went in great numbers to the Théâtre du Vaudeville; it was their intention to avenge their friends Palissot and Chénier, mercilessly ridiculed in the clever playlet entitled *L'Auteur d'un moment*, which was performed that day. But the Jacobin clique was powerless, for the great majority of decent citizens succeeded in reducing the Jacobins to impotent silence. A few of the latter, more unruly or better paid than the rest, tried to promote a disturbance, but they were put out, and the performance continued.[47]

The assured tone of these sentiments notwithstanding, the demonstration over Léger's play is noteworthy in that it was one of the last attempts by the royalists to express their feelings openly in the theatres. Respect for, even indifference to the King now rapidly disappeared. Within a few months plays passed unchallenged which portrayed Louis XVI as an imbecile, a traitor, a charlatan, a conspirator against his own subjects. He was shown deposed, imprisoned, exiled, even executed. In most such plays he was portrayed thinly disguised; a few dared even call him by name; in none did he appear in a favorable light. The patriots, after all, carried the day.

The strong feelings aroused by *L'Auteur d'un moment* discouraged neither Léger nor the Vaudeville from working the lucrative dramatic vein of parody. A mere five days after *Lovelace* opened at the Nation, Léger had staged his *Gilles Lovelace* at the Vaudeville. The target chosen for this satiric attack was less controversial and the production aroused no protest. In the meantime a new Chénier parody, *Charlot ou La Nuit des fiançailles*, had appeared at the Variétés Comiques. A less savage attack than *L'Auteur d'un moment* and directed more against *Charles IX* than against Chénier himself, *Charlot* too was accepted without rancor. The program proved so popular, in fact, that the Variétés Comiques followed it with a number of other parodies, including *Le Premier rossé*, based on the Nation's *Mort d'Abel*, and, of all things, a comic treatment of the Châteauvieux mutiny.[48]

Although they did not challenge the minor efforts of the Variétés Comiques, the patriots of Paris were not at all disposed after their success in suppressing *L'Auteur d'un moment* to allow unsympathetic productions in the major theaters. Their triumph over *Adrien* at the Opéra has already been noted; next came Cousin Jacques and his moderate comedy *Le Club des bonnes gens* at the Feydeau. Written and produced in the wake of the signing of the Constitution, Cousin Jacques' play was given on September 24, 1791, just five days after *Le Conciliateur* at the Nation and in much the same spirit. It was the first major success for the former Théâtre de Monsieur since its move to the Rue Feydeau in January. The comedy shows a village where fields are untended, friendships dissolved, marriages broken up because of overheated political discussions. A level-headed curate, who is of course a Constitutionalist, finally brings peace to the village by disbanding all the feuding clubs and setting up only one in their place—a club for all patriots with himself as president. "Let us embrace and make peace" was the closing refrain. There were verses honoring Louis XVI, and even a few kind words for the *émigrés*, those nobles who had fled the country during the first upheavals of the Revolution and whom the King was now imploring to return to support the new Constitution. The play delighted the general public, but the more extreme clubs were infuriated and Cousin Jacques was burned in effigy in more than one of them.

Undaunted by the ill feeling of scattered patriots, Cousin Jacques next created for the Feydeau *Les Deux Nicodèmes*, a sequel to his popular *Nicodème dans la lune*. But by the end of 1791, when the play was presented, the spirit of the fall had vanished. War was impending, the King suspect, the *émigrés* considered proven traitors, and moderation a much less popular view. The play survived only seven performances. *Le Club des bonnes gens* continued, however, earning the Feydeau regular patriot demonstrations, even before the riots over *L'Auteur d'un moment* at the Vaudeville. Early in February a request from certain members of the audience for a couplet to be repeated set off a violent demonstration, though the police commissioner assigned to the house, one Salliort, tried to shout above the uproar that custom allowed such a request. Shortly thereafter, a group of patriots who seemed to feel that their rights were in jeopardy at the Feydeau gathered under the balcony and loudly demanded the "Ça ira." The orchestra obliged and then attempted to balance the selection with a chorus of "Vive Henri IV." The aroused patriots stopped this attempt and forced the orchestra to play the "Ça ira" another five times, while the demonstrators shouted to the aristocrats in the boxes to remove their hats. When the play was finally permitted to begin, every possible political allusion set off a violent response. The boxes burst into applause at a line "The people must be enlightened, but not misled," and a storm of hisses and whistles from the pit forced the actors to stop. Shouts went up for Viotti, the director, who prudently did not appear. Finally Salliort managed to restore order, but only after being heavily pelted with potatoes for his pains.

At length *Le Club des bonnes gens* had amassed such a history of disturbances that Salliort convinced the municipality that it should be banned on the charge that it corrupted public manners, patriotism, and tranquillity.[49] Generally, the municipality still attempted to avoid making such decrees. The first obligation of the city officers was to preserve the peace, and this was extremely difficult in a city divided into bitter factions and swept daily by a host of inflammatory rumors. Yet the law prevented the prohibition of plays likely to create disturbances until after such disturbances had actually occurred. Tuetey lists a note of March 1 directed to the Minister of the Interior in which municipal officers were charged to restore order whenever riots broke out, since "works designed to stir up factionalism cannot be properly censored."[50] The municipal officers were not at all pleased that they could act only after a situation was already out of hand, but except in rare cases, there seemed no other immediate solution to the problem except to invite widespread protest by the open restoration of censorship before presentation.

The Jacobins were therefore not always successful in their campaigns to drive moderate plays from the boards. *Robert, chef de brigands* at the Marais was their next object of attack after *Le Club des bonnes gens,* yet this play not only survived, but even inspired a number of imitations in other theatres. Although the play was much favored by the conservative elements at the Marais, it is difficult to determine just what the Jacobins, for all their extreme patriotism, could have found objectionable in it. The play, closely modeled on Friedrich von Schiller's *The Robbers,* one of the late *Sturm und Drang* dramas, dealt heavily in spectacle, action, violence, and intrigue. It was one of the earliest examples of that new form which Guilbert de Pixérécourt would develop into the melodrama.[51] Robert de Moldar, driven from his home by the intrigues of his brother Maurice, is surprised in a forest by robbers and becomes their chief, asking their blind obedience to his plans for correcting the abuses of society. True, the hero is reconciled with the emperor at the end and cries, "Let us vow henceforth to defend our country and its laws, which will be reformed with the same courage that we have used to avenge their abuse," but such law-abiding sentiments do not characterize the bulk of the drama. Perhaps the patriots were less offended by the plot than by the attitude of the author, J.-Henri-Ferdinand La Martelière, who wrote: "As a stranger to all the sects which have in turn appeared on our political horizon, I have never embraced any opinion or party other than that of law and justice. It is not therefore a political play that I intended to write."[52]

The Jacobins were not, of course, always the outsiders in Parisian theatres. Certain houses even now catered primarily to patriots and produced the sort of fare which would become standard at most theatres under the Terror. One of these was the Louvois, which was opened August 16, 1791, by Delomel, the former director of the ill-fated Beaujolais. The new theatre, designed by the architect Alexandre-Théodore Brongniart on the site of the mansion of the Marquis de Louvois, an aristocrat the Revolution had driven from the capital, had a forbidding exterior (writers of the time said it resembled a barracks rather than a theatre) but the interior was large, pleasant, and strongly influenced by the prevalent interest in classic design. The seats were arranged in a truncated circle with two tiers of boxes ornamented with white balustrades trimmed in gold and separated by golden masks. The wall was painted to simulate white-veined blue marble with bas-reliefs of gold, and blue draperies were hung as accents. This classic *décor* was carried onto the front curtain, which showed a burning Roman temple, with priests, priestesses, citizens, and Roman soldiers saving the contents.[53]

Throughout his career, Delomel seemed destined to be plagued by the schemes of Mlle. Montansier, who had earlier evicted his Beaujolais company from the Palais-Royal. Montansier, as we have seen, considerably enlarged this theatre and built a troupe, headed for a time by Baptiste the Elder, which was one of the best in Paris after the two offshoots of the Comédie. She lived at this time on the second floor above the Café de Chartres, across from the theatre, which she could reach by a passageway. For a time her activities were largely absorbed in building up the former Beaujolais and in running one of Paris' most colorful *salons*. Almost all the noted persons of the moment, without regard for political inclination, were welcomed above the Café de

Chartres. On this neutral ground, artistic and literary discussions for a time replaced political ones. Here Napoleon Bonaparte, a young commander of artillery, met the already famous Talma and struck up a friendship which was to last for many years. Here young artists came to meet the great actors and actresses and to learn the secrets of the trade. Here, most surprisingly, men of all political colorings met for a time without bitterness—Dugazon, Paul François Barras, Danton, Robespierre, Martainville, the Duc d'Orléans, even the irascible Jean Paul Marat. Such halcyon days soon passed, of course. By the summer of 1792 the onrush of events made such gatherings more and more turbulent until at last, on the advice of her good friend Fabre d'Eglantine, Mlle. Montansier regretfully closed her *salon*. Her faithful followers, now predominantly of a moderate political cast, continued to gather in the foyer of her theatre.[54]

Even while engaged in her *salon*, Montansier continued to develop plans for her theatre. Further expansion in her present location was impossible, so she purchased land for a totally new house directly opposite the new Louvois theatre of her old adversary Delomel. The struggle with Delomel over the Beaujolais house had aroused bitterness on both sides, and Delomel had later accused Montansier of indirectly causing the unfortunate Hugot's suicide.[55] Although there is no evidence of actual vindictiveness in Montansier's choice of the new site, it is not unlikely that she was grimly pleased that the location she had selected for building what she envisioned as Paris' greatest theatre was so near to her enemy's house.

Still, the threat was not immediate, and in the meantime, Delomel attempted to win patriot sympathy by his unswerving devotion to the national cause. His was the only theatre of any importance to support the mob spirit which led to the storming of the Tuileries on June 20; Ronsin's *Arétaphile ou La Révolution de Cyrène* was presented only three days after the uprising. It followed what was becoming a popular dramatic pattern—the adaptation of Plutarch to contemporary events, catering to Revolutionary fervor with such lines as, "Without you the people is all and you are nothing without them," and, "The gods have shown us that crime is always punished, but they are never greater nor more just than when they take up arms to punish tyranny." Strong on spectacle, but weak on dramatic structure, the play's most distinct characteristic was its condemnation of royalty. The sudden rise in popular support of the King took both Ronsin and

Delomel by surprise, and aside from some extremist support, the play won little praise.[56]

Delomel's views came into favor again as the national situation deteriorated during July. The major theatres had closed after the proclamation declaring the nation in danger on July 22, but Delomel dropped the aristocratic name Louvois, rechristened his venture the Théâtre des Amis de la Patrie, and remained open with a drama called *Les Emigrés aux terres Australes ou Le Dernier Chapitre d'une grande révolution.* Representatives of the entire old society are shown in this play emigrating to Australia. In addition to a prince, a baron, a marquis, a bishop, an abbot, a president, a financier, a monk, and so on, there is a common laborer, Mathurin, who is the only one wise enough to bring a plow. The emigrants fall to arguing over which of them should be king of Australia, but the natives recognize Mathurin's worth and propose him for the position. He refuses to change his red bonnet of liberty for a crown, and concludes the play with a patriotic hymn.

Another theatre which, as we have already seen, devoted itself to extremist patriotism from its very beginning in June, 1791, was Boursault-Malherbe's Théâtre National Molière. *La Ligue des fanatiques et des tyrans,* playing at the time of the flight to Varennes, was representative of the fare which this theatre continued to offer. The Molière was therefore the scene of one of the few disturbances to mar the period of conciliation following the adoption of the Constitution. For several days the theatre, known for its antiroyalist tendency, escaped condemnation by presenting Pierre Chaussard's humanitarian *La France régénérée,* but on September 17 two new plays were posted which were rumored to be extremist statements more typical of the Molière's offerings. Hardly enough of either play was presented to substantiate this suspicion, however, for an angry crowd descended upon the theatre, jeering and whistling until the disheartened actors gave up the performance.[57] The undaunted director continued, despite such protests, to advance his unfavorable view of the monarchy, with such dramas as *Louis XIV ou Le Masque de fer,* and his equally unfavorable view of the aristocracy, with plays like the Marquis de Sade's *Comte Oxtiern ou Les Effets du libertinage.*

The evening after the attack on the Tuileries, a soldier named Desvernois wrote an account of the atmosphere at the Molière. In the pit, he notes, members of both sexes wore red caps, a patriotic emblem considerably less in evidence in the boxes. During the performance one of Desvernois' neighbors expressed the wish that all actors could become Jacobins. Desvernois, more interested in hearing the play than in discussing politics, replied brusquely that he had no desire either to see or hear Jacobins. His neighbor then loudly condemned the soldier as "an evil *muscadin* (dandy) who does not like the Jacobins." The audience shouted for the disputants to be turned out. Desvernois slapped his antagonist, for which he was cheered by some and threatened by others. He was asked why he disliked the Jacobins, and he replied that they were largely fools led by their chiefs Pétion and Robespierre. This was too much for the patriots, and the terrible cry "To the lamp-post" was heard. Patrons from the boxes now entered the quarrel, either to save Desvernois or to quiet the uproar so that they might hear the play. In the ensuing confusion, Desvernois escaped unscathed.[58]

While such theatres as the Louvois and the Molière still appealed primarily to distinctly minority factions, the period of crisis in the summer of 1792 brought much more of the general public to share their opinions. A new set of leaders came to the fore, far more Revolutionary in their goals than the men who had guided the young republic since 1789. These new leaders—men like Danton, Desmoulins, and Robespierre—viewed their moderate predecessors with the same suspicion that those predecessors themselves had entertained of the old aristocracy. Of the new leaders, none was more extreme or more violent than the infamous Marat, a journalist who styled himself "the friend of the people" and who championed a ruthless purge of all conservative parties. He branded as aristocrats all elements ranging from the royalists to the moderate Girondins, and he proposed that the Assembly require every aristocrat to wear a white ribbon on the arm for identification. This would presumably make it easier to enforce another of his proposals—that all aristocrats be killed when found in gatherings of three or more. But Marat, though widely read, was still a man of limited power, and such ravings were lightly dismissed by most of those he condemned. A member of the Assembly inquired, with some amusement, how Marat proposed to decide who were aristocrats. The journalist answered in all seriousness that mistakes were impossible; one had only to fall upon those who possessed carriages, servants, silk clothes, and who were coming out of theatres. All such were assuredly aristocrats.[59] Who could foresee that before a year had passed, condemnation on terms even more arbitrary than these would become commonplace in the suffering capital?

New strength was given to the Revolutionary extremists on July 28 when there appeared in Paris a manifesto signed by the Duke of Brunswick, advancing at the head of the Prussian army. Camille Desmoulins gave the document its first public reading in the popular foyer of Mlle. Montansier's theatre.[60] Reprinted by patriot papers and publicly read in other political gathering places, the manifesto raised tempers throughout the city by its haughty and insolent demands for French capitulation and restoration of royal power. Many wavering spirits now became convinced that the King was indeed responsible for all their troubles. On August 3, accordingly, Jerôme Pétion, who had replaced Bailly as mayor the previous November, put before the Assembly a petition from various sections of Paris demanding the dethroning of Louis. The Assembly set aside a week to consider this proposal.

During the week of deliberation tension steadily rose in the capital. The major theatres reopened, but carefully avoided controversial works. A city official, Jean-François Marmontel, wrote to the directors of the Opéra thanking them for their "very wise precaution" of "changing four verses in *Roland*" likely to stir up public feeling.[61] There were insurrectional leaders, however, who were by no means equally anxious to avoid disturbance. Irritated by the deliberateness of the Assembly, these conspirators planned to seize all municipal authority during the night of August 9 and force the dethronement of the King. At midnight the tocsin was sounded and the populace, fearing new military reverses, hurried to gathering places in all the Revolutionary sections. Angry mobs again descended on the Tuileries, and the threatened royal family fled to the Assembly for protection. The deliberations of that body were punctuated by cannon fire from the beseiged palace. When word came of the palace's fall, and with it threats to the Assembly itself, the legislators surrendered. Louis XVI was declared provisionally dethroned, and a proposal was accepted for a National Convention with far broader and more Revolutionary powers than the National Assembly had enjoyed. At last, at three o'clock in the morning, the historic sitting adjourned and the Revolution entered a new phase.

V

The Fall of the Comédie

August, 1792–September, 1793

THE weeks just before the establishment of the Republic and of the National Convention on September 21, 1792, saw strife and bloodshed in the capital, and theatre closures were frequent. Then the new government seemed to promise a fresh beginning, symbolized perhaps most obviously in a new calendar which took September 22 as the first day of year one of the new era. There was considerable cause for optimism; calm had come back to Paris, and the armies on the frontiers were at last reporting victories. On the negative side, however, freedom of thought and expression was steadily diminishing, and here the theatres were particularly vulnerable. Many sought to prove their patriotism by sending volunteers to join the armies or by specializing in plays calculated to flatter patriot taste. Certain theatres, most notably the Nation, now made up of the conservative members of the old Comédie, refused to compromise, and continued to preach conciliation and respect for tradition even in January, 1793, while the King was on trial. When the more extreme patriot elements came to power, these theatres were soon marked for destruction. One of the first acts in the Reign of Terror was the mass arrest of the Nation company.

During the month after the events of August 10, 1792, described in the last chapter, a powerful body emerged in the capital to challenge the Assembly, now in its last days. The Jacobins, unsatisfied with the mere temporary suspension of the monarchy and the generally conservative attitude of the National Assembly, rallied behind Robespierre, who made himself leader of the Commune of Paris, a legislative body with a *de facto* power even greater than the Assembly's. Its first concern was the control of the police, which in times of revolution gives any group a tremendous advantage; this it accomplished by creating a Committee of General Security, headed by the sanguinary Marat. His committee assigned police representatives to all parts of the country, establishing a vast spy system to seek counter-Revolutionaries throughout the nation, even amid the defending armies.

Every hour brought new terror to the suffering capital. On August 18, Lafayette, now commander of an army in the north, fled into the Netherlands after his troops refused to rally to the support of Louis and the Constitution. He was replaced by Charles Dumouriez, whose star had been rapidly rising in the preceding months. The Prussians continued to advance; the terrified citizens of Paris fancied themselves threatened by Prussians from without and by aristocrats at home, especially after rumors spread that the aristocracy of Longwy had betrayed that city to the enemy. This news caused the Committee of General Security to authorize the immediate arrest of all persons suspected of supporting the royalist cause. On August 29, domiciliary visits were instituted, and soon twelve to fifteen thousand suspected aristocrats filled the city's prisons. The Assembly was too concerned with the Prussians to worry about the Jacobins, and it took no steps to prevent these measures.

During these terrible weeks the theatres of Paris suffered greatly. They joined most businesses in the capital in closing after August 10, and it was late in the month before sufficient calm returned to allow the majority of them to reopen. Proceeds remained understandably low, however, and the theatres donated much of the profits to the widows and orphans of the patriots killed on August 10. The major theatres inaugurated benefit performances, and most of the others were quick to follow, unwilling to display a lack of patriotic fervor when so many persons suspected of this lack were being sent to prison.[1] By September, many theatres were on the brink of ruin. The artists of the Richelieu, represented by Dugazon, Talma, Monvel, Mme. Vestris, Angélique Desroziérs, and Augustin-Gervais Devigny, appealed to the Executive Council of the Commune for a subsidy of 30,000 livres to prevent the closing of the theatre. Boursault-Malherbe, director of the Molière, made a similar appeal to Danton.[2] Apparently only the more patriotic houses made such appeals to the authorities, for their reputations assured them some sympathy from the new regime. In response to the Molière request, Danton wrote to the Minister of the Interior, "It is for you in your wisdom to decide, Monsieur, how far our generosity can stretch in these difficult times to aid a theatre which has never presented anything to the public but plays suited to hastening the progress of the Revolution."[3] The Minister proved generous indeed, for a week after Danton's letter the Executive Council took time out from its considerations concerning the mobilization of the country to grant 25,000 livres each to the Molière and the Richelieu, which had in the meantime abandoned its aristocratic title for that of the Théâtre de la Liberté et de l'Egalité as further proof of its commitment to the national cause.[4]

Theatres with less patriotic records than the Molière and the Richelieu had few friends in the new government and accordingly suffered far more grievously. Some, like the Marais, had depended on an upper-class audience now mostly in hiding or in prison. Others, like the Nation, had drawn much of their repertoires from such aristocratic works as *Mérope*, *Didon*, *La Partie de chasse de Henri IV* and *Athalie*, all now proscribed. They were therefore forced either to close their doors or to prepare unfamiliar patriotic offerings such as *Brutus*, *La Mort de César*, *Guillaume Tell*, *Caïus Gracchus*, and *Le Despotisme renversé*.

The shift in government had its effect too on the administration of a number of theatres. Dorfeuille, one of the directors of the Richelieu, was imprudent enough to put into writing a comment that the theatre should remain politically neutral, that one should not "turn a gymnasium into a gladiatorial arena." When this paper was brought to the attention of the Commune, Dorfeuille fled the capital, leaving the Richelieu to his codirector Gaillard. The Commune itself appointed new directors, with a sharply reduced budget, at the Opéra, which it had appropriated as a municipal enterprise. Louis-Joseph Francoeur and Cellerier, the new directors, had both been associated with the old aristocratic Opéra, and were not enthusiastic about the new conditions, but like many others, they become republicans in spite of themselves.[5]

Within the next year, the repertoire of the Opéra was totally revised. Mythological and gallant spectacles disappeared, replaced by somewhat more ambitious versions of the same sort of patriotic fare which now filled the other theatres of the capital. Chénier wrote the words and Gossec the music for a militaristic review called *Le Camp de Grandpré ou Le Triomphe de la République. Fabius, Horatius Coclès* and *Miltiade à Marathon* exploited the popular taste for Revolutionary sentiments in classic guise. *L'Apothéose de Beaurepaire, Toulon soumis, La Réunion du dix août* and *La Journée du dix août, 1792* went directly to Revolutionary events for inspiration, and still other works, such as *La Montagne ou La Fondation du temple de la liberté*, presented the new ideas in allegorical form. Such traditional works as *Roland, Iphigénie en Aulide, Chimène, Oedipe à Colone* were no longer presented "since they showed kings and might offend the delicate eyes and ears of the republicans who now frequent the theatre," as the *Almanach des spectacles* explained. The same article went on to advise: "It is indeed time to forget the old chimerae of our fathers and to offer no longer anything in our theatres but models of ardent patriotism and burning love for the fatherland, and for liberty and equality."[6]

Thus by 1793 even the aristocratic Opéra had become republican not only in repertoire, but in audience. A police report on the opening of *Le Siège de Thionville* (June 14) gives us a picture of the new patrons:

> Overwhelming applause greeted the lines "We have a king no more; we are republicans. The sceptre is broken forever." When the inhabitants and the garrison of Thionville, gathered about the altar to Liberty, decided to sustain the siege and commander Wimpfen began the "Marseillaise," its stirring words turned all the audience into actors and their voices spontaneously supported those on stage. It was pleasing to hear the women in the audience join in the singing of the hymn, but it was noble and glorious to hear the men do the same. . . . D'Autrechamp was generally hissed, and applauded only by a few spectators who resisted the illusion; at such plays the Frenchman is a citizen first, a spectator after.[7]

The play proved so popular that it was often demanded even when it was not scheduled. When, after one such demand, a group of citizens complained to the Commune that their request for the play had gone unheeded at the Opéra, the Commune passed a resolution complaining of "aristocratic influence" in the theatre and requiring that "*Le Siège de Thionville*, a play of proven patriotism, be presented *gratis* and solely for the entertainment of the *sans-culottes*, who have ever been the true defenders of liberty and the pillars of democracy."[8] Such a decree was not to be taken lightly, and the directors replied that they had been only awaiting the approval of the Commune to give free performances of the play in question. Fearing that even this ready acquiescence might not remove all suspicions of "aristocratic influence," they sent also a list of recent patriotic offerings and a reminder that the Opéra repertoire had been purged of all works likely to give offense. The free performance of *Le Siège* proved enormously popular, and within a few months the state had established a policy of encouraging such free performances of patriotic works at several theatres, supporting them out of the public treasury.[9]

So the Opéra, the Richelieu, and the Molière, each by some form of concession to the new order, gained subsidies to offset the unfortunate summer of 1792. A number of other houses sought relief by appealing to the Assembly for a relaxation in the law concerning the rights of authors. On August 30, 1792, therefore, a set of compromise measures was passed providing that plays printed and sold before the decree of January 13 could now be presented without royalty on any stage which had given them before that date, and that all plays should enter the public domain after ten years. These measures satisfied no one, but the authors feared to make a strong protest lest they be accused of selfishness and a lack of patriotism in these dangerous times. They accordingly contented themselves with a letter of mild demurrer sent to the Assembly in mid-September.[10]

On September 1, a report arrived in Paris that Verdun had fallen without a struggle, as Longwy had earlier. Although the report eventually proved false, it aroused great concern in the capital; the tocsin was sounded, and all citizens were called to gather at the Champ de Mars to march to the relief of the fallen city. Many Parisians, encouraged by such extremists as Marat, reasoned that there was no need to go so far to find the enemies of the nation; the prisons were now packed with them. Uncontrollable mobs descended on the prisons of the capital and began slaughtering their occupants—a frightful butchery which lasted for several days. The Assembly, as always, proved powerless against the public and devoted what energies it had left to supervising the establishment of the Convention—the popularly elected body which was to supplant it and, hopefully, restore order to the city. By the time the elections were held, the violence of the rioting had somewhat diminished, and there seemed a prospect that the dark weeks from August 10 to mid-September would prove in retrospect only an unhappy period of transition which the newly elected body would bring quickly to a close. The representatives from Paris gave little encouragement to such a hope, however, for they proved to be largely from the very faction which had inspired the popular uprisings.

After the frightful events of September 2, all theatres had closed once again, and it was late in the month before any of them reopened. Yet the troupes were not idle. It was now dangerous to refrain from demonstrations of patriotism, and one after another of the theatres of the capital sent representatives to the Assembly with offers of service and, much more surprising in these difficult days, monetary contributions for the war effort. Montansier, whose royalist background made her particularly suspect, was the first to make such a gesture. The very day after the theatres closed, a corps of eighty-five artists and technicians from her theatre volunteered to form a company ready to march for the frontier at the first opportunity. The Assembly accepted the offer, and the new company was dispatched almost at once to join the Butte-des-Moulins battalion in the north.

Other theatres quickly followed the Montansier example. Actors from the Richelieu also volunteered to form a company, declaring that "after having preached the love of Liberty and Equality on the stage" they would consider it "glorious to defend or to die for them." More circumspect actors from the Palais volunteered to work on the fortifications which were being thrown up around Paris. On September 5, the Feydeau sent volunteers and a donation of 1,583 livres, 16 sols for the defense of the nation.[11] By the time the theatres had been closed a week, so many had made similar gestures that the rest were openly accused of antipatriotism. *Le Courrier français* accused the Opéra, one such theatre, of secretly planning productions to be presented when foreign aristocrats took over the city. The directors' reply in another paper on September 9 did not deny the accusation, but simply stated that their artists had contributed 9,000 livres to the nation since Easter and that thirty of their number were now fighting at the frontiers. The charges were immediately dropped.[12]

On September 22, the Republic was proclaimed, the Convention assembled, and sufficient calm returned to the capital to guarantee some audiences for theatrical presentations. As the theatres reopened, many showed evidence of increasing concern with national problems. Several more changed or amended their names as a gesture of their patriotism, and most repertoires were seriously abridged, partially to drop nonpatriotic plays from the bills, and partially to adjust to the absence of so many actors and technicians. Patrons who were accustomed to attending the theatre for diversion were often irritated to find that both audiences and plays were growing increasingly republican in sentiment. An aristocrat named Kolly complained of the change in a letter to his wife written just after the reopening of the theatres:

> Those who cannot view the theatre as a church now find it impossible to go there; for it has finally become necessary, so I am told, for all to drop to their knees, pit and box alike, to chant hymns to liberty. Adeline at the Feydeau was disgraced just a few days ago for refusing to sing the "Carmagnole." Madame Dugazon no longer wishes to return to Paris. All the Italian actors have left; they dance at the Opéra as if they were on crutches.[13]

The "Carmagnole" mentioned by Kolly rounded out the trinity of Revolutionary songs begun by the "Ça ira" and the "Marseillaise." Like the "Ça ira," it was a popular song which suddenly swept the city, defying future attempts to trace its authorship. It appeared in Paris during the dark days of September and was lustily sung by the patriots as they attended the reopened theatres. The music seems to have come from Marseilles, perhaps brought by that same company which brought the song that bears their city's name, but the words were conceived in Paris; and, since the melody was easier to sing than the "Ça ira," new verses appeared almost daily, particularly suited to the events of the hour.

Fortune seemed to smile on the new government in its earliest days. Almost as soon as the Convention assembled, word came of victories at the front. The conquered French suddenly found themselves conquerers, driving the enemy from Champagne and invading his own territory in the Palatine, Savoy, and the county of Nice. At the Belgian frontier, Dumouriez was preparing an invasion in accordance with his proposals of a year before. On October 11, the general came to Paris to consult with the ministers before putting his plans into action. Politically, Dumouriez was out of favor, for the violence of the Jacobins repelled him and he had broken with even the more moderate Girondins several months before. Yet his victories assured him a welcome from both of these strong parties, and he was warmly applauded not only at the Convention but even at the Jacobin club itself.

The general's popularity and success must have been galling to the Jacobins, who were well aware that he had little sympathy for either their aims or their methods. Still, none of them dared to attack openly a man at the height of his glory—none of them that is except Marat, who had long made it his policy to attack almost anyone in the public favor. Mirabeau, Bailly, and Lafayette had suffered his displeasure when no other voice was raised against them, and he now sought occasion to arouse suspicion against Dumouriez. Someone informed the journalist that the general had severely disciplined two battalions of volunteers which had slaughtered some *émigré* deserters taken in battle. Since Marat was appalled at the idea of a general disciplining patriots for killing traitors, he considered Dumouriez nothing but an aristocrat of the most dissolute habits. Marat denounced the general before the Jacobins, and demanded two commissioners to go with him to question Dumouriez concerning his conduct. After a fruitless search at the general's home and at several theatres, Marat and his companions discovered that he was attending a party at Mme. Talma's, and there the irate Jacobins repaired.

Julie Talma had accepted the new ideas of the Revolution with even greater enthusiasm than had her husband, and her home in the Rue Chanterêve became a regular gathering place for the Girondins. The Marquis de Condorcet, Victor-Maurice Gaudet, Armand Gensonné, Jean-Marie Roland—all later to perish on the guillotine—were among its members. It was not a *salon* in the manner of the brilliant gatherings of a few years past—such places had vanished completely—but a *salon* in the Revolutionary manner, a simpler but equally polished gathering where selected political and artistic figures met twice a week to dine on a single course and exchange brilliant conversation. The artistic world was represented at Mme. Talma's primarily, of course, by friends from the Richelieu—such artists as Chénier, Méhul, and Arnault.[14]

On the evening of October 16, the assembly at Talma's home was larger than usual because of the presence of the famous Dumouriez. Chénier, David, a great crowd of actors and actresses, and almost all the more noted Girondins were present. At the height of the festivities Antoine Joseph Santerre, who was at the door, announced the arrival of Marat. The journalist and his companions headed directly for the main party, gathered about Mlle. Candeille at the piano. According to Louise Fusil, one of the guests, Marat's physical appearance alone was jarring in that refined company. Like most extreme patriots, he considered attractive or even clean dress an aristocratic affectation. He wore a dirty Revolutionary jacket, with a red madras handkerchief "in which he had apparently slept for some time" around his head. Thick hair escaped from this in locks and fell upon an equally dirty handkerchief around his neck.

This unkempt figure advanced on Dumouriez and announced, "Citizen, a deputation of friends of liberty has come to the War Office to discuss matters which concern you. We went to your home but found you gone. We did not expect to find you here, in such a house, in the midst of concubines and counter-Revolutionists." Talma stepped forward and demanded to know by what right Marat felt he could so insult the guests, while Dumouriez coolly refused even to listen to the angry patriot. Realizing that further conversation was out of the question, Marat turned on his heel and left, denouncing the house as a "den of counter-Revolution." The guests were all well aware of Marat's growing power, and his angry departure was followed by an uneasy silence. Finally Dugazon, the company's comic spirit, set fire to some sugar, announcing that this would perhaps purify the air. This jest broke the tension and the party was resumed.[15]

The following morning Marat reported his version of this incident in his paper, the *Ami du peuple*. The article bore the heading: "Details of the party given to honor the traitor Dumouriez by the aristocrats at the home of the actor Talma, with the names of the conspirators who meant to assassinate the friend of the people." The whole of the lengthy diatribe need not be reproduced here; the opening and closing sections are sufficient to indicate its tenor:

> At the door was Santerre, general of the Army of Paris, performing the service of a lackey. He announced me in a loud voice the moment he saw me, which displeased me exceedingly, inasmuch as this was likely to drive away certain persons I should like to have encountered there. However, I saw enough to gain a key to their intrigues. I shall say nothing of the half score of nymphets chosen to grace the entertainment; politics were probably not the object of their meeting. Neither shall I say anything of the national officers who were paying court to the great general, or of the old court lackeys who formed his retinue, dressed as aides-de-camp. Lastly, I shall say nothing of the master of the house, who was amongst them in costume. . . . I was indignant at all I had heard, and at the atrocious manner in which our generals seem to have acted. As I could no longer bear to stay, I left the party, and I saw with astonishment through the half-open doors to an adjoining room, several of Dumouriez' brigands

with drawn swords. I don't know what may have been the object of this farce. If it were contrived with the idea of intimidating me, I must say that the valets of Dumouriez have a very low opinion of liberty. Be patient, gentlemen, we shall teach you about it. Meanwhile I assure you that your master dreads the point of my pen much more than I fear the swords of his vagabonds.[16]

The time was not far off when such a denunciation from Marat could be fatal, but happily for the actors at the Richelieu, the journalist still lacked that power. His reckless attacks had gained him many enemies, and he was himself accused in the Convention shortly after his denunciation of the guests at Talma's party. Marat defended himself successfully, but the preparation of this defense distracted his attention for a time from the "counter-Revolutionists."

Dumouriez, meanwhile, returned to the front, having won wide support in Paris for his military plans if little for his political inclinations. He entered Belgium late in October, and on November 6 at the battle of Jemmapes made that country, willingly or not, a republic. Among the troops which participated in that victory were a considerable portion of Mlle. Montansier's volunteers, whose presence added a definite theatrical note to the campaign. They had ridden to join the army of invasion in garlanded triumphal chariots drawn from the theatre stock, and now their directress, who had remained behind in Paris, conceived the idea of staging a victory pageant on the battlefield itself. Dumouriez willingly accepted the plan, apparently feeling that the reputation of patron of the arts would add to his luster as a conquering general. Soon, much to the astonishment of the Belgians in the area, a huge outdoor theatre arose on the plain at Jemmapes. The day of the production a notice appeared on an immense post near the amphitheatre describing the spectacle:

By the Authority of the Commander-in-Chief, the troupe of patriot artists, under the direction of Mlle. Montansier, will give today, November 12, 1792, in the face of the enemy:

THE FRENCH REPUBLIC

A cantata sung by MM. Elleviou, Gavaudan, and Lartique of the Théâtre Favart, Paris,

THE AUSTRIAN DANCE

or The Mill of Jemmapes

A ballet staged by M. Gallet, author of the *Ballet Bacchus,* given at the Opéra,

Principal roles: M. Seveste and Mlle. Rivière of the Théâtre Montansier.
This play will be terminated by a *Sauteuse,* executed by the Austrians.
NOTICE: The public is advised not to forget that the Austrians are Frenchmen thus disguised for the purposes of the presentation.

THE DESPAIR OF JOCRISSE

A play by M. Dorvigny

Given by MM. Baptiste the Younger, Durand, Gilbert, Mlle. Carolin and little Truffant, drummer of the 27th.
The spectacle will be concluded by a fireworks display provided by the cannoneers of the 1st battery.
The plain will be open from morning on.
The spectacle will begin at two o'clock.[17]

The day following their triumphant presentation, Mlle. Montansier and her artists remounted their garlanded chariots and returned to Paris in glory. When her theatre reopened, the public swarmed to applaude the patriot artists and to shower their stage with flowers. Montansier followed up this advantage by presenting a whole series of plays on contemporary events—Joseph de Lavallée's *Le Départ des volontaires,* Louis Dorvigny's *La Carmagnole à Chambéry,* François Devienne's *La Bataille de Jemmapes.*[18] The Théâtre Favart, as the Italienne was now called, had provided several members of Montansier's company, shared in their triumph, and now helped reap the rewards by producing a most popular *Siège de Lille.* The play combined the common themes of sentiment and national defense, featuring a patriotic family, a dashing young soldier and his love, and a ridiculous old aristocrat as a comic foil. The author, Joigny, was an actor at the theatre whose chief claim to attention apparently was that he lacked a nose. Although a *sans-culotte,* he advanced his political convictions with good-natured humor.

Turning now again to the two theatres descended from the Comédie, we find a rather darker picture. Marat's public condemnation aroused great concern at the Richelieu, despite that theatre's past record of patriotic sympathy. Production of Revolutionary plays and donations to the public treasury sharply increased. Dugazon felt himself moved to authorship, and on October 25 the Richelieu presented his *L'Emigrant ou Le Père Jacobin,* a drama clearly calculated to demonstrate the theatre's patriotic convictions. The wife of the "Jacobin father," an honest patriot, steals money from him and plots with an evil abbot to marry their daughter to a fugitive marquis. Happily, the son-in-law favored by the father discovers the plot and turns the abbot over to the authorities. Dugazon himself played the father, wearing his Jacobin card in his lapel, and was heartily applauded. This demonstration apparently allayed most suspicions of the theatre, although the *Moniteur* complained that Dugazon's hero had rather an unpleasant character and that it would be better to oppose a good Jacobin to the "aristocrats and priests who considered Jacobins blood-thirsty monsters."[19]

Hyacinthe Dorvo's *Patriote du dix août*, given November 12, was less acceptable. This "patriot" is a royalist marquis who dismisses his Jacobin concierge, breaks off his daughter's engagement to a republican, and scorns his liberal brother until the riots in the Tuileries bring him to reconsider his opinions. He thereupon embraces the concierge, refuses asylum to the defenders of the king, and burns all his royalist periodicals. Although many persons actually did behave in such a manner, the violent conversion proved unattractive to patriots and moderates alike, and the play did not succeed.[20]

After the battle of Verdun in September, a hero of that day entered the first rank of Revolutionary demigods. Nicolas Beaurepaire, the commander of the first battalion of Maine-et-Loire, was charged with defending the city. When faced with the prospect of surrender, so the report went, he blew out his brains. The Convention had his body placed in the Panthéon and the name Beaurepaire took its place beside Voltaire and Rousseau. A series of spectacular dramas celebrated this apotheosis. The version at the Nation ended with the goddess Liberty descending on an azure cloud to place a laurel crown on the hero's urn, but this spectacle was quite dwarfed by *La Patrie reconnaissante ou L'Apothéose de Beaurepaire* at the Opéra, which after tremendous funeral rites featured the goddess Destiny and her entire entourage descending on a huge cloud to promise victory to the French and glory to the hero.[21]

During the catastrophic month of August, 1792, when the King was dethroned, the only successful offering at the Richelieu had been Ducis' *Oedipe chez Admète*, given August 7. With Monvel and Mlle. Simon in the leading roles it had brought to the theatre large audiences. On November 26 the Richelieu again turned to Ducis, presenting his *Othello*. Although Ducis had already completed a number of adaptations of Shakespeare's plays, this was clearly his most daring. Even Talma hesitated at some of its innovations, though Ducis took great pains to "soften" the drama for French sensibilities. Carbon de Flins des Oliviers, the author of *Le Réveil d'Epiménide*, sought to allay Talma's fears:

The French theatre, though it can ascend no higher in talent and genius, can become much greater in detail and variety. Louis XIV enslaved the taste of artists, as he enslaved the liberty of his subjects. I have no doubt that the men of the court would have mocked Héldemone who, young and beautiful, loves a Moor; but the men of the Tenth of August will not employ the aristocracy of color at the theatre, and they will find it quite acceptable that a white woman loves a man of a color somewhat different from her own if that man is young, handsome, and passionate. They will not be scandalized to see a bed upon the stage; for the republicans, who have more manners than the subjects of a monarchy, are not, as the latter, slaves of a false delicacy, which is the hypocritical affectation of decency.[22]

Talma's concern would seem to indicate that Ducis had given *Othello* a less "French" cast than he gave his earlier works, but in fact the adaptation is as complete as ever. All events take place in Venice, in strict regard for unity of place; narrative is constantly employed to advance the action; each character of importance is trailed by a confidant. Ducis' Iago (Pézare) is far less villainous than Shakespeare's and his Othello far less black. Said the adapter, "I thought that a yellow, copperlike complexion, which is, in fact, suitable also for an African, would have the advantage of not revolting the public, and especially the ladies." Apparently Ducis was not so convinced as Oliviers of the color-blindness of republicans.

The play follows its original in broad outline, but the differences in detail are tremendous. Ducis' Othello, like Shakespeare's, has saved Venice and fallen in love with the daughter of a senator. The bitter father accuses Othello before the Senate of seducing his daughter Héldemone, and the Moor recites the exploits the telling of which won the girl's heart. When the Senate allows the girl to choose father or lover and she chooses Othello, the disillusioned father gives Othello the warning which plants a germ of doubt in his mind. Now the plots begin to diverge. Lorédan, son of the Doge, is secretly in love with Héldemone, and seeking the release of death, he begs her to ask Othello to take him on his next expedition. He also reports that the Senate is planning to condemn her father for his immoderate outbursts. Othello sees the young man leaving the house, and his suspicions begin. Soon the senator forces his daughter to sign an unread paper—a renunciation of her vows to Othello. When she refuses to marry Lorédan, however, her father gives her the paper and leaves. When the senator's enemies close in on him, Héldemone sends this paper and a necklace Othello gave her to Lorédan, asking him to use them to help her father win the Doge's support. In return, he asks her to delay her marriage a day. Othello is furious at this request, and when his friend Pézare brings him the necklace and note, saying that he killed Lorédan to get them, the Moor dashes distracted to Héldemone's chamber and stabs her to death. The Doge and Lorédan arrive and Othello realizes too late that Pézare has lied. He dies of remorse.

Such an ending proved much too strong for theatre audiences of 1792. The public that could look back with equanimity, even with a touch of pride, to the September massacres could not bear to see a sympathetic heroine stabbed to death in the illusory world of the theatre—a strange victory for sensibility. On the opening night the house arose with a cry of protest. Women fainted and men shouted condemnation over the weak applause of Ducis' friends. The easygoing author bowed to the storm and wrote an alternate ending for stage managers to substitute if they so chose. "To satisfy part of my audience who found the weight of pity and terror excessive and too painful in my conclusion," he explained, "I have taken advantage of the plot of my play, which made this change a very easy matter, to substitute a happy ending for the one which offended them." In this version Pézare is discovered, Héldemone and Othello reconciled, and the happy bridegroom pardons his friend's actions. With such changes, *Othello* became accepted as one of Ducis' best works, and Talma created one of his greatest parts as the Moor.

Othello was Ducis' last adaptation from Shakespeare. Though he lived until 1816, the events so soon to come upon Paris drove him into a retreat where he passed the remainder of his days. When, a few months later, a friend chided him for giving up a career when his fame was at its peak, Ducis replied, "Why talk to me, Vallier, of composing tragedies? Tragedy walks the streets. If I put my foot out of doors, I have blood up to my ankle." So, alone and aloof, Ducis spent his days in the company of a bust of Shakespeare crowned with laurel, polishing his adaptations.[23]

In the closing weeks of 1792, interest in public events again emptied the theatres. All during the month of November the Convention debated whether to bring Louis XVI to trial, and at last on December

3 passed a decree to do so. The King appeared before the gathering on December 11, and his examination and defense lasted into the middle of January. As the time for a vote on his fate approached, tension mounted, and the public flocked to the Convention as, in more normal times, they would have flocked to the Nation or the Richelieu. A description of the scene in Hazlitt's *Life of Napoleon* suggests nothing so much as a theatre:

> The farther end of the hall was converted into boxes, where ladies, in a studied deshabille, swallowed ices, oranges, and liqueurs and received the salutations of the members, who came and went as on ordinary occasions. . . . The upper gallery, reserved for the people, was during the whole trial constantly full of strangers of every description drinking wine, as in a tavern. Bets were made as to the issue of the trial in all the neighboring coffee-houses.[24]

With the central authority of the country on trial, the actors at the Nation began rehearsing a play which stressed order, security, and peace. Laya's *L'Ami des lois* was first presented on January 2, 1793. Laya had supported the early stages of the Revolution, but its recent manifestations concerned him deeply; his play was a passionate cry for freedom with order and a slashing attack on Jacobin extremists. With the latter growing in power daily, such a presentation was sure to be difficult, if not actually dangerous, for author and actors alike. That they were willing to undertake such a venture at such a time shows the strength of their feelings about the political situation.

The play was all the more certain to arouse protest because it did not disguise its didacticism under biblical or classic trappings. It was set in the France of the day, and its characters were drawn from the immediate acquaintances of the audience. Forlis, a former marquis, is in love with the daughter of Versac, a former baron. Versac favors the match, but his wife, influenced by Jacobin propaganda, is opposed. Although such a situation could be found in a host of dramas of the period, in *L'Ami des lois* the ordinary sympathies are reversed: the former aristocrats are loyal and patriotic, while the Jacobins are portrayed as opportunistic villains. Nomophage, the Jacobin favored by Mme. Versac, is clearly modeled on Robespierre. He attempts to dispose of Forlis by employing two incendiary journalists—Duricrâne, who is copied from Marat, and Claude—to stir up the populace against his aristocratic rival. Forlis, however, faces down a mob and gains their confidence. Nomophage is exposed and sent to prison; Mme. Versac, chastened, consents to the match with Forlis. Fleury played the aristocrat lover; Vanhove, Versac; Mme. Suin, his wife; Saint-Prix, Nomophage; Larochelle, Duricrâne; and Dazincourt, Claude. The patriots in the audience loudly protested this attack, but their protests were covered with hearty applause. Thanks to the Nation's known conservatism, moderates and royalists still made up the majority of that theatre's audience. Formal complaints were sent to the Convention, but the trial of the King took precedence over all regular business. The complaints were passed on to a Committee of Instruction, and while that body deliberated, the play continued.[25]

Given time and the distraction of the King's trial, *L'Ami des lois* might have been forgotten, if not forgiven, by the patriots. On January 5, however, another theatre mounted a production which raised Jacobin anger to such a pitch that accommodation between moderates and extremists in the theatre was no longer possible. There had been no serious disturbances at the Vaudeville since the riots over the Chénier parody, *L'Auteur d'un moment*, the previous February, and its new offering, *La Chaste Suzanne*, seemed an unlikely source of new discontent. Its authors, Jean-Baptiste Radet and George Desfontaines, departed from the theatre's usual genre of parody to tell a fairly straightforward legend from the Apocrypha—that of Suzannah and the Elders. Aside from a slightly comic cast given to the old men in the first act, and the change of their ultimate punishment from stoning to banishment, the play departed little from the original. Nothing at first glance could be further removed from the kind of immediacy which caused disputes over *L'Ami des lois*, yet the script of *Suzanne* contained a number of lines which in these tempestuous times added to the fires of factionalism. One line in particular, delivered to the two old men by the judge Azarias, aroused a storm of reaction: "You were her accusers; you cannot be her judges also." Both parties interpreted the line as a direct reference to the current proceedings at the Convention, and it was as ecstatically applauded by the moderates as it was furiously condemned by the patriots.

La Chaste Suzanne was denounced, not to the Convention, where the discussion over *L'Ami des lois* was now lost in a committee, but to the more patriotic Commune of the city. Faced with the anger of this body, the authors hastily adapted the play, changing the most offensive line to "Accaron, Barzabas, you cannot be her judges," the version which appeared in printed copies of the play.[26] Encouraged by this success, the enemies of *L'Ami des lois* resolved to bring their grievances before the Commune too. Thus on January 10, following the fourth performance of Laya's play, the Revolutionary districts of the Cité and the Réunion sent delegates to the Commune to protest against further performances. The following day their stand was reinforced by representatives from the Féderés, and the Commune shortly thereafter passed a resolution which stated:

> The Council General, considering the complaints which have been made to it against the play entitled *L'Ami des lois* in which malevolent propagandists have made insinuating statements against certain outstanding citizens in an attempt to stir up public feeling against them, and informed that the performance of this play creates alarming distrubance in our present perilous circumstances, and further, that a free performance of the play has been announced:
>
> Since it is the duty of the Council to stop, by any means in its power, the disorders which the spirits of factionalism attempt to encourage;
>
> Since the police have always had the right to stop the performance of such a work (a right which they used with the opera *Adrien* and other works);
>
> The assistant to the public attorney of the Commune therefore decrees that the performances of the play entitled *L'Ami des lois* shall be discontinued and that this present decree shall be sent to the police for immediate enforcement, with the further injunction that all theatres are to be watched for the appearance of any play which might disturb public tranquillity.[27]

This decree, posted all over Paris on January 12, drew an immediate reaction. Laya sent a letter of protest to the Convention, pleading that his work preached peace and order and, like *Tartuffe*, was being condemned by the hypocrites it attacked. He noted that no serious disturbance had yet been caused by the play, despite the charge that it disturbed the peace. Perhaps his strongest argument, however, was that the Commune was attempting to replace the old royal censor with one reflecting their own arbitrary and narrow concept of propriety. He pointed out that the Commune had condemned a production of *Le Cid* at the Nation solely because it contained a king, at the same time that it allowed a king in *L'Orphelin de Chine* at the Richelieu. He concluded by complaining that the new despots were even more inflexible than the old, for they would tolerate no opposition to their own views, while the censors at Versailles had permitted such revolutionary dramas as *Brutus, La Mort de César,* and *Guillaume Tell.* The letter was carefully phrased and convincing, and Laya added further to its force by dedicating his play to the Convention, hoping thus to place himself under the protection of that body.[28]

The Convention would probably have postponed discussion on this question had not circumstances forced them to act. The afternoon following the posting of the Commune's decree, angry crowds filled the theatre demanding the banned play. In vain the actors protested that they were under an interdiction from the Commune. A major riot seemed in the making, and Santerre, the commander of the Parisian National Guard, arrived at the Nation with a body of troops and, after training two cannon on the doors, entered the theatre with twenty armed men to announce that the play would not be given. The mob, far outnumbering Santerre's forces, was not cowed, and the discomfited general retired amid hisses and reported to the Commune that counter-Revolutionists were in control of the theatre. The Commune appealed to Nicolas Chambon, Pétion's successor as mayor, who arrived at the theatre to find some two thousand spectators demonstrating inside and several thousand more filling the square in front of the building. Chambon was an honest and peace-loving man, if not a strong one, and he attempted to satisfy the crowd by offering to represent them personally before the Commune. Loud voices in the crowd denounced the Commune as a pack of brigands and insisted that the decision be taken to the Convention.[29] The situation was now so dangerous that Chambon was forced to agree. He dispatched representatives to the Convention with such urgency that that body suspended its deliberations on the fate of the King long enough to hand down a decision on censorship. Soon Chambon's delegates were back at the Nation, and frenzied applause greeted their report that the Convention had ruled that no municipality had the right to ban plays. It was now about nine o'clock in the evening, the usual hour for plays to be finished (they began about five o'clock). Nevertheless, *L'Ami des lois* was immediately presented to an enthusiastic but orderly house which finally dispersed, to the great relief of Chambon, about one in the morning.

Too much feeling had been aroused by the struggle of January 12, however, for the affair to end with this victory for the moderates, and the very next evening brought further trouble. The Nation announced performances of *Sémiramis* and *La Matinée d'une jolie femme,* but between the two plays, the audience demanded *L'Ami des lois.*

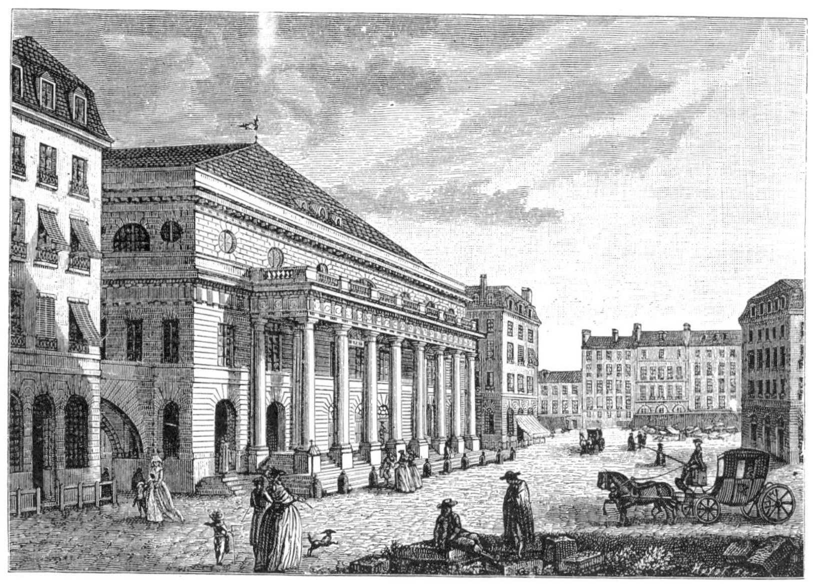

X. The Théâtre de la Nation. The building shown here housed the parent Comédie company until their arrest during the Terror. It was destroyed by fire in 1799. (Arthur Pougin, *Dictionnaire du théâtre.* Reproduced by courtesy of Imprimerie Firmin-Didot et Cie.)

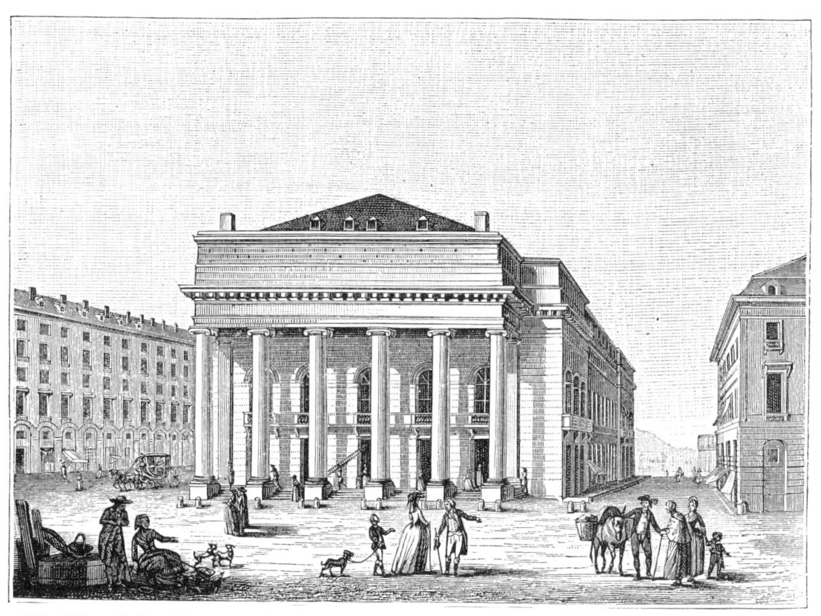

XI. The Salle Favart. This building, constructed in 1783 not long before this sketch was made, housed the Comédie Italienne. (Arthur Pougin, *Dictionnaire du théâtre.* Reproduced by courtesy of Imprimerie Firmin-Didot et Cie.)

XII. François-Joseph Talma (1763–1826). Talma's interest in historically accurate costume, especially of the classic period, is clearly indicated in this drawing of him as Sylla, one of his greatest post-Revolutionary roles. (Reproduced by courtesy of the Harvard Theatre Collection.)

The actors were well aware that continued challenges to the patriots could prove dangerous for them, and Dazincourt appeared to ask for a few days respite to "perfect the play" and to allow calm to return. This reasonable offer was rejected by the audience and Dazincourt was able to calm them only by promising a production of Laya's play for the following evening.[30]

Word of this production soon reached the Commune, and that body, unable to ban Laya's play but determined to prevent it, ordered a general closing of every theatre in Paris, in the interest of "public tranquillity." Complaints poured into the Convention, forcing it once more to override the Commune's actions by a decree which stated that circumstances did not justify closing of the theatres and that they should be immediately reopened.[31] Pétion, formerly mayor and now a member of the Convention, displayed the innocence of an outsider in a statement wondering why the Commune should be driven to such measures:

> The law puts plays under the responsibility of actors and authors. That is the true, the only responsibility in the theatre. Magistrates may make "suggestions," by summoning directors of theatres and advising them that it may be imprudent to play such and such a piece. I myself have made such "suggestions," and they have always been successful.[32]

The general closing once again warned the actors of the Nation how serious was the determination of their enemies. The promised performance of *L'Ami des lois* was therefore replaced on January 14 by *Le Médecin malgré lui* and *L'Avare*. The first play was accepted quietly enough, but *L'Avare* was refused, and a demonstration in favor of Laya's play lasted until nine o'clock, again undeterred by the arrival of Santerre with troops and cannon. At last the actors agreed to read the play, since this could not technically be called a presentation, and they did so amid the wildest enthusiasm. The following morning the worried company posted a bulletin all over the capital tracing the history of the disputed play and explaining their reluctance to repeat it.[33] This rationale proved unnecessary, however, for the Convention had at last decided upon the particular questions to be resolved concerning the King, and on January 15, the momentous voting began. All thoughts were directed toward the delegates, and the harassed actors of the Nation faded into a welcome obscurity. Demonstrators shrank from the thousands to the hundreds, and except for one embarrassing occasion when Santerre had to lead troops to the rescue of several magistrates beseiged in a box in the theatre, the authorities were able to keep peace at the Nation.[34]

On January 20, the Convention condemned Louis XVI to death, and news of this action was posted on the doors of all theatres, as well as in other public places. On this same day the Revolution gained a new hero and martyr, Louis Le Pelletier de Saint-Fargeau. A former nobleman with great wealth, Le Pelletier had eagerly embraced the Revolutionary cause, holding high posts in the Assembly and the Convention. Condemned as a traitor by other aristocrats when he voted for the King's death, Le Pelletier was shortly after assassinated by a guardsman in the Palais-Royal. He was widely mourned as the "first martyr of the Republic." After elaborate funeral ceremonies on January 24, for which most of the theatres in Paris closed, he was laid to rest in the Panthéon, and a great number of plays honoring him followed shortly after.

The execution of Louis XVI followed so quickly upon the sentence that even extremists were somewhat stunned. During the relatively quiet period which ensued, average citizens considered in awe the magnitude of this event, royalists reassessed their now dangerous position, and patriots anxiously watched for reactions to Louis' death. Aside from scattered Le Pelletier plays, few dramas of primarily political content appeared during this period; the safer vein of military drama was worked instead. The national armies had continued their triumphant advances all during the trial, and their victories made obvious dramatic subjects for theatres anxious to demonstrate their patriotism but unwilling to arouse further partisan feeling.

On January 23, the Richelieu presented its offering to the militaristic spirit of the day—*L'Entrée de Dumouriez à Bruxelles* by Olympe de Gouges, an ugly and irascible old lady whose works proved that *pièces de circonstance* were not necessarily successful even in the receptive surroundings of Revolutionary Paris. In December of 1789 she had presented a play at the Nation, *L'Esclavage des nègres,* which showed a negro couple throwing off the bonds of servitude in a West Indian colony. Despite the appropriateness of its subject matter to the sentiment of the times and superlative interpretations by Molé and Suin, the play was hissed from the stage. In October, 1790, the authoress tried again with *Le Couvent ou Les Voeux forcés* at the Théâtre-Français Comique et Lyrique, perhaps the only totally unsuccessful convent drama produced that year. The fate of her topical *Mirabeau aux Champs-Elysées* at the Italienne the following April has already been noted. Yet Olympe remained undaunted.

L'Entrée de Dumouriez à Bruxelles consisted primarily of marches, combats, and military maneuvers. Its bizarre and confused plot encouraged laughter and hisses throughout, ceasing only at the end when the authoress, missing no opportunities, had performed the "Marseillaise," the "Ça ira," and the "Carmagnole" in rapid succession. The hisses soon resumed, however, when Mlle. Candeille stepped forward to announce the dramatist. The actress' attempts to quiet the audience were interrupted by a grotesque figure which clambered out of the first box. It was the authoress herself, who pushed Mlle. Candeille aside and strode to the footlights to cry, "Citizens, you ask for the author. It is I, Olympe de Gouges. If you did not enjoy my play, that is not because it was badly written, but because it was execrably played." Hisses and hearty laughter greeted this statement, and Mlle. Candeille came forward to defend herself. Olympe argued valiantly until the aroused audience stormed the stage and put the infuriated old lady to flight. A second performance of the play was even less successful, for the audience climbed onto the stage in the middle of the presentation and began dancing the "Carmagnole." *L'Entrée de Dumouriez à Bruxelles* was not offered again. The angry authoress published a protest, noting that she had unsuccessfully offered to defend Louis XVI at his trial and that a cabal of antiroyalist actors at the Richelieu had for this reason purposely destroyed her play. The actors did not even deign to reply, and the incident seemed closed. These were dangerous times to attack antiroyalists, real or imaginary, however, and Olympe's words were not forgotten by those who had destroyed the King.[35]

After the trial and execution of Louis XVI, the Convention could again turn its attention to less significant matters. Still chafing over their defeat with *L'Ami des lois,* the patriots brought a series of complaints against moderate plays before the assemblage. On January 28, Jacques René Hébert called for complete suppression of *La Chaste Suzanne,* still running in its amended form at the Vaudeville, on the grounds that it "disturbed public tranquillity and corrupted republican morals." Hébert's complaints were substantiated by a letter to the Convention from Delpeche, an actor at the theatre, who reported that at a recent performance of the play a group of citizens had taken offense at certain lines, seeing, the actor felt, "a resemblance between Suzanne and Marie Antoinette." These patriots stopped a song being delivered by Delpeche and descended from their boxes into the orchestra with drawn swords, scattering public and actors alike. The police commissioner tried in vain to restore order as the insurgents mounted the stage to announce that if the play were repeated they would turn the theatre into a hospital. The Convention, motivated either by concern over the disturbance of the peace or fear of Jacobin anger, voted to ban *La Chaste Suzanne*, and shortly thereafter its authors Radet and Desfontaines and Barré, the director of the Vaudeville, were placed under arrest.[36]

The Nation was the patriots' next target, for the theatre had announced *L'Ami des lois* once again for February 5, hoping to escape patriot recrimination by donating the receipts to the war effort. On February 3, however, the Bureau of Police protested against the impending production to the Commune, recalling that the decree of January 13, 1791, held theatre directors responsible for trouble arising from their offerings.[37] Once again, seeing their enemies gathering, the actors of the Nation decided not to present Laya's play. On February 4, the theatre gave *Le Conteur ou Les Deux Postes*, the first major work by Picard, who was to become a comic writer of some stature. The play was a great success, but a cloud came over the evening when Dazincourt, who played the lead in Picard's play, came forward at the end to announce that *L'Ami des lois* had aroused such adverse feeling that it would not be given. This time the public, taken off guard, did not force a crisis and left in anger but quietly. Laya himself protested to the Convention the dropping of a production which could contribute 6,000 livres to the defense of the nation, but his letter had no effect.[38] His enemies in the national body were in the ascendant, and soon a whole series of charges were brought against the unhappy author, a typical one being that Jean Cléry, *valet de chambre* of Louis XVI, had purchased a copy of the play for his master.[39] Formally denounced by Collot d'Herbois, the condemned author went into hiding and did not reappear until after the Reign of Terror had passed. *L'Ami des lois* disappeared with its author, and when it was finally revived after the Thermidorian reaction, it passed almost unnoticed.

The only new play presented in February at the Nation was a much milder plea for tolerance. Louis-Laus de Boissy's *Maire du village ou Le Pouvoir de la loi* concerned a marquis converted to patriotic ideas and the marriage of his son with the daughter of the patriot mayor.

This inoffensive comedy still aroused anger among the *sans-culottes*, who could not tolerate a sympathetic and virtuous nobleman on stage, whatever the circumstances. Boissy was subjected to such brutal attacks in the following months that he felt obliged to demonstrate his patriotism by producing such dramas as *La Vraie Républicaine ou La Voix de la patrie*, which was given at the Lycée des Arts in 1794.

The controversy aroused by *L'Ami des lois* at the Nation increased the caution of the rival troupe at the Richelieu. In the six months following Olympe de Gouge's pathetic failure, this company produced only two new plays, both of strong Revolutionary sentiment. The remainder of the repertoire was composed of a bizarre collection of dramas catering to the tastes of the time, with few of the classics represented. The first of the two new plays, however, Chénier's *Fénélon ou Les Religieuses de Cambrai*, was hailed as the outstanding play of the year. *Fénélon*, given February 9, was in the convent drama tradition, but was much better written than its precursors. The trials of the young novice Amélie and her long-imprisoned mother expressed virulent antimonasticism in the most moving terms, but all religious orders having been banned early in 1790, the play was less a statement of anticlerical sentiment than a plea for humanity and tolerance in general. Chénier, who two years before had been in the vanguard of the Revolution, now found himself less and less in sympathy with its developments. Still, his reputation and the superb interpretations of Monvel and Talma saved *Fénélon* from any shadow of the enmity that *L'Ami des lois* had produced.

Two days before the opening of *Fénélon*, Chénier turned from his own concerns to aid a brother dramatist—Carlo Goldoni. A bitter rivalry with the popular and aristocratic Carlo Gozzi had driven Goldoni in 1762 to accept an offer to come to Paris as a dramatist for the Comédie Italienne. His success there was only moderate, but friends at court encouraged him, obtained him a position as tutor of Italian when his contract with the Italienne expired, and eventually, in 1768, convinced Louis XVI to grant the aging dramatist a life-long pension of 4,000 livres annually. In July of 1792, however, the King's civil list was suspended, and with it Goldoni's pension, leaving the dramatist, now in his eighty-fifth year, with no resources but a payment of 1,200 francs from the Comédie Française for *Le Bourru bienfaisant*, his only successful comedy in his adopted tongue.

Six months later Chénier learned of the penurious state of the Italian author and appealed to the Convention, barely a fortnight after the execution of the King:

Kings encourage letters through pride. From a spirit of gratitude, justice, and healthy policy, free nations should also uphold them. I need not belabor this point for Frenchmen and, above all, for legislators. Now, acting in accordance with a petition submitted to your Committee of Public Instruction, I have come to appeal to our national honor in behalf of an old foreigner, an illustrious author who, for thirty years, has called France his home, and whose talents and probity have won the esteem of all Europe.

Goldoni, this wise author and moralist whom Voltaire has called the Molière of Italy, was called to France in 1762 by the former government. Since 1768 he has enjoyed an annual pension of 4,000 livres; this pension, comprising his whole fortune, being paid to him during that time from the civil list funds. Since last July he has received nothing, for one of your decrees has reduced to penury this octogenarian whose writings should guarantee him the support of both France and Italy. At the age of eighty-six, with no other resource than the generosity of a nephew who shares with him the proceeds of his unremitting toil, he sinks to his grave, oppressed by infirmities and miseries, yet blessing Heaven that he dies a Frenchman and a republican.[40]

Goldoni's republicanism is still a matter of considerable doubt,[41] yet Chénier's plea stirred the Convention to restore the annual subsidy that the recently executed monarch had awarded to a court dramatist. This remarkable achievement was tragically ill-timed, however, for even as Chénier spoke before the Convention, Goldoni lay in his coffin at his home on the Rue Saint-Sauver. The dramatist had died in want on the previous day.

The months of February and March, 1793, saw more and more of Europe uniting against the Revolutionary government in France. A shortage of food and a steady inflation joined with this external threat to inspire an outbreak of riots and a general air of unrest in the capital. Theatre disturbances continued to increase in number and in violence, and on March 8, the day after the Convention declared war on Spain, the mayor ordered all theatres in Paris closed for several days until the populace had calmed. Volunteers were once more called to defend the frontiers, and, as in the fall of 1792, these patriots hesitated to depart until the capital had been purged of their enemies. In 1792 this feeling had led to the September massacres; in 1793 it led to the Revolutionary Tribunal.

Many delegates in the Convention feared the establishment of a body which could accuse and dispense judgment with no appeal, but the pressure of circumstances forced the majority to approve it. The Tribunal was set up on March 10 and 11, and on March 12, committees of surveillance were established in Paris. Such committees, eventually numbering over 150,000, sprang up all over France and served as a vast police network. The members, about 540,000 in number, were given three francs a day by the government for their services. All too often these committees came from the dregs of society, and given absolute power with virtually no check, it is little wonder that they frequently went to excess.

A series of disasters now undermined the central government and turned the newly formed Tribunal almost immediately into the engine of tyranny its opponents had feared. First, a full-scale insurrection broke out in the Vendée, an area of France still intensely royalist in sympathy. Hard upon the news of a wave of insurgent victories in the very heart of France came word of a major defeat in the north. Dumouriez' successful Belgian campaign had been suddenly halted at Neerwunden, and most of his conquests in that country imperiled or already lost. The general was retreating toward Paris, and according to rumor, blamed lack of support from the central government for his defeat. These somber events seemed to justify the most extreme measures. The terrible Committee of Public Safety was formed, emigrants were forever banished and their property seized, and the voices of moderate elements in the Convention were drowned by the shouts of would-be protectors of the nation's security.

The most immediate result in the theatre world from all these changes was that the Commune, now far more powerful, showed itself again determined to chastise the "royalist" theatres. On March 31, the unfortunate *Ami des lois* was again formally banned, and the Commune sent an "invitation" to the Convention to revise the repertoires of all theatres through the Committee of Public Instruction, "purging them of all plays which might corrupt republican spirit."[42]

Late in March, Dumouriez, discouraged by his lack of support from the government and revolted by the sanguinary turn the Revolution was taking at home, openly refused to obey directives sent him from Paris. When a commission was sent to remove the general from his command, the former national hero preferred the disgrace of desertion to the fate he suspected awaited him in the capital, and defected to the enemy, taking the commissioners with him as prisoners. News of this treason soon arrived in Paris, and was eagerly spread by such propagandists as Marat, long one of the general's enemies. Political moderates and conservatives known to have been friendly with Dumouriez swelled the ranks of the politically suspect.

Even half-mad old Olympe de Gouges was not forgotten for her unsuccessful eulogy on the general, especially since she had kept herself in ill favor with the patriots by a flood of pamphlets directed against Robespierre, to whom she had taken a bitter aversion. Robespierre was surely not particularly concerned by an adversary who suggested that he jump into the Seine with her, their feet weighted, to rid France of his menace; it is more likely that her much-publicized offer to defend the King, rather than her violent pamphlets or her praise of Dumouriez, brought her before the Revolutionary Tribunal. The only charge brought against the eccentric old aristocrat, however, was that of supporting the duplicity of Dumouriez. She was asked if she had written the drama presented at the Richelieu and if she still subscribed to its sentiments. Haughty as ever, the old lady proudly claimed the unfortunate work so clearly destined for oblivion, lauded its virtues, and swore that she would not renounce a word in it. Consigned to prison, she was within a few months marked for execution. For the first time, Olympe shrank from an encounter. The octogenarian pleaded for a stay of execution on the grounds that she was pregnant. Her plea was refused, and on November 2 she went to the guillotine.[43]

On April 3, the Richelieu gave its first new production since *Fénélon*. This was La Martellière's *Robert, chef de brigands*, which had already enjoyed a successful run at the Marais. Although at the Marais, as we have seen, it came under patriot attack, the play was strangely enough now lauded by those who a year before had found it objectionable. Robert's actions in taking the law into his own hands were interpreted as justifications of the Revolutionary Tribunal, and the play, according to contemporaries, contributed strongly toward stifling feelings of humanity in the public.[44] Certainly Robert and his band were close in spirit to the judges in the Conciergérie, and the same public applauded them both. Baptiste the Elder, who had created the role of Robert at the Marais, continued to play it at the Richelieu to much acclaim.

Aside from *Robert*, the major theatres enjoyed little success in this eventful spring. The Nation offered a series of insubstantial dramas calculated to offend no one. Its company was perhaps somewhat intimidated by the inscription that the district required on its façade on April 1: "To the Unity and Indivisibility of the French Republic. Liberty, Equality, Fraternity—or Death."[45] The traditional Easter closing was this year for the first time universally ignored. The smaller houses had prepared the way for this step the previous year by appealing to Manuel, a procurator of the Commune, for permission to remain open, arguing the inconvenience of losing fifteen days' business by "catering to a sect" when the season was not yet far enough advanced for attendance to drop off. Manuel upheld this view to police officials:

> Under what pretext can the municipality, guardian of all rights, condemn to inaction a group of citizens who live by the theatre and an even larger group who are amused and enlightened by it—particularly after a Revolution which has demonstrated so clearly that nations are built on the tragedies of Voltaire rather than on the sermons of the Abbé Maury? The theatres seem to me not only a means of instruction in the hands of a philosopher who enlightens the people; they are also a way of maintaining order for the administrator who controls them.[46]

Thus many of Paris' smaller houses were permitted to remain open for Easter of 1792, and the new practice was followed by all the next year.

Even so, a succession of military reverses in May led the Jacobins to call for the closing of the theatres as one of a series of emergency measures. New and serious defeats were reported in the north, the revolt in the west was growing in strength, and certain rich cities—Lyons, Toulon, and Marseilles—were drifting from the Revolutionary cause. As the situation worsened, panic increased in the capital. On May 31, a general uprising there gave the Jacobins their opportunity; in a few confused days they deposed the moderate Girondins, their only serious rivals, and assumed control of the Convention. While this struggle went on, the tocsin rang almost incessantly, shops and theatres were closed, and the streets were deserted. Thus began the Reign of Terror.

The anarchy in Paris prevented most theatres from opening early in June, and it was more than a month before either the Nation or the Richelieu mounted a new play. The threat of mob rule had been growing ever since the storming of the Tuileries, and now, with the Revolutionary Tribunal at the height of its power, the guillotine in constant use, and patriotic citizens supplementing its activity with impromptu hangings of suspected royalists, any gathering was potentially riotous. The pits of the theatres were filled with unruly crowds as capricious as they were violent, and pleasing such audiences was extremely difficult. The Richelieu, with a more patriotic record, had relatively little trouble, even though Talma was suspected in some circles for his friendship with Dumouriez and his wife's conservative *salon.* The less Revolutionary Nation suffered much more. Fleury has left a detailed description of the terrible conditions under which these actors now had to perform:

We were put nightly to the rack; insulted by the sarcastic jokes of the *Beaux*, and tormented by the vociferations of the *Tape-durs!* How pitiable was the condition of an actor of genius, compelled to submit to the caprice of such spectators! They did not know what they wanted. The piece announced was not appropriate to the times—or the performer was deficient in patriotism. The company to which I belonged, having been long marked out as object of popular disfavor, were the most persecuted. My hand trembled as I rubbed the rouge on my cheeks, at the thought of the vulgar attacks to which I was in the next moment to be subjected.

The *Beaux* were the precursors of the *Muscadins*, with this difference, that the latter were opposed to the *Tape-durs;* while between these and the *Beaux* the most perfect harmony prevailed. These Adonises of the Revolution, however, were but short-lived; their season lasted only six weeks. They fluttered away their ephemeral existence, and disappeared, like flies that usher in the plague, and die its victims.

At the theatre, the *Beaux* acted the parts of fuglemen to the *Tape-durs.* They assumed the task of dramatic commentators, and would criticize certain passages as reprehensible, or find fault with an actor for dwelling too much on what they chose to consider words of suspicious import. Lyncæus, we are told, could see the fish through the timbers of a ship; but his keenness of vision was not to be compared with these worthies. Lyncæus, after all, saw nothing but what really was in the sea, while these critics espied in our plays things which had actually no existence.

The *Tape-durs* amused themselves by making a noise in the theatre; singing, or rather roaring, their patriotic songs, to the annoyance of all who were less boisterously inclined than themselves. . . . With their tattered garments, mud-bespattered and often blood-stained, they presented a certain wildness of aspect, which in my eyes was not unaccompanied by a certain degree of savage grandeur. They might have furnished Shakespeare with models for his Caliban. They seemed like colonies of strangers, suddenly transported to the French soil, and having learned nothing of the language except blasphemy, menace, and the *Carmagnole.* They went about in bands, frequently accompanied by females of their own party, who were, if possible, more savage than themselves. It was the business of these harpies to surround the scaffold at public executions, exciting the passions of the mob, and to strain their lungs at the theatres, in order to make as much uproar as possible. The old females of this class were called *Tricoteuses,* and the young ones were denominated *furies de guillotine.* As for me, when I first saw these *Tape-durs* performing their rude dance, and uttering their coarse sneers before some unfortunate individual whom they had selected as an object of attack, I could have fancied I beheld Satan's condemned legions as depicted by Rubens, animated into hideous reality. After the catastrophe of the 10th August, such were the audiences who occupied our pit; and the reader may guess whether the classic productions of the French drama were entertainments suited to their taste.[47]

During the terrible summer of 1793, the Nation presented only one new play, a thin comedy by Louis-Guillaume Vigée called *La Vivacité à l'épreuve.* The Richelieu, less harassed, was more productive, although equally unsuccessful in its productions. Brienne's *La Liberté des femmes,* given July 22, showed a man and woman, hastily married, who fall in love with others and turn to divorce to end their ill-advised union. The old regime had tolerated only separation, but with the passing of the power of the clergy, a divorce law was passed on September 20, 1792. A previous play, by Desfontaines, had dealt with this new law with some success at the Vaudeville, but Brienne was not so fortunate. Despite the official sanction, divorce remained an unsympathetic action, and Brienne made the mistake of presenting it sympathetically. The theatre's police observer suggested dryly that the title should be changed from *La Liberté des femmes* to *La Licence du vice* and called the play "an open insult to decency and social conventions."[48] The next play at the Richelieu, though no more popular, gave Talma the opportunity to create his second and last new role in 1793 (the first had been Delmance in *Fénélon*)—the title role in Luce de Lancival's *Mutius Scévola.* The author, a former professor of rhetoric at the College of Navarre, had penned what he considered to be three acts of burning patriotism, but the Jacobins found his tyrant Porsenna too sympathetic and denounced Scévola as a "moderate." The play soon disappeared.[49]

As the fourth anniversary of the fall of the Bastille approached, the patriots gained a new martyr, far more illustrious than the simple Le

Pelletier. On July 13, Marat himself was fatally stabbed by Charlotte Corday, a partisan of the persecuted Girondists. His death caused an enormous sensation. The Convention attended the funeral in a body, and the Jacobins insisted on an immediate interment in the Panthéon. Busts of the journalist appeared in public places almost overnight, and the theatres lost no time in capitalizing on the sudden burst of sympathy which followed the assassination. The very day after Marat's death a letter was sent to the *Journal des spectacles* from Cammaile Saint-Aubin, an actor, author, theatre director, and warm partisan of the extremist cause:

> I have written a play entitled *L'Ami du peuple ou Les Intrigants démasqués.* This play, finished two months ago, has been for several days in the hands of citizen Monvel whom I have asked to present it to the directors of his theatre. From this it may be seen that I have not waited for the heart-rending situation which now afflicts us to unmask and deliver over to infamy the odious intrigues of the pretended friends of the laws who preach peace to you and then slit your throat. If my play had been presented sooner, perhaps we should not have to mourn one of the most courageous defenders of political equality. . . . P.S. I am a member of no club and have never spoken to Marat.[50]

Despite some public pressure, the actors of the Richelieu, who had little reason to mourn Marat's passing, did not present the play. The day of the funeral Dugazon was arrested and released that evening. When he asked to know the reason for such treatment, Fusil reports, he was informed that he was not worthy to attend the apotheosis of so great a man. The members of Talma's circle now saw clearly that their past difference with Marat had not been forgotten, and they began to gather at the actor's home to distribute parts and act out hypothetical scenes before the Revolutionary Tribunal, so that they might face that body without trembling when they were called.[51] As for Saint-Aubin's play, the little Cité-Variétés finally presented it on September 6, and the *Journal des spectacles,* while rendering all due homage to Marat, denounced the drama as the pitiful exhibition of style and invention which it undoubtedly was.

It was upon the Nation, however, that the wrath of the now-powerful Jacobins descended. The memory of *L'Ami des lois* was still fresh, and now an occasion was sought to punish this theatre for its presumption. The occasion came in August with the presentation of François de Neufchâteau's *Paméla.* The adaptation of Samuel Richardson's novel to the stage was not a new idea; Boissy and Pierre La Chaussée had produced rival versions in 1743, six years later Voltaire borrowed the central idea for his successful *Nanine,* and later still Goldoni too produced a rather free adaptation called *Paméla nubile.* Neufchâteau's version followed Goldoni much more than Richardson, but certain touches were Neufchâteau's own. In this new retelling, Bonfils having vainly pursued his servant Paméla, resolves to wed her despite the reproaches of his sister and a friend. Then Andrews, the girl's father, falls at Bonfils' feet and reveals himself as Count Oxpen, a wanted Scottish chief. Bonfils obtains the Count's pardon and weds Paméla.

Neufchâteau's major addition to the story was a strange one, particularly in 1793; he made his heroine of noble birth, hinting that nobility, and not virtue, was rewarded. The Revolutionary papers were quick to notice this and to protest, but the Committee of Public Safety made no immediate move against the play, possibly fearing a repetition of the public outcry raised against the banning of *L'Ami des lois.* Thus the play was allowed nine performances, long enough for public curiosity to be generally satisfied, before a ban was pronounced on August 29. This unexpected action drove Neufchâteau to protest. He pointed out to the authorities that his play had been written in 1788 and might therefore contain some "outdated" ideas which he would now be more than willing to remove. So prompt a capitulation seems to have placated the authorities, and on September 1 a rather ironic note from Neufchâteau appeared in the papers announcing the reappearance of his revised work. Even so, the *Feuille du salut public,* the major Jacobin paper, added to Neufchâteau's announcement an editorial comment calling for the closing of the Nation and condemning the author for "allowing his work to be performed in a rallying place for royalists, Prussians, and Austrians."[52]

The Jacobins turned out in force for the next performance, on September 2, to demonstrate their displeasure at the lifting of the ban, and the house was unruly all evening, though no serious trouble arose, possibly because of a ruling by the municipality forbidding "all canes, sticks, swords, or other offensive weapons" at the performance. Then in the fourth act came the interchange:

Andrews: Ah, only the persecutors are to be condemned
And the most tolerant are the most rational.
Bonfils: All honest men agree with that.

At these words, one Jullien de Carentan jumped to his feet and cried that the players were delivering forbidden lines. Fleury, playing Lord Bonfils, quietly replied that he was giving the play as it had been approved by the Committee of Public Safety and appealed to the audience for permission to continue. The great majority of the house supported Fleury, and Carentan was turned out. He repaired at once to the Jacobin Club, where he reported that the audience of the Nation, all wearing the trappings of aristocrats, were applauding royalist lines and permitting no patriotic protest. Robespierre went directly to the Committee of Public Safety to complain that the theatre in question had long been a source of irritation and to demand action against it.

A decree was passed on the spot noting that the actors of the Nation had "given continual proofs of their determined opposition to the state since the beginning of the Revolution," and that patriots were subject to insult in their theatre. For these reasons, the theatre was declared closed, and the actors and author of *Paméla* were ordered arrested and their papers confiscated.[53] So rapidly did all this occur that municipal authorities were informed of the decree before the evening's entertainment at the Nation was even finished. Fleury notes that the actors were preparing for the afterpiece, *L'Ecole des bourgeois*, when friends arrived with word that the Jacobins had denounced the theatre and that arrest was imminent. "What do you think, Fleury?" asked Dazincourt. "Shall we be off?" "By no means," Fleury replied. "Wherever we fly, we shall be pursued. Let us stay where we are; this is our 10th of August." As troops surrounded the theatre, the curtain rose and the play began. The actors remained at their posts, but Fleury did seize the occasion, while the attention of the audience was directed elsewhere on stage, to warn his friends Mme. Jeanne-Françoise-Louise de Sainte-Amaranthe and her daughter Amélie, who were seated in one of the boxes giving directly onto the stage.[54]

Mme. de Sainte-Amaranthe left the theatre unchallenged, and so, the play completed, did the astonished actors. Their respite, however, was very brief; that night the police called on each member of the company and all were placed under arrest. The following morning Bertrand Barrère presented the charges against the Nation to the Convention, and that body, now scarcely more than a rubber stamp, proved no longer willing or able to oppose the enemies of the theatre. The *Feuille du salut public* of September 3 devoted much space to praising the arrest of the actors as a triumph of equality over aristocracy.[55]

Tuetey notes an example of bureaucratic confusion which injected a single note of grim humor into this, one of the darkest moments of French theatre history. On September 3, a request was sent out from the Committee of Public Safety asking certain actors from the Nation to appear and assure the Committee that further disturbances such as the previous evening's would not occur. The actors replied, with bitter irony, that they would be unfortunately unable to appear, as they were being detained at Madelonettes and Sainte-Pélagie prisons.[56]

The men of the company—Dazincourt, Fleury, Vanhove, Bellemont, Joseph Florence, Saint-Prix, Saint-Fal, Dunant, Marsy, Larochelle, Gabriel Champville, Dupont, Gérard, Ernest Vanhove, Alexandre Duval, and Jules Fleury—were sent to the Madelonettes. The women—Marie La Chassaigne, Marie Suin, Raucourt, Louise and Emilie Contat, Joly, Magdeleine Perrin-Thénard, Devienne, Marie Fleury, Petit-Vanhove, Montgautier, Lange, Mézeray, and Ribaut—went to Sainte-Pélagie. Only three members of the company escaped: Molé, who was not at home when the police came and who strangely enough was not disturbed later; Naudet, who was traveling in Switzerland; and Desessarts, who had gone to Barèges on the advice of his doctors, and whom this sad news confined to his bed, where he soon died.[57] On September 20, the Nation troupe was joined in its imprisonment by Léger, the author of *L'Auteur d'une moment,* Radet and Desfontaines, the authors of *La Chaste Suzanne,* and Piis and Barré, the directors of the Vaudeville who had persisted in the presentation of these plays in the face of Jacobin anger.[58]

The agonies of the Nation and the Richelieu notwithstanding, interest in the drama was never greater than during this darkest year of the Revolution. In its course, one historian estimates, between 200 and 250 new plays appeared, almost half of them political in nature, by almost 140 different authors.[59] The great host of tiny theatres spawned by the Revolution naturally contributed most heavily to this total. There were now over forty playhouses in the capital, some of them born at the very peak of Revolutionary fury. One such, the Lycée, opened on July 16, announcing in the *Journal des spectacles* that its aim was "to present a relaxation to supplement the useful works which occupy the rest of the day." It attracted audiences by a series of bizarre ballets and pantomimes—*La Révolte des nègres, Les Capucins à la frontière, La Guillotine d'amour.*[60]

Most of these new houses were strongly patriotic, but one was so virulent in its Revolutionary fervor as to deserve particular mention. This theatre opened in the heart of Paris near the Palais de Justice late in 1792, taking the name Palais-Variétés from its imposing neighbor. The site upon which it was built had a strange history. For almost nine hundred years it had been the location of a church; the original structure was raised about 890 and in 915 received a great number of relics, among them the bodies of eighteen saints. By the early eighteenth century, the building, though many times remodeled, was dangerously old, and stones regularly fell from it. In 1787 the major part of the church collapsed at last and the most valuable objects still in it were moved elsewhere. Reconstruction was begun, but halted by the Revolution, and for a time a public dance hall called the Prado occupied the ruins. Then the architect Lenoir converted the remains of the old building into a theatre and served as its first director. In 1793 he abandoned the original title of his venture as too royalistic and rechristened it the Cité-Variétés.[61]

The first success of this theatre was Charles-Louis Tissot's *Tout pour la liberté*, a fairly typical offering. Here the Spirit of France is shown traveling incognito with Phanes, the play's *raissoneur*, to the borders to watch the loyal inhabitants repulse foreign invaders. The play swarms with patriots, described by the Spirit of France as "just even in their vengeance," and is composed for the most part of interchanges such as this one concerning the "Marseillaise":

> Father Thomas: Citizens! I am going to sing a song which has just arrived from Paris. It begins with the words "*Allons, enfants de la patrie.*" Jullien, surely you know it!
> Jullien: Know it! Father, we sing it constantly. It is the soldiers' prayer.
> Father Thomas: And the citizens', *morbleu!* I never hear it without tears springing to my eyes.

The play ends with the Spirit revealing itself in celestial glory and assuring the citizens that it will bless their cause.

The Cité-Variétés survived for fifteen years, opening and closing some twenty times during that period. Every sort of entertainment was attempted there—vaudeville, opera, comedy, pantomime, ballet, drama—but during the years just after its opening the dominant genre of the theatre was *pièces de circonstance*, and by a peculiar twist of fate this theatre, erected on a site sanctified by the prayers of nine centuries, a theatre entered only by traversing a series of somber cloisters, presented the most irreligious of the patriotic dramas. Nor did the irony of fate end there, for the patron saint of the departed church, a saint associated with this site from the days of Huge Capet, was none other than St. Bartholomew.

The very names of the most popular genres here and elsewhere testify to the ephermeral nature of the drama now presented: *faits historiques, faits patriotiques, divertissements patriotiques, comédies patriotiques, impromptus républicains, tableaux patriotiques, scènes patriotiques, sans-culottides, opéras* and *vaudevilles patriotiques*, and so on. Songs of the Revolution were sung during such productions and were apparently on occasion supplemented with gruesome reminders of the progress of the Terror. According to one diarist:

> During the entr'actes, an actor stepped forward to tell the audience the number of victims which had died that same day on the Place de la Révolution; and this announcement was accompanied by a song during which, as often happened in the prisons, the singers imitated the heavy sound of the ax and the contortions of the dying, while singing the praises of liberty.[62]

All suggestions of the old regime were now ruthlessly banished from the stage; demands from the public and decrees from the government seriously abridged the old repertoire. *Andromaque*, *Phèdre*, *Britannicus*, *Mérope*, *Zaïre*, *Tancrède*, *La Vestale*, and *Mahomet* were banned outright, while many other plays were extensively revised for republican ears. Kings became republican generals in the service of their native land. Titles of nobility disappeared—marquis became Damis and baron, Cléon. The Place Royale, mentioned in *Le Menteur*, became the Place des Piques. All references to royalty in Racine and Corneille were rewritten after the fashion of the line in Molière's *Tartuffe:* "We live under a prince who is hostile to fraud," which became, "Now those days are past of imposture and fraud."[63]

Audiences were even more intolerant of forbidden words than were the officials, as an occurrence of July 23 at the Favart indicates. An actor wished to announce to the public that one of his company would not appear that evening and began, as was customary, with "Messieurs . . . " He was interrupted by the observation that there were no longer any titles but "citizen." "Citizens," he began again, "Mlle. Jenny . . ." Again an angry interruption drowned his words. "So be it. Citizen Jenny being indisposed, we beg you to accept in her place Mlle. Chévalier." This set off a new protest, which drove the actor to explain that long custom made him forget himself and say Monsieur and Mademoiselle instead of citizen. This further repetition of the hated words set off a new demonstration, and the actor was driven from the stage.[64]

Fear of accusation hung over all those houses with any previous relations with the court. In March a medal was circulated at the Convention, bearing on one side a portrait of Louis XVI with the words "King of France and Navarre" and on the other "Louis XVI, born at Versailles August 23, 1754, king May 10, 1774, martyred January 21, 1793." An accompanying note accused Mlle. Montansier of having such medals struck in Brussels and distributed there through Mme. Crumpipen, mistress of the recently disgraced General Dumouriez. Mlle. Montansier would certainly never have run the risk of associating herself with such a project, and the evidence against her was so slight and so circumstantial that no direct action was taken. Her repertoire was carefully examined for indications of royalist sentiment, however, and some of it banned. Her popular play in residence, *Cadet-Roussel au Café des Aveugles*, was spared despite its lack of patriotic sentiment, and inspired an innumerable series of plays about the irrepressible title character.[65]

Such scattered policing of individual repertoires continued in the succeeding months; then, toward the end of July, came a general statement. The Committee of Public Safety sent out a "suggestion" to all theatres requesting that more patriotic plays be given. The major houses hastened to report their agreement. On July 29, Saint-Prix reported that the Nation, now just a month away from its doom, had been in the process of revising its repertoire when the Committee's suggestion arrived, and promised satisfaction. The following morning a deputation arrived from the Favart with a similar promise, and shortly thereafter Francoeur and Cellerier, the directors of the Opéra, came to state that plans for more patriotic plays were already under way at their theatre. The next morning Gaillard, director of the Richelieu, reported that he too was at work on such changes. On August 4, the directors of the Théâtre Comique et Lyrique and the Cité-Variétés submitted copies of their projected repertoires for approval.

Then came the directors of the Délassements, the Louvois, the Gaîté, and the Ambigu-Comique, and finally, on August 6 and 7, Montansier and the directors of the Vaudeville, Piis and Barré.[66]

The success of this measure encouraged the patriots in power to make still further demands on the theatres, and on August 2, the Convention passed a decree which required that certain theatres of Paris should present *Brutus, Guillaume Tell, Caïus Gracchus* and "other plays relating the glorious happening of the Revolution and the virtues of the defenders of liberty" one day each week at the expense of the Republic. The decree further noted that "any theater at which plays are presented tending to lower public spirit and to reawaken the shameful superstition of royalty will be closed, and the directors arrested and punished to the full extent of the law."[67]

The theatres, faced with closure or worse, hastened to comply. Only the most blatantly Revolutionary dramas were safe, because officials and audience could condemn anything on the merest caprice. The entrepreneur, with not only his investment, but perhaps his life, at stake, had to resign himself to flattering the taste of the day, indeed of the hour. This policy, which directors initiated for self-protection, was soon codified into law. On August 14, Silvain Lejune, speaking before the Convention, made three suggestions for stimulating spirit among the citizens of the capital—the installation of public forges for producing instruments of vengeance, the cessation of all frivolous amusements, and the closing of the theatres. Charles Delacroix arose to protest the third measure, arguing that the theatres could serve to enkindle public spirit; that no one could leave a production of *Brutus*, for example, without a desire to stab the rascals who would enslave the country. He proposed instead that the Committee of Public Safety take steps to see that only patriotic plays be given.[68] The proposition was adopted, and under the encouragement of the Committee, patriotic dramas did indeed dominate most of the theatre fare in Paris for the rest of 1793.

These new plays tended to fall into three types, all of which were already popular before the Convention's resolution. First came the patriotic spectacles based on the classics, which, with their heavy reliance on costumes and scenery, were generally produced at the larger theatres. Typical of this type was Marie Joseph Martin's *Fabius*, presented on August 9 at the Opéra. The tenuous plot was built around songs of praise to the conquerer of Hannibal, the would-be king of Rome, and the production ended with a triumphant civic festival. Second came the anticlerical plays, growing steadily more depraved. *La Journée du Vatican*, given at the Louvois in mid-August, showed a drunken pope singing coarse songs in the company of debauched cardinals and riotous bishops. At the end of the play, the pope marries his mistress, accepts the French Constitution, and after dancing the fandango, sings:

> To lose in a day the papacy
> And right of infallability
> Is truly most distressing;
> But to reign instead by liberty
> O'er Romans who are truly free—
> I find this most consoling.

The Abbé Maury gave evidence of his Revolutionary convicitons by appearing in the cast under his own name.

Most common of all, however, were the occasional pieces based on contemporary events. Typical was the extremely popular *L'Ami du peuple ou La Mort de Marat*, by Gassier Saint-Armand, offered on August 8 by the Variétés Amusantes. In the opening scene, the playwright sympathetically portrays Marat's "marriage by nature" to his housekeeper Evrard (later declared his widow and maintained at the expense of the state). Says Marat, "This is the happiest day of my life. Oh my loved one, in this vast temple of Nature I take for witness of the eternal fidelity I swear to you the Creator who hears us. Let this kiss seal the union I have so long desired." The second scene showed Marat's death, and as Charlotte Corday is seized by an angry crowd, one of her attackers cries, "Never forget that the friend of the people will survive in the heart of all the French, in the Panthéon itself!" It was the third scene which dominated the play, however. The scene showed a dais raised in a public square, with classic candelabras burning perfumes in the four corners. With somber music a funeral cortege slowly entered the stage. It reflected all the contemporary ideas of significance and solemnity: six warriors, lances lowered, two drummers in black, four musicians with trumpets, a chorus of female mourners, two children bearing the inscriptions Liberty and Equality on banners, a chorus of Romans, a soldier bearing the bust of Brutus, six members of the National Guard, four children bearing censers, a child with a box of incense, two Romans with banners bearing the words Justice and Innocence, the body of Marat, its wound conspicuously showing, borne by four Romans, a child carrying a banner saying, "He died for the Republic," Evrard in a black veil, accompanied by two other women, carrying the martyr's heart on a cushion, a chorus of deputies, citizens, and more members of the National Guard. The procession over, the body was placed on the dais to a

7. An entr'acte at Nicolet's theatre. Even after Nicolet turned to serious dramatic fare, spectacular scenes such as this were still often interspersed with the plays as part of the ever-increasing competition for audiences. (Arthur Pougin, *Dictionnaire du théâtre*. Reproduced by courtesy of Imprimerie Firmin-Didot et Cie.)

funereal hymn. Then the sky opened and a shower of roses fell on the body. Liberty descended on a cloud to address the people and place a crown on the martyr's head, while Fame sounded a trumpet and drums beat. Surely an impressive spectacle, although one might question the dramatic effect of casting the same actress, Marie-Jacqueline Lévêque, as both Charlotte Corday and the goddess Liberty.[69]

Although such fare provided a large portion of the entertainment offered Parisian audiences in the summer of 1793, there were naturally other attractions little concerned with the decrees of the Convention. Despite the pressures of the time, Arlequin maintained his indifference to new ideas, and within a few weeks during this summer Parisians were offered *Le Ménage truc d'Arlequin* at the Gaîté; *Arlequin friand*, *Arlequin tailleur*, *Arlequin machiniste* and *Le Duel d'Arlequin* at the Vaudeville; *Arlequin marchand d'almanachs* at the Variétés; *Arlequin journaliste* and *Le Lendemain des noces d'Arlequin* at the Montansier; and *Arlequin marchand d'ésprit* at the Comique et Lyrique.

Nicolet seems to have been the only director to keep his theatre entirely free from patriotic drama, despite his vow to the Committee of Public Safety. Pierrot, pantomime, magic, and tumbling—all the attractions of happier days lived on at the Gaîté. Still, other theatres varied their nationalistic offerings with such neutral fare, and audiences seem to have been attracted by these opportunities to forget for a few hours the preoccupations of the outside world. On July 14, the Lycée drew a large audience with *Le Goûter*, a simple story of three children who give money to an old beggar. The day of Charlotte Corday's death one of the most popular offerings on the boulevard was a comedy, *Mieux fait douceur que violence*, which despite its suggestive title, had nothing to do with the events of the hour. A play based on the love affair of the fairy Urgande and the sorcerer Merlin brought crowds to the Favart on the day of Marie Antoinette's execution and on the afternoon when the Girondists went to their death, the Variétés Amusantes premiered a successful production of *Arlequin gardien des femmes*.

It is not difficult to sympathize with those who sought even ephemeral distraction from the horror that surrounded them this terrible summer in Paris, but amid such horror, these trivial amusements often seem somehow even more ghastly than the chauvinistic dramas which fired patriot passions. One shudders before such reminiscences as André Gréty's, who recounts how one afternoon he was crossing the Place de la Révolution and his attention was caught by the sounds of an orchestra, the joyous cries of performers, and the laughter of patrons issuing from a near-by theatre. At the same instant he saw the blade of the guillotine rising for its next victim.[70]

VI

The Theatres under the Terror September, 1793–July, 1794

THE year following the arrest of the Nation's actors was the darkest of the Revolution. Denunciations and executions spiraled, and the hopelessly exposed actors and authors of Paris' theatres for the most part tried to escape condemnation by desperate presentation of anything likely to flatter or please those in power. Dramatic activity did not lessen, but shifted more and more to pure propaganda—revolting debasement of Church, monarchy, or aristocracy, fulsome praise of the nation and its defenders. Such presentation was made even more frantic by the necessity of adapting to sudden shifts, or even reversals, in official conviction, as when Robespierre early in 1794 attacked the then-prevalent doctrine of atheism. It was a year that saw the government undertake the reopening of the Nation as a state theatre for patriots, even while the dispossessed actors stood under sentence of death. For the theatrical world, however, it was a year of miraculous good fortune along with the evil, for it saw the escape of the Nation's actors from the guillotine by a last-minute rescue as exciting, and surely as unexpected, as anything ever offered on the stage.

For several days after the arrest of the Nation company, the papers of Paris exalted in this triumph of democracy. Not a few called for the immediate execution of the "royalists," and the *Feuille du salut public* seemed almost conservative in its recommendation that they simply be locked away until peace was restored and then "cast upon the shores of some despotic country, where they can carry on their aristocratic and effeminate talent." The former *Point du jour*, which had embraced the Jacobin cause and rechristened itself the *Journal de la Montagne*, enlisted the aid of Plancher Valcour, that former director of the Délassements-Comiques and inveterate enemy of the old aristocratic theatres. Under the classic pseudonym of Aristide which he now adopted, he warmly supported the new regime and condemned his former competitors:

> These gentlemen, by taking on the costume of Vendôme, of Bayard, or the glittering garb of the *Glorieux*, and by stepping into the red-heeled pumps of the little marquises, have foolishly identified themselves with their parts, thinking themselves aristocratic personages. . . . Plays recalling the old regime should no longer be given, even if they attack it, recall its vices, its follies, and its monstrous abuses. It is not enough to decree that counter-Revolutionary plays must not be given. We should dispense with all classics for at least half a year. When simplicity and republican fellowship have replaced the folly and ostentation of the old regime, our children can again laugh at the follies of our fathers.[1]

This influential paper was directed by Jean Laveaux, a friend and admirer of Robespierre. The fight against aristocracy in the theatre seemed to him a worthy one, and in an editorial of September 6 he condemned not only *L'Ami des lois* and *Paméla*, but even Chénier's *Fénélon* for containing "subtle poison." "Will not the presentation of a prelate under the old regime make weak souls regret the passing of these hypocrites?" he asked. On the same date in the *Journal des débats* he added to his list of suspect dramas a pantomime called *Adèle de Sacy* at the little Lycée des Arts, opened barely six weeks before. The pantomime depicted a persecuted woman waiting with her son for the arrival of a husband and a brother to free her from a tyrant who is holding her prisoner. Laveaux was convinced that the woman was intended to represent Marie Antoinette awaiting release by the courts of Provence and Artois; he "restricted" himself to demanding "that the author, actors, actresses, and even the musicians of this theatre—for, make no mistake, they are also in the plot and delight in scraping out tunes dear to the enemies of the people—that all these be arrested and prosecuted as disturbers of the peace and that their theatre be closed."

Jouan, Gervais, and Desaudrais, the directors of the Lycée, were well aware of the seriousness of this accusation and immediately appeared before the Jacobins. Jouan announced, "A good republican does not fear denunciations, since they are the touchstone of citizenship; but all denunciations should be tested and examined." He referred to the theatre's record of overwhelmingly patriotic presentations during its brief existence, submitted a scenario of *Adèle de Sacy* for examination, and offered a performance *in camera* for the Society to judge. The directors voluntarily closed the play until a decision could be reached, despite the loss involved, in the interest of "public tranquillity." Such manifestations of contriteness won over the prosecutors, and the play was allowed to continue without further complaint.[2]

All during September denunciations spread through the theatres as they spread through all walks of life. The Opéra, with its aristocratic background, was so clearly vulnerable to such attack that the actors of the theatre appeared voluntarily before the Commune early in September to pledge their support of Revolutionary plays. The Public Prosecutor observed that the Opéra was a known center of counter-Revolution, but since it seemed to be the directors and not the actors who were aristocratic in sympathy, he promised the latter his protection. This protection was granted none too soon, for on September 16 the administrators Francoeur and Cellerier were arrested, after a directorship of just thirteen months. The actors immediately pledged "to purge the operatic stage of all works which might offend the principles of liberty and equality which the Constitution has guaranteed, and to substitute patriotic works for them." The satisfied Commune turned the directorship of the theatre over to the actors themselves.[3]

The theatre was, however, still too firmly equated in the public mind with aristocracy for this change to remove all suspicion. The following week a spectator in one of the boxes stood up during a performance of *Oedipe à Colone* to shout that it was shameful for republicans to continue tolerating kings and princes on their stages. A municipal officer restored order on this occasion but the criticism continued. The *Journal des spectacles* asked: "How can it be tolerated that in a republican theatre the execrable doings of the House of Atreus are still celebrated; that the names of Agamemnon and of Achilles are offered for public acclamation; that *Iphigénie en Aulide* is still given—a shameful monument to the adoration which Frenchmen of old held for an aged Capet?" Soon *Iphigénie* disappeared and the kings were demoted to generals. Admetus' Thessaly became a republic and Alcestis' husband a chief of police.[4]

The Opéra's moment of greatest danger came late in September when the police received a circular from the theatre bearing the inscription "Académie Royale de Musique, by the grace of the King" with three *fleurs de lis*. The actors, called upon to explain, stated that the circular dated from 1790 and had been sent to the police to injure them. As protection against further such happenings, the entire company gathered at noon on September 30 before their theatre and publicly burned all documents relating to royalty. The Council General of the Commune accorded them a civic citation for the ceremony, and accusations against the theatre thereafter diminished sharply.[5]

Elsewhere, however, attacks continued. One police observer called for the suppression of three-quarters of the theatres in the capital, accusing even Talma and his company of "amusing themselves at the expense of liberty and equality" by presenting unpatriotic plays. "Burn if necessary the Molières and the Regnards," the report concluded. "The arts will lose something but surely public morals will gain. Moreover, the void will not last long. The genius of liberty will inspire the French muses and republican poets will soon make us forget the poets of the court."[6]

In November came the downfall of the hitherto irrepressible Mlle. Montansier. The directress, it will be remembered, had in the summer of 1792 purchased property in the Rue de la Loi near the Louvois theatre directed by her old adversary Delomel, planning to build there the most magnificent theatre in Paris. The architect Louis, who had remodeled the old Beaujolais theatre for her with such success, supervised the construction, which was not finished until the following August. The directress christened it the Théâtre National de Montansier, but the public, more impressed by the structure's expense in these inflationary times than by its patroness, persisted in calling it the Théâtre des Neuf Millions. Louis had done his work well, incorporting all the latest ideas in theatre design. Since Montansier planned to produce all genres—comedy, tragedy, dance, pantomime, and opera—the scale of the building was neceassrily unusually large; the theatre extended to the streets on all sides, although the major façade faced the Rue de la Loi. Thirteen arches opened onto this street with grills which opened for the play or which, closed, served as ticket offices. A balcony hung out over these arches, extending the full width of the building. The vestibule had two rows of Doric columns supporting a roof covered with arabesque reliefs, and was heated by three great ovens. At either end was a grand staircase leading up to lateral corridors and smaller flights of stairs. On the ground floor, passageways led to the pit, the orchestra, the grilled boxes and *baignoires*. Directly above the vestibule was a columned foyer with mirrors and carved panels and with frequent openings out onto the balcony.

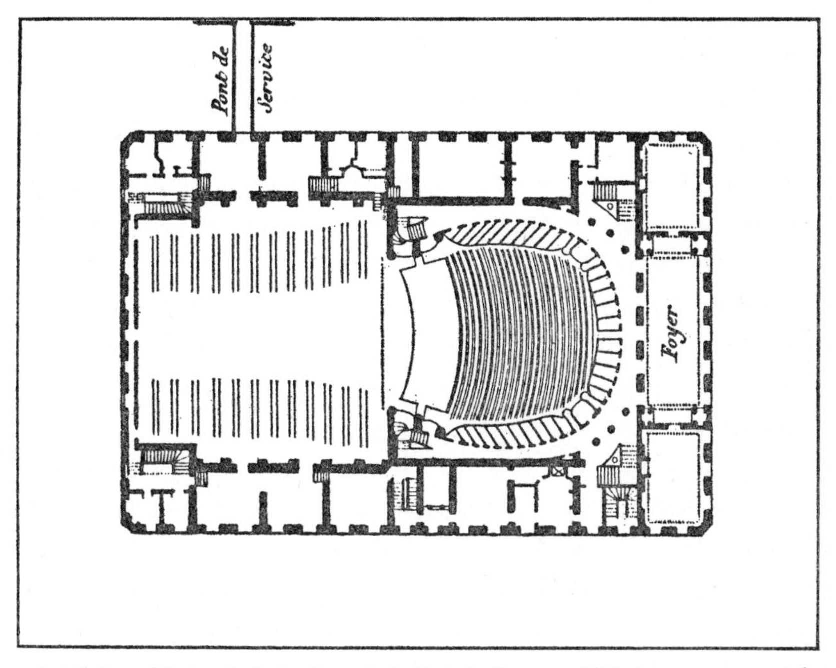

8. Théâtre National de la Rue de la Loi, built 1793. This huge structure, the largest and most elegant theatre of the period, became the home of the Opéra in 1794. (Alexis Donnet and Jacques-Auguste Kaufmann, *Architectonographie des théâtres.*)

Inside the house, ten Corinthian columns with rich entablatures supported four great double arches which in turn supported a cupola about fifty-four feet in diameter. The boxes were richly ornamented in blue and gold, with red draperies hung in front. The *Almanach des spectacles* noted that "for the first time a theatre has been built without forestage boxes." This innovation reflected a growing feeling that a clear demarcation should exist between actors and audience. The sides of the forestage therefore terminated in two rows of three columns each, but instead of the customary "intercolumn" boxes, statues of comedy, tragedy, music, and dance appeared between them. The stage proper was some seventy-five feet square and one hundred feet high, from basement to ceiling, but above the stage itself there was a rather low false ceiling which supported a painters' attic and higher yet, ventilating devices. Property shops, rehearsal areas, and dressing rooms surrounded the stage. The lighting was quite bright for the time, even though the sources of illumination were cleverly concealed behind cloud formations which formed part of the decorations of the ceiling.[7]

The first program in these impressive surroundings featured drama, spectacle, music, even performing horses. But the actors did not live up to their new home, and the audience expressed strong displeasure. Undaunted, Montansier presented ten new productions in the next three weeks and was soon attracting larger crowds than any other theatre director in Paris. The resourceful proprietress seemed to have reached the goal she had set for herself when she first followed Marie Antoinette to Paris, but her very success caused her new difficulties. Many resented the competition of the new theatre, and Montansier's past relations with the court and support of Dumouriez weighed heavily against her. Her large gifts to the war effort, her frequent presentations of patriotic dramas, and her lavish pageants in honor of the "immortal Marat" only succeeded in postponing the inevitable attack from the directress' many foes. On November 4, she was denounced to the Commune by Hébert and Pierre Chaumette, who charged her with having received money from the English and from Marie Antoinette to finance her new theatre. Moreover, this huge, ornate structure had been built, Montansier's accusers averred, to distract attention from her real object, which was to set fire to the near-by Bibliothèque Nationale.[8] Even a charge so patently absurd was sufficient in these terrible days to unleash the wrath of the public, and a few days later police had to empty the new Théâtre Montansier when its pit became a virtual battlefield between moderates and *sans-culottes*. Shortly after, Montansier and her assistant Neuville were arrested at their homes, the directress was taken to the Petit Force, and both the theatres under her direction were closed.[9]

The actors of the smaller Variétés Montansier immediately objected to this arbitrary cutting off of their only means of livelihood, arguing that their theatre could not also be involved in the plot against the National Library. The authorities relented for this minor house, allowing it to reopen after a few days with the cumbersome but politically safer name of the Théâtre du Péristyle du Jardin Egalité. Neuville was even released to direct the company. After a few weeks, the troupe petitioned the government to change their name again to the Théâtre de la Montagne, in honor of that extremist element in the Convention. The officials replied that the "impurity" of the actors made it difficult to tell "if they merited so honorable a title and if they would continue to aid in the propagation of patriotism and public spirit." Yet after a long discussion the title was approved, the delegate Louis-Marie Lulier observing reasonably enough that if the actors did not live up to their new name, the active surveillance of the police would curb their audacity.[10]

With the closing of the Nation, the Richelieu became indisputably the first theatre of Paris, and its actors, well aware that in these days pre-eminence encouraged attacks, hastened to demonstrate their loyalty. It may be remembered that as early as 1792 this theatre had found its title too reminiscent of the old regime and rechristened itself the Théâtre-Français de la Liberté et de l'Egalité. Even contemporary references rarely used this ponderous title, however, and to reduce the confusion we have continued up to this point to use the theatre's more popular older name. In 1793 the title Théâtre de la République was first employed and, after the disappearance of the Nation, accepted as the official title of the one remaining branch of the Comedie.

The République's first offering after the fall of its rival was *L'Ami du peuple,* the eulogy of Marat by Cammaile Saint-Aubin which the theatre had refused when it was first submitted, just after the journalist's death. Throughout the play the hero, Démophile, lauds Marat and berates the moderates. These were fast becoming stock comic characters, and Saint-Aubin went so far as to include three of them. The theatre's next two offerings, *Bathilde* and *Le Hulla de Samarcande* were hissed from beginning to end, although after the latter the audience was somwhat mollified by an announcement from Desprez that the author was at the moment in La Vendée fighting the enemies of the nation. On September 26, the actors sent a gift of 1,441 livres to the Convention for military expenses, and with it went an announcement reaffirming the company's patriotic goals and expressing a desire to become a monument of public instruction and inspiration meriting the theatre's new name.[11]

Despite such precautions, clouds still gathered about Paris' new first theatre. During a performance of *Timoléon* on October 5, a patriot deputy named Antoine-Louis Albitte who was just back from a mission in southern France took offense at the speeches of Timophane and loudly denounced the play and the author. The memory of *Paméla* was still fresh in everyone's mind, and chorus and extras fled in panic. The auditorium and boxes were soon emptied, though Chénier, who was present, begged the audience to wait for the ending. Many expected the playwright to be arrested that night, but he was not disturbed. Even so, the actors resolved not to risk another patriot outburst, and replaced *Timoléon* with *Caïus Gracchus.* It was a fruitless substitution, for the intractable Albitte appeared again, and during the applause which followed the line "laws and not blood," arose in a fury. He condemned the audience for fearing to shed "the blood of conspirators," boasted of his own recent shedding of such blood in Marseilles, denounced Chénier as a bad citizen, and abruptly departed. The play continued peacefully enough, but from this time on Chénier was considered a marked man. His plays were withdrawn from the repertoire, and few people came near him.[12]

Extreme measures were called for to insure the good opinion of the authorities, and the République attempted to silence its critics by presenting one of the most infamous plays of the Revolution, Pierre-Sylvain Maréchal's *Le Jugement dernier des rois.* The author's only previous writing, his *Livre échappé au déluge*, had earned him a certain notoriety as an atheist and lost him his job as sublibrarian at the Collège Mazarin. What was punished under Louis XVI was often praised under the Revolution, however, and Maréchal's position and reputation were restored by the new regime. *Le Jugement dernier des rois* was an expression of his gratitude. The setting is a volcanic isle, savage and desolate, where the *sans-culottes* of fifteen European nations bring their rulers, chained by the necks, to leave them. A Frenchman heads the expedition, although he has no monarch to exile, having already disposed of his. The kings are shown as petty, cruel, quarrelsome monsters. The Pope blames his present impotence on the schismatists and thus sets off a fight with Catherine of Russia. A blow of her scepter shatters the Pope's cross, and the beaten churchman offers her absolution if she will spare him. "Absolution!" laughs Catherine. "Before I let you go you must repeat after me that a priest is a charlatan and a trickster." The humbled Pope so swears, and to stop further fighting the *sans-culottes* throw biscuits to the kings, sneering, "Here, scoundrels, here is your fodder; wolf it down." As the *sans-culottes* leave, a volcano begins to erupt, causing the kings to dash about in terror. "If I escape," cries the King of Spain, "I will become a *sans-culotte* myself!" "And I will marry," swears the Pope. "I will even become a Jacobin," promises Catherine. Yet all these noble vows are in vain, for at last fire surrounds the kings and they fall consumed into a pit which opens beneath their feet.

When so violent a work was read before the actors, there were naturally objections, especially from Grandménil, who argued, "If we give this play and kings are restored, we shall be hanged." "Well then, Citizen Grandménil," replied a member of the Convention, "do you wish to be hanged for not giving it?" On October 18, Grandménil appeared as the Emperor of Austria. Michot was Catherine and Dugazon the Pope.

From a political point of view, the play was a tremendous success. The authorities were so delighted that the Committee of Public Safety immediately granted an expensive, almost presumptuous, request from the directors to explode twenty pounds of gunpowder at the close of each performance. With a war being fought on several fronts and gunpowder in very short supply, such a concession was a most significant one. Alexandre Rousselin in the *Feuille du salut public* cried, "Public spirit exists at last!" when the drama opened. Hébert, in the *Père Duchesne,* lauded the production under the guise of an old merchant showing his wife the sights of Paris:

> Thus my Jacqueline, you will certainly not go to that theatre; I will take you instead to the one which is justly entitled the Théâtre de la République, where you may see the *Jugement dernier des rois.* You will see all the crowned brigands, ropes about their necks, thrown on a deserted island; you will see the Pope make amends and admit he is merely a thimble-rigger; you will see all the tyrants of Europe obliged to tear each other apart for food; and at the end of the play you will see them engulfed by a volcano. There is a fit spectacle for republican eyes.[13]

Two days before Maréchal's play was presented, Marie Antoinette went to the guillotine. The condemned Girondists were soon to follow. When these had appeared on October 27 before the Tribunal, Talma had appeared with them. The patriotic demonstrations at the République had not completely effaced the memory of that evening when Marat was insulted at the actor's home, but Talma's avoidance of political involvement in the intervening months saved him from sharing the fate of his Girondist friends, all of whom were sent to death. The lesson was not lost on the actor, who for a time was careful to avoid any notoriety.[14]

Dugazon, the other actor who had openly scorned Marat on that fateful evening, lost no opportunity to affirm his loyalty to the new order. His arrest the day of Marat's funeral had shown the comedian his danger, and he became subsequently an avid Maratist, explaining that a bit of punch was responsible for his conduct on the evening in question. On October 30, the République gave his play *Le Modéré*, in which the author played Modérantin, a perfectly harmless patriot who is destroyed simply because he is not rabid enough. Denounced by his servant, he is sent to prison so that his daughter may marry her lover, a patriot of more extreme convictions. As a comedy it was not particularly successful, but as a statement of loyalty it satisfied the authorities and Dugazon was left in peace.[15]

Dugazon's actions point up the dilemma of the playwright under the Terror. Only the most insubstantial and chauvinistic works were acceptable to patriotic audiences, and the author who wrote nothing at all was as suspect as the author who openly supported Church or nobility. The inevitable result was a flood of plays of unrelieved mediocrity wherein standards fell so low that even the most patriotic newspapers complained. A typical sentiment appeared in the *Feuille de la République:*

> Liberty should not be the shield for mediocrity and sloth; these debase it while hiding under its protection. The license and degradation in the work of today's authors lead one to think that they have not realized the worth of their subject matter and are trying to express sentiments which are not in their hearts.

Quality, however, was something that even the threat of the guillotine could not guarantee, and the deluge of bad plays continued. Authors who had retired from Paris to shun the excesses of the Revolution were called back into service under threat of accusation. Cousin Jacques reappeared to produce *Allons ça va ou Le Quaker en France* at the Feydeau, excusing himself later by saying, "If I had not written it, they would have called me a moderate." Even this sacrifice was barely sufficient, for a cabal of patriots hissed the first performance of this story of a Quaker preaching war as being still too pacifistic.[16]

The older writers Ducis and Sédaine sought to excuse themselves on the grounds of their age, but no excuses were accepted. Ducis was

XIII. The Festival of the Supreme Being, June, 1794. In this sketch by Monnet, the emerging statue of Wisdom is still surrounded by flames from the disappearing cardboard representation of Atheism. Members of the Convention are seated at the right, in front of the Tuileries palace. (Armand Dayot, *La Révolution française*. Reproduced by courtesy of Librairie Ernest Flammarion.)

XIV. *Left:* A member of the gilded youth. Costumes such as this were favored by the young men who wandered about Paris in groups during 1795 seeking quarrels with the patriots. Note the short stick weighted with lead, a common weapon, and the long powdered wig (called dog's ears) and *culottes* so despised by the Revolutionists. (Armand Dayot, *La Révolution française*. Reproduced by courtesy of Librairie Ernest Flammarion.)

XV. *Right:* Plaster bust of Marat. Such busts, erected in most theatres in 1793, formed a focus for anti-Terrorist demonstrations during the Thermidorian reaction. (Armand Dayot, *La Révolution française*. Reproduced by courtesy of Librairie Ernest Flammarion.)

forced to rework his tragedies in a patriotic vein, departing even further from Shakespeare than before. A copy of the *Sans-culotte Othello* was submitted by the author to the deputy Herault de Séchelles with a note requesting that Talma continue to play the part.[17] Laujon, the quiet little author of *Le Couvent*, managed to preserve himself during these dark days and yet maintain a clear conscience by writing patriotic verses signed "Laujon, *sans-culotte* FOR LIFE," easing his mind by a double meaning the subtlety of which escaped the perpetrators of the Reign of Terror.[18]

Although the actor and author Monvel had long given indisputable proofs of his patriotism, his fairy-play *Urgande et Merlin* at the Favart drew down the wrath of Rousselin in the *Feuille du salut public* for being too easygoing for the times. Monvel quickly withdrew the play, explaining in a public letter, "You feel this play too insignificant for a time of revolution; I have suppressed it. The play was to have been presented today, but it will disappear from the bills. I would make many such sacrifices for the good of the nation." So abject a submission should have satisfied any critic, but Rousselin demanded a clearer proof of patriotism, the creation of truly patriotic plays. The *Feuille du salut public* therefore next accused Monvel of "letting his pen grow moldy in the ink." No play was forthcoming, however, and Monvel and Rousselin were not reconciled until November, when a common cause united them at last. Rousselin had turned his attention to public expressions of religious feeling, writing, "We charge the *citoyennes*, especially those connected with the theatres, no longer to wear crosses when they play the parts of villagers. This emblem of fanaticism which the sex made an ornament should be banned forever." Then, on November 30, Monvel mounted the pulpit in the church of Saint-Roch to deliver a violently atheistic speech, concluding with the exortation: "Marat! Le Pelletier! Beaurepaire! Rousseau! Voltaire! Your immortal names will never be pronounced among us without inspiring in us an overwhelming feeling of gratitude and admiration." Rousselin was delighted, and Monvel was thenceforth accepted by even the most extreme of the patriots.[19]

Talma's narrow escape made the actors of the République understandably cautious, and Dugazon's *Le Modéré* late in October was the last new play they mounted in 1793. Later programs were devoted primarily to revivals of proven patriotic works, a tendency reinforced the following year. The first new play of 1794 was *Les Contre-Révolutionnaires jugés par eux-mêmes* by Hyacinthe Dorvo, now a Revolutionist cannoneer. Ideally suited to this period of denunciations, it portrays a priest, a parliamentarian, a noble, and a merchant who condemn themselves by discussing aristocratic ideas before a patriot disguised as a Spanish ambassador, who delivers them up to "justice." Dugazon, as usual, played the patriot.[20]

On January 14, a large crowd was attracted to the theatre by the appearance of Mlle. Joly as Dorine in *Tartuffe*. Shortly after the mass arrest of the Nation company in September, a few of their number had been released. The wrath of the Jacobins was clearly directed less at specific plays than at actors and directors unsympathetic to their cause, for Léger and Neufchâteau were released after a few days, but the majority of the actors who presented their works remained in prison. Only Mézeray, Duval, and Bellemont, "for his favorable sentiments toward the Revolution," were freed shortly after the arrests. No other actors were freed until Mlle. Joly gained her release in January of 1794. There is no record of whether the authorities suggested as a condition of release that the former Nation actors demonstrate their conversion by serving their old rival, the more patriotic République, or whether the actors themselves saw the wisdom of such a gesture, but in any case Dupont followed Mlle. Joly to the République stage on February 4, and was followed in turn by Dunant, Vanhove, Mme. Petit-Vanhove, and others.[21]

This series of pardons encouraged Joly, Dupont, and the rest to hope that soon their imprisoned companions would be allowed to join them, but a representative sent to Collot d'Herbois to inquire about this possibility was soon disabused of any such hope. "You and your companions are all counter-Revolutionists," he was informed. "The head of the Comédie Française will be guillotined, and the body deported." A short time later, d'Herbois sent an order to Antoine Fouquier-Tinville, the public prosecutor of the Terror, stating:

> Citizen, the Committee is sending you papers concerning the former Comédiens. You know, as do all patriots, how counter-Revolutionary these people are. You will bring them to trial the 13 *messidor* [July 1]. As for the others, there are some among them that deserve only deportation; for the rest, we shall see what is to be done with them after the following are judged.

A list of those still in prison followed. The names of Dazincourt, Fleury, Louise and Emilie Contat, Raucourt, and Lange were marked in red with a large *G* (to be guillotined). Others were given a *D* (to be deported) or an *R* (to be released). The secretaries of the Tribunal began to sift the evidence.[22]

Early in February, amid the debuts of the former Nation actors, the République opened *Epicharis et Néron*, a new tragedy by the popular Legouvé. The play dealt with the crimes of Nero, and the career of that tyrant showed more than a few parallels to that of Robespierre. Danton and his followers, now at odds with Robespierre, warmly supported the piece, but it was saved from censorship less through their support than through the foresight of its author, who prefaced his work with a fulsome dedication to Liberty.[23] This play was one of the few works written under the Terror to survive that dark period. Talma added to his reputation in the role of Néron, and Monvel and Baptiste the Elder played supporting roles. Guillaume Pigault-Lebrun's *Charles et Caroline ou Les Abus de l'ancien régime*, a successful but certainly undistinguished work, was the République's only other new offering this month.

The most serious uprising against the Revolutionary government within the borders of France had taken place a few months before in La Vendée, to the west of Paris. After a bitter struggle, the power of this insurrection was broken by the battle of Savenai on December 22, 1793, but anti-Vendée plays continued to be popular throughout much of 1794. Many stories were circulated about republican valor in this internal strife, and a new martyr from it joined Le Pelletier and Marat in popular veneration. According to the stories circulated in Paris in the spring of 1794, a drummer boy named Barra was surprised by rebels and ordered to cry, "Long live the King," then beaten to death on his refusal. Historical evidence suggests that young Barra actually was taking some horses to a watering place and was shot when he refused to turn them over to the enemy. A number of plays now drew their inspiration from young Barra, but few paid any attention to the details of either story.[24]

Briois' *La Mort du jeune Barra ou Une Journée de la Vendée* was the first new play attempted by the République after several months of revivals of *Brutus*, *La Mort de César*, *Guillaume Tell*, and *Caïus Gracchus*. Briois' play opens with old Gilbert and his wife and daughter making clothing for republican soldiers. Old Gilbert sighs wistfully, "If I could only kill two rebels before dying, I would die content," but unhappily his advanced age prevents him from this noble action.

Others make up for his failings, however; Barra, a young hussar, almost a child, stops as Gilbert's guest and kills half a dozen rebels in a single morning. In his absence Aimée, Gilbert's daughter, kills three more. "A good day's work," observes the young hero on his return. Clearly a match is in order, and Gilbert offers his daughter to Barra, but their bliss is short lived. Young Barra soon leaves for battle, where, after great feats of valor, he is mortally wounded. His grieving companions carry him back to Gilbert's cottage, where he rouses himself to cry before expiring, "Aimée, I die worthy of my country. I have deserved you. I die content. Long live the Republic!"

This play, produced early in June, was followed shortly by two bagatelles, *Les Dangers de l'ivresse* by Jean Pujoulx, and Colin d'Harleville's *Rose et Picard ou La Suite de l'optimiste*. Neither play had much to commend in it, and d'Harleville especially was surely capable of writing something better. *Rose et Picard* was clearly a product of the times, however, a hastily written contribution to the Reign of Terror. D'Harleville's earlier *Optimiste* had been banned for a scene in it showing a former noble teaching patriotism to a *sans-culotte*, and the poet, knowing well that Robespierre and his party had long memories, hastily composed this less questionable sequel to insure his safety. It was the last new work produced by the République before Robespierre's fall.[25]

The ubiquitous secret police with their confidential reports contributed in no small measure to the success of the Terror, but at least one small bit of good has come from their activities. Their detailed and on-the-spot reports of the people and places of the Revolution have provided historians with a great amount of invaluable primary material. We have already quoted from one of these men, Perrière, on audience reactions to *Le Siège de Thionville* at the Opéra. On September 8, 1793, we find him again, submitting the results of several weeks' observations of public reactions to patriotic paintings and plays in the art museums and theatres of the capital:

> The small theatres, frequented by the less well-to-do citizens, show in the spectators and in those who entertain them a spirit of patriotism pleasant indeed to the true republican; while the more elegant houses, excluding all but the rich by their high prices, receive only the enemies of liberty or those indifferent to it. But, as I said before, these are general observations, and there are exceptions, such as the République. This theatre truly merits its name; the most ardent patriots gather there to applaud the

smallest action, the least reference favorable to patriotism. Last night this theatre gave *Robert, chef de brigands,* and one might say that no play exists more in keeping with our present spirit. It breathes virtue, true republican virtue, worthy of the founders of Rome. . . .

The République is, however, only a heartening exception to the rule I have stated regarding the larger theatres. The one on the Rue Feydeau, on the other hand, still retaining the name Monsieur, sadly confirms the rule, or so it seems to me. There I was surrounded by impudent enemies not only of our Revolution, but of all revolutions. . . . The light, bantering tone of the actors whenever they touched upon a Revolutionary ideal made them no better than the spectators. The glorious and sacred title of citizen was to them an object of comedy; and this abuse of so respectable a title was all the more unpardonable as it was committed in a play whose subject and details came from an era long before our new age. It was therefore a clear attempt on the part of these gentlemen to render this title vile in the eyes of the spectators rather than using it to elevate their spirits. They were well aware of what their audience wanted.[26]

Of all the major theatres in the capital, only the Feydeau after the fall of the Nation continued to serve as a rallying place for the spirits of moderation. For a number of weeks after Perrière's report, this theatre was therefore closely watched by the patriots. On September 21, the patriotic piece *L'Officier de fortune* was applauded, but on September 25, a dispute arose as to whether the "Marseillaise" should be played before the production. A group of Jacobins, swords drawn, issued a challenge to the house at large which no one accepted.[27] As a result, the officials seem to have decided that despite scattered unfortunate incidents, patriots were holding their own at the Feydeau, and no action was taken. The theatre continued to avoid dramas of extreme patriotism, producing a number of politically neutral works, the most successful of which was Alphonse Dubreuil and Jean Lesueur's *Paulin et Virginie*, given in January, 1794. The play catered to eighteenth-century sensitivity, and crowds who watched dry eyed, through conviction or fear, while the guillotine carried on its grim work wept profusely at the imagined agonies of this drama's delicate lovers.

Representatives of the Feydeau and of other major theatres in the capital were called before the Committee of Public Safety in January to receive "advice" on their repertoires. After this, patriotic drama because somewhat more frequent at the Feydeau. *La Prise de Toulon,* written by Picard, appeared in February, and Léger wrote for the theatre a version of the Barra legend, *L'Apothéose du jeune Barra,* which virtually ignored the young hero to portray the effects of his martyrdom on his family. All are inspired to praise the Republic, and Barra's mother glows with pride at the honor of his sacrifice.

The Feydeau's near-by rival, the Favart, despite its former position as one of the three houses supported by the crown, had abandoned all traces of the aristocratic sympathies it displayed as late as 1792. Although after the fall of Robespierre it became again the Théâtre Favart, during the Terror this house adopted the title Opéra-Comique National. Under this name it offered such works as the popular *Marat dans le souterrain des Cordeliers ou La Journée du 10 août*, presented December 7, 1793. A source of great difficulty for the venerators of Marat was the indisputable fact that on August 10, when the Tuileries were stormed, the journalist was hiding in a cellar. This drama explained Marat's action on the grounds that he was hiding from royalists seeking his life, and showed him giving inspiration and guidance to a great number of patriots come to seek him out in his shadowy retreat. The prospective martyr is full of love and forgiveness, crying when word comes of the storming, "Great heavens! What a misfortune! The blood of patriots is being spilled!" He prays to the goddess Liberty to let only the wicked be harmed. Then, when the Tuileries fall, more patriots come, despite Marat's modest refusal, to carry him out in triumph.

Further patriotic dramas followed in rapid succession. On December 23 came *La Veuve du républicain* and on December 28 *Le Cri de la patrie*. Armand Chastenet's *L'Intérieur d'un ménage républicain*, given January 4, expressed many Revolutionary ideals by showing a governess being instructed on how to teach children in these enlightened days. The governess does her job so well that she is herself converted to republicanism, and when at the end of the play she marries a curate, her pupils thoughtfully present her with a tricolored cockade as a wedding present. This stirring statement of the new society was followed by the equally chauvinistic *Le Plaisir et la gloire* on January 19 and *La Prise de Toulon par les français* on January 21.

The theatre remained quick to adapt to any shifts in official opinion so that, for example, when religious tolerance returned to favor at Robespierre's insistence, the Favart responded almost immediately with Picard and Alexandre Duval's *Andros et Almona ou Le Français à Bassora*, given February 4. Intolerant proponents of various "cults"—a Brahmin, a Spanish Dominican, a rabbi, and a Moslem—are urged to practice tolerance by Andros, a Frenchman and philosopher. Says he: "Be a good citizen, a good father, a good husband, a good friend; serve others and your country, and you will have fulfilled all the demands of the Supreme Being, the God of all religions." The Spanish priest cries, "After this, our reign is finished," and Andros concludes by singing:

> Then all embrace, and cease your strife.
> To love, to serve all human life,
> That is the true, the only way
> To worship the divinity.

Despite such caution, the Favart found it impossible always to please the officials in power. Late in February came a spectacular but inept drama called *Le Congrès des rois.* It was a strange production, for although the author, De Maillot, was unknown and his play insignificant, twelve of the most outstanding composers of the day collaborated on the music—Gréty, Méhul, Cherubini, Berton, Dalayrac, Kreutzer, Devienne, Solié, Jadin, Blasius, Deshayes, and Trial the Younger. The play showed the kings of Europe meeting at the court of Russia where Cagliostro, republican in sympathy, diverts them with a shadow play depicting the ultimate triumph of France. The kings scoff at this display and are discussing the partition of France among themselves when cannons are heard and triumphant *sans-culottes* arrive to put them to flight. The tree of liberty is planted, symbols of royalty burned, and patriotic songs and dances performed. For all its host of collaborators, the play was hissed for two evenings, then withdrawn as hopelessly badly written. Shortly thereafter it received the further indignity of an official ban for its "aristocratic tendencies." The Commune viewed with distrust a play wherein "the infamous Cagliostro is sanctified with the exalted title of patriot and with all the republican virtues, while the immortal Marat, that illustrious father of liberty, is exposed to malignant eyes, and passes like a Chinese shadow-figure behind a translucent curtain."[28]

The Favart's *Andros et Almona,* as we have noted, reflects a major shift in the Revolutionary attitude toward religion, a shift which will become clearer as we trace the fortunes of our next two theatres under the Terror. In mid-October of 1793 Piis and Barré, the directors of the Vaudeville, were released after six weeks' imprisonment. Piis disappeared from the public eye, but Barré hastened to demonstrate his conversion to the national cause by collaborating with Léger and

Lecouppey de la Rosières in a play called *La Heureuse Décade.* Written, learned, and presented in five days, and to all accounts as badly acted as written, it was none the less rapturously received.[29] The play supported every advanced idea of the day, from socialism ("A Frenchman thinks a loss a gain, when it is for his brother's good.") to free love ("Run off with a good patriot," a mother advises her daughter. "He is the best of companions."). "Since we have had liberty," cries one enraptured character, "the weather has always been superb." He had apparently not attended any civic festivals.

After *L'Heureuse Décade* had demonstrated his own patriotism, Barré attempted to secure the release of his imprisoned authors Radet and Desfontaines, the creators of *La Chaste Suzanne*, by presenting an ultra-Revolutionary drama which they had written in prison called *Au retour.* In it, a young soldier vows not to wed his fiancée until the country is out of danger, and an old friend assures him grimly as he leaves for the front, "If you leave traitors here at home, they'll not be here when you return." A series of submissive letters to the Commune and a promise to present to the nation all profits from this exemplary drama finally did indeed procure Radet and Desfontaines' release. Anxious to prove the sincerity of their conversion, they immediately followed Barré's example in producing another play suited to the tastes of the persecutors. *Encore un curé*, given November 20, shows a country priest, married and beloved by the poor of his parish, who abjures his calling to become a soldier and protect the nation. His faithful flock assure their departing leader that there will be no backsliding into religion during his absence.

November of 1793 saw antireligious sentiment at its highest pitch. Not content with destroying the appurtenences of Christianity, the *sans-culottes* sought to eradicate all traces of it even among human beings. J. B. Gobel, the Bishop of Paris, was asked to abjure his faith publicly as an example to others. Actually, the bishop agreed to abdicate rather than abjure, but the subtlety of this quibble passed unnoticed and his action was a strong stimulus for further renunciations. Gobel made his statement on November 7, accompanied by a great crowd of vicars and other priests, bishops, curates, and protestant ministers:

> Born a commoner, I gained the love of liberty early. Called by my fellow citizens to the Constituent Assembly, the will of the people was always my first law, submission to it my first duty. When the people wanted

bishops, I became a bishop. Now that they no longer want them, I cease to be one. My vicars and I renounce our priestly titles. Long live the Republic!

He then cast aside his miter and put on the red bonnet of the Revolution.[30] Many priests and ministers followed Gobel's example, and the public renunciations lasted several days. One after another of the Paris districts officially abjured any religion other then the worship of truth and reason. At the request of Chaumette, one of the chiefs of the Commune, Notre Dame cathedral was converted into a Temple of Reason.

Since the proclamation of the Republic, a reformed calendar had been in general use, with a ten-day week, and civic festivals were now organized for the last day of this week, the *Décadi*, to replace the Christian ceremonies of Sunday. The first such festival was held on November 10. A young woman representing the Goddess of Liberty was carried into the ancient cathedral on a classic chair entwined with ivy. She wore white robes, a blue mantle, and the inevitable bonnet of liberty. Young girls robed in white and wearing crowns of roses followed the goddess and were in turn followed by busts of Le Pelletier and Marat, musicians, and soldiers. Hymns, speeches, and favorable news from the frontiers composed the ceremonies. On later occasions the mayor, the municipal officers, and the public officials of Paris came to the new Temple to read the Declaration of the Rights of Man, analyze news from the front, and relate the week's patriotic actions for the edification of the public.[31]

The Vaudeville's first production of 1794 was Thierry and L.-T. Lambert's *La Plaque retournée*, an undistinguished drama featuring celebrations over the taking of Lyons and Toulon and the subjugation of La Vendée, an illustrious patriot named La Montagne, and a hero who weeps when he sees the busts of Marat and Le Pelletier on the the stage:

Since of these deaths I learned
My mind is overturned.
Dear pillars of the state
Be certain that your fate
Determined my ambition
To carry on your mission.

Late in January the theatre again turned to the subject of religion, but with a marked change, for, in the interim since November, Robespierre, fearing the excesses of a populace cut free from all religious bonds, had denounced atheism as an aristocratic doctrine and proposed the worship of a supreme being in the spirit of freedom and reason. This doctrine had not yet been formally sanctioned by the government, but was already widely accepted by the people. Thus, the young lovers in J. S. Rafford-Brienne's *Les Volontaires en route ou L'Enlèvement des cloches* are still wed outside the Church, but the mayor who unites them expresses the latest approach to religion:

> 'Neath the Great Being's watchful eye
> Why need we priest to ratify
> The vows here made?
> We'll let the bigots rail and shout
> For battles can be won without
> The chaplain's aid.

On January 30, Jacques Deschamp's *Le Poste évacué*, full of patriotic sentiments and Revolutionary slogans, again encouraged young men to go fight at the frontiers. The following evening at last risked another satire, though of a very mild sort, and still packed with Revolutionary feelings. Léger and Barré's *Le Sourd guéri ou Les Tu et les vous* drew its inspiration from the custom which had arisen late in 1793 of universal use of the familiar forms of the second person pronoun. While such speech was not required by law, the old forms, now regarded as aristocratic, became as dangerous to employ as the titles "monsieur" and "mademoiselle." A number of plays appeared making fun of members of the older generation scandalized by this freedom of speech—Valcour's *Le Vous et le toi* at the Cité-Variétés, Dorvigny's *Les Tu et toi* at the Opéra, and Barré and Léger's *Le Sourd guéri* were the most popular. The Vaudeville play shows old Poli, suddenly cured of deafness, who makes a fool of himself by imagining an affair between his wife and his doctor, who address each other in the new fashion.

After this hesitant foray into satire, the theatre returned to purely chauvinistic works. Near the end of February, Radet and Desfontaines' spectacular *La Fête de l'Egalité* lauded Rousseau and preached a sort of mystic socialism amid a setting with an altar to liberty and the inevitable busts of Marat and Le Pelletier. Late in the spring Desfontaines contributed an attack on the Vendée rebels entitled *Les Chouans de Vitré*, while Radet, not to be left behind, praised the republican military in *Le Canonnier convalescent.*

It will be remembered that in September of 1793 the artists of the Opéra lost their directors and were themselves suspected of aristocratic sympathies, a suspicion alleviated only by a public burning of most of the Opéra records the last day of September. Sensitive to public opinion, the artists of the Opéra quickly embraced the next manifestation of the Revolution, the short-lived atheist movement which began in November. The noted atheist Pierre-Sylvain Maréchal, whose brutal *Le Jugement dernier des rois* was at this moment drawing warm patriot praise at the République, was approached for a play. The resulting *La Fête de la raison* took as its subject the renunciation of the symbols of religion by a patriotic curate.

If reason became the faith of the day, the saints of this new faith were Marat and Le Pelletier. The sale and display of all religious images or tokens was forbidden as "harmful to public tranquillity," but busts of these martyrs were sold everywhere. They were ceremoniously unveiled in many public places and in almost every theatre, and they filled the niches built for saints in many a Parisian church. The day after the opening of Maréchal's play, the Opéra unveiled its busts of the martyrs in one of the most impressive ceremonies of the kind which the capital had seen. A huge mountain was built to cover the entire façade of the theatre. On its summit stood a Temple of Arts and Liberty with tombs of the martyrs to its right and left and their busts on an altar before it. The mountain, made of stone, extended to the middle of the street, and across from it another mountain was built to receive deputies from the Convention and other dignitaries come to attend the ceremony. As soon as these high priests were seated, a procession appeared, bearing the goddesses Liberty and Equality. While the orchestra of the Opéra played, these two divinities mounted to the Temple, where they were welcomed by a crowd of girls in white tunics, floral crowns, and tricolored sashes, bearing garlands, palms, urns, and similar classic properties. The goddesses crowned the busts with civic palms, and after a hymn of praise from the chorus, Apollo and the Muses appeared to welcome the busts into the Temple.[32]

So dedicated was the Opéra to demonstrating its support of atheism that the theatre was caught unaware by the next shift in official opinion. Thus in January the production *L'Inauguration du Temple de la Vérité ou Le Tombeau des imposteurs*, which parodied songs and ceremonies of the Church, was banned by the Committee of Public

Safety as "an attempt by counter-Revolutionists to disturb public peace by provoking religious quarrels" and "an attack on the peace and freedom of all faiths." Robespierre himself led the signers of the decree. Shortly after, Ducancel's *Sainte Omlette* disappeared from Montansier's Variétés, now called the Théâtre de la Montagne, for the same reason.[33]

Although Montansier remained in prison, her assistants were granted permission by the Committee of Public Safety to visit her several times a week for consultation.[34] The Variétés Montansier, as we have seen, reopened under its new name almost immediately after her arrest in November. A few weeks later the released Neuville and another Montansier apprentice named Paché reopened the Théâtre des Neuf Millions. Molé, one of the few Nation actors to escape the mass arrest in September, soon appeared on this stage, giving continual demonstrations of his loyalty to the new order. The actor who had specialized in playing the foppish marquis now became the most ardent of republicans. Engaged as a "leading actor," he hastened to ask the papers to suppress this distinction, and although his earnings were the highest in the company, he contributed most of them to his Revolutionary district. No one was more active than he in changing outmoded lines, and his "check on the tyrant" in *Le Bourru bienfaisant* became the standard phrase among chess players of the day. When Mlle. Devienne was released the following March, she broke the pattern of République debuts to appear with Molé at this theatre.[35]

Both the theatres under Montansier's indirect direction now dedicated themselves to the most violent of Revolutionary dramas. Even Molé was unable to stomach *Les Catilinas modernes* by Feru the Younger, and he pleaded illness rather than portray the deified Marat in this offering. The unhappy Girondists were brutally degraded, for public feeling against them was by now so strong that the actors who played Girondists often made public apology before the play began, explaining that their profession forced this odious task upon them. Such manifestations of patriotism did not, however, avert jealous eyes from the fabulously expensive theatre in the Rue de la Loi, now considered one of the wonders of the capital. In mid-April the Committee of Public Safety ordered the transfer of the Opéra from the wooden theatre Lenoir had built at the Porte-Saint-Martin to this handsome new building. Thus, on April 17, the actors of Montansier's company presented their last productions in the home which had been theirs for only seven months.[36]

Despite the great effort already expended on this theatre, the government arranged for further alterations before the Opéra moved in. The parterre patrons were for the first time seated on permanent stepped benches on an inclined plane which ran from the orchestra to the first boxes, and the theatre was made even more elegant than before by the addition of decorations from the theatre at Versailles.[37] The same authorities who had imprisoned Montansier then solemnly declared, after receiving a report from David, Leroi, Hubert, and Lanoix, that the proximity of the Opéra to the Bibliothèque Nationale put the latter in no danger from fire. Soon this danger was forgotten entirely, and indeed within a few months another Convention member seriously proposed that the government itself should burn the library as a "dark receptacle of the old wounds of humanity." In the meantime Montansier, the supposed incendiary, remained behind bars.

The first production mounted by the Opéra in its new home was *La Réunion du 10 août ou L'Inauguration de la République française,* a sort of symbolic résumé of the Revolution in operatic form. Act I showed symbolic offerings and dances on the site of the Bastille; Act II was a ballet of "heroines of October 5 and 6"; Act III depicted the Place de la Révolution and the destruction of symbols of royalty; Act IV showed a colossus symbolizing the French people crushing the monster of feudalism on the Place des Invalides; Act V featured the president proclaiming the Constitution on the Champ de Mars. The drama was conceived by Gabriel Bouquier, a member of the Committee of Public Safety, and his colleagues found the work so worth while that its expenses were paid by the government, and two other houses, the Favart and the Molière (now called the Sans-Culottes), were ordered to add it to their repertoires. In January of 1795 it disappeared from all three theatres, and its author Bouquier disappeared with it, retiring to the country to take up painting.[38]

March of 1793 was the first month in which the number of persons condemned to death by the Revolutionary Tribunal in Paris had exceeded one hundred. In the months that followed, this total increased ever more rapidly. The year 1793 had numbered monthly sacrifices to liberty in the tens; 1794 would number them in the hundreds. The struggle for political control grew more desperate daily. When the ultra-Revolutionary Hébertists attempted an insurrection in March and failed, Hébert and his followers swelled the number of the condemned, and his passing left two major parties with strong support—the moderates, headed by Danton, who viewed with horror the geometrical progression of executions, and the Jacobins, headed by Robespierre, who looked upon this purgation as inescapable. These two fractions had united to destroy Hébert, but once he was removed, a split between them was inevitable. At last Danton and his followers were denounced as reactionaries in the tradition of Dumouriez and Lafayette, and despite Danton's formidable reputation, few members of the Convention dared oppose the Jacobins who denounced him. On April 5, 1794, Danton followed Hébert, and with him went his secretary, the dramatist Fabre d'Eglantine, who, ironically, had always been among the most outspokenly Revolutionary authors. The colorful dramatist carried his manuscripts with him to the scaffold and threw them amid the spectators as he passed with pitiful cries of "My friends! Save my glory!" At least one comedy was indeed saved in this way—*L'Orange de Malte,* revised after the Terror by Charles-Guillaume Etienne and Charles Nanteuil and successfully presented under the title *L'Espoir de faveur.*[39]

Shortly after the execution of Danton, a decree was passed forbidding accused persons the right of pleading their cases, and subjecting them to immediate sentence. For three more months, the Terror continued with no voice of opposition raised against it. All clubs except the Jacobins' were closed, and Robespierre became the virtual dictator of France.

Controls on the theatres now increased sharply. In April a decree from the police commissioners Jean Faro and Jacques Lelièvre officially banned all titles from the stage, and citizen and citizeness replaced duke, count, marquis, baron, monsieur, and madame regardless of rhyme, meter, or context. Greeks, Romans, Venetians, and Gauls appeared now in the national colors, and the tragic heroines of Racine suffered their agonies with large patriotic cockades pinned to their breasts. Actors were expected to be citizens first and professional persons second, and audiences were often asked to wait patiently because Citizen X was on patrol duty or Citizen Y was meeting with a committee. Such actors were praised for their loyalty and quickly forgiven if they arrived so late to the theatre that they were forced to perform in their street clothes. Under such circumstances, many actors lost all respect for their art and plays were presented in the most haphazard way; actors appeared through doors, windows, even fireplaces quite indiscriminately, improvising lines and relying upon Revolutionary slogans to bridge the gaps in their memories. That audiences were apparently quite willing to accept such slovenliness is an indication of the extent of the debasement of drama under the Terror.[40]

The stifling decrees of the government drove many actors to flee the capital this spring even when they were not in danger politically. Requests for passports so increased that on April 5 several members of the Commune reported their suspicions that nobles were "hiding in the wings of theatres" as extras or machinists until six months' service gave them the right to be approved by the theatre director for foreign travel. The Commune therefore decreed that an actor applying for a passport must thenceforth furnish a birth certificate, a certificate of residence, and a statement on the length of his professional career.[41] The actors protested this measure, as they had protested earlier abridgments of their liberty, and in May Claude Payan, a spokesman for Robespierre, supported the actors and encouraged modifications in the more offensive of the recent laws. The April decree was revoked, and the restrictions imposed on the classic repertoire slightly relaxed. Payan's note, dated May 3, said in part:

> Without doubt it is as ridiculous to say Citizen Cataline as it is to see Jupiter or Armide in a tricolored cap. Therefore, the police have today informed all directors that they may leave intact all tragedies written before the Revolution, or later ones dealing with non-Revolutionary subjects. The titles "Monsieur," "Seigneur," etc., need not be changed. As for the classic comedies, we leave it to the sagacity or patriotism of the directors to decide when these should be altered. In short, we ask only that new plays use the words "citizen" and "citizeness," and that in them "Monsieur" and "Madame" be used only as an insult or to distinguish an enemy of the Revolution.[42]

Most directors, of course, having this choice left to their "sagacity of patriotism," and knowing that whatever the officials decided the theatres were still answerable to the mobs that now composed their audiences, did not choose to profit by the apparent freedom of action opened to them.

Among the smaller theatres already discussed, only the Marais succumbed under the Reign of Terror. Located in an aristocratic section of Paris now almost depopulated by emigration and execution, and deprived of the support of Beaumarchais, who was abroad on a secret mission, the theatre declined rapidly. The final blow came through a bureaucratic tangle which would be amusing if the consequences of it had not been so grave. Beaumarchais was dispatched to buy guns for the nation on a mission so secret that he was inadvertently branded an emigrant, his property seized by the government, and his family imprisoned.[43] Official suspicion then fell on the Marais, so closely associated with the dramatist, and under this new threat, the failing theatre disbanded.

Though theatre management was in every sense a hazardous occupation in these times, the other houses managed somehow to survive, stimulating public interest as always by constantly changing repertoires and flattering the government with strongly chauvinistic presentations. Even Lazzari, at the Variétés Amusantes, was careful to alternate political drama with his harlequinades. On November 21, he presented *A bas la calotte ou Les Déprêtrisés*, by Pierre Rousseau, a former abbot now preaching against organized religion. In this work, typical for the time, Aline, daughter of a protestant minister, refuses to wed Nicaise because she loves a vicar. Nicaise's mother reproaches the vicar for encouraging the girl, but he amiably replies:

> Heaven, in giving me a heart
> Told me how it should be employed
> And the creator I adore
> By loving his most lovely work!

It is, strangely enough, precisely the same argument which Molière gave to his hypocrite Tartuffe, but now used with total seriousness. The vicar resolves to marry the girl, and casts aside his black robes to don the national dress. The protestant minister cries, "My friend, your example inspires me to do likewise. From this moment I renounce my ministry; let us unite in the abjuration of all cults and preach to all citizens the gospel of the rights of man!" An old curate joins the lovers in marriage, urging them, "My children, be united under the auspices of Liberty and Equality."

Later offerings at this theatre included *La Mort de Marat* and *Les Brigands de la Vendée* along with such traditional fare as Arlequin in *La Boîte enchantée* and *Le Moulin brulé*. Nicolaïe Clairville's *La Fausse Dénonciation*, given at the height of the Terror in the summer of 1794, praised a political system which denounced innocent and guilty alike and subjected all to domiciliary visits. "We must take these harsh measures for the general good," explains the president in the play. "But the innocent person is soon recognized and is given the justice he deserves. There is nothing unpleasant in such visits; they are by elder brothers who simply want to watch over the conduct of young families."

The Ambigu-Comique and the Gaîté provided similar fare, but this saved neither of their directors from spending several weeks in prison early in 1794—not for lack of patriotism, but for staging obscene works. Picardeaux, Audinot's successor at the Ambigu, and an actress named Juliette, in an effort to attract audiences to the theatre, passed the limit of government tolerance in a play calle *La Pomme*. At the Gaîté, Nicolet and Rhamin, one of his actors, were arrested on a charge of "violating all principles of decency and honor [in a play called *L'Amante au tombeau*] and committing the most disgusting obscenities while disguised as a dog." On January 25, representatives from both houses were called before the Committee of Public Safety and warned to purify their repertoires of grossness and obscenity.[44]

The little Cité-Variétés, built amid the ruins of the old church of Saint-Bartholomew, was apparently the only theatre of any importance to pass the entire period of the Terror without running afoul of the authorities. Its constant manifestations of patriotism were so favorably received that when the Committee of Public Safety began its review of the capital's theatres in January, the Cité was heard on the first day with the patriotic République. Their representatives were urged by the Committee to continue the propagation of "good sentimental plays and plays showing true patriotism,"[45] and the Cité soon obliged with a work unusually violent even for this extremist theatre—Jean Lebrun-Tossa's *La Folie de Georges ou L'Ouverture du Parlement d'Angleterre*. Ten months before, war had broken out with the English, making them ideal subjects for patriot wrath. The war had been discouraging at first, but on December 19, 1793, Bonaparte gave the French cause fresh impetus by delivering the city of Toulon, held by the enemy since the previous summer. Jubilation over this victory was so great that few patriotic plays of the time omit a reference to it. By January 9, the Théâtre des Sans-Culottes had mounted *L'Heureuse Nouvelle ou La Reprise de Toulon*, the first play dealing exclusively with this victory, and other Toulon plays soon followed, as we have seen, at the Favart, the Feydeau, and elsewhere.

Lebrun-Tossa's version at the Cité assumes that the recapture of Toulon has upset the reason of England's monarch. In the opening scenes George is shown dashing through the palace in a dressing gown, a whip in his hand, cursing all he meets and crying that his son is plotting his assassination. Pitt, declared an enemy of mankind by the French government six months before, is the villain of the piece, plotting to seize the British government during this confusion. In the midst of a stormy session of Parliament, however, the English people overrun the chamber, disperse the royalists, massacre Pitt and the prince of Wales, and place their heads on pikes. The insane king is locked in a cage and a triumphant procession is formed with certain ministers —Burke, Grenville, and Chesterfield—pulling the cage, preceded by a donkey covered with the royal robes and wearing the crown between his ears. Behind the cage come many lords in chains and behind them the "patriotic" ministers Fox, Grey, and Sheridan, wearing red bonnets and proclaiming the advent of liberty. After the king is thus escorted to Bedlam, Fox declares England a republic, and Grey says, "Now let us join the French; now we are worthy of them." Oddly enough, by the standards of the time even this work was considered not extreme enough by some members of the Committee of Public Instruction. One representative insisted that George be hanged instead of locked away, and the play was finally approved only after the author inserted a line for Fox suggesting that George be delivered to the scaffold as soon as he is cured, "so that he may die with the knowledge of his crimes."[46]

Shortly after this production, a new *Prise de Toulon* was offered to Saint-Edme, the director of the Cité. Well aware that Toulons were flooding the market, he refused the play. As a result Bizet and A. Faciolle, the authors, denounced him to General Bonaparte, and Faciolle even went so far as to accuse the director of signing his name *de* Saint-Edme. This affectation of aristocracy was a terrible charge during the Terror, and only the theatre's obvious devotion to the national cause saved its director from the unpleasant consequences of his refusal.[47]

L'Epoux républicain, the theatre's first important success in the spring, glorified family betrayal. The hero is a locksmith named Leroi who has changed his name to Franklin and married a former prioress. When he discovers that his wife is plotting with a former priest to flee the country, taking his son with them, the republican husband promptly denounces them to the authorities. As the would-be emigrants are led away, the priest asks: "Can you desire the death of your wife? Of your son?" Franklin replies: "It is nothing to me, since they deserve it. Long live the Republic!" The author Pompigny appeared amid tremendous applause on the opening night wearing a red cap and *carmagnole*, a Revolutionist jacket. "Citizens," he said, "I do not deserve the credit for creating this little patriotic scene; when the heart guides the pen, one always does well, and I am sure that there is not a husband in the house who would not be ready to follow the example of my *époux républicain*."[48] A storm of applause showed the truth of his observation, and the next day Pompigny was lauded in the *Conservateur des principes républicains*, which observed:

> Both art and patriotism owe a eulogy to citizen Pompigny, author of this work. To the merit of presenting manly and touching lessons in civic duty he adds that of rejecting the timidity which makes so many of our Revolutionary authors unwilling to show aristocrats on the stage unless these are ridiculous, characterless, and completely lacking in that cunning which they employ in their perfidious conspiracies.[49]

The Cité's next offering was Pierre Duplessis' *Les Peuples et les rois ou Le Tribunal de la raison*, conceived in the same spirit. The staging was as spectacular as the tiny stage could manage, and allegorical characters, generalized characters, and specific persons were indiscriminately mixed in the cast. During a bloody battle in the first act, Jacques, a worker, steps to the footlights to shout, "People, love kings, for here is their work!" The goddess Reason appears and rallies the people, who turn upon the Duke and the King, shown seated in a pavilion of bones cemented with human blood. When the deposed tyrants are brought in chains before an altar to humanity to witness the burning of symbols of royalty, the ground opens to swallow them in flames. Out of the inferno rises a banner with the words "The Republic, one and indivisible." A strange company of figures emerges from the wings to salute this banner—Fraternal Love, Conjugal Love, Filial Love, Modesty, Charity, Citizenship, Paternity, Maternity, Courage, Work, Genius, and Agriculture. Amid resounding applause, this odd assortment of allegorical beings raises statues of Rousseau, Marat, Le Pelletier, and Brutus.[50]

Almost nothing concerning the Revolution was too trivial for the adulation of the Cité, so that authors were often led to ludicrous extremes in their subject matter. Charles-Louis Tissot, whose *Tout pour la liberté* had been the Cité's first big success, was now chief of the bureau concerned with arms, powders, and saltpeters. His *Les Salpêtres républicains,* presented June 26, glorified those who minded this important product. The lovers in the play are united before a loaf of saltpeter which serves as an altar, and their proud fathers sing:

> Approach us, dearest children ours
> We see ourselves reborn in you
> Swear on this loaf of saltpeter
> That you'll be faithful to your vows
> And if this union should be blessed
> And you be fathers in your turn
> Instruct your children every day
> To cherish deep within their hearts
> The love of country.

Even poor Arlequin was pressed into Revolutionary service, and in *Arlequin imprimeur,* given June 16, the poor fellow assures the audience that he now prints only patriotic works, since the printers who do otherwise are as guilty as the authors they publish. Clearly the Committee of Public Safety agreed with this observation, for a decree of June 30 placed all publishers under the surveillance of the Committee of Public Instruction.[51]

One of the last items of correspondence issued by the Committee of Public Instruction in 1793 made a proposal indicative of the official attitude toward drama at this time:

> In all towns of 4,000 inhabitants there should be a theatre where the students of public schools and other persons may practice, but only upon thought-provoking plays in the spirit of the Revolution. . . . No building will be necessary, as almost all such towns have vacant churches. Nothing would be more suitable to instruct the public, to make them forget the apish antics of the priests, and at last to regenerate morality.[52]

Yet Paris itself had as yet no such theatre, and the authorities looked about for a suitable location. The deserted Nation was the obvious choice, and a decree of March 10, 1794, stated the strange terms upon which the former Comédie was to be reopened:

> 1. The former Théâtre Français, being a national building, shall be reopened without delay, and it shall be solely dedicated to performances given for and by the people, several times each month.
>
> 2. The building will be designated by the title "Théâtre du Peuple," and shall contain all the emblems of liberty. The companies of artists in various Parisian theatres will be called upon to give performances in turn three times a *décade,* according to the wishes of the municipality.

3. No citizen may enter the Théâtre du Peuple without a particular identifying card given only to proven patriots by the municipality.

4. The municipality of Paris will take all steps necessary for the execution of this decree and will report on the measures taken.

5. The repertoire of plays to be given at the Théâtre du Peuple will come from each theatre of Paris, according to the desires of the Committee.

6. In towns where no theatre exists, the municipality is charged with organizing civic performances according to the regulations of this decree, to be given free to the people each *décade*. Only patriotic plays, chosen from a repertoire approved by the municipality, shall be given, under the surveillance of the district, answerable in turn to the Committee of Public Safety.[53]

This program was scarcely inaugurated when the Committee decided that the Nation was unfit for its purposes, being built according to the old "aristocratic" plan, with boxes and balconies for the upper classes. Extensive remodeling was begun on April 24, while the Committee directed its attention toward further purification of the repertoire. Almost all of Molière now disappeared, as did *Henry VIII*, *Calas*, *Horace*, *Macbeth*, and *Fénélon*. Of Chénier's Revolutionary works, only *Charles IX* escaped, and the persecuted author was even forced to publicly burn his *Timoléon* before the Jacobin Club.[54]

The remodeled Nation opened on June 27. The title, since March, had changed again, and the venture opened as the Théâtre de l'Egalité. The Revolution had brought certain decorative and architectural modifications to many Parisian theatres, but here for the first time evidence of the new order was visible in every detail of the interior. Most striking was the change in seating, for all distinctions had been repressed as aristocratic and the house changed into a vast circular gallery with no boxes and no balconies, only one huge sweep of seats extending from pit to ceiling. The old foyer had been narrowed to enlarge the stairways, and the removal of boxes allowed the installation of long promenades where one could smoke a pipe (cigars and cigarettes were as yet unknown) during the intermissions. The stage boxes had, of course, disappeared with the others, and in their place stood panels painted the color of marble, backing niches which contained statues of Liberty and Equality. The old decorations were all torn down or covered with tricolored paint or paper. The baroque painted ceiling disappeared under alternating bands of red, white, and blue, and the same colors indiscriminately covered gilded and sculpted friezes, laurel branches, floral garlands, lions' heads and pilasters. The main curtain too was red, white, and blue, with a giant bronze statue of Equality in the center. Above the audience rose a vast tricolored dome, giving the entire theatre something of the appearance of a colorful circus tent. The only relief from these bold colors was given by occasional columns in bays ornamented with busts of the usual martyrs and defenders of Liberty—Marat, Rousseau, and all the rest.[55]

Something of the Committee's first title for the theatre remained in an inscription on the façade: "Pour le Peuple," but this all-inclusive sentiment was deceptive. Robespierre had no desire to allow this new temple of patriotism to be profaned by counter-Revolutionary outbursts such as sometimes occurred in other theatres even in these despotic days, so only certified patriots were admitted to the new "democratic" house. Even so, the Egalité was filled to capacity for the opening on June 27. After the "Marseillaise" was sung and patriotic dances performed, actors from the République presented Dorvigny's *La Parfaite Egalité*, Goldoni's *Le Bourru bienfaisant*, and Kreutzer's *Le Serment civique de Marathon*. The opening was a huge success, and the already enraptured audience was raised to new enthusiasm when in the midst of the performance an actor rushed onto the stage with the news that national troops had taken Charleroi in one of the major encounters of the war. Hats and handkerchiefs filled the air, and the public finally departed glowing with patriotic pride.[56]

The very day that the new national theatre opened, Collot d'Herbois sent to Fouquier-Tinville his request for the accused artists who had once performed there to be brought to trial, setting July 1 as the date of execution for those condemned. At this point, one of the strangest figures in the history of the Revolutionary theatre appeared almost from nowhere to save these apparently lost artists. All documents assembled against accused persons were sent to a Bureau of Evidence at the dismantled Tuileries. There many of them passed through the hands of a certain clerk, Charles-Hippolyte Labussière, who until this time had led a most insignificant life, once a minor actor, but more recently a wastrel and general drifter. He entered service as a clerk for the Committee of Public Safety on April 21, 1794, possibly only to show his patriotism in this dangerous time, but possibly also with an idea of hindering the work of that dread Committee.[57] At any rate, within three weeks he had begun systematically destroying incriminating papers from certain accused families, thus preventing their trial and condemnation. Such an action was certainly dangerous, but not necessarily as suicidal as it might appear, for between April and June the average number of persons executed daily doubled, and the number of accusations was staggering. The courts worked almost around the clock, and Labussière's office processed such a flood of papers that even the most patriotic clerks could not avoid losing or misfiling important documents. Concealing even a large number of papers without arousing suspicion was moderately easy, and Labussière was careful and ingenious.

When Collot d'Herbois' order came concerning the Nation actors, Labussière resolved to save them, but he could do so only by abandoning his customary caution. The evidence against the actors was primarily in the form of plays, and Collot d'Herbois had spared no pains in the collection of this evidence, sending a huge dossier to the Bureau. Such a mass of material was impossible to hide, and d'Herbois had demanded a trial in so short a period of time that carrying off the evidence bit by bit was also impossible. Yet Labussière was determined enough to take the only possible course left—boldly removing and destroying the entire dossier at once. Unable to risk a fire in the summer for fear the smoke might betray him, he conceived the idea of taking the papers to the public baths, located near the Bureau, soaking them until they became unrecognizable, and then throwing them into the Seine.

The papers could hardly be removed during the day, so Labussière returned for them at one A.M., when the Committee was in deliberation and he would not be disturbed. He got the documents safely out of the building, then suddenly realized a new danger. The baths did not open until six in the morning and he did not dare dispose of the papers until they had been rendered unrecognizable. Despite the danger of encountering a Revolutionary patrol, the nervous clerk decided to walk about until the baths opened. Several hours later he sat down to rest in a café on the Boulevard des Italiens, and dozed off in spite of himself. He was awakened by a hand on his shoulder and a harsh voice demanding to know the business which kept him abroad at such an hour. When Labussière refused to give any explanation, his interrogator identified himself as Aillaume, a well-known patriot. "I wish to know your name as little as I wish to tell you mine," replied Labussière.

Aillaume, now convinced that he had discovered an enemy of the Republic, shouted for a Revolutionary patrol. Labussière was placed under arrest and taken to a near-by station. Still refusing to identify himself, he was recognized there by a member of the Committee of Public Safety named Pierre who happened to be in the station. Pierre warned Aillaume to be careful with his accusations or he would get into trouble. Aillaume thereupon denounced Pierre as Labussière's accomplice. Pierre produced his Committee badge and received an immediate apology from the patriot. Aillaume then turned to Labussière, considerably less confident, to ask if he too belonged to the Committee. By way of answer, the clerk boldly drew the incriminating papers from his portfolio, showed only their official seals, explained that he was on business of the utmost secrecy, and promised Aillaume that he would commend his zeal to the Committee. This bravado succeeded and Labussière departed unmolested. Shortly thereafter, the papers were in the Seine.[58]

On July 1, rumors of the impending execution spread throughout Paris and much larger crowds than usual lined the streets through which the tumbrils passed. They were disappointed, however, for the actors from the Nation did not appear. Collot d'Herbois was furious, and wrote to Fouquier-Tinville demanding an explanation. The embarrassed prosecutor instituted a frantic search for the missing papers, but after three weeks of seeking, he was forced to send a dispatch to d'Herbois confessing:

> Within the last ten months the utmost disorder has prevailed in the documents of the Committee. Of every twenty cases marked out for trial, only ten, or at most fifteen, are brought forward. A great deal of interest has been recently excited throughout Paris by the expected trial of the actors of the Comédie Française; and *as yet I have received no papers relating to this affair.* I must therefore await further instructions on the subject. It is impossible to proceed to the trials of any of the individuals under accusation unless we are furnished with papers telling at least the names of the prisoners, the prisons in which they are confined, etc.[59]

The prosecutor set to work gathering fresh evidence against the actors, but time for such action had run out. Only four days after this letter to d'Herbois, Robespierre was toppled from power and the Reign of Terror came to an end. Labussière's work had gained the actors a crucial delay, and saved the Comédie.

Never was Robespierre's power or influence greater than shortly before his fall. On May 7 the Convention supported by legislation his campaign against atheism, acknowledging the existence of a Supreme Being and sanctioning worship of the deity. A series of festivals were established in His honor, and the *décadis* were each consecrated to the celebration of some principle, person, or virtue. There was a *décadi* devoted to truth, one to justice, one to the human race, one to filial piety, one to agriculture, even one to frugality and one to disinterestedness—hardly likely raw material for festive occasions.

A solemn festival in the Revolutionary tradition was planned for June in the Champ de Mars to launch the new religion officially. A series of victories at the front and the promise of a bountiful harvest seemed to bless these plans, and Robespierre's pride and assurance grew as the great day approached. Although David was as usual given responsibility for the planning of the ceremonies, and Gossec for the composition of suitable music, Chénier did not participate. The chorus of the Opéra had actually begun rehearsal of a great new anthem by Chénier and Gossec when word came that the people alone would sing the "Hymn to the Supreme Being," and that Gossec should write new music for verses by Joseph-Théodore Desorgues. It was Robespierre himself who was responsible for this order, and Chénier realized that his past sympathies would not be forgiven him, even though he had displayed his repentance by burning his *Timoléon* at the Jacobin Club the day before the festival was declared. He left his home and went into hiding.[60]

All professional theatre persons were now officially supported by the Revolutionary government and therefore obliged to serve in this national festival. Preparations for the ceremony began as soon as the decree was passed; a great amphitheatre with enormous statuary was erected in the Tuileries. On June 4, the Convention unanimously appointed Robespierre to lead the celebration. When the great morning arrived, drums were beaten in all quarters of Paris, all the church bells sounded, cannons fired, and the populace began to assemble at the Tuileries. Artists from various theatres showed citizens to their places and distributed wreaths and garlands to the multitudes. It was not until noon that Robespierre appeared among the Convention members in an extravagant costume with tricolored plumes in his hat. All the delegates carried bouquets of flowers, fruit, and ears of corn, but a special one designed for Robespierre had been mislaid after being carried about all morning. Even so, his costume was clearly the most striking in the assembly.

When the Convention was seated in the amphitheatre, a hymn was sung and Robespierre stepped forward to deliver an introductory address. In the midst of it, he seized a torch, descended from his rostrum, and set fire to a great cardboard figure representing Atheism which had been erected facing the amphitheatre. As it crumbled in flames, a plaster statue of Wisdom appeared inside—"of dazzling whiteness," according to David's plan, although it was widely remarked in the audience that the experience had somewhat blackened the goddess.[61] Robespierre concluded his discourse, and a grand procession was formed to march to the Champ de Mars. In front came cavalry blowing fanfares and a hundred drummers, then the great throngs representing the twenty-four Revolutionary sections of Paris. Just before the Convention came the actors and artists of the capital, one hundred and fifteen in number, with six hundred apprentices. The actors, who had had no sustenance since early that morning, began to complain during the march of heat and hunger, but Robespierre apparently believed that the smell of incense was sufficient nourishment on this memorable day, and Talma and David were forced to distribute food to their companions surreptitiously to avoid attracting the attention of the Jacobins.[62]

Robespierre headed the Convention, walking far ahead of his companions. Never had his pride been greater, and such insolence strengthened the determination of his enemies. Murmurs against such affectation ran through the Convention, and a number of deputies were heard to remark that Brutuses still existed. One even came forward, like the soothsayer in *Julius Caesar*, to address to Robespierre the prophetic words, "The Tarpean Rock is very near to the capitol," but the triumphant leader marched on unaffected.

The procession which filed into the Champ de Mars found that great field much altered in appearance. On the site of the altar to the fatherland now rose a huge artificial mountain, large enough to hold several thousand persons, picturesquely decorated with grottoes, trees, rock ledges, and streams, and with incense burning on all the slopes. The Convention ascended to the summit, with actors and musicians grouped immediately below. Twenty-four hundred singers sent from the various sections covered the slopes, and battalions of youths surrounded the base, with the general populace spread out across the field beyond, men and women separated to sing different parts in the ceremony. A tricolored flame was lit at the summit to start the rites, and Gossec led this huge gathering in the hymn to the Deity, surely one of the most imposing feats of musical direction ever attempted. Cannon and trumpets signaled each verse, and at the conclusion mothers raised their children, soldiers their arms, young girls threw flowers, and all raised a cheer of triumph. Public spirit was so fired by this event that several Parisian theatres risked the danger of anticlimax that evening to recreate the festival in song and dance on their stages. The Cité-Variétés presented *La Fête de l'Etre Suprême* by J. G. A. Cuvelier almost as soon as its artists returned from the celebration. Most houses, however, waited until later to demonstrate their enthusiasm, closing that evening to give their exhausted companies a rest from patriotic observances.[63]

The last days of Robespierre's rule were dominated by the veneration of a new martyr to liberty. Another drummer boy, Agricole Viala, was killed in circumstances similar to young Barra's and was similarly mourned and celebrated by the public and the theatres. Typical of the plays based on the young hero was *Agricole Viala ou Le Jeune Héros de la Durance* at the Louvois, still struggling along under the direction of Delomel. During the Terror this theatre took a new name. The *Spectacles de Paris* had advised, "It is to be hoped that this theatre will rechristen itself; the name of the minister Louvois does not sound suitable in a republic, and its eradication is a sage bit of advice which we offer the director."[64] Such "advice" was not to be ignored during these days, and Delomel renamed his venture the Théâtre des Amis de la Patrie. The young hero of *Agricole Viala* lives near a ferry with his mother. On the day of his cousin's wedding he is given a red bonnet as a gift, with the observation:

> Upon your forehead wear with pride
> This hat of liberty,
> And if a tyrant should decide
> It should removéd be,
> What glory then to cry instead—
> "Remove it only with my head!"

Happy thoughts for a wedding day, surely! Leaving the feast, Agricole surprises a rebel company crossing the ferry. Mortally wounded in stopping them, he is carried back home to gasp, "I die content, because I die for liberty." His mother observes, "My son died for his country. I need no other consolation."

Robespierre, delighted by the success of his Festival of the Supreme Being, planned a similar observance for July 28, when the remains of Barra and Viala would be placed in the Panthéon. This celebration, however, was never held. The ever-widening attacks of the Terror finally spurred the members of the Convention to unite in denouncing their tyrant, and on the ninth thermidor according to the Revolutionary calendar (July 26, 1794), he and a number of his most ardent supporters were placed under arrest. Although the greater part of the government remained unchanged, Robespierre was so closely associated with the policy of terror that his arrest was immediately and correctly interpreted by the populace as the end of these horrible days. The very night of the dictator's fall many theatres echoed popular relief by presenting reactionary and anti-Jacobin plays for the first time in many months. Légouvé's *Epicharis et Néron*, full of references applicable to the fallen leader, was presented amid great ovation at the République, where public feeling ran so high that the performance lasted until one in the morning. Similar pieces were given at the Variétés Amusantes, the Sans-Culottes, and, of all places, at the Cité-Variétés, which followed its policy of shifting with the political winds by now damning the Jacobins as readily as a week before it had deified them.[65]

The next morning the Committee of Public Safety began to accept petitions for the release of political suspects, and within ten days after the execution of Robespierre, most of the ten thousand persons in this category were freed. Among them were, of course, a great number of actors, directors, and playwrights who welcomed this change in the political scene with great joy. Many of their number had been sacrificed during these dark days—Grammont and Roselly from the Comédie; Jean-François Papillon, a former director of the Opéra; Mlle. Leroy of the Feydeau; Pascal Boyer, editor of the *Journal des spectacles,* whose crime seems to have been the editorial use of "monsieur" instead of "citizen"; the dramatist Fabre d'Eglantine, and many others. Nor had all of the victims been claimed by the guillotine; Montansier's faithful friend and financier, the Abbé de Bouyon, had been seized by a mob and hanged from a lamp post, a fate narrowly escaped by the actor Michot and by Arnault, the author of *Marius à Minturnes.*[66] At a time when suspicion was so easily aroused, it is not surprising to find so many victims among the people of the theatre, whose actions have always been so much in the public eye. Indeed, it is perhaps more surprising that, thanks to the efforts of Labussière, and of faithful friends who provided shelter and protection, a majority of these menaced authors and actors did survive.

VII
The Reaction
August, 1794–November, 1795

THE fifteen months between the fall of Robespierre and the establishment of the Directory were characterized above all by a growing power and demonstrativeness in those elements of society most opposed to the Terror. The Convention, in which the Jacobins still possessed a certain strength, had no wish to encourage public reaction to Robespierre's period of authority, but after the crushing oppression of the Terror had been so suddenly lifted, demonstrations from those most oppressed were inevitable. Revolutionary plays were hooted from the stage, patriotic emblems torn from the walls, actors who had supported the Jacobin cause subjected to constant abuse. The patriots did not, of course, stand idle in the face of such demonstrations, and bloody riots erupted in many Parisian theatres.

After the fall of Robespierre, the freed members of the Nation returned to their old theatre, rendered almost unrecognizable by its conversion into the Théâtre de l'Egalité under the Terror. New galleries replaced the familiar boxes, and among them rose strange pillars topped with busts of Marat and other heroes of the new order. The stage box where on the night of that final, fatal performance Fleury had warned Mme. de Sainte-Amaranthe and her daughter had been purged along with its aristocratic inhabitants. Despite Fleury's aid the Sainte-Amaranthes had perished under the guillotine, and where their box had stood the saddened Fleury now found a block of yellow marble on which stood a colossal statue of Equality.[1]

The actors settled into these unfamiliar surroundings and on August

16 presented a special program officially reopening the theatre. An immense crowd applauded *Métromanie* and *Les Fausses Confidences* in a program lasting eight hours. Even Talma, forgetting the past, was on hand to congratulate his former comrades on their triumph. "My friend," Louise Contat is reported to have said bitterly to him, "an even larger crowd gathered to see us guillotined."[2] Four days later, Préville completed this family reunion by returning to give his famous interpretation of *Le Bourru bienfaisant*. It was a joyous occasion, for the old actor had only recently regained his reason. Possibly out of sympathy for his old comrades, he fell into the delusion during the Terror that he was living in a dungeon, and only by putting him through a pretended trial in which he was acquitted were his friends at last able to restore him to sanity.[3]

A month later the company mounted its first new play, Nicolas-Julien Forgeot's *Le Bienfait de la loi ou Le Double Divorce*, which shows a husband and wife separating to marry more congenial mates. The husband evidences some of the speculative fever which was soon to grip France, and he regrets his action when he finds his new wife not so rich as he had supposed. Such politically neutral fare characterized for a time the offerings at the Egalité. After their recent trials the actors were understandably cautious, as indeed were most persons in public positions. Despite strong popular feelings against extremists, the Jacobins were still powerful, so although a more moderate tone had been assumed in the government, its new leaders wished to avoid the perils of too severe a reaction and continued to pay respect to the party they had forced from power. Before the fall of Robespierre a measure had been passed to place Marat's remains in the Panthéon on September 21, and this plan was carried out with great ceremony. All the usual accoutrements of a national festival were present, but the majority of the Convention members were not. Already there were many who felt that Marat was not so exalted, nor Mirabeau, whom he replaced, so guilty as opinion of six months before had found them.[4]

The République was somewhat bolder, and on September 10 revived the condemned *Timoléon*, of which Chénier had preserved a copy. The plot, dealing with a would-be dictator that his own brother assassinates to preserve liberty, seemed timely, and Jacobin condemnation gave the play an added attractiveness. It was produced with great splendor and a number of new choruses adapted to the times by Méhul. The success of this revival was tinged with bitterness for its author, however, for Chénier now began to be the target of widespread attack. No one seemed to remember the dangers the dramatist had faced during the reign of Robespierre, only the successes he had enjoyed earlier in the Revolution, and the unhappy Chénier, associated by terrorists with moderatism, was now linked by the moderates with the Terror. One paper, *La Quotidienne,* so conservative as to be almost royalist, attacked Chénier on what was surely his most sensitive spot, the death of his brother André. This promising young writer and orator had been one of the last to fall during the Terror, going to the scaffold on July 25, the very day Robespierre's fellows rose against him in the Convention. André and his friend Jean Roucher rode to their death quoting passages from *Andromaque* for solace, and this stoic resignation impressed many, even among the hardened observers of these horrors.

The memory of this striking young man, who missed reprieve by a single day, remained fresh, and not a few wondered why his brother, who was generally presumed to be on good terms with the leaders of the Revolution, had not acted to save him. Marie-Joseph's disappearance from the public eye during the last days of the Terror was interpreted not as a measure to save his own life, but as a sign of unwillingness to witness his brother's fate. Even those who realized that Marie-Joseph had been in some danger wondered whether he had allowed André to be sacrificed to save himself. *La Quotidienne,* with savage mockery, reprinted almost daily a phrase from Chénier's play *Caïn:* "Cain, what have you done with your brother?" For more than a year Chénier suffered under this horrible quotation. It arrived with his mail, was pushed under his door, was left in his box at the theatre, was shouted at him in the streets. No defense was possible against such attacks, and the miserable author bore them in silence.[5]

After the fall of Robespierre, a new sort of popular hero replaced young Barra and Agricole Viala in the theatres, indicating the sort of virtues which now appealed to the public. This hero was a certain Cange, the commissioner of the Saint-Lazare prison, who, according to the reports, became interested in the fate of one unfortunate family in his keeping, and taking his last 100 francs, gave half of it to the man, saying it came from his wife, and half to the wife, suggesting it was sent by her husband. Hardly a heroic gesture this, but so receptive was the public to any manifestation of human feeling reported under the Terror that the story was widely repeated. Sédaine set it to verse and presented the poem to the Convention, whose president noted, "We applaud Cange's generosity and love in him the virtue which is shown by this deed." A whole series of Cange plays soon appeared: Jean Villeneuve's *Le Commissionnaire* at the Egalité, Pierre Villiers and Gouffé's *Cange ou Le Commissionnaire bienfaisant* at the Cité-Variétés, Marsollier and Dalayrac's *Les Détenus ou Cange commissionnaire de Lazare* at the Théâtre des Amis de la Patrie, Augustin Hapde's *Le Commissionnaire de Saint-Lazare* at the Variétés Amusantes. On October 30, Cange himself and his entire family attended the premiere of Gamas' *Cange ou Le Commissionnaire de Lazare* at the République, where they were conducted to the stage amid thunderous applause and shouts of "Long live virtue!" and "Long live the Republic!"[6]

The République's next offerings were received with much less enthusiasm. The last new production in 1794 was Arnault's *Quintus Cincinnatus*, which attempted to trace a parallel between the rise and fall of the tyrant Melius and that of Robespierre. The play was composed of political discussions rather than action, and, despite the timeliness of the theme, the public condemned Arnault's effort. The next opening, *La Bayadère*, on January 24, 1795, was the occasion of a full-scale riot.

Demonstrations of anti-Jacobin feeling from theatre audiences were now becoming increasingly common, and those houses which had profited most from the rule of the *sans-culottes* now began to pay the penalty for that profit. At the République, Fusil, Talma, Dugazon, and others were, like Chénier, attacked for their presumed close ties to the previous regime. Here the storm broke with the production of *La Bayadère*. It was the most disastrous failure the theatre had ever mounted; the hissing and the cries of disapproval were so continuous that the plot could not even be followed. Mlle. Candeille, who played the lead, was rumored to be the authoress, but if so, her name was never announced in the uproar.

The final curtain in no way diminished the storm. The afterpiece was supposed to be *Crispin rival de son maître* with Fusil in the title role, but Fusil was known to have served on a Revolutionary committee which condemned many to death in Lyons, and loud cries of horror burst forth at his entrance. Several persons demanded that he sing the "Réveil du peuple," the melody the forces of reaction had adopted

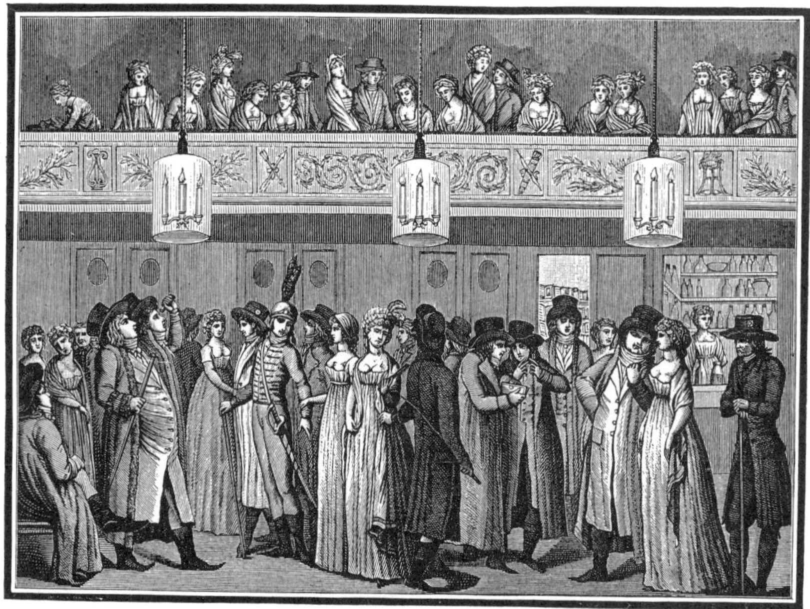

XVI. The foyer of the Théâtre Montansier. Under the Directory, crowds like the one shown, including parvenus, soldiers, speculators, and courtesans, were common in this most popular gathering place. (Armand Dayot, *La Révolution française*. Reproduced by courtesy of Librairie Ernest Flammarion.)

XVII. The Théâtre du Marais, built 1791. The gothic interior, of which this is an outstanding example, was almost as popular as the neoclassic in smaller theatres of this period. The Marais was truly a theatre of the Revolution, for most of its building materials came from the demolished Bastille nearby. (Reproduced by courtesy of the Harvard Theatre Collection.)

XVIII. *Left:* The Tivoli Gardens. In this engraving, several of the most popular features of this first Revolutionary pleasure garden may be seen—the striking vistas, pleasant paths for strollers, pyrotechnic displays, and balloon ascensions. (Paul Lacroix, *Directoire, Consulat et Empire*. Reproduced by courtesy of Imprimerie Firmin-Didot et Cie.)

XIX. *Right:* Caroline Petit-Vanhove (1771–1860). One of Paris' most popular actresses under the Directory, Mme. Petit-Vanhove later became Talma's second wife. She is pictured here in a costume from Duval's post-Revolutionary *Jeunesse de Henri V*. (Paul Lacroix, *Directoire, Consulat et Empire*. Reproduced by courtesy of Imprimerie Firmin-Didot et Cie.)

to sing in opposition to the "Marseillaise" of the Jacobins. Trembling, Fusil began the first verse of the song, but he was soon shouted down. A young man from Lyons stood on a bench in the pit to read aloud a judgment Fusil had signed condemning the youth's father to death. This redoubled the wrath of the audience, and many expressed the opinion that the actor was unworthy to sing so noble a song. As Fusil stood quaking under the storm, the house demanded the director Gaillard, who was also suspected of Jacobin sympathies. At this point Talma, still somewhat more popular than Fusil, came forward to explain that the director was not present and that he would be pleased to read the "Réveil du peuple." This offer was readily accepted, and Talma read the verses of the song while the wretched Fusil stood beside him holding a torch, subject to a steady hail of insults.[7]

Fusil attempted to justify himself after this unpleasant incident by a public letter to the *Journal des Théâtres* in which he explained that while he had served on a committee in Lyons, his duties had concerned only persons released, not those condemned. The public was not convinced, however, and for some time after the poor actor was followed wherever he went by cries of "Down with the brigand! Down with the assassin!"[8] Dugazon was similarly condemned, and was generally greeted by hisses whenever he came on stage. On one occasion, playing the valet in *Les Fausses Confidences,* he was informed by his master, "We have no need of you, nor of your brand of scoundrel!" a line welcomed by the audience with delighted applause. Public opprobrium concerned Dugazon considerably less than it did Fusil, however, and the volatile comedian drew the line at a forced singing of the "Réveil du peuple." When this demand was made, therefore, he not only scornfully refused, but threw his wig into the pit and took to his heels. The audience swarmed onto the stage seeking revenge, but could find no trace of the actor and had to content themselves with destroying a bust of Marat in the foyer on the way out.[9]

Talma's willingness to accede to the demands of his audience spared him from many such attacks, but he too was occasionally forced to stop in the midst of a performance to reaffirm his love of peace and order. "Citizens," he said on one such occasion, "I swear that I love and have always loved liberty; and that I have always detested crime and murder. The Reign of Terror cost me many tears, and many of my friends died on the scaffold. I beg your pardon for this brief interruption. I shall do my utmost to make you forget it by my exertions and my zeal." The audience applauded, and Talma continued undisturbed.[10]

After the Thermidorian reaction, the area around the Palais-Royal became the center of the capital's theatrical life. The Saint-Germain quarter, long the district of rank and opulence, had been almost depopulated by the Terror, and the former Nation found itself now in a remote and unattractive location. "Most of these stately homes stand tenantless," a writer of the time notes. "Grass is flourishing in the empty streets."[11] Refugees from Montansier's Théâtre des Neuf Millions, dispossessed by the Opéra, alternated productions in the Egalité with the returned actors from the Nation, but even the talents of these two outstanding troupes could not attract audiences to the deserted suburb. The two companies quarreled bitterly over the distribution of the meager profits, and the Nation actors decided to look about for another home. Finally, in the last days of 1794, they accepted an offer from M. B. Chagot-Defays, then director of the Feydeau, to alternate with the company of his theatre at his far more favorable location.[12]

The Nation actors agreed to appear in alternation with the Feydeau troupe for three months, an arrangement launched on January 27 by *La Mort de César* and *La Surprise de l'amour* with Saint-Prix, Molé, Dazincourt, and Mlles. Contat and Devienne in leading roles. The audience of the Feydeau were eager to demonstrate their interest in a company which they viewed as martyrs of the Jacobins, and crowds waited for places from daybreak for this first appearance. Chagot-Defays encouraged the company to follow up this success with works capitalizing on the public sympathy, and productions of the plays which had brought the Nation's downfall—*L'Ami des lois* and *Paméla*—were immediately put into rehearsal.

All during the spring, demonstrations continued against the "patriot" actors of the République. On March 25, a crowd of young people marched on the theatre to demand the removal of the "Jacobins" Talma and Michot, but were unable to arouse general support. On March 27, however, Michot was called by a sizable portion of the audience to appear and defend himself. The actor pleaded that he had saved forty-three victims from the Terror, and citizens from Toulouse and Bordeaux arose in the audience to support his claim. Thus fortified against attack, Michot called upon his enemies to state their charges.

One advanced to the forestage and admitted that he did not know Michot himself but had heard it said that the actor was not enthusiastic when he sang the "Réveil du peuple." This ridiculous accusation aroused the jeers and whistles it deserved, and Michot's accuser was hustled out of the theatre. The actor concluded the incident by singing the "Réveil"—with hearty enthusiasm, no doubt.[13]

Although the actors of the République were especially tormented by anti-Jacobins, many artists in other theatres now similarly suffered. François Lays, a noted baritone at the Opéra, may serve as an example. Lays had zealously welcomed the Revolution and, according to general belief, had been sent to Bordeaux on a secret mission during the Terror. He was scheduled to reappear at the Opéra on January 24, but he sent word that he was ill. Rumors spread that the artist was afraid to face his public, and Lays was forced to reaffirm his illness in a letter to the *Journal de Paris*. Finally, on March 18, he returned to the theatre, where his enemies awaited him. Such a storm of whistles and hisses greeted his appearance as Thesée in *Oedipe à Colone* that the play could not continue, despite the pleas of police and fellow actors. Popular papers joined in condemning the singer, although the *Journal des théâtres* of March 23 noted that opinion about his guilt was divided and that in any case it was regrettable "to confuse the actor with the citizen"—an unusually clear-minded observation in those days. The outcry against Lays did not subside until he was actually placed under arrest pending investigation of his activities. When he was released several months later by the Committee of Public Safety, which ruled that there was no evidence against him, the singer immediately published a brochure reproducing this official ruling and was warmly applauded when he reappeared at the Opéra.[14]

Talma, unlike others, never deigned to write public letters in his own defense, and so came regularly under attack. During the March demonstrations, however, others came forward to defend him. During the Terror, he had apparently spent a good deal of money to obtain incriminating documents which might otherwise have been used against the accused actors of the Nation. On March 25 and 27, Louise and Emilie Contat and Larive published letters revealing this generous action, which dissolved much of the ill feeling held by both troupes since their schism early in the Revolution. The path toward an eventual reconciliation seemed to open.[15]

On April 12, Talma appeared in the leading role of Ducis' new tragedy *Abufar ou La Famille arabe*. Even though the incestuous love at the base of the plot was, according to Talma, "painted in traits of fire," the play did not prove popular.[16] The audience found the plot too complex, the misunderstandings in it too close to the comic, and its denouement too sudden for real tragic effect. Talma, supported by Mlle. Desgarcins and Mme. Petit-Vanhove, achieved only a modest success.

The end of the Terror still left Paris with many problems; among its most serious was a continuing inflation of the assignats. The city found itself short of supplies, and the more unruly sections, driven by hunger and encouraged by the Jacobins still among them, marched on the Convention. "Why were the popular societies disbanded?" their leaders asked. "What has become of the crops? Why do assignats continue to fall in value? Why are the young men who frequent the Palais-Royal the only group allowed to assemble? Why are only patriots in prison?" The governmental body stood fast, sent into exile such factional leaders as Barrère and Collot d'Herbois, and put down this insurrection after a few difficult days in early April, during which time all theatres were closed. Soon a certain measure of calm returned, but the uneasy officials increased their severity, and the underlying irritations which caused the uprising continued unabated.

Early in June, the Nation actors, who had extended their contract with the Feydeau, presented there *L'Ami des lois*. The furor of the first presentations was totally absent, but curiosity and a desire to honor the persecuted players did bring large audiences to the Feydeau. The République, anxious to quiet the memories awakened by this revival, countered on June 10 with Népomucène-Louis Lemercier's *Le Tartuffe révolutionnaire*. Although the plot line of this play came directly from Molière, almost nothing else of the master remained. The famous hypocrite was depicted as a Revolutionary extremist, finally discovered and hauled off to prison. The public, whether out of respect for Molière, disregard for Lemercier, or sympathy for the actors of the Nation, shunned this offering.

Much more successful was Legouvé's *Quintus Fabius ou La Discipline romaine*, given at the République July 31. This play, with Talma, Baptiste the Elder, and Mlle. Desgarcins in leading roles, stressed republican virtues but carefully avoided attacking any party. Five days after, the Nation actors revived *Paméla* at the Feydeau. Like *L'Ami des lois*, this fatal play seemed most innocuous when viewed afresh, but the public again came, out of respect or curiosity, to applaud the Nation actors.[17]

On October 30, a short comedy by Armand Charlemagne at the République focused upon one of the central preoccupations of the day—financial speculation. There had of course been serious fluctuations in the currency all during the Revolutionary upheavals, but in April and May of 1795 an unprecedented frenzy of speculation gripped the public and started a terrifying downward spiral in the value of the assignats. All the worst abuses of stockjobbing flourished. Articles were resold a dozen times in the course of a day; property never seen passed from hand to hand in a whirlwind of trading. Fortunes were made and lost overnight as the whole populace seemed to catch the fever for rapid profits. The Palais-Royal, center of the forces of reaction, took on the appearance of a giant fair, and dealers swarmed about it selling jewelry, silver plate, and gold ornaments in open defiance of a 1793 decree against the sale of such goods for assignats. The theatres, so dependent on the purchase of goods for costumes and the spectacular scenery which most of them favored, suffered keenly from this inflation. Between June and October box office prices doubled, tripled, quadrupled, and still could not cover expenses. Far greater pressure lay ahead, however, for in 1796 inflation became so serious as to actually threaten the existence of many theatres. At the Favart, for example, a balcony seat which cost 10 francs in June had risen to 40 by October and to 125 by the end of the year. This figure had doubled again by the following February, and again by May. At the end of a full year, the 10-franc seat was selling for 1,000 francs, and other prices had increased proportionately.[18] Financial speculation was soon, therefore, no laughing matter in the theatre, but in October of 1795 it could still provide comic capital. Charlemagne satirized frantic traders in his speculators Crusophile and Boucliac, who deal wildly in soap and sugar, and Bernard, a former attorney, speaks for the times when someone observes that his prospective son-in-law is not a man of honor. "What does it matter," says he, "so long as he has money?"

The République presented only one more new play in 1795—*Les Amis de collège*, a trifle by Picard, who was simultaneously represented by *Les Conjectures*, presented by the Nation actors at the Feydeau. Larochelle left the République to rejoin his former comrades in the latter production. Picard's two comedies were the first new plays produced at either of these theatres in 1795 without strong political overtones, and their success encouraged more such efforts. Patrons and actors alike seemed weary of the political propaganda which had filled the theatres since the Revolution began, and by the end of 1795 such plays were decidedly in the minority in almost all Parisian theatres.

During the closing months of 1794, the faction opposed to the Jacobins became steadily bolder and more cohesive. The young men in persecuted families formed the nucleus of this new group, but soon women, former aristocrats, and all the enemies of the "Revolutionary canaille" joined them. This party began to adopt distinguishing colors, manners, meeting places, phrases, and dress. The gaiety and ostentation of the old days returned in their assemblies. Brilliant entertainments replaced the affectation of simplicity, even squalidness, required under the Terror. The women, influenced by David, wore pseudoclassic tunics and sandals. The men wore large cravats, black collars, and, frequently, black arm bands as a sign of mourning for those executed during the Terror. The dead were never far from their thoughts, and one of the most brilliant of their gatherings was the Ball of the Victims, which was open only to those who had lost a near relative under the guillotine. This group, determined to restore life and light to the stricken capital, was aptly nicknamed the *jeunesse dorée*—the gilded youth. Their enemies favored the somewhat less flattering title of *muscadins* (fops), for the dress of the new party became increasingly brilliant and ostentatious as time passed. The gilded youth made no attempt to avoid conflict with their opponents, and once again the theatres were the scenes of uproarious demonstrations as opposing factions struggled for control.

The Vaudeville, devoted to satire but unable to produce much of it during the Terror, found a rich mine of material in the affectations of the gilded youth, and references to the "young fops" began appearing regularly in its plays, even though the objects of such satire rarely allowed it to pass unchallenged. In *L'Abbé vert*, the actor Auguste Bourgeois was stopped by outraged protests from the gilded youth when, following a common practice of the time by adding topical references of his own devising to his part, he observed, "this *muscadin* of an abbot." In a moment of calm, the actor excused himself by saying that the epithet was "only addressed to an abbot." A new outburst greeted this explanation, and the play was never completed. *La Perruque blonde*, a comedy by Picard given November 12, 1794, suffered a similar fate, for many in its audience were not amused by jests about the recently revived fashion of wearing wigs.[19]

The Feydeau, which had remained the most moderate of the theatres under the Terror despite the threats of the authorities, was the natural rallying place now for the forces of reaction. There the gilded youth gathered to exchange notes on the progress of their cause, admire the latest fashions, and applaud Pierre Jean Garat, the most popular actor of the hour. The plays presented for their amusement were neither satirical nor bellicose, but sentimental pieces, stressing brotherhood, charity, and equality. Pujoulx' popular *Montagnards*, for example, did not deal with the Jacobins, as one would suppose, but with simple peasant students who come to the aid of a poverty-stricken schoolmaster. Hoffman's *Callias ou La Nature et patrie* showed the mingled sorrow and pride of a father whose son died for his country, a much more realistic presentation than the parental reactions in similar plays under the Terror.

Here lavish spectacles catered to the gilded youths' love of display. In the opening scene of *La Fête americaine*, a magnificent alley of trees was displayed, in their midst a coconut palm hung with garlands of oak leaves and tricolored ribbons, these in turn fastened to the points of pikes carried by two rows of volunteers gathered about an altar to the fatherland. In the foreground stood a representative of the American people carrying a scale with two children, one black and one white, balanced in it, indicating that no distinctions existed in that happy land. In Cherubini's *Voyage au Mont Saint-Bernard* a section of the Alps was reproduced on stage, complete with crevices, forests, precipices, glaciers, and waterfalls. Such spectacular settings, and the machinery necessary to mount them, caught the fancy of many theatre directors. Even Paris' smaller houses installed highly sophisticated mechanical devices, largely the work of the popular machinist Boullé. It was a period of great interest in settings and of considerable experimentation. Even a few box sets with realistic furniture appeared, although the major trend remained toward more and more spectacular wing and drop arrangements, the sort of settings which housed the melodramas at the end of the century.[20]

The audiences which appeared in the theatres after the fall of Robespierre were better educated and more reasonable than those of the Terror, but they still lacked the intelligence and sophistication of pre-Revolutionary gatherings. They were capricious and unruly, easily bored and suspicious of any indications of the political extremism which had brought Robespierre to power. In the early years of the Revolution, audiences had diverted themselves at the theatre by seeking allusions to contemporary events in the play, then applauding or hissing according to their political convictions. Now the gilded youth introduced a new diversion, the throwing of political notes onto the stage for public reading. The first occurance of this post-Thermidorian phenomenon seems to have been at the Opéra on January 22, 1795. There two poems were thrown from a box onto the stage and the curious audience demanded to hear them. The police officer assigned to prevent disturbances at the theatre did not interfere, and the actor Augustin-Athanase Chéron read the items—both violent attacks on the "drinkers of blood" who had organized the Terror. The applause which greeted these sentiments was so great that Chéron repeated them and promised to have them set to music.[21]

This success encouraged other poets, and the fad spread rapidly. On January 24, a similar paper appeared at the Vaudeville, and at the Feydeau the singer Vallière was asked to recite some anti-Jacobin poetry. Vallière was suspected in some quarters of sympathizing with the Jacobins, despite his connection with the Feydeau, and like Fusil, he felt called upon to defend himself in a public letter. He swore that he had served on no committees, traveled on no missions, been given no power, and so on, concluding, "In short, my friends, all those who know my private life can testify that I am a drinker of wine and even of punch, but never of blood! My whole fortune has been gained by the exercise of my talent, and with this I support my wife, her mother, who is over seventy, and four children, two of them orphans." As an extra precaution, Vallière posted all over Paris a six-page leaflet reprinting documents to prove he had risked his own liberty to save three accused persons. No futher demands were then made on him.

The evening after Vallière's experience at the Feydeau, the actor Antoine Trial underwent a similar test at the Favart. Trial was suspected of having betrayed three actresses of his theatre to the terrorists, and the demand that he read some anti-Jacobin verses was tinged with particular bitterness. Shaken by the ill will shown on this occasion by a public which had applauded him for thirty years, the old actor never reappeared after reading these verses.[22] On January 29, more notes appeared at the Opéra, but this time some of the audience objected to such an interruption of the presentation, and a violent argument broke out. The police realized too late that a dangerous precedent had been established. The commissioner at the Vaudeville therefore attempted to prevent the opening of two notes at his theatre and was roughly handled by the audience, which subsided only when one of the actors struck up a song condemning the Jacobins. Similar incidents soon followed at the Feydeau, the Variétés, the Favart, the Ambigu, and elsewhere.

Although the Jacobins were silenced in the theatres and officially disbanded as an organization, they had not at all disappeared from the political scene. They met in coffeehouses in all the more Revolutionary sections of Paris—Saint-Denis, Saint-Antoine, the Temple—and plotted attacks on the gilded youth. Their opponents, knowing themselves in the stronger position, resolved now to strike a blow where the Jacobins would feel it most keenly—at Marat, the most sacred martyr of the Revolution. The campaign began quietly enough. On January 15, three gentlemen called on Barré, the director of the Vaudeville, asking him pleasantly enough to remove the busts of Marat and Le Pelletier from his theatre. Sensing a threat behind the request, but unwilling to run afoul of the authorities, Barré passed on the request to the Committee of Public Safety, which absolutely forbade anyone to touch the statues in any theatre. The next day in the Convention a speaker arose who identified himself as one of those who had made the request. He formally retracted their demand, stating that his interests were pure and that he simply was opposed to the extremists of the Revolution, but that he would henceforth confine his hatred to the living and "let the dead, whatever they may have done, rest in peace." But the "spokesman" who delivered this lofty sentiment apparently did not know his own party, for within twenty-four hours an organized mutilation of busts was under way. The image of Marat at the Favart, fortunately made of plaster, was damaged regularly every evening from then on, and every morning the distraught director was forced either to repair or replace it. On January 22, the audience even interrupted a play to carry the bust onto the stage and drop it into a well which formed part of the setting.[23]

By the beginning of February, bust-smashing was threatening to replace note-throwing as the favored expression of gilded youth exuberance. At the Feydeau, the entire house cheered a group of young men who climbed to the balcony, threw down the bust of Marat while the police tried in vain to stop them, and set up one of Rousseau in its place. Wreaths were thrown to them to crown this new idol, extempore verses covered the stage, and the building echoed with shouts of "Down with the Terrorists! Down with Marat!"[24] Shortly after, similar scenes were witnessed at the Vaudeville, Montansier's Variétés, and the République, which was rather ironically attempting to present François Poultier's *Galathée*, a romantic melodrama based on the Pygmalion story, in the midst of all this iconoclasm. At the Favart, a bust was tied to the curtain so that it was lifted from its base and upset, nearly injuring several persons. Soon after, a young man appeared at the Opéra announcing that he had just destroyed the images of Marat at the Favart and immediately roused a crowd of volunteers to join him in purging this theatre as well. All the busts were replaced, but a new round of destruction on February 7 destroyed them again.[25]

When the Committee of Public Safety heard reports that the theatres of Paris were "on the verge of anarchy," they backed down. On February 8, the Committee notified the Convention that they had discovered no decree stating that the bust of Marat should be placed in any theatre, and such busts could therefore legally be removed. The same day a decree was passed stating that no citizen could be interred in the Panthéon, nor his bust publicly displayed, within ten years after his death. Marat, Le Pelletier, Viala, and Barra were removed from the national shrine and their few remaining likenesses removed from the theatres. In many places, Rousseau took Marat's place.[26]

A decree of February 12 attempted to remove the other major source of disturbance in the theatres:

> The Committee of Public Safety, realizing that it would be possible for evil-wishers to seize the opportunity of throwing impromptu writings on the stage during the interval between the announced plays in order to propagate dangerous maxims or to disturb the peace; and not wishing to abridge the sacred rights of liberty of thought and expression; decrees that, in order to satisfy everyone and to encourage a sense of responsibility, the author of these writings, prose or verse, will be responsible for reading them himself on the stage, or for standing beside the actor who sings or speaks them.

Moreover, the Minister of Police requested Napoleon, now chief of the army of Paris, to mount a temporary watch on the Feydeau, the theatre which clearly stood at the center of such disturbances. The enforced calm which followed was short lived, and the government was finally driven on Februrary 27 to order the theatre to close within twenty-four hours. This closing lasted several weeks, much to the dismay of the actors from the Nation, who had been doing a profitable business at the theatre.[27]

When the Feydeau was allowed to reopen in March, its performances were noticeably more subdued, but the plays presented continued a steady disapproval of Revolutionary extremes. On March 17, *Le Bon Fermier*, by Ségur the Younger, portrayed a hero reminiscent of the popular Cange. The good farmer of the title hides and protects the orphans of his condemned master, eventually turning their father's property over to them. On March 28, *Pausanias*, by Charles Joseph Trouvé, attacked Robespierre through the portrayal of a traitorous Spartan general. So accustomed had the public grown to direct attacks that the author thought it necessary to explain his allegory, noting that "Pausanias is just like Robespierre, except that Robespierre was a coward and vile rascal while Pausanias was brilliant and energetic in his vices."[28] The next production, *Le Portrait d'un magistrat verteux*, described the death of the unfortunate Malherbes under the Terror and was quite successful.

At this point, a figure destined to become of major importance in the Parisian theatre during the next several years appeared at the Feydeau. This was Sageret, a grasping, speculative man, perfectly suited to these profit-centered times. Seeing others making fortunes dealing in every sort of merchandise, it occurred to him that similar profits might be made by investing in the theatre. Accordingly, he purchased the Feydeau, now Paris' most popular house, from Chagot-Defays for the sum of 1,600,000 assignats. The three-month contract which the former owner had signed with the actors from the Nation having just expired, Sageret arranged new contracts with them for a period of five years and, with this substantial base, began plans to build his investment into a theatre empire. On April 23, the day after Sageret assumed control, the Feydeau produced Demoustier's *Le Tolérant*, which stressed liberal ideals and moral and religious toleration. The play was quite successful and inaugurated Sageret's regime auspiciously, but unrest in Paris during May prevented the theatre from offering any other new works for a number of weeks.[29]

By this time it was generally realized in Paris that the events of early April had been only a prelude to a more serious clash still to come between the opposed parties. The reactionaries continued to press for the expulsion of former Jacobins from the Convention and to agitate for royalist representation in the papers. The patriots, feeling their power declining and enraged by the execution of Fouquier-Tinville and several of his assistants, planned for a final desperate attempt to regain control of the Revolution. The day before May 20, the date selected for this bid, a manifesto was circulated among the citizens of Paris recapitulating their grievances and calling for a general march on the Convention to force a return to the Constitution of 1793. One of the darkest days of the Revolution followed. The Convention was overrun by an implacable mob; one of its members, Jean Féraud, was killed by the populace; and the assembly was forced to pass an extraordinary group of Revolutionary decrees to prevent further bloodshed. At last, late in the evening, troops arrived to free the legislators, and at midnight the assembly began the work of officially annulling the decrees just passed under duress. Measures were also taken to prevent another such uprising. Orders went out for the disarming of the Terrorists, and delegates with known patriotic inclinations were arrested. The governmental body was ruthlessly purged of Jacobin influence, and the patriots' last chance to seize the reins of power passed by.

After this important victory, the gilded youth spared the general public their demonstrations for over a month. Then, in mid-July, the anniversary of the fall of the Bastille apparently triggered a new wave of *muscadin* exuberance. The troubles, as might be expected, began at the Feydeau, where the performance of July 16 was delayed while the gilded youth sang and applauded the "Réveil du peuple." The next day a similar demonstration occurred at the Opéra, where the crowds cheered a professional singer, Elleviou, who delivered the song from the first balcony. Within a few days the Vaudeville, the Favart, and the République were also treated to the musical talents of the young reactionaries. At the République several young men became impatient when the actors on stage did not join in the singing promptly enough. Six of them mounted the stage, where one got into an argument with Dugazon and drew his sword before they were separated. The actor, as usual, disappeared, but one of his fellow artists finally sang the song, amid much applause.[30] The young *muscadins* were of course not at all interested in the plays being offered in these various theatres, so it soon occurred to them to spread their influence by going in a body from theatre to theatre, breaking into song whenever they arrived, and departing as soon as their presence had produced its effect.

This new tactic annoyed those patrons who were interested in the plays, and they began to protest. Even at the Feydeau a hearty shout of "Enough of it!" greeted the song on July 19, and applause was by no means universal. At the Opéra, feelings ran even higher, and protests quite drowned out the *muscadin* efforts. The would-be singers responded by crying that the Terror was coming back, that the government was releasing the drinkers of blood, and that the Convention was sheltering these villains and betraying the people. Philippe Merlin of Thionville attempted to speak for the authorities, but could not even be heard in the uproar. When an adjutant general appeared urging concord and fraternity, the young demonstrators, unmoved, shouted, "Let the Terrorists and Jacobins perish!" They were finally driven from the theatre so that the play could continue, but as they left they shouted, "This is only the beginning."[31]

The Feydeau's rival, the Favart, had been far more favorably disposed toward Revolutionary extremists during the Terror, but after the 9 Thermidor it joined with equal gusto in condemning them. Indeed, Lebrun-Tossa's *Arabelle et Vascos ou Les Jacobins de Goa*, presented August 22, 1794, was so vindictive that the delegate Barrère even attempted to stop the play. He gave up the fight when it became clear that popular opinion opposed him, fearing that his political future might be in danger.[32] The drama contrasted Philippe, a despotic governor, with his son Vascos, a friend of humanity. Both love Arabelle, and Philippe disposes of his son and rival by turning him over to the tribunal of the Inquisition, but a popular uprising unseats the tyrant, and the young lovers are united. Despite its exotic setting, the play was full of unmistakable references to Robespierre and the Reign of Terror. Even so the author wished to leave no doubt as to his purpose and publicly proclaimed, "Putting the Jacobins of the Inquisition on the stage is to me the same as putting the Jacobins of Paris there." A similar idea underlay another work, *L'Esprit des prêtres ou La Persécution des français en Espagne*. No one seemed to find it strange now to represent the Inquisition, which the Jacobins had been quick to cite as an example of ecclesiastic evil, as a sort of Jacobin manifestation itself.

Later plays abandoned foreign trappings to attack the Jacobins of Paris directly. In *On respire* (March 9, 1795) Charles-Louis Tissot celebrated the passing of the patriots:

> They spent their days in horror and destruction; these cannibals should concern us no more except in giving them the punishment their crimes deserve. The cloak in which they wrapped themselves has been stripped away. They are exposed in all their ugliness and the populace begins to breathe again.[33]

The Favart was one of the first theatres to reopen after the minor uprising which threatened the Convention the first days of April. The theatre opened April 3, and on the following day a poem by Dalayrac was sung commenting on the uprising. On April 5, one of the actors read a poem of some two hundred lines which he had composed himself entitled "Les Crimes des terrorists." These sentiments were warmly received, as was the stongly anti-Jacobin *La Pauvre Femme*, by Marsollier and Dalayrac, which the Favart mounted on April 8. Mme. Dugazon played the widow Armand who hides two victims of Terrorist tyranny in her home. When Robespierre is overthrown she cries, "The great rule of tyranny is over. Then it was a very good thing to be a poor woman . . . . When these gentlemen with red bonnets and black mustaches, great swords and well-filled purses went searching about everywhere—accusing, arresting, injuring—they did not come to my garret." The entire cast joined in a chorus celebrating the "courageous senate" for overthrowing such tyranny and protecting the people.[34] In the light of the events of this spring, the senate needed such encouragement.

Early in April a reader suggested in the *Journal de Paris* that the *Barbier de Séville* be revived, noting that although the play was widely admired, it had disappeared during the reign of Robespierre, "whose unkempt hair and unprepossessing dress contrasted too strongly with the immaculate wig and dress of Almaviva." The letter reasoned that now that all were free to dress as they chose, Almaviva would naturally be preferred and would be restored to the stage. Despite the aristocratic overtones of the request, the Favart did revive Beaumarchais' play, which proved most popular. Performed amid a series of anti-Jacobin pieces, this gentle satire seemed a soothing note from a happier time.

The plight of the Favart was typical of Paris' theatres during the days of turmoil in May. *Blaise et Babet* was posted for the evening of May 20, the day the Convention was overrun, and was of course not presented. Sufficient calm was restored by May 22 for the theatre to post the play again, but no sooner had the curtain risen than excited persons rushed into the theatre to stop the performance. The assassin of the deputy Féraud had been arrested and taken to the scaffold that afternoon, but at the last moment a group of extremists had overcome the police and rescued him, carrying him off in triumph to the Saint-Antoine district. The audience arose in wrath, crying, "To arms," and,

"Avenge the Convention," and poured out of the theatre. The gilded youth were the first to enter the rebellious district and soon found themselves surrounded by furious citizens. Their bravado earned most of them a good thrashing, but the arrival of General Jacques Menou with cannon and several thousand men brought peace to the district, and Féraud's assassin was turned over to the authorities as this last stronghold of patriot power surrendered. Even so, turbulence in the capital was so great that the Favart did not again attempt to present the unfortunate *Blaise et Babet* until May 26. Then, as calm settled over the city, the theatre turned again to its popular anti-Jacobin fare.[35]

The disturbances which plagued the large theatres after the Thermidorian reaction were generally unknown now in their small rivals the Ambigu-Comique and the Gaîté. One contemporary credits this calmness somewhat strangely to the presence of women in the orchestra, resulting "in a less tumultuous and more tranquil parquet." It seems rather more likely that the directors of these houses were simply more interested in attracting audiences than in arousing political controversy. Nicolet, in retiring from the Gaîté, had turned the direction over to César Ribié, who had risen in a few years from ticket seller in this theatre to one of its outstanding authors and actors. Ribié took to heart a recent government recommendation to "let a laudable spirit of emulation be reborn among artists; let each theatre aspire to the first rank. The ambition to surpass one's rivals in usefulness is the only ambition a republic can endure." The Gaîté was therefore rechristened the Théâtre d'Emulation, and indeed soon did challenge its boulevard rivals in the production of a whole range of genres—political satires, like *Les Réclamations contre l'emprunt forcé;* gloomy dramas of real life, like *Marguerite ou Les Voleurs;* adaptations from other languages, like *Le Moine*, which featured frightful caves, tombs, and demons; fairy plays, like *La Belle au bois dormant;* vaudevilles, like *Le Dentiste; parades*, like *Le Galant Savetier;* even ballet-pantomimes, like *L'Enlèvement.*[36]

A crowd of directors had followed Audinot at the Ambigu—first Picardeaux, one of the theatre's actors, then Andre Coffin-Rosny and Hector Chaussier. Another actor and dramatist, Cammaile Saint-Aubin, followed these; he did not avoid serious political drama as Ribié did, for it was now too profitable, but the extreme reactionaries whose works were being presented at the Feydeau and Favart were not welcome here.[37] Known moderates were favored instead—the gentle Cousin Jacques, now come out of hiding, and the peaceful civil servants Cuvelier of the Committee of Public Instruction and Briois of the Treasury. With that important exception, the repertoire closely resembled that of the Gaîté—pantomime, exotic dramas, translations—

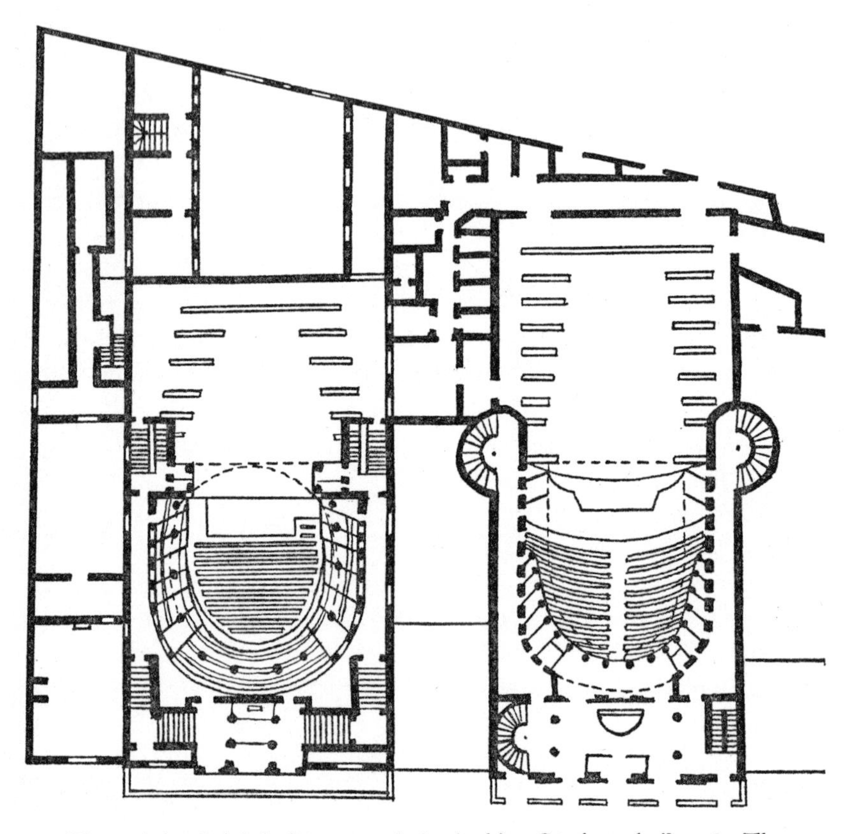

9. Plans of the Gaîté, built 1759, and the Ambigu-Comique, built 1769. The two oldest boulevard houses stood side by side on the Boulevard du Temple (Ambigu, left, Gaîté, right). Unlike most later houses, these both provided a small gallery at the rear of the auditorium instead of a complete circle of boxes. (Alexis Donnet and Jacques-Auguste Kaufmann, *Architectonographie des théâtres.*)

any sort of genre provided only that it featured much action, movement, and spectacle. A report of the times speaks glowingly of this theatre's productions:

Picturesque and well-arranged settings, novel costumes, perfectly suited to the place and the circumstances, ballet beautifully designed and executed by dancers almost the equal of those at the Opéra, military parades, combats—nothing is spared to satisfy the spectators, who are not demanding about the sort of work presented, provided only that it is entertaining.[38]

More and more, both the Ambigu and the Emulation stressed action and spectacle. Of Ribié it was said: "He invented monstrous posters and huge productions." The influence of the translations from German and English brought the somber and mysterious mood of that strange preromantic movement known as the gothic, a mood well suited to the imitation medieval auditorium of the Ambigu.[39] Quite unconsciously, these theatres were preparing the way for Guilbert de Pixérécourt, who in only a few years would crystallize on these very stages a new genre, the melodrama.

One of the rare disturbances at the Ambigu during this period occurred on Februrary 3, 1795, at the production of the anonymous *Le Concert de la rue Feydeau.* As the title suggests, this little satiric piece was inspired by the musical entertainments of the Ambigu's large rival, recently closed by the government as a source of turbulence. The Ambigu play showed a crowd of immoral young people who are represented as the source of the Feydeau's poor reputation. The attack was a lighthearted one, but it came at a moment when the gilded youth were unusually sensitive to such comment, and angry crowds surrounded the Ambigu for two evenings until the Committee of Public Safety demanded that the play be withdrawn in the interests of public tranquillity. The management of the Ambigu profited by this experience, and future offerings at the theatre were considerably less controversial.[40]

The gilded youth were not inclined to let matters rest there, however, and one of the most outspoken of their number, Martainville, began work on a violently anti-Jacobin play with the same name as the Ambigu satire. Aided by his friend Chaussier, he finished this new *Concert de la rue Feydeau* in a few days. Martainville, although a very young man, was already well embarked on a long and colorful career of public protest, and stories of his exploits were common. At the age of sixteen he had appeared before the Revolutionary Tribunal on a charge of writing a pamphlet against the government. When the judge asked his name, the young man replied, "Martainville." The judge, thinking he detected an aristocratic ring in the name, inquired "De Martainville, I presume?" "Citizen President," answered the youth, "your task I believe is to cut me shorter, not to lengthen me." It would be pleasant to report that this flash of wit under the most perilous circumstances earned Martainville's release, but this was unhappily not the case. Only his tender years and the good fortune of having a friend among the judges saved him from the scaffold.[41]

Never one for half measures, the young reactionary celebrated Robespierre's fall by establishing a royalist journal, for which he boldly frequented Jacobin haunts to gather material. One story tells that he was once recognized at the Café des Aveugles, where he was insulted and forced onto a table to sing a republican song. When he protested that he did not know any, he was told to improvise one. He therefore sang:

> Dear Jacobins, let us embrace.
> Too long I've called you ruffians base
> And pseudopatriots;
> Now let such petty rancor cease.
> Let us exchange the kiss of peace;
> I'll take off my *culottes.*

The Jacobins, who apparently never were very sensitive to humor, seem to have accepted this and let Martainville leave unscathed.[42]

The near-riot at the Ambigu provided this colorful young journalist with an excellent motive for a new broadside at his enemies, and his anxiety to present his play was such that he did not even wait for the reopening of the Feydeau, but took the manuscript at once to the Variétés Montansier, which during the closing of the Feydeau had become the new rallying place of the gilded youth.

Montansier, at last released from prison, had restored her own name to the small Théâtre de la Montagne still under her direction, married her old administrator Neuville (though both were now past their sixtieth year), and launched herself into a new whirl of activity. She had the double pleasure of revenging herself and of drawing large audiences from the gilded youth by treating her public to plays abounding in such statements as:

> Tyrant, thief, assassin,
> One word expresses all—
> That word is Jacobin!

Now engaged in a lengthy campaign to gain reimbursement for the usurpation of her theatre on the Rue de la Loi, she cordially welcomed as fellow sufferers all enemies of the Terror. Her foyer now became and remained for several years the most important gathering place in the capital for the gilded youth and the pleasure-seeking crowds of the Directory. When ladies of pleasure reappeared, Montansier was so solicitous of the needs of her patrons as to put aside fifty complimentary seats for them every evening in the balcony on the level of the first boxes, where the ladies could easily bestow their winning smiles on the assembly below. A sort of official eunuch named Robillard was even employed to watch over these creatures, an expansive, good-natured soul with huge round eyeglasses, silver buckles, and a 1787 hairdo. His pockets bulged with bonbons for the well-behaved among his charges, but the theatre had a guardroom where others could be locked away during intermissions if they misbehaved. A happy, colorful, animated company surrounded these ladies every evening, and filled the mirrored gallery between the theatre's lemonade counter and Mme. Cavanagh's bookstand, where that lady sold questionable works which she edited herself.[43]

Martainville's *Le Concert de la rue Feydeau* was received with delight by this assembly. The Jacobins were, of course, as infuriated by this play and its central figure, a rascally *sans-culotte* named Brise-Scelle, as the gilded youth had been a few weeks before by the Ambigu play. Eventually fighting broke out, and one of the patrons even fired a pistol at the actors. No one was seriously injured, but the authorities had had enough, and the Variétés Montansier joined the Feydeau in temporary closure.[44] The offending play disappeared from the theatre, but Montansier had no intention of renouncing anti-Jacobin drama. Indeed, the patriots were again the subject of ridicule in the first new play mounted after reopening, Armand Gouffé's *Arlequin sculpteur*, which opened March 7. Here Arlequin profitably sells busts of Rousseau, Voltaire, and Franklin and makes fun of his neighbor Gilles, who is going bankrupt with images of Jacobin heroes. Says Arlequin:

> Now that true freedom has been won
> Your ugly business cannot thrive.
> The wrathful portraits you have done
> Can only serve to keep alive
> The memory of brothers' deaths.

The former Théâtre Molière, which had become the Théâtre des Sans-Culottes during the Terror, had a similar grudge against the past regime. Although its founder, Boursault-Malherbe, had filled his theatre's repertoire with patriotic offerings, he was denounced to Robespierre for protecting several condemned deputies. He escaped death only because Collot d'Herbois, an old school friend, suddenly sent him to Rennes under the pretext of buying horses for the nation. His successor, Solomon de La Chapelle, was not so fortunate, and died under the guillotine.[45] After the Thermidorian reaction, Boursault-Malherbe returned to the capital to reassume direction of his theatre, which he rechristened the Théâtre de la Rue Martin, and to attack the Jacobins as brigands and assassins in such plays as *Le Faux Député* and *Le Souper des Jacobins.*

Le Faux Député, by Dorvo, depicted the members of Revolutionary committees as greedy, vindictive, and bloodthirsty petty tyrants, but Charlemagne's *Le Souper des Jacobins* was more savage still. Two different parties are shown meeting for supper in the same hotel. One group, all former Jacobins, drink and lament the passing of the good times of persecution when they could take whatever they wanted from anyone. The other group is composed of victims of the Terror: Forlis, who had his watch impounded by the police when he was arrested for laughing at Marat; a tailor, whose goods the Jacobins took without payment; and Déricour, whose father was sent to the guillotine by these "ignoble assassins and perverted judges, drunken by wine, by blood, by animal fury." As the Jacobins drink, they become quarrelsome and accuse each other of betraying the Revolution. Their shouts attract the others who recognize their former persecutors. An officer arrives to arrest the Jacobins and Forlis cries, "Shall my watch be returned?" The tailor adds, "And, I hope, my clothes?" Déricour concludes bitterly, "Ah, friends, who will return to me my father?"

Early in February, 1795, the Cité-Variétés, which the previous June had been the first theatre to press Arlequin into the service of the Jacobins, now released him in Roland and Clairville's *Arlequin perruquier*. Arlequin rejoices with his mistress Columbine to see the fashions flourish again. Says she:

Under the reign of Robespierre
How desperate was our fear;
I didn't make a single sale
For over half a year.
No one then dared show his face
Set off by ribbons or by lace
Or even a coronet
And more than one coquette
Who did so, lost her head.

She scorns the "so-called patriots" and their affectation of humble clothing, and Arlequin observes in delight that

> Since the ninth of Thermidor
> Brought joyous liberty,
> The golden things appear once more—
> Our jewels and finery!

A whole series of anti-Jacobin Arlequin plays followed this offering here and at other theatres. The Variétés Montansier, as we have seen, presented *Arlequin sculpteur* on March 7, and the Variétés Amusantes presented the most vicious of these little plays, Hector Chaussier's *Les Jacobins aux Enfers* on March 22. Chaussier, Martainville's collaborator on *Le Concert de la rue Feydeau,* portrays Arlequin as the assistant of Pluto who escorts the Jacobins to Hell, where they seek refuge after the fall of their leader. When they arrive, bearing placards saying "Calumny," "Treason," "Terror," "Brigandage," "Assassination," and "Poison," even the lord of Hell is reluctant to accept them, but Arlequin points out:

> You surely cannot hesitate
> Whatever troubles you may fear.
> The Jacobins now at your gate
> Have earned the right to enter here,
> For all those left on earth agree
> That Hell is where they ought to be.

Pluto grudgingly gives in, but the Jacobins immediately fulfill his worst expectations. They find Robespierre in Sisyphis' place, and this outrage stimulates them to attempt to overthrow Pluto himself. They are put down, but the lord of Hell cannot decide what to do with mortals who shame even his own demons in evil. At last Arlequin suggests that the Jacobins be fitted with beaks and claws to replace the vultures which torment Prometheus. This is done, and the Jacobin women find suitable occupation as supplementary furies.[46]

The Cité also depicted Robespierre in Hell during a phantasmagorial scene in *La Tentation de St. Antoine,* which also featured gardens, military parades, and a temple with dancers, all rendered with tremendous detail. The decree allowing the removal of Revolutionary statues from either side of the stage was a great blessing for the Cité, for while most other theatres restored the side boxes in this area, the

Cité gained great flexibility by using the space thus freed for scenic background. In this way, it was able to mount spectacles often rivaling the most ambitious in the large theatres.[47]

It was the spirit of partisanship, however, and not spectacle, which made the Cité's next offering the most successful play in Paris during the spring of 1795. *L'Intérieur des comités révolutionnaires ou Les Aristides modernes*, first presented near the end of April, was one of the most violent of the anti-Jacobin dramas. Its author, Charles Pierre Ducancel, had attempted dramaturgy only once before, with the ill-fated *Sainte Omlette* which was banned during Robespierre's campaign against atheism. Early in April, according to Ducancel, he attended a dinner where the talk turned to the Revolutionary committees and their injustice. As the anecdotes flowed, the young man was inspired to work a number of them into a satiric comedy. Within three weeks his play was put on the stage, and such was its advance publicity that the five small balconies of the Cité were completely filled for the opening. The curtain rose in silence, but the audience began to shout in recognition as soon as the Revolutionists appeared.[48]

The play is set in Dijon, a city which, as was generally known, had sent a protest to the Convention when Robespierre was removed from power. The members of the committee reveal their intrigues almost at once:

> Caton: I have just sold some soap for six francs above the legal maximum.
> Aristide: Aren't you afraid that you will be denounced by the man to whom you sold it?
> Caton: Never fear. I will have him arrested this evening.

Jealous of the possessions of old Dufour, they plot against him and his son, now home after having been gloriously wounded at the frontier. Deschamps, Dufour's servant, is tricked into making compromising statements against his master. Dufour and his son are arrested and left alone briefly in the conference room of the committee. They find it piled high with papers containing atrocious denunciations. "How horrible," cries young Dufour. "The correspondence of cannibals would be less frightful!"

In the midst of these tragic circumstances, comic relief is provided by the Revolutionary judges. They cannot write; they suspect a request to go to Bourges because they think it is in Belgium, and they applaud a prisoner reading Montaigne, saying, "Oh, since it is of the Mountain, bravo!" Naturally, they find Dufour guilty and also order the arrest of his wife, who is discovered to possess Spanish and Hungarian wine. Dufour prepares to leave his son, saying, "The scaffold is now the place of talent and virtue." Then an officer arrives with the news of Robespierre's fall, and the Jacobins are arrested in Dufour's stead. The officer concludes:

> Generous Dufour, the reign of the brigands is over. Justice and humanity will rule in their place. Stamp out these persecutors who nearly destroyed your family. Use the courage which allowed you to face death to pursue the total annihilation of the vampires which devastated your country; and posterity, weeping over the ashes of innocent citizens, will bless their avengers.

Cheering filled the theatre as the curtain descended. Ducancel was received with the wildest applause; overnight he became famous and his play the sensation of Paris. The gilded youth hailed it as a rallying cry for their cause. One reactionary septegenarian subscribed to a permanent seat at the theatre so that he could come every evening to hiss the Jacobins. After a triumphant run at the Cité, the play was immediately revived at Montansier's Variétés, which brought its total presentations to over two hundred, an enormous figure in these days.[49] Ducancel's popularity was as a result so great that few recalled that he had supported the Revolution with equal vigor in 1789 and even become a Jacobin in 1791. He continued to remain in the vanguard of political sympathy, passionately supporting the imperial government, then the Restoration, which gave him a political appointment for his efforts. Finally, however, he voted the wrong way, lost his position, and retired to assemble and publish his collected works. *L'Intérieur des comités révolutionnaires,* the most popular of these, eventually aroused such strong feelings that it was banned. It was subsequently revived and banned several more times until at length it joined the rest of the author's works in well-deserved oblivion.[50]

When the Nation actors left their old home, now the Egalité, in the Saint-Germain quarter at the end of 1794, the Montansier actors soon followed, and the Egalité, converted at such great expense into a "theatre of the people" during the Terror, stood deserted. In February and March, 1795, petitions appeared before the Convention complaining of the waste in allowing so valuable a property to stand idle. It was not until June, however, that the authorities found an entrepreneur willing to undertake the expensive and uncertain task of reorganizing a new national theatre. Poupart Dorfeuille, former director of the République and of the Grand-Opéra de Bordeaux, at last assumed this responsibility, but since the Convention's course was almost run and political support was uncertain, Dorfeuille laid his plans and waited until a more settled time to put them into action.[51]

While he waited, the vacant theatre served as an assembly hall for political groups. After a series of stormy sessions in September, the Convention accepted a new constitution providing for the Convention to give way in November to a new governmental body, the Directory, two-thirds of its members to come from the existing Convention and one-third to be elected representatives from the sections. The reactionary elements, trusting that the Jacobins had been destroyed as a political force, favored greater elector strength as a means of augmenting their own party. When this effort failed, a plan was formed to force the body of elected representatives from the sections upon the Convention as a central authority. On October 3, therefore, the electors convened early in the deserted Théâtre de l'Egalité under the protection of several battalions of the National Guard. The menaced Convention declared itself in permanent session, ordered the electors to disperse, and sent a party of police officers to the theatre to enforce this order.

The electors and their supporters, pacing about on the stage of the dimly lighted theatre and huddling together in small groups in the orchestra, anxiously awaited some stimulus to action. When word came of the arrival of the police, they rushed out of the theatre to meet them, but a mob had gathered outside to await developments, and the police, seeing such a multitude, had decided to retreat. The electors returned to the theatre, congratulating each other on their firm stand and several speeches were made against tyranny. No one had any decisive action to propose, however, and as the night wore on without further incident, the assembly gradually drifted away. When at last an armed force arrived to enforce the Convention's decree, they found the theatre deserted.

Despite the ineffectiveness of this demonstration, the Convention was alarmed. The menace of the Jacobins had been stamped out, it appeared, only to be replaced by a new menace from the opposite party. Agitation in Paris increased rapidly until October 5, when a major insurrection broke out, the first since those inspired by the patriots in April and May. Napoleon, attending a production at the Feydeau, learned of the disturbance from friends and went at once to the Convention to volunteer his services. He was placed second in command to Barras in putting down the revolt. By the following day all was quiet in Paris, largely due to the efforts of the young officer. The government profited by this uprising of the 13 Vendémiaire to put severe restrictions on future gatherings of the gilded youth, and their domination of the theatres now sharply diminished.[52]

The Convention gave way to the Directory in November without further incident. The new, predominantly conservative legislative body was composed of two houses, a lower house called the Council of Five Hundred and a senate called the Council of Ancients. Executive authority was vested in a board of five men, nominated by the Five Hundred and elected by the Ancients. This board, the Directory, gave its name to the next stage of the Revolution.

VIII

Three Comédies

November, 1795–October, 1797

ALTHOUGH the first two years of the Directory saw a continuing struggle for power among political factions in Paris, the new government seemed to reduce the threat of internal violence, and the citizens of the capital flocked to places of entertainment. Political plays became rarer, as did military plays, though the European war continued unabated. Interest in manners and theatrical spectacle increased, and new forms of amusement competed heavily for theatre audiences. Actors and theatre directors no longer had to fear the guillotine, but inflation and increased competition brought serious financial worry to many.

The new audiences of the Directory were more sophisticated and less demonstrative than their predecessors, but they had failings of another sort. The almost universal pursuit of profit and diversion in these times led to a general decline in morality; theft, prostitution, crime of all sorts flourished. Even women of the highest social rank appeared in public in transparent gowns in the classic designs popularized by David, so that it became impossible to tell demimondes from aristocrats. The public ballrooms, now over a hundred in number, and the host of theatres in the capital were filled with libertines, speculators, parvenus, and criminals. As might be expected, those houses around the Palais-Royal particularly favored by the gilded youth were the ones with the worst reputations. The Feydeau and the Variétés Montansier naturally headed the list, shortly followed by the Vaudeville and the neighboring short-lived Petit Théâtre du Lycée.[1] Here prostitutes openly pursued their trade, and on occasion brigands would even assault their victims in the pit while the play was in progress.

The new government would probably have closed its eyes to the moral abuses in these theatres (as it did to those of the public balls) had not the same houses also favored plays of a reactionary nature whose seditious passages were warmly applauded by the *muscadin* audiences. After the insurrection of October, the government could hardly be expected to tolerate such demonstrations, and the favorite haunts of the gilded youth were now closely watched by the authorities.

A police report of November 26 notes, "The Vaudeville always offers scandalous scenes. The 'Marseillaise' was just hissed there." The Feydeau, Montansier, and Lycée are condemned in the same report: "Royalist sympathizers impudently display themselves; frightful luxury abounds; the foyers of these theatres are filled with brigands sparkling with their thefts." Once again the Feydeau was closed by the authorities, and shortly after, at the beginning of December, the Lycée, the Vaudeville, and the Montansier were also closed. Little was gained by this measure, however, for the *muscadins* who were the chief source of trouble simply moved their activities to other theatres. Reports came from the police that the Favart was being invaded, and on December 8 one Houdeyer warned:

> The closing of the Lycée, the Variétés, and the Vaudeville was applauded by all friends of manners; but if prompt and firm action is not taken at once, the République will soon be deserted by good and quiet citizens and given over to libertines. Already all the dissolute males and females of the area are gathering there. The boulevard theatres too require more strict surveillance than is now in effect. Only severe regulation, the safeguard of propriety, will hold these theatres to their true duty—providing instruction and wholesome entertainment.[2]

On December 13, one exasperated official even called for the closing of all theatre foyers, but this extreme measure received little support. The little Lycée theatre did not survive this closing, but by the end of 1795 all the other *muscadin* houses were open and again drawing complaints from the police.[3]

The first new play of 1796 at the Feydeau was *Myrrha*, a tragedy by a young author named J. M. Souriguières. Despite its questionable subject matter—the criminal passion of a Greek maiden for her father—the play was well written and warmly received. This tranquil opening did not lessen the apprehension of the authorities, who on January 4 attempted to decrease the probability of future *muscadin* demonstrations at the Feydeau and elsewhere by decreeing:

> All directors, producers, and owners of Parisian theatres are held, under their individual responsibility, to have their orchestras play before the rising of the curtain songs dear to republicans, such as the "Marseillaise," the "Ça ira," "Veillons au salut de l'empire," or the "Chant du départ."
>
> In the intermissions between plays, the "Marseillaise" or some other patriotic song must always be sung.
>
> The Théâtre des Arts [Opéra] will present every evening *L'Offrande à la liberté* with chorus and accompaniment, or some other republican play.
>
> All are expressly forbidden to sing or to allow others to sing the homicidal "Le Réveil du peuple."
>
> The Ministry of Police will order the arrest of all those who in the plays call in their speeches for the return of royalty, urge the abolition of the legislative body or the executive power, incite the populace to revolt, destroy public peace and order, or insult good manners.[4]

This decree set off a long running battle between Merlin of Douai, the Minister of Police, and the artists and patrons of the Feydeau. The obligatory patriotic songs aroused bitter memories here and were shown so little respect that within a few days Merlin was forced to write for support to Napoleon, then general in chief of the Army of the Interior:

> I am informed, General, that last night at the Théâtre de la Rue Feydeau the cherished songs of the Republic were greeted only by hisses. What will therefore become of the executive decree which demands that all entrepreneurs and theatre owners play them every day before the raising of the curtain? I charge you to stand ready to arrest immediately all those who defy the orders of the executive directory, and in this I rely upon your zeal and steadfastness.[5]

The general promised to investigate the matter personally.

In the meantime, on January 8, the Feydeau mounted a play which could only substantiate the authorities' fears. Dorvigny's *Les Réclamations contre l'emprunt forcé* dealt with a recent drastic measure taken by the government to diminish its terrible financial problems. A forced loan of six hundred million real value, to be paid either in specie or assignats, was divided among the wealthy classes. It was a violent solution to the problem of getting money back into circulation, but at this time of crisis it seemed warranted. Naturally, the enemies of the Directory insisted that the loan would only make matters worse, and those on whom the burden fell were furious.

Dorvigny's play was a mediocre attempt to justify this forced loan. The author himself played Dorval, the leading character, who hopes to marry the daughter of old Dupont. The old man fears that his prospective son-in-law, in charge of collecting the forced loan, will make many enemies, and insists that Dorval must convince three wealthy persons of the validity of the loan before he can wed Dupont's daughter. Dorval is so persuasive with the first two victims that the old man himself becomes the third, and the happy lovers are united. The audience was not so easily convinced, however, and a storm of hisses burst from them. The theatre continued stubbornly to revive the play, which ironically raised more anger by its weak defense of the measure than open attack would probably have occasioned. Merlin was well aware of this, and sought some excuse to close the theatre. In the meantime, the controversy aroused by Dorvigny's play was so great that the Théâtre d'Emulation and the Variétés Amusantes both mounted their own versions of it.[6]

On January 13, Napoleon submitted to Merlin the results of his personal investigation of six major theatres. The République, Vaudeville, and Louvois appeared orderly; the Favart had accepted the patriotic airs with gusto and they were universally applauded there; the Cité-Variétés accorded the singing quiet respect; only the Feydeau continued to resist the decree of the government. Constant friction was observed there between the *muscadins* and other patrons, who found the "royalists" offensive. This situation was apparently not the fault of the directors, who were well aware of their unfortunate reputation and anxious to accommodate the authorities. A complaint about the lavish uniforms in the ballet *Déserteur*, for example, had been quickly acknowledged and national uniforms substituted. All sources of trouble could not be anticipated either by Merlin or the directors, however, and reports were daily submitted by police observers that *muscadins* at the Feydeau and elsewhere were interrupting presentations by violent applause of apparently innocuous lines: "Cannot crime or innocence always be distinguished on mortal brows," in *Phèdre;* "Let us enjoy ourselves, for in three weeks, perhaps, we shall no longer exist," in *Le Barbier de Séville;* "The people judge, but do not assassinate," in *Tarare;* "Instead of one tyrant, you will have a hundred," in *Brutus.*[7] Actors attempting to please the authorities were subjected to constant ridicule. On January 28, after *L'Emprunt forcé,* one came forward to sing a republican song and was prevented by shouts and whistles. He pleaded that the Directory had demanded the song, whereupon a spokesman for the public informed him that it had a profound respect for the Directory, but that they should no longer request such tedious songs. The actor retreated amid general applause.[8]

Thus trapped between public censure and governmental decrees, the artists of the Feydeau hit upon an ingenious compromise of which Merlin complained in a letter to the central authorities written early in February: "The 'Hymne à la liberté' was sung by a man who, because of his little experience on stage, and his gauche and embarrassed air, could only dishonor what he sang by arousing laughter in the spectators. Thus the law was evaded and its effect nullified while it was apparently obeyed." On February 21, Merlin was forced to call upon Bonaparte to maintain order at the theatre, and he demanded that a body of dragoons be stationed in the street near the building. "I am sure," he observed, "that the sight of these defenders of liberty will reduce the royalists to silence and thus prevent any disturbance."[9]

Yet as soon as the troops disappeared, the disturbances resumed, and a week later Merlin finally ordered the theatre closed. This action was probably none too soon, for the Feydeau was then rehearsing *Le Tribunal révolutionnaire,* a violent new anti-Jacobin piece by Ducancel, the author of *L'Intérieur des comités révolutionnaires,* and the repercussions from it would surely have been severe. After the closing of the Feydeau, Ducancel tried to get his work accepted at other theatres, but all took warning from the Feydeau's fate, and the play was everywhere refused. Ducancel finally gave up and wrote for Montansier a much gentler work, *Le Thé à la mode ou Le Million de sucre,* which derived quiet amusement from the manners of the day.[10]

No new plays were presented at the République for several months in early 1796, but the reopening of the rival Feydeau on April 2 after a month's closure encouraged Talma's theatre to mount Lemercier's *Lévite d'Ephraim* in competition. The new tragedy had a certain poetic power, but its unpleasant subject matter (a man who kills and dismembers his wife) prevented it from gaining much approval. Two other original tragedies, Philippe de Saint-Marcel's *Caton d'Utique* and

Arnauld's *Oscar*, set in Scotland in the time of the bards, soon followed *Lévite*, but neither was any more successful. The Feydeau, apparently cautious after its chastisement, presented no new plays for several months.[11]

On July 13, a new stimulus was added to the uninspiring Parisian theatre scene when the Directory passed a decree authorizing Dorfeuille to proceed with his plans for a new national theatre. The new director promised to restore the deserted Egalité to its original condition, to assemble the best actors in all genres to perform there, to establish a related school for declamation and singing, to leave the theatre at the disposal of the government for national celebrations, and to establish a fund with his profits from plays by dead authors for pensions for retired actors. The new venture was to be called the Odéon, from the Greek word *odeion*, "a place where one sings."[12]

Dorfeuille's first concern was finding a near-by building where he could establish his school. This he found in August, and in September he published a prospectus in seven articles, promising to regenerate the ailing national theatre. Three Conservatory professors were selected to teach comedy and tragedy, and having successfully organized the school, Dorfeuille turned again to the theatre.[13] The architect Le Clerc was engaged to remove taints of the Terror. He took down the busts of Marat and Le Pelletier, destroyed the niches by the stage and replaced them again with boxes, tore down the tricolored streamers and restored the ceiling paintings. A great chandelier of argand lamps was hung, and new decorations were added according to the taste of the day—neo-Greek imitations of cameos and Parthenon friezes showing gods, goddesses, horse races, and athletic combats. The project was a huge one, and the work was not completed until the following year.[14]

While Dorfeuille organized his theatre, his two potential rivals seemed to compete only in apathy. After Hoffman's *L'Original* on July 30 at the Feydeau, two months passed without a single new offering. The République at last stirred into activity in September. *La Journée difficile*, given September 9, was a failure, but the following evening *Le Chanoine de Milan* proved to be a delightful *pièce de circonstance*. The author, Duval, had fought under Dumouriez and for this service been suspect under the Terror. His play was not surprisingly a plea for conciliation, showing two French soldiers who stop by a canon's home in Italy where they end by becoming fast friends with the churchman. Michot played the canon, Dugazon and Baptiste the

Younger were the soldiers. Duval himself was generally lauded as a most promising young comic writer.

On September 16, Monvel played Descartes in a poorly attended play of that name by Bouilly. Then came two months of dispirited revivals. On November 9, Colin d'Harleville's *Artistes* finally brought the theatre a new success. Even so, the public found this comedy boring in places, and an abridged version, with four acts instead of five,

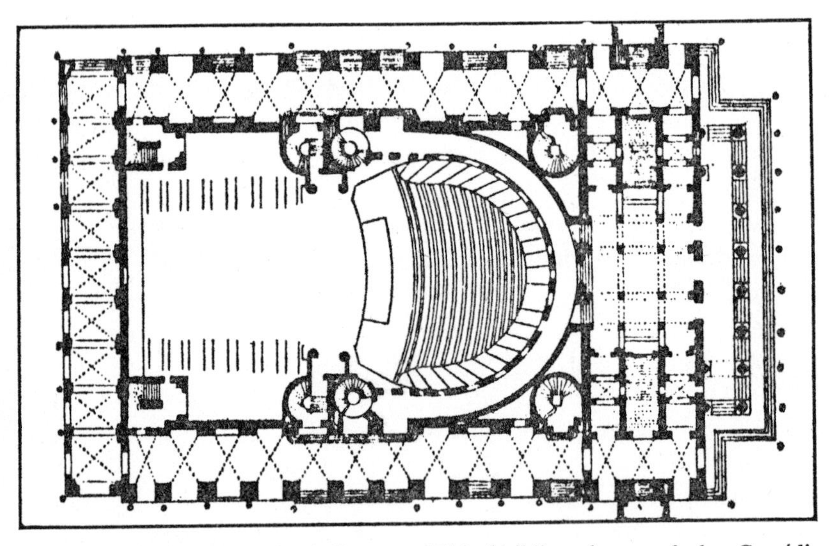

10. The Théâtre-Français, built 1782. This building, home of the Comédie before the Revolution, was subsequently renamed the Nation and, when the Comédie divided, sheltered its more conservative branch. Later still it became the Odéon, which Napoleon established in its present position of France's second national theatre. (Alexis Donnet and Jacques-Auguste Kaufmann, *Architectonographie des théâtres.*)

shortly replaced it. The Feydeau, which had now produced nothing original since midsummer, was stirred by this success to present *Les Deux Voisins ou Etre et paraître*, also by Colin d'Harleville. The dramatist's name was insufficient to save this minor effort, which was pitilessly hissed and quickly withdrawn. The République followed up this victory with a new comedy by Duval called *Héritiers;* starring the same three actors as the author's earlier *Chanoine de Milan*, it rivaled that play in popularity. As 1796 drew to a close, the République seemed about to eclipse its less productive rival.[15]

But now came a new blow. With the theatres already suffering terribly from the combined pressures of competition and inflation, the government suddenly re-established the *impôt des pauvres,* a tax which had been abolished in the first weeks of the Revolution. This sudden removal of 10 per cent of all income wiped out any gains the République had made in recent months and piled even greater burdens on the struggling Feydeau.

At this point, Mlle. Raucourt, long one of the pillars of the Comédie, conceived the idea of improving the theatrical situation by reuniting the scattered troupes to form a theatre which could regain the power and prestige enjoyed by the former Comédie. Realizing that bitter memories still clung to both of the major offshoots of the old theatre, she proposed a third house, the Louvois, as the place of reunion. The theatre was not difficult to obtain; its original director, Delomel, had long since abandoned it, and his uninspired successors had mounted no real success in almost four years. Raucourt's plea was seconded by Larive, Marie Fleury, Magdeleine Thénard, Naudet, Saint-Prix, Saint-Fal, Dupont, Joly, and Mézeray, the majority of the Nation actors now at the Feydeau, and had the government also supported the plan, the République actors might have agreed. The government, however, had given its support to Dorfeuille's Odéon project, still in the preparation stages, and hoped that this enterprise would itself become the projected new Comédie. It therefore ignored Raucourt's proposal. As a suggestion from a few individuals, her scheme had little drawing power, and most of the République actors decided to wait and see what would happen. At the Feydeau, the frightened director Sageret promised extra wages for the artists who remained with him, and so kept the majority of that troupe. Raucourt nevertheless went on with her plan, opening the new venture, the third branch on a languishing tree, on December 5 with an incomplete roster of actors. Dressing rooms with certain players' names hopefully painted on their doors stood empty; Fleury and Dazincourt remained at the Feydeau; Talma and Dugazon stayed at the République. Despite this, the opening production, *Les Deux Soeurs,* a new play by Laya, was a success. The two sisters were Thalia and Melpomene, and the play a sort of allegory on the contemporary theatre situation, with Picard, Saint-Fal, Dupont, and Mlles. Joly, Simon, and Mézeray in the cast. A few days later Mlle. Molière of the Vaudeville joined the troupe and enjoyed a great success in the little comedy *Minuit,* presented December 31.[16]

One of the major activities of the three rival stages in the following months was the raiding of actors from each other, and this constant turmoil in all three theatres contributed heavily to a general decline in the quality and quantity of new works offered. Fleury good-humoredly describes the strange situation:

The actors, turning with every breeze, offered themselves to all directors, and went here out of fear, there out of interest, elsewhere out of conviction, friendship, or simple whim. What else could they do? Nothing was fixed, nothing was settled, nothing was permanent; everything was, as they say in financial circles, to come due this month, or to come due next month. It was a time when kings lasted three months, books an hour, plays half an evening, and constitutions fifteen days. The scene shifted constantly, the nation lived in tents, and as we were part of the nation, we followed the trend. Larochelle and Joly went to the République and later rejoined us; Devienne joined Montansier and then came back to us at the Feydeau; Molé tried various audiences, coming, going, returning again, and leaving again, still fickle despite his sixty years.[17]

The day after the opening of Raucourt's venture, the République countered with *Le Lovelace français ou La Jeunesse du Duc de Richelieu.* Once again the theatre had turned to Duval, assisted this time by Monvel. The play was based on an incident in which the young duke under a pseudonym allegedly seduced the wife of his upholsterer and left her to die of a broken heart. Despite its inauspicious subject matter, the play was brilliantly interpreted by Baptiste the Elder, who played the duke, and Mme. Petit-Vanhove, who portrayed the unhappy wife. Auguste Damas, Michot, and the two authors gained much applause in supporting roles. The second offering by the Louvois was *Cécile*, a mediocre translation from the German by Souriguières, the author of *Myrrha.* The play was unsuccessful, but interesting as an early example of that flood of German translations which would come to the Parisian stage in the next two decades.

About this time, Mlle. Raucourt heard the distressing story of a direct descendant of Corneille who was living in great poverty. Seeing in this another opportunity for lowering the barriers between the three major rival stages, she proposed a combined benefit with the Feydeau and the République. This noble plan was not carried through, but the other theatres did help to alleviate the woes of the indigent relative, and the Feydeau turned over to him all the rights to *Le Festin de pierre* and *Le Menteur.* This gesture of good will, while not so spectacular as Mlle. Raucourt's proposal, nevertheless showed that the theatres could unite at least in the respect of their heritage, and gave some small hope for further accord in the future.

The opening month of 1797 produced only one new play from the three major houses, and that, Desforges' *Le Mari jaloux* at the République on January 31, was a failure, despite the considerable talents of Mme. Petit-Vanhove. The weeks that followed were more dispirited still. The République presented no new plays at all. The Louvois attempted to introduce a new tragic heroine, but the girl could not compete with Mlle. Raucourt and soon disappeared. On February 12, Saint-Fal was applauded as Duval in Ségur's *Verseuil et Saint-Elmont ou Le Danger du soupçon*, but the production as a whole failed. The Feydeau on February 26 mounted Demoustier's *Les Trois Fils ou L'Héroisme filial*. It was a dismal failure, and the last new offering by this theatre for four months.[18]

Saddest of all in these depressing weeks was the total failure of Dorfeuille's project. In mid-February the impressively redecorated Odéon opened with *Les Philosophes amoureux* and *Les Apparences trompeuses*. Dorfeuille, it seemed, lacked nothing: one of the best theatres in Paris was under his direction with a thirty-year lease, he had the blessing of the government and its encouragement to put the theatre in order and to bring to it the best actors available, and he could draw on his years of experience as a director in major theatres elsewhere. All this, however, proved insufficient. The public looked upon the new venture as a weak fourth effort in the Feydeau, République, and Louvois category, and attendance was very small. Lacking the capital to attract actors from his rivals, Dorfeuille soon found himself facing ruin. He temporarily closed the Odéon on March 17, explaining to the authorities that without aid he could not compete with other theatres for actors. The government showed no inclination to give Dorfeuille any such aid, and after a few unsuccessful attempts at reopening, he gave up completely and on June 19 signed his lease over to his assistant, Le Page, and his architect, Le Clerc. Except for two grand balls in honor of the Turkish ambassador, the theatre then remained closed until August 17, when it reopened with a troupe described by one contemporary as "of the power of a third or fourth class provincial company."[19] The fate of the Odéon was of so little concern to the Paris public that its March opening was quite overshadowed by the opening of *Laurence*, a successful new tragedy by Legouvé at the

Louvois. Mlle. Raucourt was widely praised for her portrayal of a woman whose son, not knowing his parentage, comes to love her.[20]

In the early months of 1797, the name most frequently associated with the République was that of the popular actress Mme. Petit-Vanhove, but in April two figures rather in the shadow again became prominent: Talma and Chénier. These two idols of the early Revolution had paid the price for their previous celebrity during the Thermidorian reaction, and both countered the attacks by retiring from the public eye. Talma appeared in no major new roles, and Chénier gave up dramaturgy to devote himself to gambling and amatory adventures. Even these private pursuits did not, as a matter of fact, completely protect the dramatist. During March he entered into an argument with a young man named Kerboux who had taken advantage of Chénier's momentary absence from his box at the République to install himself next to Chénier's attractive companion. A duel followed in which Kerboux was wounded, and a number of papers condemned Chénier, not for duelling, apparently, for that was acceptable enough, but for winning.[21] This affair was scarcely over when Talma attempted to regain his following with a new play closely suited to his style called *Junius ou Le Proscrit*. Rumors spread that Chénier had written this play, and the feeling against the dramatist was still so strong that a large cabal was formed to hiss down the production. Actually the author was Monvel, and the directors of the theatre attempted to forestall demonstrations by writing on all the posters, "The public is notified that the tragedy of *Junius* is not by Chénier." Talma was most impressive as the villain of the play's title, so terrifying that when he raised a dagger against his wife a cry of fright came from the audience. For all that, much of the public remained convinced that the drama had been written by the unpopular Chénier, while others found it badly done, whoever the author had been. As a result, *Junius* was deserted in favor of *Le Jaloux malgré lui*, a successful new comedy at the Louvois, and the long-awaited benefit for Corneille's family, which was held there on April 5.[22]

Talma's next attempt to reassert himself as the first actor of Paris was much more successful. On April 24, he played the lead in Lemercier's *Agamemnon*, which was hailed as "the best tragedy in thirty years." This production was one of the few bright spots in the République's later years and the only durable play Lemercier ever wrote. The plot, of course, dealt with the often-reworked story of the House of Atreus. In Lemercier's version, Agamemnon returns to find Egiste abusing his authority and condemns him to exile. When the villain arouses Clytemnestre's jealousy by telling her of Agamemnon's love for Cassandre, Clytemnestre stabs her husband as he sleeps and poisons her rival. Oreste runs to his mother for comfort when the deed is discovered, while Cassandre dies swearing that she will appeal to Minos for revenge. The play was tremendously successful, although posterity has hardly echoed the contemporary critics who adapted Voltaire's comment on his *Oedipe* ("Applaud, Athenians; this is pure Sophocles") to "Applaud, Frenchmen; this is Aeschylus improved upon."[23]

The triumph of this presentation was soon dimmed by a tragic loss. Mlle. Desgarcins, barely twenty-five years of age, attempted to kill herself as a result of an unhappy love affair. Her fellow actors arranged for her to retire to a country home near Paris until she recovered, but there one night she found herself face to face with a gang of burglars, a shock which totally unsettled her reason. She died shortly thereafter.[24] The Feydeau too suffered a major loss in May when Molé, former dean of the Comédie, decided to join Mlle. Raucourt's company at the Louvois. His appearance there followed two lesser *coups* for the theatre, the successful debut of Mlle. Nanine in *Le Glorieux*, and a popular new tragedy by Petitot entitled *Géta*.[25]

Although Talma's brilliant interpretation of *Agamemnon* restored his public, he was no longer influential enough to impose his ideas on other actors, and he struggled almost alone for accuracy in costume now that ostentation and display had become the rule outside the theatre. The most exaggerated traditional costumes of pre-Revolutionary days reappeared. The French cavalier, for example, was now invariably dressed in a plumed helmet and a yellow tunic bordered in black and decorated with suns or golden palms, with the addition of buff boots if he were also a prince. Actresses tended to follow the fashions of the day, appearing in plays from all periods in Greek tunics or whatever else the *merveilleuses* who set the styles were wearing. The result was a fantastic mixture of costumes. At the Opéra in *Anacréon*, the princesses wore costumes out of paintings by Gainsborough or Lawrence, while their confidantes wore Greek tunics and the soldiers wore Arlequin costumes, with pigtailed wigs under their helmets. In Lemierre's *Guillaume Tell*, which the République continued to revive, Talma and Monvel designed their costumes from a medal struck only a few years after Tell's death, but they cut sorry figures against the rest of the company, composed of Swiss mountaineers in powdered wigs, tight waistcoats, fine linen chemises, snug breeches, white linen stockings and pointed shoes, and of peasant women with fashionable bonnets, stylish taffeta gowns, and maline lacework.[26]

Only plays with contemporary settings or those set in classic Greece provided any sort of basis for costume unity, although even in these the whims of the individual actors generally dictated whether any particular costume really suited the character. The République's *Oedipe à Colone*, by Ducis, was one of the few dramas of the period with visual unity. With Monvel playing Oedipe, this proved one of the summer's greatest successes. Almost as well received was the theatre's next offering, Vincent Lombard de Langre's *Journaliste ou L'Ami des moeurs*, wherein a journalist interested in correcting public manners provided an opportunity for many amusing comments on contemporary concerns.[27]

The declining Feydeau passed this spring and summer without a new work and with only one revival of any interest. This was Beaumarchais' *La Mère coupable*, last seen in a relatively undistinguished production at the Marais in 1792. Beaumarchais, after months of exile on a highly involved mission for the state, had returned to Paris, where he was enjoying a period of relative quiet and the tacit approval accorded by most of his fellow citizens to anyone known to have suffered injustice during the Terror. At the request of Sageret of the Feydeau, the author consented to rework his last play to bring in more contemporary concerns, and the play was presented on May 5. The same characters appear as in the earlier plays, although the count and countess are, of course, no longer addressed by their ceremonious titles. Figaro and Suzanne remain faithful and devoted, but all their ingenuity cannot save their master and mistress from injury, loss of wealth and position, and attacks from false friends under the new order. An emphasis on sentimentality dominates the play, but even more typical of the period are references to divorce, political pamphlets, and the general instability of society and government. Bégearss, the play's villain, is a thinly disguised portrait of an enemy of Beaumarchais named Nicolas Bergasse, but the character shows traces also of the Robespierre-modeled villain found in many plays of the time. After the production, Mlle. Contat conducted the old dramatist onto the stage, where he was heartily applauded.[28]

Neither the République nor the Feydeau presented very serious competition during this spring and summer for the popular Louvois. Mlle. Raucourt's constantly changing program, the successful debut of Mlle. Beffroy shortly after that of Molé, and the plays of Picard, who now developed a great flair for judging the taste of the public, kept her theatre indisputably in first place among Parisian houses. The known royalist sympathies of the directress made her theatre attractive to a predominately aristocratic audience, but aroused suspicion against her in certain high places. The aura of government defiance which surrounded the theatre was thus financially beneficial, but dangerous, as the actors were soon to discover.

On August 4, the Louvois presented Joseph de Lafont's *Les Trois Frères rivaux,* a revival from the old repertoire. A valet in it bore the same name as the contemporary Minister of Justice, so that when at one point the valet's master observed, "M. Merlin, you are a rascal," the audience interpreted the line as an attack on the government and roared with delight. When the actor continued, "M. Merlin, you will end on the scaffold," the amusement of the audience was so uncontrolled that the play could not continue for some time. The actors and director, realizing their mistake, did not repeat the play, but the damage had been done. Enemies of the theatre made certain that the minister heard of the insult, and Merlin was not long in seeking his revenge.[29]

A few years before, so impolitic a mistake would have spelled immediate doom for the theatre, but strong government action was difficult in mid-1797 with the public still suspicious of any movement suggesting a return to the Terror. The reaction was now at full tide. The emigrants were returning; Catholicism was reviving with the reappearance of the priests; churches were full and services celebrated; streets once named for saints and retitled during the Revolution were restored to their original appelations. Although little open advocacy of monarchy was heard, many looked back with nostalgia to the quiet and settled life under Louis XVI. The elections of March and April of 1797 reflected such feelings, bringing to the governing bodies representatives almost all of whom were hostile to the Revolution, its laws, and its leaders. This shift in temper became apparent as soon as the new Councils met. One of the five Directors was due to be replaced, and the Councils elected François Barthélemy, a man of notoriously royalist opinions. Moreover, the legislative bodies now pledged themselves to such conservative measures as ending the costly foreign wars, stabilizing the currency, restoring complete religious freedom, and subduing Revolutionary propaganda. Terrorist laws still in force against refractory priests and the families of emigrants were promptly repealed.

The new conservative forces could not carry all before them, however. Serious divisions concerning the extent of the reaction appeared in their own ranks, the older Council members united against the newcomers, and among the Directors, only Barthélemy and on occasion his friend Lazare Carnot supported the new measures. With no legal recourse to oust these troublesome new elements, the republicans turned to force. Barras, one of the Directors, arranged with Napoleon for a military coup. On September 4 (18 Fructidor), the Tuileries were surrounded by troops and the Councils were forced to renounce their moderate elements. One hundred and ninety-five deputies were unseated, and with them Barthélemy and Carnot. The Terrorist laws against emigrants and priests were restored, the press was placed under police supervision, and rightest papers closed down. Elected to the empty Directors' seats were Merlin of Douai, Mlle. Raucourt's enemy, and François de Neufchâteau, whose *Paméla* had brought about the imprisonment of the Nation actors.[30]

The events of the 18 Fructidor resulted in a revival of many of the manifestations of the Terror. A program of bloodshed would no longer be tolerated, but the reaction to rightist influence inaugurated a governmental attitude that would have been much to Robespierre's liking. Priests were again persecuted, emigrants forced to flee, a strict observance of Revolutionary holidays and calendar demanded, and rigid censorship imposed on all forms of expression. For the theatres, it was a familiar story. Once more the repertoires were expurgated; Roman emperors again became republican magistrates and aristocratic titles disappeared. There was even some discussion of standardizing all costume, and David went so far as to design a "uniform for citizens," but this step at least was never taken. Even so, classic heroes in tricolor cockades were by no means unusual in productions of the day.

The changes in the government also provided Merlin with the power to avenge his insult at the Louvois, and the Director was not long in employing it. On September 10, with the new regime less than a week in power, an order arrived at the Louvois just as the curtain was about to rise on *Le Barbier de Séville*. Without explanation, it prohibited any further productions of any kind in the theatre. In vain

Mlle. Raucourt protested that she had scrupulously followed official "suggestions," never presenting such questionable works as *Athalie* and *Les Comités révolutionnaires;* the decree was final, and Mlle. Raucourt's dream of uniting the Comédie was shattered. The distinguished troupe she had assembled was suddenly left homeless. The actors Molé, Larive, Vanhove, Florence, Larochelle, Saint-Prix, Saint-Fal, Naudet, Dunant, Marsy, and Dupont; the actresses Raucourt, Joly, Thénard, Mézeray, Simon, Fleury, and fifteen other artists of considerable talent were once more scattered to the winds.[31]

No other theatre suffered so heavy a blow from the new government, but all the old burdens of police surveillance and forced changes in scripts returned. Only two months before the 18 Fructidor, a Parisian paper, the *Quotidienne,* felt it safe to make the reasonable observation:

> Several theatres, in their announcements, have preceded the names of their actors with the title Monsieur or Madame. The Central Bureau has forbidden this, answering one folly with another. Actresses are neither citizens nor madames, they are actresses, and it is enough to let the public know they are performing without adding a meaningless title to their names. It makes no difference to me to know whether Monsieur Molé or Citizen Molé will fill a role, provided I know that it will be Molé.[32]

By November, however, such reasonableness had disappeared, officially at least, and a police report on November 2 on *Alphonse et Léonore* at the Feydeau calls the attention of the authorities to abuses in it: "A French officer continuously uses the word "Monsieur," speaks of Madame *de* Gercont, and believes the son of a farmer fortunate to be his valet."[33]

The major theatres and many of the minor ones labored also under a new disadvantage. A certain portion of their audience no longer had any interest whatsoever in the factional disputes within the government, and those who were interested were generally aristocratic in sympathy. Thus anything which would flatter the present regime might lose audiences, a painful fact which the République was the first to discover. Although the closing of the Louvois at first benefited this rival house, the events of these days recalled the Terror to the minds of many, and there were unpleasant associations concerning the République in such a context. Word circulated that on the 18 Fructidor the République had been one of the few places in Paris where cheers were heard for an upheaval which meant exile or prison for so many. Thus by October 7, when the theatre offered Duval's *Le Sot intrigant ou La Manie d'être quelque-chose*, the house was almost deserted, and *Les Véritables honnêtes gens*, a comedy presented October 20 celebrating the proscriptions of the 18 Fructidor, literally emptied the theatre. Soon the République was forced to turn to magicians and jugglers, the mainstays of the boulevards, to attract audiences.[34]

The Feydeau ultimately profited most from the 18 Fructidor. Its production on October 15 of *L'Amour et la raison* exploited the sensibility of the time in the manner of Marivaux, and was the only important success of the month.

The Odéon reopened on August 17 under the direction of Le Clerc and Le Page, but the new managers were no more successful than Dorfeuille had been. Added to the problems of an uninspired repertoire and an undistinguished company was the clause in Dorfeuille's lease from the government which placed the theatre at the disposal of the authorities whenever a large hall was needed. On September 4, amid the upheaval which led to the 18 Fructidor, the Council of the Five Hundred moved into the theatre and did not depart until September 9, with never a thought of indemnity for the dispossessed actors. Shortly after, a military commission charged with persecuting the enemies of the new regime moved into the theatre to hold trial, and the actors were again forced to plan their productions around these unwelcome guests. Under such adverse conditions, the theatre steadily declined.[35]

While the Feydeau and the République struggled half-heartedly for prominence and their unwilling subsidiaries, the Louvois and Odéon, rose and fell, the minor theatres too faced troubled times, and many of these disappeared. The majority of the Parisian theatres had followed the example of the Feydeau and République in abandoning political drama during 1796, despite the potential subject matter offered by the unsuccessful Baboeuf conspiracy organized by the Jacobins in September. The government's shift from encouragement to disparagement of political theatre had been generally effective, and the Jacobins, the natural target for theatrical attack, were sufficiently humbled to provide little stimulus for such attack except in the theatres with the bitterest memories. The Cité-Variétés continued to present works such as Bizet's *Les Boîtes ou La Conspiration des mouchoirs,* given September 5, which showed the Jacobins as cowards, thieves, and drinkers of blood, and the Molière still sponsored Armand Charlemagne, whose *Soirée de Vaugirard* once again condemned the conspiracies of the vanquished party, but these two theatres stood almost alone in their condemnation. The populace at large considered the Terrorists completely purged from their society, and turned more and more to the concerns and amusements of the day. Far more typical of Directory theatre fare was that at the Variétés Amusantes, where Arlequin, freed again from political concerns, returned to his old fantastic adventures.

The young iconoclast Martainville was apparently the only dramatist who willfully flouted the new government's disapproval of politically controversial drama. Now, just over a year after his anti-Jacobin *Concert de la rue Feydeau* had brought about the closing of the Variétés Montansier, he was represented at the recently opened Théâtre des Jeunes-Artistes by *Les Assemblés primaires ou Les Elections.* In the play, presented March 19, 1796, Martainville shifted his attack to the Directory, which he dismissed as merely a new version of the Revolutionary government that had condoned the Terror. Although the play was heartily applauded, it was closed almost at once by the police. Most playwrights would have accepted such a closure simply as part of life under the Directory, but Martainville thrived on opposition. He went to Limodin, chief of the central Bureau of Police, threatening to make an issue of the decree if it were not revoked. According to Martainville, this interchange followed:

> Martainville: The public demands this play and you have no right to deprive them of it!
>
> Limodin: What is the public to me? I don't give a damn whether the public is satisfied or not!

This conversation was soon reproduced on posters at the theatre and in the major streets of the capital with the additional comment:

> The public, for which M. Limodin does not give a damn and who I am sure will requite him for this, yesterday loudly demanded the play. Since I am not a member of the infamous central bureau and therefore do give a damn for the public, I have had the play printed so that they can judge it for themselves all the same. It is for sale at Barba's, 27 Rue Saint-André des Arts.

Each day for some time after, the theatre appended to its announcement for the day the note: "Awaiting *Les Assemblés primaires ou Les Elections,* vaudeville by Citizen Martainville, banned by order of the government." The play was not, however, presented again.[36]

Later political plays at the Jeunes-Artistes stressed compromise, forgiveness, and toleration, as in Jean-François Corsange and Hapde's *Le Dernier Couvent de France,* given August 13. This work strove to please both those who approved the suppression of convents and those repelled by irreligious excesses by showing a convent transformed into a hospital and school directed by a woman of the world—benevolent, philosophic, and free from prejudice. It proved very successful.[37]

The sudden financial flourishing of the lower classes in this period of speculation made the *nouveaux riches* a significant element in society, and much of the comedy of the day was based on the ludicrous attempts of the dregs of society to assume a pseudonobility. Antoine François Eve's *Madame Angot ou La Poissarde parvenue* was by far the most successful of these, causing all Paris to flock to Ribié's little Théâtre d'Emulation to laugh at the misadventures of the old lady from the Halles plunged suddenly into aristocratic circles. The idea was not a new one; Madame Angot, as the subtitle of Eve's play suggests, was directly in the *poissard* tradition of burlesques of lower-class Parisian life going well back into the preceeding century. Madame Angot herself was a direct descendant of Mme. Engeuele, an ambitious and well-to-do fishwife who first appeared on the stage in 1754.[38] Still, the shifting social classes under the Directory made Madame Angot seem particularly apt in 1796, and the drama was further enhanced by the interpretation of Labanette Corsse, who made himself famous in the title role, and by lively lyrics sung to all the popular tunes of the day, much in the manner of John Gay's *Beggars' Opera.* The subsequent stage history of the ambitious fishwife with her mispronounced words, her grotesque costumes, and her overdone gesticulations, was as spectacular as her debut. For two years no play produced in Paris could rival the attractiveness of this old lady, and a host of imitations of Eve's work soon appeared, Eve himself penning one successful sequel the following year, to which Leblanc wrote the music. Other theatres mounted not only Madame Angot, but also Père Angot plays. Favart the Younger attempted to kill off the popular old lady at the Théâtre des Jeunes-Artistes in *Joseph, ou La Mort tragique de Madame Angot,* but his presumptuous posters were torn down almost as soon as they appeared, and that evening a storm of vengeful hisses drowned out the play which pretended to put an end to this colorful career. Gaussier Saint-Armand's *La Mort de Madame Angot*, produced October 31, 1797, met a similar fate.

The old lady seemed indestructible, especially after a more talented dramatist, Joseph Aude, took up her story in 1798. *Madame Angot dans son ballon ou Le Voyage aérien* provided amusing comments on balloon ascensions, the fashionable novelty of the day, and *Cadet Roussel misanthrope et Manon repentante*, done in collaboration with two other writers, combined Madame Angot with another popular comic figure, Cadet Roussel, in a parody of a recent tragedy by Kotzebue. Aude's next Angot play, presented in 1800, was his most successful—*Madame Angot au Sérail de Constantinople*. So it went, well into the nineteenth century. Eve and Aude continued to produce new Madame Angot adventures, and other dramatists supplemented their efforts. Play after play appeared—*Le Débarquement de Madame Angot*, *Le Lovelace des Halles*, *Madame Angot au Malabar*, *Madame Angot au muséum*, *Madame Angot dans son grénier*, *Les Dérnieres Folies de Madame Angot*, *Les Deux Angot*, and so on. Angot novels, pamphlets, even parlor games appeared. Plays portrayed the adventures of her son, her daughter, her grandchildren.[39] Almost a century after her first appearance, the durable old fishwife was still active, serving as the basis for Paul Siraudin and Victor Koning's popular comic opera *La Fille de Madame Angot*. One of the opera's most delightful songs casts a nostalgic eye back over her adventures:

Fish of all kinds she carried
And well she held her own.
Both single men and married
All trembled at her tone.
When her shrill vocal organ
She raised or high or low,
'Twas a foregone conclusion
She'd raise her fist also.
Handsome nearly, vulgar clearly,
Thus contempt for all she'd show.
Chin protruded, all things rude did,
Such was she, Madam Angot.[40]

Despite such occasional successes as *Madame Angot*, the minor houses of Paris declined greatly under the Directory. Suspected by the police, prostituted by unscrupulous speculators, driven to the most absurd expedients in their competition for audiences, over half of those houses still open as 1797 began had disappeared by the following fall. No existence could have been more unstable than that of the artists connected with such ventures. Managers changed monthly, even weekly, and theatres opened and closed with bewildering rapidity. The final blow for many of these little houses came not from political upheaval, for even at the height of the Terror Parisians had demonstrated a willingness to seek dramatic entertainment, nor from inflation, though this was serious enough for most of them, but from a new sort of competition. This new diversion was the "pleasure garden," which proved so popular with the public of the Directory that during the summer of 1797 it almost completely emptied the minor theatres of Paris.[41]

The first of these gardens to attain great success, and the model for most later ones, was the Tivoli, which Claude Ruggieri and his brother opened late in 1796. Their park, with its promenades, allowing the dandies of the day to display themselves, and its pyrotechnic exhibitions, catering to the public love of spectacle, proved immensely popular, and a host of imitations appeared the following summer. In May the Jardin Biron opened, with illuminations, dances, and fireworks, then the Jardin Idalie, with similar features. Parks and châteaux deserted by the nobility during the Revolution were ideally suited for such exploitation, and soon the Parc Saint-Cloud and the Château on that estate opened, then the Hermitage and the Petit-Trianon at Versailles, the latter converted into an elegant restaurant. Others followed—the Château de Belle-Vue at Sèvres, the Bagatelle in the Bois de Bologne, the Hameau at Chantilly, and the Hôtel de Richelieu were among the most popular.[42]

At first all such gardens followed the example established by the Tivoli of a general admission charge of six francs, allowing the patron to stroll along the richly landscaped promenades and witness an evening of fireworks displays. The sudden burgeoning of such establishments, however, soon led them into the same sort of competition which had in the last several years characterized the minor theatres, and new experiments constantly appeared in an ever more frantic search to entice the public. First, two-franc gardens appeared for the lower classes—the Marbeuf, the Paphos, and the Mousseaux. Then came more expensive experiments, but the price of the most lavish, the Elysée-

Bourbon, proved prohibitive for everyone, even though the garden featured concerts by Martini, a Venetian carnival, Chinese dances, and whole crowds of Arlequins, Pierrots, and Colombines.[43]

Garnerin, an aerialist who had launched balloons for the civic festivals in 1790 and 1791, had been almost forgotten in succeeding years, until the managers of the Jardin Biron realized the potential drawing power of such a spectacle. In July, posters announced not only a balloon ascension, but also a parachute jump. A great crowd assembled, and the income, almost 36,000 francs, was the largest ever received at a public garden. Garnerin after this triumph went to the Parc de Monceaux, where he successfully repeated his demonstration three more times during the year, always before huge crowds. Other gardens sought to emulate this attraction. At the Idalie the Chûte de Phaéton failed miserably, although the crowd drawn for it was almost as large as that gathered for Garnerin's first flight. The proprietors attempted to win back their disappointed public by featuring an aeronaut named Calais who undertook a flight with taffeta wings. A perpendicular fall and a broken nose were his reward, and the garden soon closed. More successful was a spectacle at the Château de Bellevue, where a certain Brissi surpassed even Garnerin by going aloft mounted on a horse. Ruggieri alone managed to keep his garden steadily among the most popular without resorting to such aerial displays, but even he had to add more and more attractions to maintain his position. Fireworks alone were no longer sufficient, and constant ramifications were added to his displays. *La Descente d'Orphée aux enfers* found him in the business of regular theatrical production, for it was a full-scale opera, with chorus, musicians, scenery, and elaborate costumes set against a background of pyrotechnic displays. Little wonder that few of the boulevard theatres could compete.[44] The small houses closed, one by one, until by late 1797 there were only about twenty professional theatres left in Paris. Even those which survived did so under the most unstable conditions, changing actors and directors with bewildering rapidity.

The theatrical situation was further confused by the competition of amateur theatres; their number had grown steadily throughout the Revolution until there were now more than two hundred in the capital, in every quarter, and almost in every street. Plays were presented in wine shops, in cafés, in cellars, in garrets, in stables, and in sheds. All classes of society now participated in this activity, which was formerly an amusement only of the aristocracy. A writer of the time reports that the humblest laborers willingly sacrificed two or three days a week to produce plays marked by an engaging lack of ostentation: "I have seen Agamemnons with calloused hands, Iphigénies with chilblains on their fingers, Célimènes with holes in their stockings."[45]

Such humble productions contrasted sharply with the stylish affectations of the major theatres and their audiences. The fashions worn in Paris all during the Revolution had, like the theatrical fare, closely followed the sudden political changes. In 1789 and 1790, while the King was still generally respected, styles followed court fashions. In 1791 Spartan and Roman styles appeared in David's paintings, Talma's costumes, theatrical settings, and street wear. The Terror imposed dirty and ragged dress upon everyone hoping to avoid suspicion of aristocracy, and a wave of dandyism naturally followed with the reaction of 1796. In 1797, under the Directory, the gilded youth gave way to the *incroyables*, and these products of an affected, pleasure-seeking society truly did carry foppery to incredible extremes. Athenian influences predominated, and Pericles, Socrates, Alcibiades, cameos, tunics, and sandals became standard household words. Classic purity did not distinguish this new classicism, however: transparent tunics were worn readily with diamond-studded slippers and Egyptian bracelets, all in the name of the *antique*.[46] At first exhibited in the pleasure gardens, such dress was not long in finding its way to the major theatres, which sought to appeal to the same public.

Extreme daintiness and delicacy likewise appeared in the thought, sentiment, and language of those who wished to be in the fashion, and clarity and precision, so long the foundations of French expression, were widely abandoned. Certain letters, such as *R* and *G*, were now considered "harsh" and virtually purged from the language. In the speaking and writing of persons of refinement *paole d'honneu* replaced *parole d'honneur*. Such influences were naturally felt in the theatre, especially in the larger and more fashionable houses. New plays stressed grace, euphony, and light themes. Corneille and Racine were replaced by Marivaux; acting style became more studied and subdued. Talma's bursts of passion diminished, Louise Contat turned her strong humor into an elegant *finesse*, and even Raucourt's notorious masculinity took on an air of affectation.[47]

IX

The Comédie Reunited
October, 1797–June, 1799

THE final two years of the Directory brought to the theatres of Paris at least a relative calm. The vigilance of the Censor and the indifference of the audience did little to stimulate the drama, but, with one or two isolated exceptions, helped to restore dignity and decorum to its presentation. Political drama tended to disappear, and with it the riots and disturbances so common in the theatres earlier. Some minor houses continued to decline, but others which had proved hardy enough to withstand the competition during 1795 and 1796 found the last days of the Directory stimulating and profitable. With the popular new melodramas and other diversions they attracted enthusiastic new audiences. The scattered branches of the Comédie, after many months of strife, instability, and exploitation, at last, in the final months of the directory, merged to re-establish their original society.

The last time during the Directory when the theatres and the general public joined in enthusiastic response to a political event came in October, 1797. On October 17, near the little Italian village of Campo Formio, Napoleon signed a treaty with representatives of the Austrian Emperor which brought peace to France for the first time in five years. The theatres of Paris were prompt and unanimous in adding to the general jubilation, some putting the news on stage the very evening of its arrival. At the Vaudeville, which was capitalizing on the vogue of pleasure gardens and of Garnerin's balloon ascents at the Monceaux with a play about these popular amusements, the balloonist dropped a note from the heavens saying, "When I descend, I shall bring you celestial news." The news was, of course, news of the treaty. At the Feydeau, Lesage, playing in *Le Traité nul,* announced, "But listen, sir, I just met Gros-Pierre, who told me that peace has been signed with the Emperor; now you surely must make peace with your wife!" At the Favart, Gouthier, playing the nurse in *Farfar et Colas,* appeared crying, "Ah, madame! What happiness I feel! Peace is signed with the Emperor!" In all three theatres the news was received with tremendous applause.

By early November these theatres, and most of the others in the capital, had mounted plays celebrating the peace. The Feydeau presented *L'Heureuse Nouvelle* by Gauderd de Saint-Just, Charles de Longchamps, and Marie-Jacques Boieldieu, and commissioned Méhul to write a "Hymn to Peace" to play at intermissions. The Vaudeville gave *Le Pari* by its standard authors Desfontaines, Barré, Radet, Desprez, and François Deschamps. At the Favart, Joigny and Berton offered *Le Dénouement inattendu.* Aude's *La Paix,* at the République, was one of the most noteworthy efforts among the larger theatres. The Odéon presented *Le Mariage à la paix* by Gamas. The Ambigu-Comique offered J. Corisandre Mittié's *La Paix ou Les Amants réunies.* At the Variétés Amusantes, Lazarri gave *Le Pied de nez ou La Nouvelle de la paix* by Joseph Dusaulchoy, and anonymous occasional pieces were offered by Montansier and the Délassements-Comiques.[1]

When Napoleon himself arrived in Paris to reap the rewards of his accomplishments, the government organized an impressive ceremony in his honor for December 10. The great court of the Luxembourg palace was richly decorated for this occasion. The Directors, in Roman robes, were seated on a platform at one end of the court surrounded by lesser ministers and backed by the altar of the fatherland. Captured enemy flags surrounded the court, while artillery units and bands supplemented the throngs in the hall. After the conqueror was hailed and his short speech delivered, a huge chorus sang a hymn written for the occasion by Chénier, who since the recent changes in the government had been reaccepted by the authorities, if not by the people.[2]

Here, as 1797 drew to a close, France entered the last full year of the Revolution, before Napoleon came to power. There were only fifteen professional theatres left in Paris, a number the new Emperor would reduce further still. The two surviving branches of the old Comédie—the République and the Feydeau—along with their lesser rival, the Odéon, spent much of this final year in a merry-go-round of disintegration, which we shall consider presently. The less-involved fortunes of the capital's other theatres can be summarized more quickly.

If little has been said concerning the Opéra under the Directory, it is because there is little to say. After its abrupt move to Montansier's Théâtre des Neuf Millions in the Rue de la Loi, the Théâtre des Arts, as the Opéra was shortly renamed, did not produce a new play in two years. On July 17, 1796, the *Journal de Paris* described the theatre's affairs as "in a disorder promising imminent ruin." A committee was appointed to administer the theatre's business, but a full year passed and their administration witnessed only one new work, Gréty's *Anacréon chez Polycrate.* Although successful, it was hardly sufficient in itself to restore the theatre's financial balance. Dispirited revivals did nothing to aid the situation, nor did a Directory decree of February 2, 1797, which tied the theatre more openly to the government, renaming it the Théâtre de la République et des Arts. A pathetic occasional piece, *La Pompe funèbre de général Hoche*, produced at the close of 1797, was so complete a failure that the theatre was forced to a temporary closure for reorganization. After several weeks, the venture was turned over to Francoeur, who had directed the Opéra with Cellerier earlier in the Revolution until the Terror brought his arrest.

Few men could have brought more experience to the position, for Francoeur had spent forty-five of his sixty years in the theatre. Still, the new administration began as inauspiciously as the old. In order to flatter the government, now involved in an antagonism with England, Francoeur mounted Rouget de Lisle's anti-British pantomime, *Chant des vengeances.* The public in May, 1798, was not interested in a new "Marseillaise," however, and the work failed. *Apelle et Campase*, in July, fared little better, and an ambitious operatic version of Voltaire's tragedy *Olympie* opened December 18 and lasted only three performances. Francoeur set to work at once to prepare a final effort with his remaining funds. This time his success seemed assured; the opera, *Adrien,* was well written, its author, Méhul, widely known and admired. But the same political considerations which in 1792 killed a work concerning this Roman emperor were still present in 1799. The opera was banned after its fourth performance, all the money expended in its mounting gone for naught, and Francoeur's direction, seventeen months old, was bankrupt. Once again, in 1799, the Opéra stood closed for reorganization.[3]

The Favart, with a rich repertoire and a seasoned troupe, did not suffer from the instability which plagued Sageret's Feydeau, and it steadily drew customers from its once far more popular rival. This continuing prosperity in turn allowed the Favart to reinvest its profits in the scenic accoutrements now so much in favor. A contemporary critic thus assessed the theatre's popularity:

> Few theatres have expended so much effort and expended it to such good effect . . . . Painstaking presentations, new and effective settings, striking costumes faithfully copied from those centuries when the action is supposed to take place—these actors have spared nothing to please the public.[4]

The Favart's greatest success during the Directory was *Elisca*, presented early in 1799. Grétry, its composer, was hailed as immortal, and at the opening performance a crown was thrown onto the stage for Mme. Saint-Aubin, the leading lady, to place on the musician's head. Four days later the actress herself was similarly honored, amid tumultuous applause. It may be imagined with what coolness such royalist procedures were viewed by the municipal authorities, but since the play itself offered no grounds for complaint, the demonstrations at the Favart continued unchecked.

Jean-Etienne Championnet's suppression of an Italian uprising later in January provided an opportunity for the government to make some modest suggestions to the erring theatre. The King of Naples, angered by French occupation of Rome and encouraged by the British, had initiated an abortive attack which in seventeen days toppled his own government and left the French more firmly entrenched in Italy than before. A few years earlier such a victory would have swept the Paris stages; now it was not even mentioned. This indifference seems only to have disturbed the authorities in one case, however; it was significantly to the Favart alone which the Minister of the Interior appealed for a theatrical acknowledgment of the victory:

> Citizens, the Greeks and Romans announced to the populace assembled in the theatres the honors of new victories; the games were interrupted and the same tribute was paid to courage as to genius.
>
> Such a solemn occasion took place yesterday, and your patriotism should stimulate you to acknowledge it. Rome reconquered, the vast development of Neapolitan perfidy checked in its course, eighty thousand men dispersed

by a few republican phalanxes, a new war begun and ended in seventeen days, a great example given to Europe—all this great news should be proclaimed by all true citizens. It would have been praiseworthy to anticipate my call upon your patriotism and to do yourselves the honor of proclaiming our national glory. Doubtless you will immediately correct the silence you are maintaining. . . .[5]

Despite this warning, the Favart refused to interrupt the run of the successful *Elisca,* and aside from reading a few verses in honor of the occasion, continued to maintain its "silence." The authorities had to content themselves with a number of patriotic pieces presented at such other houses as the Odéon and République on January 21, the sixth anniversary of the execution of Louis XVI. The Favart continued its quiet defiance of government wishes, with no unhappy consequences. When trouble came to the theatre, it came from another direction. On April 14, the Favart was the scene of as stormy an opening as any experienced during the Revolution, all the more striking since it came after several years of comparative calm. *Montano et Stéphanie,* with lyrics by Dejaure and music by Berton, was eventually accepted as one of the theatre's standard repertoire pieces, but bitter strife marked its opening. A police report of the following morning describes the occasion:

Last evening the public flocked to the opening of *Montano et Stéphanie,* a new lyric drama. Calm reigned throughout the first act, but the setting of the second—representing a church and showing a high altar with a cross, Christ, angels, lighted candles, and all the ornaments and accoutrements of the Catholic cult—aroused partisan feeling, and a disturbance grew all during the act.

Whistles were heard as soon as the curtain rose, but the partisans of the formerly privileged cult were apparently in the majority at the theatre and applause soon drowned out the whistles. Several satisfied cries were even heard: "The altars have come back!"

Several whistles followed the thunderous applause, and one of the spectators in the parquet arose and said in a moment of silence: "Let those who are displeased depart!" This suggestion raised a new storm of applause, which continued as a bishop arrived on stage and began a prayer to the "Almighty." Then, ascending the altar steps, he began to administer the sacrament of marriage, quite according to the Catholic rites. This service aroused fresh antagonism and new whistles mingled with applause as the atmosphere became more and more menacing. A lengthy demonstration followed the priest's line: "Respect this sanctuary and fear to bloody it!"[6]

After such an opening, the government justifiably feared a repetition of the *muscadin*-Jacobin riots of a few years before if the play were allowed to continue. The work was therefore banned until extensive revisions could be made, including the suppression of all religious decoration and a modification of the bishop's costume. Upon its return to the stage, however, the modified work enjoyed a long and tranquil run, belying its dubious distinction as the source of the last theatre riot of the Revolution.

The Cité-Variétés, outstanding in its production of Jacobin plays under the Terror and anti-Jacobin plays during the reaction, held to contemporary political themes longer than any of its rivals. It was thus the first to react, in December of 1797, to a change in the country's military strategy. After the Treaty of Campo Formio in October, the Directory could no longer hope for further conquests in the south, but Britain, the only one of France's old enemies which had not suffered from the treaty, remained a potential area for military expansion. Napoleon was named general of the Army of England, and an intensive campaign was launched by the government to stimulate public enthusiasm for a projected invasion. Large signs were posted in the theatres and other public places saying, "War to the Government of Great Britain." On January 5, 1798, another forced loan helped defray the expenses of the military preparations, and by February Napoleon was embarked on a tour of inspection along the British coast.

On December 24, before the general public was even aware of the possibility of war with England, the Cité presented Mittié's *La Descente en Angleterre*. The play chiefly concerns comparisons between the qualities of French and English soldiers, with the latter faring rather badly until an English commander, forced to surrender, blows out his brains. "He was worthy to be French," the opposing general grudgingly admits. This work, somewhat in advance of its time, did not prove particularly successful, and Mittié did better with *L'Anniversaire ou La Fête de la souveraineté*, showing the English defeated near Calais. Given over a month later, it capitalized on the public feeling which in the meantime had been aroused.

After Mittié's two plays, even the Cité turned from occasional pieces to favor another sort of presentation already dominating the programs of the Ambigu and Emulation—*pantomime dialoguée*, a form now very close to the earliest melodramas[7] and an important part of the repertoires of these three major boulevard houses. Before 1791, it will be remembered, minor houses were ordinarily required by law to present only various forms of truncated drama, often pantomimes. When the decree freed the actors in these houses to speak, they often merely added words to their actions, creating the *pantomimes dialoguées*, but as the competition among the theatres increased, action and spectacle grew. Fads in subject matter came and went rapidly; at first fairy plays were popular, then late in 1797, horror plays. Although the gothic movement in England was in full stride long before 1789 and both Horace Walpole's *The Castle of Otranto* and Clara Reeve's *The Old English Baron* had been translated into French, it was not until 1797 that the gothic made any real impression in France. Then within a few months translations of Ann Radcliffe's *Mysteries of Udolpho* and *The Italian* and Matthew Gregory Lewis' *The Monk* appeared and became the rage of Paris.[8] Naturally, horror soon entered the theatre. *Le Moine*, drawn from Lewis' book, was given at the Théâtre d'Emulation on December 27, 1797, and *Le Château d'Udolphe*, Duval's version of Radcliffe's tale, was offered at the Cité the following year. One of the fathers of the melodrama, Joseph-Marie Loaisel de Tréogate, was represented by *Roland de Montglare* at the Cité in January, 1799.[9] The *pantomimes dialoguées* needed only the dramatic craftsmanship of Loaisel de Tréogate and Pixérécourt to turn them from these spectacular horror plays to the comparatively sophisticated melodramas. In the meantime, the pantomimes at the Cité continued: *La Mort de Turennes, La Fille Hussard, La Tentation de Saint-Antoine, Les Incas, Le Mongol ou La Fête du Sérail.* Late in 1798 Brunet, Duval, and Tiercelin, who produced many of these strange dramas, left the Cité for the Variétés Montansier, and after their departure the former house rapidly declined.[10]

The Théâtre d'Emulation readopted its original title, Théâtre de la Gaîté, in 1797. There Nicolet's successor Ribié also presented spectacular pantomimes, like *L'Amazone de Grenade, La Fille sauvage, La Morte vivante*, and *La Tête de bronze.* Notable among these was one of Pixérécourt's first important plays, *Victor ou L'Enfant de la forêt*, given May 12, 1798. The success of such works plus the tremendous vogue of *Madame Angot* made Ribié a rich man, and he began to dream of a theatre in the very center of Paris.

He first approached Montansier, whose Variétés was now, according to the *Almanach des spectacles*, "the most frequented and flourishing theatre in Paris, thanks to the enchanting voice of Mlle. Carolin, the original talents of Brunet and Tiercelin, the zeal of the administrators, and the delightful plays given."[11] All the flower of the Directory continued to congregate in Montansier's famous foyer; her gallery of mirrors reflected crowds of dashing young hussars, wealthy courtesans, *merveilleuses* in classic garb and their admirers, even the Madame Angots and Cadet Roussels whose dramatic counterparts drew much laughter on Montansier's stage. Montansier indicated an interest in renting her theatre, so long as she was guaranteed a share of the profits, and Ribié even organized a committee of four to manage the venture before an even more grandiose scheme diverted his attention. He arranged with Mlle. Raucourt for rights to the Louvois, abandoned since the government closed it in September of 1797. An agreement was reached, and boulevard fare was permanently installed for the first time in a major Parisian theatre. *Madame Angot*, *Arlequin qui file*, and *Le Capucin qui se marie* were now produced in the same hall which had for a brief period of time sheltered one branch of the Comédie itself. Ribié, still not satisfied, added two expensive pleasure gardens to his holdings, the Elysée-Bourbon and the Tivoli. Under the weight of such investment, Ribié's empire collapsed, and early in 1799 he was forced to renounce his ambition and return to the simple but profitable business of managing the Gaîté alone.[12]

By 1798 Lazzari's Variétés Amusantes too was presenting spectacular dramas as well as its arlequinades, but one such drama brought disaster to the theatre. On May 13, Lazzari presented *Il Convitato di pietra*, an anonymous imitation of Molière's *Festin de pierre* which demanded the most elaborate settings: Naples, Marseilles, Castille, even Hell, where Don Juan was shown being tortured before he was engulfed by a rain of fire. After a presentation of this play on May 30, the director was retiring when he smelled smoke. He returned to find the whole stage in flames. All the patrons had long since left and the theatre's water supply was low. One of Lazzari's actors, a son of Ribié, rushed off on horseback to summon aid, but although the fire was bravely fought, it raged out of control all the next day. The theatre was totally destroyed and two neighboring cafés seriously damaged. Lazzari appealed to the government for permission to move his company to the old home of the Opéra near the Porte Saint-Martin, deserted since the national theatre had moved to the Rue de la Loi, but the authorities brusquely refused the request, apparently viewing the loss of one of the boulevard houses as an improvement. In his despair this most famous arlequin of the Revolution committed suicide.[13]

Audinot's old Ambigu-Comique experienced a much happier change of fortune during this spring. Corsse, who had won such success with Madame Angot, resigned from the Montansier to assume direction of the Ambigu. Once again Madame Angot revived an ailing theatre, and the Ambigu soon again rivaled the Gaîté for first place among boulevard houses. The new melodramas seemed perfectly suited to this gloomy old theatre with its heavy draperies, huge bas-reliefs, and dark gothic *décor*. For the next thirty years it enjoyed an almost unbroken prosperity by presenting the works of Pixérécourt and his followers.

The Vaudeville, so long a theatre of lighthearted but consistent opposition to the government, had since Napoleon's victories in the south seized every opportunity to laud the popular general. This zeal continued on into the Empire, and the Vaudeville enjoyed an unaccustomed period of official favor when Napolean came to power. In 1798 and 1799 the only rival vaudeville theatre was the former Molière, an unstable venture subject to frequent openings, closings, and changes of name and director. Most recently a dramatist named Joigny and redecorated and reopened Boursault-Malherbe's old theatre with the pretentious title Théâtre des Amis des Arts et des Elèves de l'Opéra. A dispute between singers and actors broke out, forcing Joigny to resign in 1799. He was followed by Piis and Léger, formerly of the Vaudeville, but though these more experienced directors managed to produce two new plays a week for several months, they were unable to bring prosperity to the venture.

Three other small theatres, all unsuccessful in a variety of genres and therefore subject to frequent closings, complete the roster. The Délassements-Comiques, moderately successful in 1796, and the Théâtre sans Prétention, never particularly successful, were both by 1799 slowly expiring in the hands of a series of unfortunate administrators. The Jeunes-Artistes never recovered from Martainville's challenge to the authorities. Its directors in 1799, Cantiran de Boirie and André Cailleau, managed to keep the theatre operating for several years more, but only by the most desperate determination, for they never produced a single successful play.[14]

The story of the Comédie, it will be remembered, we left in 1797—the group split into four companies, all unstable, and one, the

Louvois, actually lacking even a theatre. At the end of that year the Feydeau, under Sageret's direction, remained the undisputed leader of the theatres of Paris, still favored over its struggling rivals despite the weakness of Lemercier's *La Prude,* which opened on December 4 and lasted only four performances. On December 16, the roving Molé was

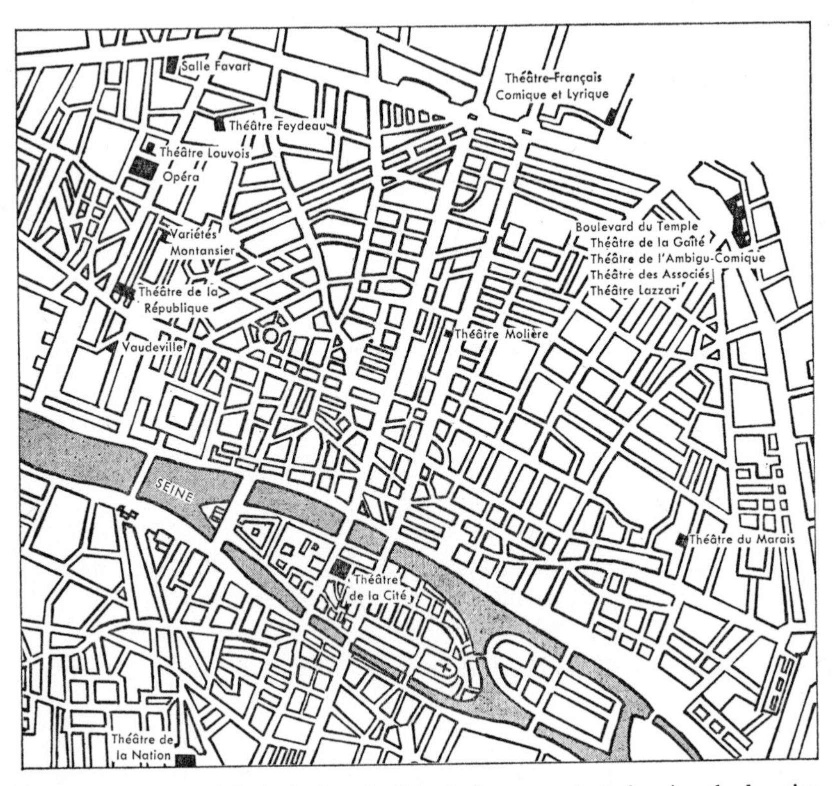

11. Map of central Paris during the Revolutionary period, showing the location of the principal theatres.

enthusiastically welcomed as Dorson in *Le Jaloux sans amour.* The République attempted to compete with this attraction by mounting *Les Modernes enrichis,* a new comedy by Pujoulx which condemned the speculators of the time in its ridiculous Truchant family. These Revolutionary *bourgeois gentilhommes,* come to vast fortune by the most dubious and dishonorable means, provided excellent comic situations. The son satirized all the affections of the *incroyables:* the ridiculous costume, the strange tastes (as for warm ice cream), and the affected language. The police, fearing that the theatrical public of the day would take offense at much of the play, demanded extensive revisions, including (for no apparent reason) a change of the title from *Les Nouveaux Parvenus.* The new version was so greatly changed as to be almost a new play, but it was received with enthusiasm and it postponed for a time the closing of the now almost totally deserted République.[15]

On January 9, 1798, the anti-British declarations of the government stimulated the République to mount Sauvigny's *Scipion l'africain,* which despite its southern setting consisted mainly of violent imprecations against France's neighbor across the Channel. The Parisian public was not yet generally convinced of the wisdom of launching another war, and Sauvigny's work would probably have failed had he not added an apologetic prologue, delivered by Dugazon, and dedicated the play to the popular hero Napoleon, whose virtues it extolled.[16] Thus protected, it gained a moderate following, even striking a certain prophetic note in its choice of setting, for when the general returned a month after from his inspection of the Channel, he suggested invading Egypt, a possibility never considered before that time. Sauvigny's work even established a sort of pattern, in that later anti-British dramas similarly pleased the authorities by vitriolic denunciation of the enemy while courting public approval by glorification of the new national hero. Thus, for example, in *Les Prisonniers français en Angleterre* at the Variétés, Jean François Dognon and Rebory showed Englishmen rising in revolt against their leaders upon hearing from captured Frenchmen that Napoleon was coming to deliver them.[17]

January found the majority of the dispossessed Louvois troupe still seeking a home. The République seemed the most likely place for them to turn, since that theatre desperately needed some stimulus. Financial problems were strangling the venture; audiences were scant; and the authorities were inflexible in their demands. The innocuous *Minuit* was closed on January 1 because one character in it wished another a happy new year and "it would be most improper," felt the police, "to reproduce on the stage a custom abolished by the republican calendar." *Alexis ou L'Erreur d'un bon père* suffered a similar fate shortly after because one of its characters gave away twenty-four louis, a name now banned in the theatre.[18] Caught between such official hostility and public indifference, the République could surely have profited by a coalition, but the feelings from old feuds were still too strong, and the Louvois actors had to try elsewhere.

The Feydeau had in recent months devoted itself entirely to comedy and opera and was simply not interested in harboring a troupe whose forte was serious drama, so an agreement was finally reached with Le Clerc at the undistinguished Odéon. That theatre was completely redecorated for the fourth time and reopened on January 18 showing *Phèdre,* which featured the majority of the Louvois company, most of them originally from the Nation. Although some of the public complained of the remoteness of the theatre and others still expressed suspicion of Mlle. Raucourt's royalist leanings, large numbers were attracted by the lure of the old names, and the Odéon entered a period of prosperity which lasted well into the summer. Mlle. Joly, prevented by a serious illness from ever appearing at the Louvois, rejoined her companions on January 22 in *Le Dissipateur.* The success of the new coalition completely ruined the République, and February 19 saw the closing of the house which had, for a brief period after the fall of the Nation, been the first theatre of France. Once again a major body of actors was left homeless.[19]

Despite the new prosperity of the Odéon, the Feydeau had now unquestionably replaced the République as the most popular and influential theatre in the capital. Its director was wise enough to specialize in sentimental comedies such as Jean-François Roger's *L'Epreuve délicate,* which pleased the public and yet avoided offending a sensitive government. The first failure of 1798, Marsollier's *Trop de délicatesse,* adapted from an English comedy, received one of the theatres' rare reproofs from the authorities. The report, dated March 9, is interesting in the shift it indicates in certain quarters of opinions about America:

> The play is set in America, but nothing indicates this very strongly, and moreover, we no longer consider the Anglo-Americans much different from the English. To allow the presentation of this play would be to sanction the portrayal of Englishmen on our stages, where they should never appear except as objects of ridicule.[20]

This small check was of little concern to the prosperous Sageret, who was attempting to capitalize on the downfall of the République by hiring its dispossessed actors for his own projects. The same pride and partisanship which prevented the merger of the Louvois and République troupes a few months before emerged again, but Sageret had resources the other theatres had lacked. By offering extremely high wages, the entrepreneur succeeded in overcoming the hesitation first of Grandménil, then of Michot and Baptiste the Elder, then of Monvel, Talma, and Mmes. Vestris and Petit-Vanhove. Last to be hired was Dugazon, whose past was still a liability at the moderate Feydeau. The months of April and May, therefore, saw a brilliant series of debuts at Sageret's theatre. First came Grandménil and Michot in *L'Avare* on April 1, then Baptiste in *Le Glorieux* on April 17. On May 3, Napoleon, his wife, and Barras attended the debut of Talma and Mme. Vestris in Ducis' *Macbeth*, on the eve of the general's departure for Egypt. Two days after, Mme. Petit-Vanhove appeared in *Andromache*, and Monvel followed on May 15 in *Britannicus*. Only Dugazon's debut, in *Les Fausses Confidences*, was unsuccessful. The public which had neither forgotten nor forgiven the actor's past reserved all their acclaim for Dazincourt, playing opposite Dugazon. The series of debuts was climaxed by a production combining the talents of the Feydeau and former République companies, and Laya's *Falkland* was chosen for this great occasion. Molé, Talma, Monvel, and Mlle. Mézeray filled the leading roles, and attracted overflowing houses.[21]

During this same spring, pressures mounted on the government for some sort of theatre reform. Chénier, as a representative of the nation's dramatists, submitted a report complaining of the steady decline in the quality of dramatic works produced since 1791 and requesting a serious abridgment or even a repeal of the decree of 1791 that he and others had then so heartily welcomed.[22] Ribié's experiment with boulevard entertainment in the Louvois added new fuel to the dispute which had flared up between the national and popular theatres sporadically all during the Revolution. Most ministers refused to tamper with the decree of 1791, however, fearing that a reversal of position now would cast doubt on both the justice and wisdom of the authorities. Still, the Minister François Lamarque pointed out that some of the troubles of the Directory might be alleviated if a curb were put on the theatres, many of which "encouraged the factions behind the successive uprisings."

In the face of this argument, the Council of the Five Hundred finally passed a resolution restricting the liberty of the theatres before it adjourned in April. The resolution placed all theatres officially under the supervision of the Directory and restricted their number to six; the Opéra, for tragedy and lyric drama; the Favart, for poetic comedy and vaudeville; the Odéon, for conventional comedy and tragedy; the République, to serve as a rival to the Odéon for those who insisted that competition was necessary for artistic excellence; and two new subsidiary theatres, for training young artists, one in tragedy and poetic plays, the other in drama and comedy. After its passage, the bill went to the upper legislative body, the Council of Ancients, but that body felt its restrictions too severe and on June 6 voted against it. The majority of Paris' theatres were thus granted a few more years of grace.[23]

Deprived of the strength this legislative blessing would have offered it, the Odéon declined steadily. Léger's *L'Homme sans façon ou Le Vieux Cousin,* given early in February of 1798, was the last success the theatre enjoyed. François Larnac's tragedy *Thémistocle,* presented March 1, was very coolly received, but the blow which doomed the theatre was the death on May 5 of Mlle. Joly, who had suffered for some time from an illness contracted during her imprisonment. The already weakened company could not support the loss of its most popular actress, and on June 1 it gave its final performance, a presentation of Voltaire's *Oedipe* for the benefit of the disillusioned Mlle. Raucourt.[24]

The closing of the Odéon suggested new opportunities for expansion to the insatiable Sageret at the Feydeau. He was now director of the only branch of the old Comédie left in Paris, and he could not resist this chance to reorganize that venerable body to further his own ends. His profits at the Feydeau gave him enough capital to rent the République, empty since its closing in February. A whole army of workmen labored day and night until September 5 when it reopened, a virtually new theatre. A great crowd filled even the aisles and the corridors to cheer the opening presentation of *Le Misanthrope;* the orchestra's opening selection of "What happier place than the bosom of one's family?" was heartily applauded and the acting won high praise. The theatre itself was less appreciated. Jean Moreau, the architect, had positioned enormous pillars so as to deprive most of the balconies of views of the stage. It is difficult to imagine why even Sageret, who was often enough mistaken in artistic matters, should have selected Moreau to redecorate the République. The architect even before this commission had made himself notorious by placing a huge column in the middle of one of Paris' favorite views. It was popularly said that Moreau designed for the blind.[25]

Such minor irritations Sargeret passed over in proceeding to his greater plans. At the Feydeau, he had been forced into the expensive practice of alternating opera with comedy and tragedy. The opening of another theatre allowed him to separate the genres. Yet even this did not satisfy the ambitious director, for no sooner was the remodeling of the République under way than he approached Le Clerc and Le Page with a proposal to rent the Odéon as well. He obtained a three-year lease on this theatre and on September 16 installed an opera troupe at the Odéon, leaving comedy and tragedy actors at the République. This left the Feydeau vacant in its turn, and Sageret this time commissioned a committee of architects to plan its redecoration. On October 22, rechristened the Théâtre-Lyrique de la Rue Feydeau, it was ready for the public, and Sageret's grand plan went into operation. The Feydeau was reserved exclusively for musical productions, the République for dramatic offerings, while the Odéon was to repeat the most popular offerings from both of the other theatres interspersed with other activities. The programs at this third theatre were set up according to the *décade*. On odd days, national festivals, civic banquets, and distributions of Conservatory prizes were held in the theatre. On even days, student matinées were given, and in the evenings the Feydeau and République companies alternated contributions, so that on *duodi* the Feydeau would send a comic opera, on *quartidi*, the République would send a comedy, on *sextidi* the Odéon orchestra gave concerts, on *octidi* the Feydeau company reappeared, and on *décadi*, the République sent a tragedy.[26]

It is typical of the times that the first new play mounted at the reopened République was banned by the censor. Arnault's *Blanche de Montcassin* opened with lines condemning the abuse of power; the author willingly suppressed them at the request of the authorities, but even with this and other corrections, the play was considered too controversial by many ministers. Only the personal support of Jean-Baptiste Treilhard, a member of the Directory, at last brought the play to the stage.[27]

Blanche de Montcassin was by no means an isolated case. During the fall and winter of 1798, censorship became more rigorous than it had been at any time since the Terror. The authorities apparently wanted to run no risk of a return to the theatre riots of a few years before, and scrupulously banned any references which might give rise to partisan feeling. One decree purged from the stage "persons in the trappings of aristocracy"; another forbade "the revival of all heraldic art in any works which recall the feudal regime." Attendants in theatres were forbidden to address patrons as "monsieur," an appellation also banned on the stage, although for the play *Amélie* the authorities proposed a slight compromise in this ruling: "No addresses of 'monsieur' will be allowed unless they refer to foreigners, valets, or ridiculous or odious characters, or unless the scene is set in Madrid or elsewhere and France is not mentioned." Thus Marsollier was able to avoid official condemnation of his opera *Adolphe et Clara* and still use the old titles by placing the action in Berlin.

Many of the official pronouncements on the theatre of this period recall those of the Terror. The words *château* and *seigneur* were suppressed in *Le Pari.* Hoffman was forced to change the name of the lover Louis in his play *Léon* when an official statement informed him, "This name cannot be used in our theatres, especially for a virtuous person." Extensive revision was required in *Mathilde* because "the principal characters are barons and counts—titles which offend republican ears."

Religious references were similarly purged. *Zaïre* was banned from the stage on October 25 because of the "religious principles embraced by the play." A police report on *Les Vénitiens* noted, "Reprehensible situations are found here; a Roman priest is called to conduct a marriage in a Catholic chapel decorated with an altar and all the customary ornaments. . . . This scene is intolerable. It can only scandalize true republicans and encourage a spirit of fanaticism and opposition to the new marriage ceremonies." The play was allowed to continue, but the chapel, cross, and priest disappeared from it.

The Directory censor proved even more difficult to please than had been his predecessor under the Terror, for plays were now condemned on the grounds of bad taste alone, aside from political or even moral considerations. *Le Combat de taureaux,* for example, was banned on September 22 as "a cruel play which could serve only to dull sensitivity, the mother of all republican virtues."[28] The far-ranging demands of the censor brought almost every theatre under government discipline. Since the beginning of the Revolution at least certain of the large and small houses had regularly worked hand in hand with the dominant political party, but under the Directory, amity of this sort did not exist.

The government's single venture into state-supported drama, at the Odéon, had added little to official enthusiasm for the art of the theatre, and by autumn of 1798 the administration's opinion of the theatre seemed to be that it was a necessary evil, to be held severely in check and discouraged whenever possible. In November, Sageret found himself in financial difficulties and appealed to the Council of the Five Hundred and the Council of the Ancients for support. He was certain that each member would gladly contribute two hundred francs to maintain the national theatre. The ministers, however, haughtily refused.

Sageret was stunned to discover that his efforts meant no more in official circles than those of Lazzari, who had been similarly rebuffed six months before. Panic seized him. The huge empire he had built was sinking under its own weight, and without official subsidy he had no way to increase his income. He therefore proposed a cut in the salaries of most of his leading actors. Molé was dropped from 24,000 livres annually to 18,000, Dazincourt from 19,000 to 12,000, Petit-Vanhove from 15,000 to 10,000, Louise Contat from 30,000 to 18,000, Raucourt from 24,000 to 18,000, and so on.

The actors were furious, and with good reason, for Sageret had unmercifully exploited them since the inaguration of his tripartite theatre. Actors were forced to change theatres daily and sometimes even between matinees and evening performances. Hardly was one show finished on such days when the actors were bundled into carriages and rushed across the Pont Neuf for the next production. This frantic shifting about left positions open for new actors, whom Sageret had hired at high rates only to leave them idle when the older artists insisted upon their rights to perform.[29] All this was ruinously expensive, and the actors were almost certainly mistaken when they accused their director of using his profits for his own pleasures—covering a famous courtesan with jewels, buying three homes in his wife's name, a farm in his father's, and so on.[30] Sageret appealed to the government, and the ministers, although unwilling themselves to support his venture, were quite willing to impose such support on others. A quarter drop in wages was decreed for the entire company, even for Talma and Mlle. Mars, who had been previously spared.

It was a Pyrrhic victory for Sageret. Talma and Mme. Petit-Vanhove abruptly left the company to play in Bordeaux. Others followed. The harried director was forced to give up the Odéon, which after a few days' closure was reopened by deserters from his company—Dupont, Saint-Fal, Saint-Prix and others. A series of resounding failures at the République completed Sageret's ruin. *Michel Montaigne*, a comedy given November 12, featured Molé in the lead, but the ancient actor could no longer remember his lines and was hissed throughout.[31] Sageret then staked almost everything he had left on a lavish production of *Ophis*, an Egyptian tragedy by Lemercier. It opened December 22 and failed totally. Sageret, a gambler to the last, plunged deeply into debt with two further productions, hoping to recoup some of his losses. He revived *Charles IX* and recalled Mlle. Bellecour from retirement to play Nicole in *Le Bourgeois Gentilhomme*. Chénier's tragedy, however, had lost its power to attract audiences, and Mlle. Bellecour, although she drew a large crowd to her opening performance, showed beyond doubt that her talent had fled with her youth. On January 24, 1799, the République closed and Sageret's amazing empire ended. Shortly after, the government initiated proceedings against the bankrupt director on charges of fraud.[32]

At the Odéon, a series of mediocre tragedies and one moderately successful comedy, *Le Voyage interrompu*, by Picard, gained little distinction for the deserters from Sageret's administration, but in December, 1798, a new play by Mlle. Molé brought all Paris to the theatre. The play was *Misanthropie et repentir*, based on *Misanthropy and Repentance* by the contemporary German dramatist Kotzebue. German translations had been appearing on the French stage for some years, but until this success they remained merely a novelty for jaded audiences or a stimulus for unimaginative playwrights. Now German plays opened everywhere, as a host of imitations of Kotzebue's work entered the theatres. The vogue of *Misanthropie et repentir* was thus a powerful influence in the coming of the "German movement" which was to stimulate so much of French and English Romanticism. In the theatre, its heavy sentimentality and its appeal to bourgeois values helped mold the *bourgeois tragédie larmoyante*, the domestic melodrama, and later the domestic drama of the following century. The misanthrope of the piece is the Baron de Mello, who withdraws from the haunts of men when his young wife Eulalie is seduced by one of his friends. Both the Baron and his sorrowing wife seek refuge with a Count de Walker; after many painful scenes of recollection and one agonizing encounter, they are reunited by their love for their children. The words of a contemporary critic give some idea of the impression made by this simple story:

> There is perhaps not a man or a woman in Paris who has not gone to admire this masterpiece. Women have fainted, men have wept in agony when seeing this serious treatment of adultery, taken until now as a mere

bagatelle. Many marriages have been dissolved, many engagements broken off when husbands or suitors showed too great a sympathy for the accused or when wives or fiancées showed a cold heart by laughing or smiling during this play.[33]

The success of *Misanthropie et repentir* sustained the Odéon for two full months; the next new work, Laya's *Une Journée du jeune Néron*, was not offered until February 16, 1799. Despite the talents of Dupont, Saint-Fal, Saint-Prix, and Grandménil, this mediocre comedy did not prove attractive. On the day following this failure, the government revoked the thirty-year concession given to Dorfeuille, and officially removed him and his associates or lessees from the Odéon. The Directory itself took over the theatre, allowing the actors to remain until the inevitable reorganization was completed. A committee composed of Dorfeuille, Le Page, Le Clerc, and three governmental representatives was appointed to inventory the theatre's goods and examine its books to determine how much the enterprise owed the Republic. The governmental representatives drew up a balance sheet showing a deficit of 150,000 francs, so disastrous a reckoning that Le Page refused to sign the report, stating that he "would rather set fire to the theatre than agree to its destruction in this way."[34]

That very night, March 18, the Odéon presented *L'Envieux*, a comedy by Dorvo. The play was not the spectacular success it had been when first performed in Nantes, but the public was pleased and the future encouraging. Then, late that evening when the audience had departed, a terrible fire broke out in the theatre. Two soldiers and several firemen lost their lives in a holocaust which by morning had reduced the Odéon to a heap of cinders, with virtually nothing preserved but Grandménil's costumes. The cause of the fire was never determined, but since there was not nearly enough combustible material in the building to cause such a catastrophe, arson was suspected and two persons arrested: Le Page, apparently on the evidence of his injudicious and highly ill-timed remark, and Sageret, whose speculations were now closed to investigation by the destruction of the Odéon records. Sageret was soon released, but Le Page remained in prison for two months, even though no evidence except his own words could be discovered against him. Since Sageret's best actors had long since left his Feydeau, a theatre now barely able to hold its own against the popular Favart, Paris suddenly discovered that within a few months its three Comédies had dropped to none.

The homeless Odéon company first sought refuge at the Louvois, where Ribié's financial burdens brought him willingly to agree to sponsor a series of Odéon revivals. By the end of March, the government became interested in the plight of the only remaining branch of the national theatre, and an official decree was passed opening the Opéra to the Odéon troupe on nonperformance days. This could, of course, be only a temporary measure, and the dramatist Neufchâteau, now minister of the interior, began laying plans for a definite settlement of the continuing theatre crisis.[35]

Rumors that Neufchâteau was planning to restore the Comédie predictably stirred up afresh all the old controversies. The dramatists again demanded a second state theatre to protect their interests before the Minister had even set up a first, arguing that the struggle for freedom in the theatre would have been in vain if a single national house like that of pre-Revolutionary days were the ultimate result. A petition to this effect was organized by Beaumarchais and signed by Laya, Colin d'Harleville, Ducis, Legouvé, Arnault, Demoustier, Picard, and others—all the leading playwrights of the day. This petition was Beaumarchais' last contribution to his art, for he died on May 11, 1799, just after its completion.[36]

Beaumarchais' death weakened the opposition, and the petition failed. As Neufchâteau and his assistant Mahérut made arrangements to refurbish the République as a home for the reunited Comédie, Dazincourt invited all the scattered members of the company to his home for a festive dinner to celebrate the end of their rivalry. After the dinner, Michot arose to speak, saying that he wished to deliver a small apologue:

> In a certain assembly, some persons affected to be embarrassed in solving the very simple arithmetical problem, how many are six and six? They appealed for information to a deputy on the left side, who quickly replied: "Six and six are twelve."
>
> "Those who hear a bell hear nothing but a sound," remarked one of the members of the assembly, a profound thinker. "Let us ask a deputy on the right side." Accordingly the question was proposed to another honorable member, who after some minutes of profound reflection, gravely said: "Six and six make fourteen." The enquirers felt not a little embarrassed by these conflicting statements. They resolved to refer the question to some one more expert at calculation. They looked around, and fixing upon a member in the middle of the assembly, they asked him the question. "How many do six and six make?" repeated he; "that is a rather difficult

problem. What said the gentleman on the left side?" "Twelve." "And what was the answer of the member on the right?" "Fourteen." "Well then," said he, "I will be impartial—you shall hear the truth—six and six make thirteen."

Now, it appears to me that this is the history of our past opinions—the history of our errors and mistakes, of our friendships and antipathies. The fact is, ladies and gentlemen, that six and six make twelve, in spite of any differences of opinion that may exist on the subject. Let us unite in friendly concord; for that is the way to promote the interests of the French drama. I again repeat that six and six make twelve, and let those who are of that opinion hold up their hands.[37]

Nearly every hand was raised, and Michot was cheered by all. Talma delivered a poem on the New Jerusalem, and Fleury rushed to embrace Dazincourt's bust of Molière. The evening ended with the entire company joining hands around the revered image to swear an oath of unity.[38]

Within a few weeks the administrative details were settled and the new theatre opened on May 31 with *Le Cid*, given by Talma, Vanhove, and Mme. Petit-Vanhove, and *L'Ecole des maris*, with Grandménil, Dugazon, Mlles. Mars, Mézeray, and Devienne. All of the surviving actors from the original Comédie were reunited, their dates of reception stretching back almost forty years: Molé, Monvel, Dugazon, Dazincourt, Fleury, Vanhove, Florence, Saint-Prix, Saint-Fal, Naudet, Larochelle, Talma, Grandménil, and Mmes. La Chassaigne, Raucourt, Suin, Thénard, Devienne, Louise and Emilie Contat, Petit-Vanhove, Vestris, Fleury, and Mézeray.

The troupe was supplemented by a number of artists from the République: Alexandre Duval, Michot, Baptiste the Elder, Baptiste the Younger, and Damas. From the Feydeau came Caumont, and from the Montansier the young Mlle. Mars. Benoît-Roussel Armand, Pierre Lafon, Bourgoin, and Volnais, four artists who had made their fame in the provinces, completed the company.[39] It was one of the most brilliant assemblies of actors the capital had ever seen, but what sufferings lay behind their premiere in May of 1799! Torn asunder by the same forces which divided their nation, persecuted under the Terror, and buffeted by the opportunistic cross-currents of the Directory, the Comédiens had lived out in their microcosm the experience of all France in these turbulent years. Now re-established and placed once more in their position of theatrical pre-eminence, they seemed almost ready to resume a course interrupted abruptly ten years before.

EPILOGUE

The End of Liberty

THE summer of 1799 ended with France close to anarchy, as internal uprisings and external threats of invasion steadily weakened the crumbling central authority. Napoleon, now in Egypt, sensed the nation's desperate desire for a strong leader, and late in August he responded to this desire. After a perilous crossing of the Mediterranean, he landed at Fréjus on October 8, then marched in triumph to Paris. On October 16, the evening of his arrival in the capital, all theatres enthusiastically announced the coming of the man already widely regarded as the future savior of France. The enormous popularity of the military leader caused many politicians to fear that Napoleon would immediately make a bid for power, but the general assured the Directors, "My sword will never be drawn except in defense of the Republic and its government." He then shut himself up in his home, seemingly deaf to the acclaim which surrounded him.

The theatres echoed popular sentiment with such offerings as *Le Retour à l'espérance ou L'Arrivée du général Bonaparte*, given at the Troubadours, as the Molière was now called, on October 20, and *Le Héros de retour d'Egypte*, given the next week at the Gaîté. Napoleon himself avoided such demonstrations; when he attended the theatre, he favored the politically neutral larger houses, on occasion leaving even them if he were noticed and acclamation seemed forthcoming. This reserve, however, was of brief duration. Scarcely a month after his return, Napoleon decided that the moment to strike had arrived. Relying on his popular support and the indecision of the Directory, he forced the governing bodies to adjourn to Saint-Cloud and there dissolved them on November 9 (18 Brumaire, an VIII). The executive power of the government passed into the hands of three administrators called, according to the classic taste of the time, Consuls: Napoleon, Emmanuel Joseph Sieyès, and Pierre Roger Ducos.

This open military coup won far more praise than censure in a nation seeking any sort of security after ten years of political upheaval. The boulevard theatres hastened to capitalize on public feeling, presenting celebrations of the 18 Brumaire within three days after the event. The first of these was Saint-Victor's *Le Premier Rayon de soleil* at the Jeunes-Artistes, a thinly disguised allegory showing a beloved general, believed dead, emerging from his tomb to confound his enemies. Other works shortly followed: Charles Augustus Sewrin's *Les Mariniers de Saint-Cloud* at the Opéra-Comique; *La Girouette de Saint-Cloud* at the Vaudeville; Léger, Réné de Chazet, and Gouffé's *La Journée de Saint-Cloud* at the Troubadours; and an anonymous *Journée de Saint-Cloud* at the Ambigu.

All of these pieces were much the same, all hastily conceived and staged. *La Girouette de Saint-Cloud* was written, learned, and performed in less than twenty-four hours. All such pieces, too, were characterized by fulsome praise of Napoleon. Typical of the sentiments expressed is the stanza:

> A flight to Egypt in the past
> Preserved the savior of mankind
> Although today some spiteful mind
> May doubt upon the story cast.
> But whether that is true or not
> One fact is quite beyond debate—
> That a return from Egypt brought
> A savior to preserve our state.[1]

Finally, almost all of these dramas indulged in the customary deprecation of the vanquished parties, and the Directors now joined the Jacobins and royalists in the gallery of theatrical villains. The new regime, however, indicated almost immediately that it did not share the inclinations of its predecessors in such matters. *Les Mariniers de Saint-Cloud* was banned after two extremely successful presentations, and Joseph Fouché, the Minister of Police, made it clear to the directors of the theatre that the work was banned for its partisan sentiment, even though this was manifested in favor of the new government.

"Your intention is doubtless praiseworthy," he wrote, "but too many details recall bitterly old memories, which are best forgotten." He closed by suggesting, "Your patriotism leads me to expect that you will give up your play without my requesting it, since public tranquillity demands it." This, of course, was done at once.[2]

A general directive went out to all theatres on November 17, repeating the warning already given to the Opéra-Comique:

> In the succession of parties which have in turn come to power, the theatre has usually resounded with unnecessary insults for the vanquished and idle flattery for the victor. The present government scorns and disdains the support of factions; it desires nothing from them, and is concerned only with the Republic. Let all Frenchmen rally to the same concern, and all theatres promulgate it. Let feelings of harmony, maxims of moderation and wisdom, the expression of noble and generous sentiments alone be presented on our stages. Let nothing of that which divides spirits, encourages hatred, prolongs unhappy memories, be tolerated there. It is time at last that only Frenchmen dwell in the French nation.

A ruling from the Bureau of Manners in December further stipulated that no theatre post any play "the title of which seems to refer to the events of Brumaire or the laws resulting from them, even if the play is unrelated to these matters."[3] In the face of such strong directives, Napoleon's assumption of the title of First Consul in mid-December went officially unnoticed by the theatres. This moratorium on political drama lasted until the summer of 1800, when the Cité, the Troubadours, the Vaudeville, the Gaîté, and the Ambigu joined in the general celebration of the battle of Marengo, which ended Napoleon's second Italian campaign and won Italy for France. The theatres apparently assumed that celebrations of victory and praises of peace would not arouse charges of partisan sentiment from the authorities, and they were right. In this way, eulogies of Napoleon could be staged without arousing official condemnation.

In 1800 the First Consul became interested in the fortunes of the national theatres, and before he left in June for Italy, Napoleon received a delegation from the recently merged Comédie. He listened sympathetically to their plans and fears for the future, and expressed surprise at the unanimity in the new organization. "How," he asked, "have you been able to reconcile so many interests and such diverse spirits?" "Like you," Dazincourt responded, "we have pleased the querulous, forgiven the weak, and redoubled our efforts."[4] Napoleon was pleased and promised to consider the future of the company. On his return, he invited representatives from the Comédie to attend the laying of the first stone of the Vendôme column, an honor accorded no other theatre.

On August 11, the Comédie was officially placed under the protection of the government and guaranteed a theatre. The following month the First Consul and his wife attended *Le Cid* at this theatre, a special performance given in celebration of the proclamation of the Republic, and were warmly applauded by actors and audience alike.

Napoleon seems early in his regime to have conceived the idea of restoring a theatre system quite similar to that of pre-Revolutionary Paris. Thus, while he encouraged and supported the Comédie, he did not neglect the other former national theatres. In September of 1801 the Feydeau reunited with the declining Favart, and a month later Jean-Antoine Chaptal, the Minister of the Interior, granted the combined venture a government subsidy, took it officially under the protection of the Consulate, and rechristened it the Théâtre National de l'Opéra-Comique. The First Consul gave the national theatres the further unofficial support of his presence, especially favoring the Comédie, which he visited eight times in 1801 to view such works as Voltaire's *Nanine*, *L'Orphelin de Chine*, *Oedipe*, and *La Mort de César*, d'Harleville's *Vieux Célibataire*, and Legouvé's *La Mort d'Abel*. The only other theatres so honored were the Opéra, on three occasions, and the newly formed Opéra-Comique, on two. The minor theatres, despite their flattery of the new regime, were ignored.

Official attempts were next made to restore the tradition of the old Comédie Italienne with new artists from Italy. A subsidy was given to Montansier to install such a troupe in the Cirque Olympique in 1801, but Montansier's ability to turn the most extravagant schemes into financial successes had vanished, and before the end of the year this venture was threatened with bankruptcy. The directress convinced the government that her remote location was the reason for her lack of popular support, and she was granted a further subsidy to allow her to rent the recently vacated Favart. Here her theatre, called the Opéra-Buffa, moved in January, 1802.

Napoleon was now approaching the peak of his popularity. Peace had been concluded with France's enemies in terms highly favorable to the Republic. Internal disputes had been quelled; the government and the economy had been stabilized. No honor seemed too great for a man strong enough to accomplish so much in so little time. With an almost total unanimity, the electorate showed its gratitude in August, 1802, by making Napoleon Consul for life and according him the privilege of choosing his successor. Monarchy was only a step away. Since his assumption of power, Napoleon had continued the public celebrations of July 14 and September 22, to which many theatres contributed free performances for the public. On August 14, 1802, a new yearly holiday was added to these, indicating the direction the Republic was taking. This was Napoleon's birthday, and the Comédie, the Opéra-Comique, the Louvois, the Vaudeville, and the Ambigu staged special programs for the occasion. A week later the Comédie, which a month before had been granted a permanent government subsidy, expressed its gratitude by setting aside a permanent seat for the First Consul at the theatre.

Napoleon next turned his attention to the Opéra, hearkening to a request for aid from that theatre which late in 1801 had informed him, "The arts live only in peace, and all Europe regards you as its peacemaker. You have upheld the arts during war; you can help them to prosper and flourish during peace. The arts will not be ungrateful; they immortalize their benefactors." On the threshold of an empire, Napoleon was impressed by such promises. The Comédie had been launched, and a few years more would see it fully reorganized by its powerful overseer. A decree of November 27, 1802, brought the Opéra also under the protection of the Consuls, and a further ruling of January 10, 1803, accorded it, too, a permanent subsidy.

On April 5, 1803, Napoleon joined a great number of Parisian citizens in paying homage to Labussière, who had preserved so many of the city's best actors during the Terror. The Comédiens honored their savior, who was now living in great poverty, with benefit performances of Ducis' *Hamlet,* played by Talma, and *Théodore ou Les Deux Pages.* The profits from the performances totaled over 14,000 francs, to which Josephine added an extra contribution from the First Consul. It was a handsome and fitting gift to the savior of the Comédie, but Labussière did not long enjoy it. Whatever his virtues may have been, economy was not among them. The proceeds of the benefit were soon thrown away, and Labussière died in great want a few years later.

All during 1803 Napoleon continued to work on his reorganization of the theatre despite the tremendous responsibilities put upon him by the breaking of the Treaty of Amiens and the resultant threat of imminent war with England. Late in the year a decree from the Palais de Saint-Cloud set up a tentative constitution for the Comédie, and by April of the following year the Comédiens had reorganized their society along the lines proposed. This decree, with future additions, formed the basis of the Moscow Decree of 1812, which became the definitive constitution of the society.

In the spring of 1804 totalitarianism was re-established, under a new title, when Napoleon was elected hereditary emperor. The Comédie, with the new name the Théâtre de l'Empereur, became associated with a subsidiary, the Théâtre de l'Imperatrice, established in the reopened Odéon. Another important merger encouraged by the government joined the Odéon company, now playing at the Louvois under the direction of Picard, and those of Montansier's actors not involved in the Italian venture, to form a new Opéra-Comique.

The preoccupations of his military campaigns prevented Napoleon from considering the nation's theatres during the remainder of 1804 and 1805, but a series of decrees in the two following years nearly completed the theatrical reorganization which he had begun during the Consulate. The first of these, enacted in June, 1806, required that no new theatres be established without special permission, that all plays be submitted to a censor, that the repertoires of the Opéra, Comédie, and Opéra-Comique be reserved for those theatres alone and that the Minister of the Interior should prescribe the genres to be permitted at all other houses.

Jean-Baptiste Champagny, the official who held this office, issued a ruling April 25, 1807, which put this recommendation into more specific form. The first four articles, establishing the repertoires, were the most significant:

Art. I. The following are to be considered major theatres:

1. The Théâtre-Français (Théâtre de S.M. l'Empereur). This theatre is to be particularly dedicated to tragedy and comedy. Its repertoire shall be composed of: (a) All plays (tragedies, comedies, and dramas) played at the old theatre of the Hôtel de Bourgogne, at that which Molière directed, and at that which was formed by the reunion of the two organizations and which has existed under various names until the present. (b) Comedies played in the theatre called the Italienne up until the founding of the Opéra-Comique.

The Théâtre de l'Imperatrice. This will be considered as an annex of the

Théâtre-Français, for comedy alone. Its repertoire will contain: (a) Comedies written especially for this theatre. (b) Comedies given in the theatre called the Italienne up until the founding of the Opéra-Comique. These may also be presented at the Théâtre-Français.

Art. II.

2. The Théâtre de l'Opéra (Académie Imperiale de Musique). This theatre is especially dedicated to music and dance; its repertoire is composed of all works, opera and ballet alike, which have appeared since its founding in 1646. It can only present works which are entirely in music and ballets of elevated style, i.e., those whose subject matter is derived from mythology and from history, the heroes being gods, kings, or heroes. It may also give ballets representing rustic or ordinary life, but so may other theatres.

3. The Théâtre de l'Opéra-Comique. This theatre is particularly dedicated to the presentation of any kind of comedy or drama which has mixed verse, arias, and choruses. Its repertoire shall be composed of all plays given at the Opéra-Comique before and after its union with the Comédie Italienne, provided only that the dialogue of these plays is interrupted by song.

Art. III. To be considered as secondary theatres:

1. The Théâtre du Vaudeville. Its repertoire may contain only short plays with songs set to common tunes, or parodies.

2. The Théâtre des Variétés, Boulevard Montmartre. Its repertoire shall be composed of short plays in the *grivois, poissard,* or *villageois* genres, sometimes also containing songs set to popular tunes.

3. The Théâtre de la Porte-Saint-Martin. It shall be particularly committed to the genre called melodrama, to plays with great spectacle. As in all the secondary theatres, only scraps of song, to popular tunes, may be heard here.

4. The Théâtre de la Gaîté. It shall be devoted to pantomimes of all types, without ballets; to arlequinades and other farces in the manner of those formerly given by Nicolet in this theatre.

5. The Théâtre des Variétés-Etrangères. The repertoire of this theatre may contain only plays translated from foreign stages.

Art. IV. Other theatres presently existing in Paris and authorized by the police are considered to be annexes or doubles of these secondary theatres. Each of their directors must choose among the genres offered to the secondary theatres the one which best suits his own.[5]

With the national houses subsidized, encouraged, and protected, and the lesser theatres heavily restricted in types of drama permitted, only the disappearance of most of these minor theatres was needed to restore a theatrical situation almost identical to that of 1789. Napoleon had never favored the smaller houses, viewing them as demoralizing influences on public spirit, and he eagerly embraced the advice of his counselors to take this final step. On July 29, 1807, a decree came from the Palais de Saint-Cloud which stated:

> The *maximum* number of theatres in Paris is set at eight; therefore, the only ones allowed to remain open, to announce and present plays, outside of the four major theatres mentioned in the first and second articles of the ruling of our Minister of the Interior of April 25, are the following:
>
> 1. The Théâtre de la Gaîté, established in 1760, and the Ambigu-Comique, established in 1772 in the Boulevard du Temple, which will both give plays of the same type, designated in the ruling of the Minister of the Interior, Art. 3, paragraphs 3 and 4.
>
> 2. The Théâtre des Variétés, established in 1777, and the Vaudeville, established in 1792, which will both give plays of the same type, designated in the ruling of the Minister of the Interior, Art. 3, paragraphs 1 and 2. All theatres not authorized in the preceding article are to be closed before August 15.[6]

It has been estimated that up to twenty-five theatres were closed by this decree, but actually the ravages of the preceding years had left Paris with only nine regularly operating houses in addition to the eight now officially recognized. These were the Porte-Saint-Martin, the Troubadours, the Variétés Etrangères, the Jeunes-Artistes, the Marais, the Cité, the Jeunes-Elèves, the Jeunes-Comédiens, and the Sans-Prétention. Even so, the measure was a harsh and abrupt one, and a sizable percentage of Paris' theatre artists had to seek some other means of livelihood.

So at last ended the capital's debilitating surplus of theatres by the restoration of the very checks and controls cast off so eagerly almost twenty years before. Out of the agonies of those twenty years emerged stronger and better organized national theatres, one significant new boulevard house, several new genres the importance of which was as yet little realized, and major innovations in acting, costume, and theatre architecture. Yet for all that, not a few Parisians felt that in the theatre a circle had come round, and if the famous sleeper Epiménide were to awaken once again amid the theatre world of 1807, he might be forgiven for at first assuming that the *ancien régime* had come again.

Chart of Major Theatres of the Revolution

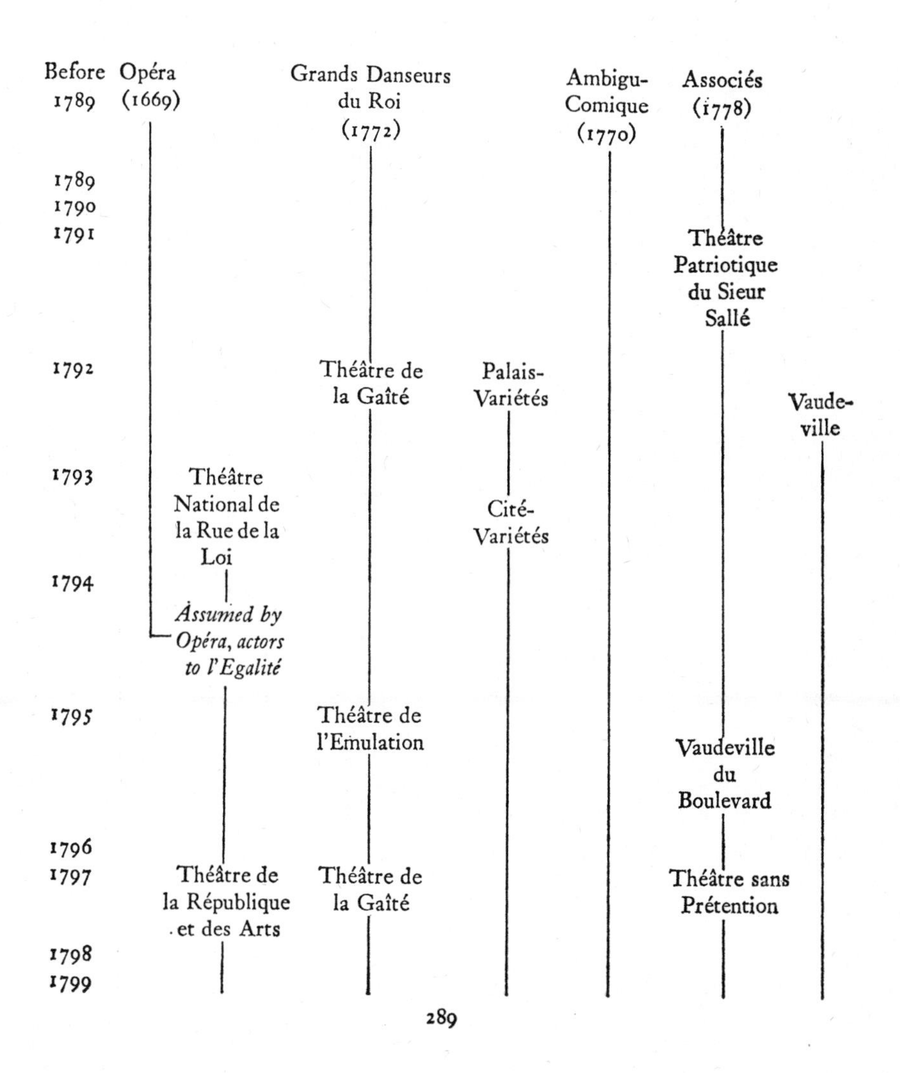

Before 1789	Comédie Française (1680)	Variétés-Palais-Royal (1785)			Comédie Italienne (1762)
1789	Théâtre de la Nation		Théâtre de Monsieur		
1790		Théâtre du Palais-Royal			Salle Favart
1791	*Talma —and others— move*	Théâtre-Français Rue de Richelieu	Théâtre Feydeau	Louvois	
1792		Théâtre-Français de la Liberté et de l'Egalité			
1793	CLOSED *Actors arrested*	Théâtre de la République			Opéra-Comique National
1794	Théâtre de l'Egalité			Théâtre des Amis de la Patrie	Théâtre Favart
1795	CLOSED *Actors to Feydeau*		*(Sageret's direction)*		
1796				Louvois *(Raucourt's direction)*	
1797	Odéon			CLOSED *Actors to Odéon*	
1798	*Louvois actors added* CLOSED *Reopened by Sageret*	CLOSED *Actors to Feydeau* *Reopened by Sageret*		*Reopened by Ribié*	
1799	CLOSED *Reopened by deserters from Sageret* *Theatre burns*	CLOSED *Reopened as* Théâtre-Français			

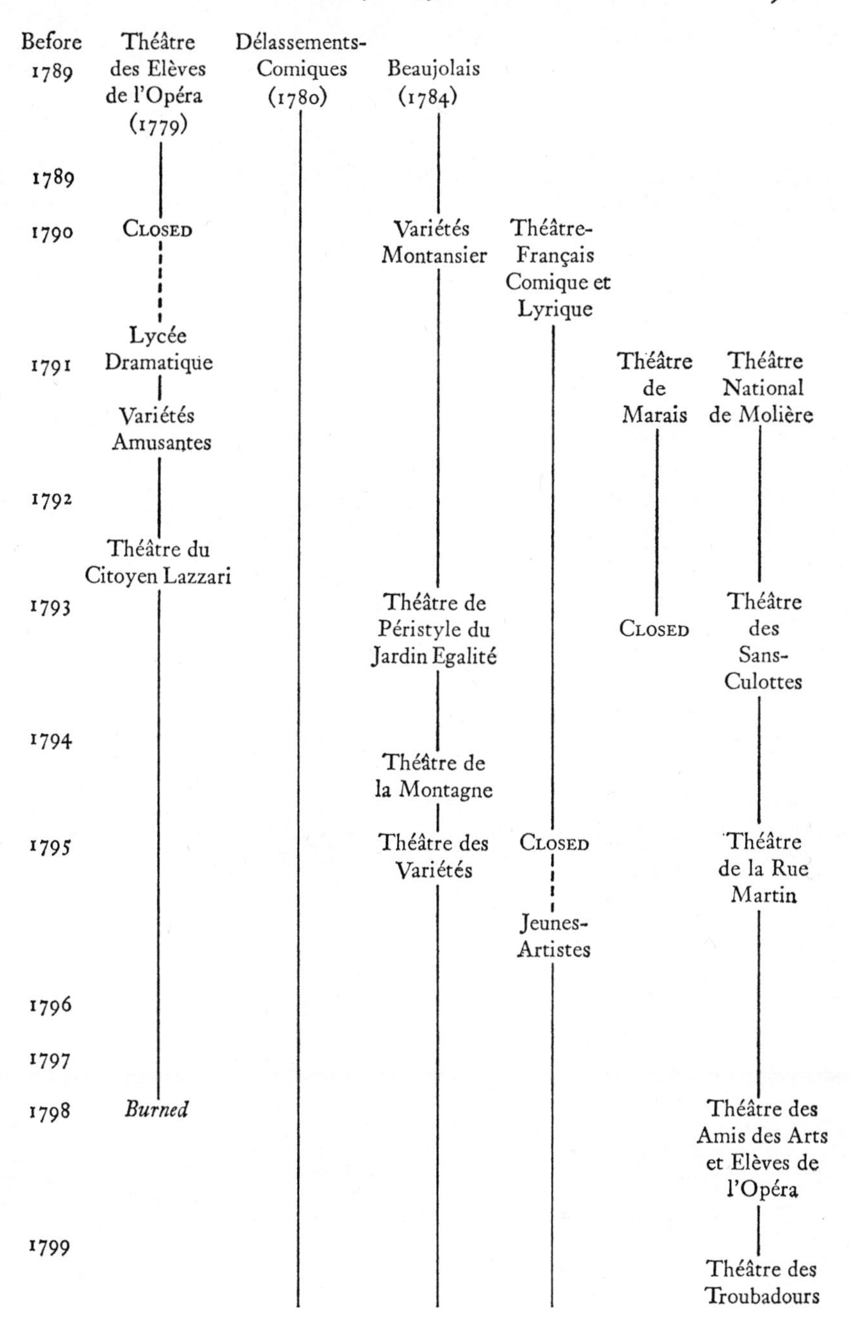
Before 1789
Théâtre des Elèves de l'Opéra (1779)
Délassements-Comiques (1780)
Beaujolais (1784)
1789
1790
Closed
Variétés Montansier
Théâtre-Français Comique et Lyrique
Lycée Dramatique
1791
Théâtre de Marais
Théâtre National de Molière
Variétés Amusantes
1792
Théâtre du Citoyen Lazzari
1793
Théâtre de Péristyle du Jardin Egalité
Closed
Théâtre des Sans-Culottes
1794
Théâtre de la Montagne
1795
Théâtre des Variétés
Closed
Théâtre de la Rue Martin
Jeunes-Artistes
1796
1797
1798
Burned
Théâtre des Amis des Arts et Elèves de l'Opéra
1799
Théâtre des Troubadours

Notes

Prologue

1. Madame de Campan, *Mémoires sur la Vie de Marie-Antoinette* (Vol. X in the series *Bibliothèque des Mémoires relatifs à l'Histoire de France pendant le Dix-huitième Siècle,* Paris, 1849), p. 203. Translations throughout the book are by the author unless otherwise noted.

2. Georges Lemaître, *Beaumarchais* (New York, 1949), p. 275.

3. Mme. Vigée-Le Brun, *Souvenirs* (Paris, [1880?]), I, 98.

4. A. Fleury, *The French Stage and the French People as Illustrated in the Memoirs of M. Fleury,* trans. Theodore Hook (London, 1841), I, 291,

5. Fleury, *Memoirs,* I, 292.

6. Recent biographies of Beaumarchais tend to follow Louis de Loménie, *Beaumarchais and His Times,* trans. Henry Edwards (New York, 1857), in crediting the dramatist with supervising the demolition of the Bastille. While Beaumarchais was in and around the structure during its razing (see Fernand Bournon, *La Bastille* [Paris, 1893], p. 205, and Frantz Funck-Brentano, *Légendes et Archives de la Bastille* [Paris, 1898], pp. 7–9), he was certainly not in charge. The Marquis de la Sallé of the Parisian Guard was appointed to watch over the building until formal demolition began, and this in turn was carried out largely under the direction of the Parisian contractor Pierre-François Palloy. For details see Henri Lemoine, *Le Démolisseur de la Bastille* (Paris, 1930).

Chapter I

1. Max Aghion, *Le Thèâtre à Paris au XVIIIe siècle* (Paris, 1926), pp. 240–45.

2. Aghion, *Thèâtre à Paris,* pp. 261–62, 267, 273.

3. Eugène Hugot, *Histoire littéraire, critique, et anecdotique du Théâtre du Palais-Royal* (Paris, 1886), pp. 7–18.

4. A situation soon ended. See Maurice Albert, *Les Théâtres des boulevards* (Paris, 1902), p. 54.

5. Edmond and Jules de Goncourt, *Histoire de la société française pendant la Révolution* (Paris, 1864), p. 92.

6. Louis Pericaud, *Théâtre de Monsieur* (Paris, 1908), pp. 7–9.

7. This description of the Palais-Royal assembly is drawn from two sources: L. G. Pitra, *La Journée du 14 Juillet, 1789* (Paris, 1892), p. 176; Louis Pericaud, *Théâtre des Petits Comédiens de S.A.S. Monseigneur le Comte de Beaujolais* (Paris, 1909), pp. 72–73. References on closely related material will be similarly gathered in subsequent footnotes.

8. Edward Rigby, *Letters from France in 1789* (London, 1880), p. 43.

9. Pericaud, *Monsieur*, pp. 60–62.

10. Arthur Pougin, *L'Opéra-Comique pendant la Révolution* (Paris, 1891), p. 23.

11. Albert, *Théâtres des boulevards*, pp. 56–57.

12. Henri Beaulieu, *Les Théâtres du boulevard du crime* (Paris, 1905), p. 62.

13. Albert, *Théâtres des boulevards*, pp. 48–50.

14. Germain Bapst, *Essai sur l'histoire du théâtre* (Paris, 1893), p. 454.

15. Aghion, *Théâtre à Paris*, pp. 290–92.

16. Beaulieu, *Boulevard du crime*, pp. 38–39.

17. Paul Porel and Georges Monval, *L'Odéon* (Paris, 1876), I, 62–63; Albert, *Théâtres des boulevards*, pp. 54–55.

18. C. G. Etienne and A. Martainville, *Histoire du Thèâtre Français depuis le commencement de la Révolution jusqu'à la Réunion Général* (Paris, 1802), I, 21–23.

19. H. Carrington Lancaster, *French Tragedy in the Reign of Louis XVI and the Early Years of the French Revolution* (Baltimore, 1953), p. 131.

20. Alfred Jepson Bingham, *Marie-Joseph Chénier: Early Political Life and Ideas* (New York, 1939), pp. 2–3, 7–8.

21. Lancaster, *French Tragedy*, pp. 103–04.

22. Jean Sylvain Bailly, *Mémoires* (Paris, 1821–22), II, 282.

23. Lancaster, *French Tragedy*, p. 104; Etienne and Martainville, *Histoire*, I, 29, 33.

24. M. A. Thiers, *The History of the French Revolution*, trans. Frederick Shoberl (Philadelphia, 1844), I, 99–100; Pougin, *Opéra-Comique*, p. 25.

25. Bingham, *Chénier*, p. 12.

26. Frederick Hawkins, *The French Stage in the Eighteenth Century* (London, 1888), II, 343–44.

27. Alfred Copin, *Talma et la Révolution* (Paris, 1888), pp. 21, 25–26.

28. E. Jauffret, *Le Théâtre révolutionnaire* (Paris, 1869), pp. 40–41.

29. Bingham, *Chénier*, pp. 13–14.

30. Goncourt, *Révolution*, p. 49.

31. Fleury, *Memoirs*, II, 166–67.

32. Bingham, *Chénier*, p. 14.

33. Quoted in Hawkins, *French Stage*, II, 339.

34. Henri Welschinger, *Le Théâtre de la Révolution* (Paris, 1880), pp. 197–98.

35. Hawkins, *French Stage*, II, 353–54.

36. Etienne and Martainville, *Histoire,* I, 49, 53–55.
37. Albert, *Théâtres des boulevards,* p. 53.
38. Pericaud, *Monsieur,* pp. 70–74.
39. Pericaud, *Beaujolais,* pp. 74–75. Curiously enough, André Antoine indulged in precisely the same grim jest a century later, by presenting Björnson's *A Bankruptcy* in November, 1893, during the declining days of the Théâtre-Libre.
40. Hugot, *Palais-Royal,* pp. 27–31. For further information on this part of Montansier's career, see P. Fromageot, "Le Théâtre de Versailles et la Montansier," *Revue de l'histoire de Versailles et de Seine-et-Oise,* VI (1904), 177–204; VII (1905), 25–46, 128–44. On the Versailles debuts, see Charles Maurice-Descombes, *Le Théâtre Français: Monuments et dépendances* (Paris, 1860), p. 175.
41. Pericaud, *Beaujolais,* pp. 81–83.
42. Ernest Lunel, *Le Théâtre et la Révolution* (Paris, 1911), pp. 30–33.

Chapter II

1. Etienne and Martainville, *Histoire,* I, 59.
2. Théodore Muret, *L'Histoire par le théâtre* (Paris, 1865), I, 43–44.
3. Jauffret, *Théâtre,* pp. 41–42.
4. Etienne and Martainville, *Histoire,* I, 67–68, 73–78.
5. Arthur Pougin, *La Comédie-Française et la Révolution* (Paris, 1902), pp. 7–10.
6. Marie-Joseph Chénier, *Oeuvres* (Paris, 1826), IV, 458–60.
7. See Alfred Copin, *Talma et la Révolution* (Paris, 1888), pp. 49–50; Jauffret, *Théâtre,* p. 42.
8. Lunel, *Théâtre,* p. 41; Muret, *L'Histoire,* I, 46.
9. Max Aghion, *Théâtre à Paris,* p. 274.
10. Augustin Challamel and Wilhelm Tenint, *Les Français sous la Révolution* (Paris, 1843), pp. 207–08.
11. Louise Fusil, *Souvenirs d'une actrice* (Paris, 1841), I, 151–53.
12. Fusil, *Souvenirs,* I, 153; Etienne and Martainville, *Histoire,* I, 108, 111–12.
13. Henri Beaulieu, *Les Théâtres du boulevard du crime* (Paris, 1905), p. 116. See also Lancaster, *French Tragedy,* p. 131.
14. Fusil, *Souvenirs,* I, 167–68.
15. Pericaud, *Monsieur,* p. 97.
16. Thiers, *French Revolution,* I, 152–54.
17. Goncourt, *Révolution,* p. 34.
18. See Pougin, *Comédie-Française,* pp. 7–24, for a full account of these political maneuvers.
19. Details of these crucial three days at the Comédie have been drawn from the following sources: Porel and Monval, *L'Odéon,* I, 73–75; Jauffret,

Théâtre, p. 43; Pougin, *Comédie-Française,* pp. 20–24; Bingham, *Chénier,* pp. 23–25.

20. Fusil, *Souvenirs,* I, 24; Etienne and Martainville, *Histoire,* I, 141–45.
21. Copin, *Talma,* p. 44.
22. Hawkins, *French Stage,* II, 359–60.
23. Hawkins, *French Stage,* II, 363–64. For full details, see the *Archives Parlementaires,* XXII, 216.
24. Albert, *Thèâtres des boulevards,* pp. 62–65.
25. Lunel, *Théâtre,* p. 52.
26. Etienne and Martainville, *Histoire,* I, 153–58; Pougin, *Comédie-Française,* pp. 27–33.
27. Hawkins, *French Stage,* II, 360–62. Bailly's discipline of Dugazon is reported in the *Chronique de Paris,* Sept. 27, 1790.
28. Pougin, *Comédie-Française,* p. 32.
29. Etienne and Martainville, *Histoire,* I, 164–68.
30. *Revue des curiosités Révolutionnaires,* II (1911–12), 394–95. Bailly's letter is noted in Alexandre Tuetey, *Répertoire général des sources manuscrites de l'histoire de Paris pendant la Révolution française* (Paris, 1890–1914), vol. III, item 1883.
31. Bingham, *Chénier,* pp. 28–29.
32. Pougin, *Comédie-Française,* pp. 45–48; Etienne and Martainville, *Histoire,* II, 7–10.
33. Etienne and Martainville, *Histoire,* I, 182–89.
34. Tuetey, *Répertoire général,* vol. II, item 4005.
35. Etienne and Martainville, *Histoire,* I, 194–97.
36. See Muret, *L'Histoire,* I, 44–45.
37. Lancaster, *French Tragedy,* p. 110.
38. Lunel, *Théâtre,* p. 82.
39. Pericaud, *Monsieur,* pp. 77–78.
40. Pericaud, *Monsieur,* p. 102. See also Jauffret, *Théâtre,* p. 101.
41. Augustus von Kotzebue, *Journey to Paris in the Year 1790,* trans. Anne Plumptre (London, 1800), p. 263.
42. See Pericaud, *Monsieur,* p. 111.
43. Tuetey, *Répertoire général,* vol. III, item 2705.
44. Aghion, *Théâtre à Paris,* pp. 292–96.
45. Muret, *Histoire,* I, 48–50.
46. Albert, *Théâtres des boulevards,* pp. 34–35.
47. Aghion, *Théâtre à Paris,* pp. 323–24.
48. Hugot, *Palais-Royal,* p. 38.
49. A list of these periodicals may be found in Pericaud, *Monsieur,* p. 106.
50. Albert, *Théâtres des boulevards,* p. 33.
51. Fleury, *Memoirs,* II, 93.
52. Aghion, *Théâtre à Paris,* p. 319.
53. Beaulieu, *Boulevard du crime,* pp. 39–40.
54. Pericaud, *Beaujolais,* p. 83.
55. Tuetey, *Répertoire général,* vol. III, item 1883.

56. Beaulieu, *Boulevard du crime*, pp. 83–84.
57. Albert, *Théâtres des boulevards*, pp. 35–37, 38n. Background material on Cousin Jacques quoted by Albert from Mouselet, *Les Oubliés et les dédaignés.*
58. Pericaud, *Beaujolais*, pp. 101–03.
59. Albert, *Théâtres des boulevards*, pp. 39–42.
60. Lunel, *Théâtre*, p. 49.
61. Aghion, *Théâtre à Paris*, pp. 283–84.
62. Albert, *Théâtres des boulevards*, p. 45n.
63. Paul d'Estrée, *Le Théâtre sous la Terreur* (Paris, 1913), p. 419.

Chapter III

1. Etienne and Martainville, *Histoire*. II, 17–19; Lunel, *Théâtre*, p. 81.
2. Pougin, *Comédie-Française*, p. 49.
3. Jauffret, *Théâtre*, p. 120.
4. Albert, *Théâtres des boulevards*, pp. 67–68.
5. Lunel, *Théâtre*, pp. 70–72.
6. Bingham, *Chénier*, p. 43; Welschinger, *Théâtre*, p. 98.
7. Jauffret, *Théâtre*, pp. 114–15.
8. Fleury, *Memoirs*, II, 240–41.
9. Welschinger, *Théâtre*, pp. 281–82.
10. Lancaster, *French Tragedy*, p. 108; Etienne and Martainville, *Histoire*, II, 79–80; see also Fusil's letter to Mme. Lemoine-Dubarry, reproduced in Fusil, *Souvenirs*, I, 155.
11. Hawkins, *French Stage*, II, 370.
12. Fusil, *Souvenirs*, I, 219.
13. Copin, *Talma*, pp. 89–90.
14. Etienne and Martainville, *Histoire*, II, 108, 115.
15. Copin, *Talma*, p. 103.
16. Etienne and Martainville, *Histoire*, II, 126.
17. J. J. Jusserand, *Shakespeare in France* (London, 1889), pp. 415 ff.
18. Hawkins, *French Stage*, II, 370.
19. The complete texts of these letters may be found in Etienne and Martainville, *Histoire*, II, 83–105.
20. From *Révolutions de Paris*, 13–20 November, 1790. Quoted in d'Estrée, *Terreur*, p. 415. D'Estrée credits the quotation to Fabre d'Eglantine.
21. Albert, *Théâtres des boulevards*, pp. 79–80.
22. Pericaud, *Monsieur*, p. 126.
23. Bapst, *Essai*, p. 458; *Almanach des spectacles*, XLI (1791), 151–52.
24. L.-Henry Lecomte, *Les Variétés Amusantes* (Paris, 1908), pp. 195–96; Goncourt, *Révolution*, p. 158.
25. Beaulieu, *Boulevard du crime*, p. 63.

26. Pericaud, *Beaujolais,* pp. 95, 117–19; Tuetey, *Répertoire général,* vol. II, item 2730; Lunel, *Théâtre,* p. 83.

27. Arthur Pougin, *L'Opéra-Comique pendant la Révolution* (Paris, 1902), p. 40.

28. Copin, *Talma,* p. 102.

29. Lunel, *Théâtre,* p. 85.

30. *Almanach des spectacles,* XLI (1791), 182–83.

31. Albert, *Théâtres des boulevards,* pp. 73–74.

32. Jauffret, *Théâtre,* pp. 127–29; Albert, *Théâtres des boulevards,* pp. 99–101.

33. Pougin, *Opéra-Comique,* p. 44.

Chapter IV

1. *Almanach des spectacles,* XLI, 30, 70.

2. Pericaud, *Monsieur,* pp. 148–49.

3. Etienne and Martainville, *Histoire,* II, 137–38.

4. Lancaster, *French Tragedy,* p. 143; Jauffret, *Théâtre,* p. 130; Etienne and Martainville, *Histoire,* II, 141–42.

5. Bingham, *Chénier,* pp. 23–25.

6. Julien Tiersot, *Les Fêtes et les chants de la Révolution française* (Paris, 1908), pp. 54, 57–60.

7. Jauffret, *Théâtre,* p. 122; Lancaster, *French Tragedy,* p. 143.

8. Copin, *Talma,* p. 106.

9. Tiersot, *Fêtes,* p. 65.

10. Goncourt, *Révolution,* p. 169.

11. Etienne and Martainville, *Histoire,* II, 46–49.

12. Jauffret, *Théâtre,* p. 145; Goncourt, *Révolution,* p. 170.

13. Etienne and Martainville, *Histoire,* II, 173.

14. Lunel, *Théâtre,* pp. 28, 89; Aghion, *Théâtre à Paris,* pp. 431–32.

15. Arnault, *Souvenirs,* quoted in Aghion, *Théâtre,* pp. 425–36.

16. Etienne and Martainville, *Histoire,* II, 162–63; Fleury, *Memoirs,* II, 180–81.

17. Voltaire, either in enthusiasm or cruel irony, once wrote "Europe awaits *Mélanie.*"

18. Etienne and Martainville, *Histoire,* II, 170–72, 181–85.

19. *Consolateur,* no. 20, March 9, 1792.

20. Bingham, *Chénier,* pp. 56–59.

21. D'Harleville biography from Laurence Hervey Skinner, *Collin d'Harleville, Dramatist* (New York, 1933).

22. Etienne and Martainville, *Histoire,* II, 197, 207–08.

23. Lunel, *Théâtre,* p. 92.

24. Tiersot, *Fêtes,* pp. 70–71.

25. Etienne and Martainville, *Histoire,* II, 213–18.

26. Thiers, *French Revolution,* I, 294–95.

27. Goncourt, *Révolution*, p. 202.
28. See Lunel, *Théâtre*, pp. 88–89.
29. Nicholas Brazier, *Histoire des petits théâtres de Paris* (Paris, 1838), I, 179–80; Albert, *Théâtres des boulevards*, p. 76n.
30. Beaulieu, *Boulevard du crime*, pp. 114–15.
31. Aghion, *Théâtre à Paris*, p. 284.
32. Lecomte, *Variétés Amusantes*, pp. 197–98.
33. At least such was the speculation of the *Almanach des spectacles*, XLI (1791), 10. The theatre's dogged determination to present works by this author earned it the nickname the Théâtre de Beaumarchais. Without the dramatist's support, these often unprofitable presentations would surely have ceased. Jacques Hillairet, in his *Dictionnaire historique des rues de Paris* (Paris, 1964), notes that Beaumarchais arranged for the construction of the Marais from materials provided by the demolition of the Bastille (II, 516).
34. Goncourt, *Révolution*, p. 160.
35. Aghion, *Théâtre à Paris*, p. 349.
36. Welschinger, *Théâtre*, p. 257.
37. Pougin, *Opéra-Comique*, p. 50.
38. Jauffret, *Théâtre*, p. 144.
39. Pougin, *Opéra-Comique*, p. 64.
40. *Almanach des spectacles*, XLI (1791), 150; Goncourt, *Révolution*, p. 165.
41. D'Estrée, *Terreur*, p. 127; Muret, *Histoire*, I, 127–28.
42. This early history of the Vaudeville is drawn from Brazier, *Petits théâtres*, I, 261–62; Albert, *Théâtres des boulevards*, p. 74; Lunel, *Théâtre*, p. 83; Aghion, *Théâtre à Paris*, p. 361.
43. Touchard-Lafosse, II, 289–99, quoted in Bingham, *Chénier*, p. 62.
44. Lunel, *Théâtre*, p. 96.
45. Bingham, *Chénier*, pp. 62–65; d'Estrée, *Terreur*, pp. 381–82.
46. Aghion, *Théâtre à Paris*, p. 351; *Annales P. et L.*, no. 59, Feb. 28, 1792, quoted in Bingham, *Chénier*, p. 66.
47. *Feuille du jour*, no. 55, Feb. 24, 1792.
48. Lecomte, *Variétés Amusantes*, p. 196.
49. Tuetey, *Répertoire général*, vol. V, items 3727, 3736, 3737; Goncourt, *Révolution*, p. 173.
50. Tuetey, *Répertoire général*, vol. IV, item 149.
51. Several early examples of this genre, called the *comédie-heroïque*, are discussed in Aghion, *Théâtre à Paris*, pp. 47–48.
52. Jauffret, *Théâtre*, p. 162.
53. Bapst, *Essai*, p. 459.
54. Hugot, *Palais-Royal*, pp. 48–50; Lunel, *Théâtre*, p. 89.
55. Pericaud, *Beaujolais*, p. 119.
56. Jauffret, *Théâtre*, p. 179.
57. Tuetey, *Répertoire général*, vol. I, item 2612.
58. D'Estrée, *Terreur*, pp. 383–84.

59. Thiers, *French Revolution,* I, 301.
60. Hugot, *Palais-Royal,* p. 50.
61. *Archives de l'Opéra, correspondance* 1792–93, 2e *registre,* p. 88, quoted in d'Estrée, *Terreur,* p. 128.

Chapter V

1. Copin, *Talma,* pp. 117–18.
2. Tuetey, *Répertoire général,* vol. VI, items 2598, 2607.
3. Welschinger, *Théâtre,* p. 80.
4. Tuetey, *Répertoire général,* vol. VI, item 2610.
5. D'Estrée, *Terreur,* p. 84; Lunel, *Théâtre,* p. 43.
6. Vol. XLIII (1793), pt. 1, pp. 118–19.
7. Welschinger, *Théâtre,* pp. 144–46.
8. Lunel, *Théâtre,* p. 108.
9. D'Estrée, *Terreur,* pp. 71–72.
10. Lunel, *Théâtre,* pp. 72–73.
11. Tuetey, *Répertoire général,* vol. IV, items 1812, 1913, 1917, 1918.
12. Lunel, *Théâtre,* p. 99.
13. D'Estrée, *Terreur,* p. 385.
14. Copin, *Talma,* pp. 108–10.
15. Fusil, *Souvenirs,* I, 277–79.
16. Thiers, *French Revolution,* I, 418–20n.
17. Hugot, *Palais-Royal,* pp. 51–55.
18. D'Estrée, *Terreur,* p. 353.
19. Etienne and Martainville, *Histoire,* III, 17–19.
20. Jauffret, *Théâtre,* p. 198.
21. Welschinger, *Théâtre,* pp. 455–58.
22. Jauffret, *Théâtre,* p. 60.
23. Jusserand, *Shakespeare,* pp. 434–36.
24. Quoted in Thiers, *French Revolution,* II, 70n.
25. Hawkins, *French Stage,* II, 380.
26. Muret, *Histoire,* I, 119–20.
27. Welschinger, *Théâtre,* pp. 389–90.
28. Pougin, *Comédie-Française,* p. 83; Etienne and Martainville, *Histoire,* III, pp. 54–59.
29. Etienne and Martainville, *Histoire,* III, 49–53.
30. Pougin, *Comédie-Française,* pp. 85–89; Tuetey, *Répertoire général,* vol. VIII, item 1070.
31. Tuetey, *Répertoire général,* vol. VIII, item 1076.
32. D'Estrée, *Terreur,* pp. 3–4.
33. Etienne and Martainville, *Histoire,* III, 62–64.
34. Tuetey, *Répertoire général,* vol. VIII, item 1082.
35. Etienne and Martainville, *Histoire,* III, 57–58, 65–67.
36. D'Estrée, *Terreur,* pp. 315–16; Muret, *Histoire,* I, 120.

37. Tuetey, *Répertoire général,* vol. VIII, item 1464.
38. Etienne and Martainville, *Histoire,* III, 69–70. Laya's letter is reported in Tuetey, *Répertoire général,* vol. VIII, item 1466.
39. D'Estrée, *Terreur,* p. 139.
40. Chénier, *Oeuvres,* V, 95–97.
41. For a discussion of this problem, see H. C. Chatfield-Taylor, *Goldoni: A Biography* (New York, 1913), pp. 577–82.
42. D'Estrée, *Terreur,* pp. 4–5.
43. Jauffret, *Théâtre,* pp. 220–23.
44. D'Estrée, *Terreur,* p. 5.
45. Aghion, *Théâtre à Paris,* p. 154.
46. Pougin, *Opéra-Comique,* p. 59.
47. Fleury, *Memoirs,* II, 285–88.
48. Tuetey, *Répertoire général,* vol. IX, item 1110.
49. D'Estrée, *Terreur,* p. 143.
50. D'Estrée, *Terreur,* pp. 339–40.
51. Fusil, *Souvenirs,* I, 53, 283.
52. Pougin, *Comédie-Française,* pp. 105–06.
53. Hawkins, *French Stage,* II, 387; Pougin, *Comédie-Française,* pp. 107, 110–12.
54. Fleury, *Memoirs,* II, 304–05.
55. Pougin, *Comédie-Française,* p. 116.
56. Tuetey, *Répertoire général,* vol. IX, item 1214.
57. Pougin, *Comédie-Française,* pp. 118–21.
58. Tuetey, *Répertoire général,* vol. IX, item 1361.
59. Jauffret, *Théâtre,* p. 203.
60. Albert, *Théâtres des boulevards,* p. 76.
61. Brazier, *Histoire,* I, 152–58.
62. Grégoire, *Mémoires de l'executeur,* p. 107, quoted in d'Estrée, *Terreur,* p. 294.
63. Goncourt, *Révolution,* pp. 310–11.
64. D'Estrée, *Terreur,* p. 391.
65. Lunel, *Théâtre,* p. 107; d'Estrée, *Terreur,* pp. 5–6.
66. Tuetey, *Répertoire général,* vol. IX, items 1112, 1115, 1118, 1129, 1132, 1138.
67. Copin, *Talma,* pp. 168–69.
68. Pougin, *Opéra-Comique,* pp. 94–95.
69. Lecomte, *Variétés Amusantes,* pp. 210–11.
70. Gréty, *Mémoires,* p. 87, quoted in Albert, *Théâtres des boulevards,* p. 87n.

Chapter VI

1. D'Estrée, *Terreur,* pp. 431, 449–51.
2. D'Estrée, *Terreur,* pp. 90–91.
3. D'Estrée, *Terreur,* p. 83; Lunel, *Théâtre,* p. 110.

4. Goncourt, *Révolution*, pp. 303, 309.
5. Lunel, *Théâtre*, p. 112.
6. Tuetey, *Répertoire général*, vol. IX, item 1273.
7. *Almanach des spectacles*, vol. XLIII (1793), pt. I, pp. 254–64.
8. D'Estrée, *Terreur*, pp. 76–78.
9. Aghion, *Théâtre à Paris*, p. 377.
10. D'Estrée, *Terreur*, pp. 14–15.
11. Etienne and Martainville, *Histoire*, III, 112–16; Tuetey, *Répertoire général*, vol. VIII, item 531.
12. Fusil, *Souvenirs*, I, 24–25.
13. Details on this play are from Challamel and Tenint, *Les Français*, p. 271, and Cleveland Moffett, *The Reign of Terror*, (New York, 1962), p. 143. The reviews are quoted in d'Estrée, *Terreur*, pp. 435, 454.
14. Copin, *Talma*, pp. 160–61.
15. Jauffret, *Théâtre*, pp. 256–57.
16. D'Estrée, *Terreur*, pp. 166, 444–45.
17. Albert, *Lettres inédits*, p. 54, quoted in d'Estrée, *Terreur*, p. 124.
18. Muret, *L'Histoire*, I, 46.
19. Pougin, *Opéra-Comique*, pp. 86–87; d'Estrée, *Terreur*, pp. 433–34; Lunel, *Théâtre*, p. 105.
20. Etienne and Martainville, *Histoire*, III, 133.
21. Lunel, *Théâtre*, p. 112; Etienne and Martainville, *Histoire*, III, 105; Tuetey, *Répertoire général*, vol. IX, item 1216, vol. X, items 1568, 1578, 1602, 1610–12.
22. Etienne and Martainville, *Histoire*, III, 145.
23. D'Estrée, *Terreur*, pp. 142–43. The dedication is reproduced in Welschinger, *Théâtre*, p. 375.
24. Welschinger, *Théâtre*, p. 453.
25. Etienne and Martainville, *Histoire*, III, 155–56.
26. Welschinger, *Théâtre*, pp. 155–58.
27. Tuetey, *Répertoire général*, vol. IX, items 1373, 1422.
28. Pougin, *Opéra-Comique*, p. 107.
29. D'Estrée, *Terreur*, p. 186.
30. Jauffret, *Théâtre*, pp. 224–26.
31. Tiersot, *Fêtes*, p. 107.
32. *Almanach des spectacles*, vol. XLIII (1793), pt. I, pp. 100–04.
33. D'Estrée, *Terreur*, pp. 23–24.
34. Tuetey, *Répertoire général*, vol. X, item, 1933.
35. D'Estrée, *Terreur*, p. 305; Copin, *Talma*, p. 164.
36. D'Estrée, *Terreur*, p. 307; Etienne and Martainville, *Histoire*, III, 140; Aghion, *Théâtre à Paris*, p. 378.
37. Aghion, *Théâtre à Paris*, p. 212.
38. D'Estrée, *Terreur*, pp. 269–73.
39. Welschinger, *Théâtre*, p. 209.

40. Aghion, *Théâtre à Paris,* p. 256; Etienne and Martainville, *Histoire,* III, 141–43.
41. D'Estrée, *Terreur,* p. 36.
42. Welschinger, *Théâtre,* pp. 149–50.
43. See Louis de Loménie, *Beaumarchais and His Times* (New York, 1857), pp. 421–41.
44. Lunel, *Théâtre,* pp. 119–20; Tuetey, *Répertoire général,* vol. X, items 1526, 1534.
45. Tuetey, *Répertoire général,* vol. X, item 1517.
46. D'Estrée, *Terreur,* p. 221.
47. Welschinger, *Théâtre,* p. 332.
48. Albert, *Théâtres des boulevards,* p. 146.
49. Quoted in d'Estrée, *Terreur,* pp. 261–62.
50. Jauffret, *Théâtre,* pp. 281–83; Welschinger, *Théâtre,* p. 205.
51. Welschinger, *Théâtre,* p. 150.
52. Welschinger, *Théâtre,* p. 186.
53. D'Estrée, *Terreur,* pp. 31–32.
54. Welschinger, *Théâtre,* p. 109.
55. Copin, *Talma,* p. 294; Bapst, *Essai,* p. 510; Porel and Monval, *L'Odéon,* I, 140.
56. Lunel, *Théâtre,* pp. 125–27.
57. Pougin, *Comédie-Française,* pp. 145–46.
58. Fleury, *Memoirs,* II, 381–86.
59. Fleury, *Memoirs,* II, 380.
60. Tiersot, *Fêtes,* p. 139. Pages 140–44 trace the discord between Chénier and Robespierre.
61. Tiersot, *Fêtes,* pp. 165–68.
62. Fusil, *Souvenirs,* II, 58.
63. Tiersot, *Fêtes,* pp. 165–68; Welschinger, *Théâtre,* p. 274; Pougin, *Opéra-Comique,* p. 111.
64. *Almanach des spectacles,* XLII (1792), 271.
65. Fusil, *Souvenirs,* II, 61; Beaulieu, *Boulevard du crime,* p. 89.
66. Pougin, *Opéra-Comique,* p. 79n; Hawkins, *French Stage,* II, 397.

Chapter VII

1. Fleury, *Memoirs,* II, 389–90.
2. Hawkins, *French Stage,* II, 408.
3. Fleury, *Memoirs,* II, 267–79.
4. Tiersot, *Fêtes,* pp. 199–200.
5. Marc Mauret, *Ça Ira* (Paris, 1948), p. 201.
6. Welschinger, *Théâtre,* pp. 243–44.
7. Etienne and Martainville, *Histoire,* III, 171–75.
8. Pougin, *Opéra-Comique,* p. 136; Welschinger, *Théâtre,* p. 112.

9. Victor Fournel, *Les Hommes du 14 Juillet* (Paris, 1890), p. 168; Copin, *Talma*, pp. 172–73.
10. Welschinger, *Théâtre*, p. 111.
11. Hawkins, *French Stage*, II, 409.
12. Copin, *Talma*, p. 102.
13. Pougin, *Opéra-Comique*, pp. 145–46.
14. D'Estrée, *Terreur*, pp. 308–09.
15. Lunel, *Théâtre*, p. 109.
16. Hawkins, *French Stage*, II, 411.
17. Etienne and Martainville, *Histoire*, III, 185–99.
18. Pougin, *Opéra-Comique*, p. 168.
19. D'Estrée, *Terreur*, p. 273; Etienne and Martainville, *Histoire*, III, 163.
20. Bapst, *Essai*, p. 512; Paul Lacroix, *Directoire, Consulat, et Empire* (Paris, 1884), pp. 178–79.
21. Jacques Hérissay, *Le Monde des théâtres pendant la Révolution* (Paris, 1922), p. 285.
22. Pougin, *Opéra-Comique*, pp. 130–38.
23. Hérissay, *Monde des théâtres*, pp. 286, 293–94.
24. Thiers, *French Revolution*, III, 199.
25. Etienne and Martainville, *Histoire*, III, 180; Pougin, *Opéra-Comique*, p. 152; Welschinger, *Théâtre*, p. 160.
26. Hérissay, *Monde des théâtres*, p. 297.
27. Pougin, *Opéra-Comique*, pp. 182–84. The February decree is quoted on p. 158.
28. Welschinger, *Théâtre*, p. 495.
29. Goncourt, *Révolution*, p. 303.
30. Pougin, *Opéra-Comique*, p. 154.
31. Welschinger, *Théâtre*, pp. 161–62.
32. Welschinger, *Théâtre*, p. 410.
33. Jauffret, *Théâtre*, pp. 321–22.
34. Welschinger, *Théâtre*, p. 497.
35. Pougin, *Opéra-Comique*, pp. 160–64.
36. Albert, *Théâtres des boulevards*, pp. 162–63. The contemporary is quoted on p. 158n.
37. Aghion, *Théâtre à Paris*, p. 271.
38. Albert, *Théâtres des boulevards*, pp. 150–51, 161n.
39. M. Minnigerode, *The Magnificent Comedy* (New York, 1931), p. 117.
40. Albert, *Théâtres des boulevards*, p. 150.
41. Muret, *L'Histoire*, I, 155.
42. Brazier, *Petits théâtres*, I, 10.
43. Lunel, *Théâtre*, *p.* 115; Hugot, *Palais-Royal*, pp. 78–81.
44. Hugot, *Palais-Royal*, p. 64; Pougin, *Opéra-Comique*, p. 184.
45. Aghion, *Théâtre à Paris*, pp. 285–86.
46. Lecomte, *Variétés Amusantes*, p. 232.
47. Sebastian Mercier, *Paris pendant la Révolution* (Paris, 1862), II, 191–

92; Jacques François Louis Grobert, *De l'Execution dramatique considerée dans ses rapports avec le matériel de la salle et de la scène* (Paris, 1809), p. 95.

48. Edmond and Jules de Goncourt, *Histoire de la société française pendant le Directoire* (Paris, 1864), pp. 121–23.
49. Goncourt, *Directoire*, pp. 127–29; Muret, *L'Histoire*, I, 150.
50. Albert, *Théâtres des boulevards*, p. 143.
51. Porel and Monval, *L'Odéon*, I, 199.
52. Thiers, *French Revolution*, III, 317, 320n.

Chapter VIII

1. Aghion, *Théâtre à Paris*, pp. 363–64.
2. Welschinger, *Théâtre*, pp. 163–64.
3. Aghion, *Théâtre à Paris*, p. 364.
4. Welschinger, *Théâtre*, p. 165.
5. Etienne and Martainville, *Histoire*, III, 212.
6. Jauffret, *Théâtre*, pp. 375–76.
7. Welschinger, *Théâtre*, pp. 113–14, 167–68.
8. D'Estrée, *Terreur*, pp. 409–11.
9. Welschinger, *Théâtre*, pp. 169, 178.
10. Muret, *L'Histoire*, I, 150.
11. Etienne and Martainville, *Histoire*, III, 216–21.
12. Porel and Monval, *L'Odéon*, I, 150–57.
13. Porel and Monval, *L'Odéon*, I, 159–60.
14. Bapst, *Essai*, p. 518.
15. Etienne and Martainville, *Histoire*, IV, 6–7, 11–14.
16. Etienne and Martainville, *Histoire*, IV, 19–23; Copin, *Talma*, pp. 251–53.
17. Fleury, *Memoirs*, II, 398.
18. Etienne and Martainville, *Histoire*, IV, 23–34.
19. Porel and Monval, *L'Odéon*, I, 163–65.
20. Hawkins, *French Stage*, II, 415.
21. Goncourt, *Directoire*, pp. 203–06.
22. Copin, *Talma*, pp. 253–54; Etienne ad Martainville, *Histoire*, IV, 51–53.
23. Etienne and Martainville, *Histoire*, IV, 60–63.
24. Hawkins, *French Stage*, II, 417.
25. Etienne and Martainville, *Histoire*, IV, 69–70.
26. Bapst, *Essai*, pp. 515–16.
27. Etienne and Martainville, *Histoire*, IV, 71–73.
28. Eleanor Jourdain, *Dramatic Theory and Practice in France 1690–1808* (New York, 1921), pp. 23–24.
29. Etienne and Martainville, *Histoire*, IV, 78–79.
30. Thiers, *French Revolution*, IV, 208.

31. Etienne and Martainville, *Histoire*, IV, 83–84.
32. Pougin, *Opéra-Comique*, p. 202n.
33. Welschinger, *Théâtre*, p. 122.
34. Etienne and Martainville, *Histoire*, IV, 86–93.
35. Porel and Monval, *L'Odéon*, pp. 165–68.
36. Welschinger, *Théâtre*, pp. 161–62.
37. Jauffret, *Théâtre*, pp. 392–97.
38. See A. P. Moore, *The Genre Poissard and the French Stage of the Eighteenth Century* (New York, 1935), esp. pp. 236–78.
39. Moore, *Genre Poissard*, pp. 279–82; Albert, *Théâtres des boulevards*, p. 166.
40. Translation by H. J. Byron, *La Fille de Madame Angot* (New York, n.d.).
41. Pougin, *Opéra-Comique*, p. 200.
42. Claude Ruggieri, *Précis historique sur les fêtes, les spectacles, et les réjouissances publiques* (Paris, 1830), pp. 86–93, 102–07.
43. Fusil, *Souvenirs*, II, 121–22.
44. Ruggieri, *Précis historique*, pp. 84, 89, 94, 107.
45. Aghion, *Théâtre à Paris*, p. 396.
46. Fusil, *Souvenirs*, II, 115–17.
47. Hawkins, *French Stage*, II, 413–14.

Chapter IX

1. Pougin, *Opéra-Comique*, pp. 205–07.
2. Thiers, *French Revolution*, IV, 229.
3. Arthur Pougin, *Un Directeur d'opéra au dix-huitième siècle* (Paris, 1914), pp. 93–99.
4. Pougin, *Opéra-Comique*, p. 223.
5. Pougin, *Opéra-Comique*, pp. 229–33.
6. Pougin, *Opéra-Comique*, p. 235.
7. See Alexis Pitou, "Les Origins du mélodrame français à la fin du XVIIIe siècle," *Revue d'histoire littéraire de la France*, XVIII (1911), 256–96.
8. Alice M. Killen, *Le Roman "terrifiant" ou roman "noir" de Walpole à Anne Radcliffe et son influence sur la littérature française jusqu'en 1840* (Paris, 1915), pp. 101–05.
9. Pitou, "Origins du mélodrame," pp. 280–81.
10. Aghion, *Théâtre à Paris*, p. 373.
11. Hugot, *Palais-Royal*, p. 73.
12. Hugot, *Palais-Royal*, pp. 69–71; Beaulieu, *Boulevard du crime*, p. 16.
13. Beaulieu, *Boulevard du crime*, pp. 89–90; Lecomte, *Variétés Amusantes*, pp. 280–82.
14. Aghion, *Théâtre à Paris*, pp. 271–72, 287, 320, 355.
15. Muret, *Histoire*, I, 172–73; Jauffret, *Théâtre* p. 367.
16. Etienne and Martainville, *Histoire*, IV, 106–07.

17. Jauffret, *Théâtre*, pp. 416–19.
18. Welschinger, *Théâtre*, p. 122.
19. Porel and Monval, *L'Odéon*, I, 170; Etienne and Martainville, *Histoire*, IV, 110–11.
20. Welschinger, *Théâtre*, p. 124.
21. Copin, *Talma*, pp. 277–79; Etienne and Martainville, *Histoire*, IV, 112–13, 115.
22. Hérissay, *Monde des théâtres*, p. 370.
23. Albert, *Théâtres des boulevards*, pp. 170–74.
24. Hawkins, *French Stage*, II, 418; Etienne and Martainville, *Histoire*, IV, 128–36.
25. Porel and Monval, *L'Odéon*, p. 307; Etienne and Martainville, *Histoire*, IV, 127n.
26. Porel and Monval, *L'Odéon*, pp. 173–77.
27. Copin, *Talma*, pp. 279–80.
28. Pougin, *Opéra-Comique*, pp. 225–26; Welschinger, *Théâtre*, pp. 126–30.
29. Goncourt, *Directoire*, pp. 308–09.
30. Muret, *Histoire*, I, 98.
31. Goncourt, *Directoire*, pp. 308–10.
32. Etienne and Martainville, *Histoire*, IV, 145–49, 155–57; Porel and Monval, *L'Odéon*, p. 308.
33. Etienne and Martainville, *Histoire*, IV, 165–75.
34. Porel and Monval, *L'Odéon*, p. 180.
35. Pougin, *Opéra-Comique*, pp. 238–39; Porel and Monval, *L'Odéon*, pp. 181–82.
36. Etienne and Martainville, *Histoire*, IV, 184–89.
37. Fleury, *Memoirs*, II, 403–05.
38. Hawkins, *French Stage*, II, 425.
39. Muret, *Histoire*, I, 99–100; Copin, *Talma*, pp. 285–87.

Epilogue

1. Jauffret, *Théâtre*, pp. 426–28.
2. Pougin, *Opéra-Comique*, pp. 244–46.
3. L.-Henry Lecomte, *Napoléon et le monde dramatique* (Paris, 1912), pp. 34–35.
4. Lecomte, *Napoléon*, p. 54.
5. Lecomte, *Napoléon*, pp. 108–10.
6. Lecomte, *Napoléon*, p. 113.

Selected Bibliography

THIS bibliography contains the nondramatic sources that have been particularly useful in the preparation of this history. Plays mentioned in the text are generally accompanied by the author's name and by the place and date of first presentation. Readers desiring further bibliographic information are urged to consult the comprehensive *Bibliothèque dramatique de M. de Solienne*, 6 vols., compiled by P. L. Jacob, Paris, 1843–44 and the supplement, *Table des pièces de théâtre*, by Charles Brunet, Paris, 1914.

Aghion, Max. *Le Théâtre à Paris au XVIIIe siècle*. Paris, 1926.
Albert, Maurice. *Les Théâtres des boulevards*. Paris, 1902.
Bailly, Jean Sylvain. *Mémoires*. Paris, 1821–1822.
Bapst, Germain. *Essai sur l'histoire du théâtre*. Paris, 1893.
Beaulieu, Henri. *Les Théâtres du boulevard du crime*. Paris, 1905.
Bingham, Alfred Jepson. *Marie-Joseph Chénier: Early Political Life and Ideas*. New York: Privately printed, 1939.
Bournon, Fernand. *La Bastille*. Paris, 1893.
Brazier, Nicolas. *Histoire des petits théâtres de Paris*. 2 vols. Paris, 1838.
Cailhava. *Causes de la décadence du théâtre et les moyens de le faire refleurir*. Paris, 1789.
Campan, Madame de. *Mémoires sur le vie de Marie Antoinette*. Paris, 1849.
Challamel, Augustin, and Wilhelm Tenint. *Les Français sous la Révolution*. Paris, 1843.
Chatfield-Taylor, H. C. *Goldoni: A Biography*. New York, 1913.
Chénier, Marie-Joseph. *Oeuvres*. 5 vols. Paris, 1826.
Copin, Alfred. *Talma et la Révolution*. Paris, 1888.
Dayot, Armand. *La Révolution française*. Paris, 1896.
D'Estrée, Paul. *Le Théâtre sous la Terreur*. Paris, 1913.
Dowd, David Lloyd. *Pageant-Master of the Republic*. Lincoln, 1948.
Etienne, C. G., and A. Martainville. *Histoire du Théâtre Français depuis le commencement de la Révolution jusqu'à la Réunion Général*. 4 vols. Paris, 1802.
Fleury, A. *The French Stage and the French People as Illustrated in the Memoirs of M. Fleury*. Trans. Theodore Hook. 2 vols. London, 1841.

Fournel, Victor. *Les Hommes du 14 Juillet.* Paris, 1890.

Fromageot, P. "Le Théâtre de Versailles et la Montansier," *Revue de l'histoire de Versailles et de Seine-et-Oise* VI (1904), 177–204, VII (1905), 25–46, 128–44.

Funck-Brentano, Frantz. *Légends et archives de la Bastille.* Paris, 1898.

Fusil, Louise. *Souvenirs d'une actrice.* 2 vols. Paris, 1841.

Geruzez, E. *Histoire de la litterature française pendant la Révolution.* Paris, 1869.

Goncourt, Edmond and Jules de. *Histoire de la société française pendant le Directoire.* Paris, 1864.

——. *Histoire de la société française pendant la Révolution.* Paris, 1869.

Grégoire, Henri. *Mémoires.* Paris, 1840.

Grobert, Jacques François Louis. *De l'Exécution dramatique considerée dans ses rapports avec le matériel de la salle et de la scène.* Paris, 1809.

Hawkins, Frederick. *The French Stage in the Eighteenth Century.* 2 vols. London, 1888.

Hérissay, Jacques. *Le Monde des théâtres pendant la Révolution.* Paris, 1922.

Hillairet, Jacques. *Dictionnaire historique des rues de Paris.* 2 vols. Paris, 1964.

Hugot, Eugène. *Histoire littéraire, critique, et anecdotique du Théâtre du Palais-Royal.* Paris, 1886.

Jauffret, E. *Le Théâtre Révolutionnaire.* Paris, 1869.

Jourdain, Eleanor Frances. *Dramatic Theory and Practice in France 1690–1808.* New York, 1921.

Jusserand, J. J. *Shakespeare in France.* London, 1899.

Killen, Alice M. *Le Roman "terrifiant" ou roman "noir" de Walpole à Anne Radcliffe et son influence sur la littêrature française jusqu'en 1840.* Paris, 1915.

Kotzebue, Augustus von. *Journey to Paris in the Year 1790.* Trans. Anne Plumptre. London, 1800.

Laborde, Alexandre de. *Versailles, ancien et moderne.* Paris, 1841.

Lacroix, Paul. *Directoire, Consulat, et Empire.* Paris, 1884.

Lancaster, H. Carrington. *French Tragedy in the Reign of Louis XVI and the Early Years of the French Revolution.* Baltimore, 1953.

Le Brun, Madame Vigée. *Souvenirs.* Paris, [1880?].

Lecomte, L.-Henry. *Napoléon, et l'Empire racontés par le théâtre.* Paris, 1900.

——. *Napoléon et le monde dramatique.* Paris, 1912.

——. *Les Variétés Amusantes.* Paris, 1908.

Lemaître, Georges. *Beaumarchais.* New York, 1949.

Lescure, M. F. A. *L'Amour sous la Terreur.* Paris, 1888.

Lemoine, Henri. *Le Démolisseur de la Bastille.* Paris, 1930.
Loménie, Louis de. *Beaumarchais and His Times.* Trans. Henry Edwards. New York, 1857.
Lunel, Ernest. *Le Théâtre et la Révolution.* Paris, 1911.
Mauret, Marc. *Ça Ira.* Paris, 1948.
Maurice-Descombes, Charles. *Le Théâtre Français: Monuments et dépendances.* Paris, 1860.
Mércier, Sebastian. *Paris pendant la Révolution.* 2 vols. Paris, 1862.
Minnigerode, M. *The Magnificent Comedy.* New York, 1931.
Moffett, Cleveland. *The Reign of Terror.* New York, 1962.
Moore, A. P. *The Genre Poissard and the French Stage of the Eighteenth Century.* New York, 1935.
Muret, Théodore. *L'Histoire par le théâtre.* Vol. I. Paris, 1865.
Pericaud, Louis. *Théâtre de Monsieur.* Paris, 1908.
——.*Théâtre des Petits Comédiens de S.A.S. Monseigneur le Comte de Beaujolais.* Paris, 1909.
Pitou, Alexis. "Les Origins du mélodrame français à la fin du XVIIIe siècle," *Revue d'histoire littéraire de la France,* XVIII (1911), 256–96.
Pitra, L. G. *La Journée du 14 Juillet, 1789.* Paris, 1892.
Porel, Paul, and Georges Monval. *L'Odéon.* Vol. 1. Paris, 1876.
Pougin, Arthur. *La Comédie-Française et la Révolution.* Paris, 1902.
——. *Dictionnaire du théâtre.* Paris, 1885.
——. *Un Directeur d'opéra au dix-huitième siècle.* Paris, 1914.
——. *L'Opéra-Comique pendant la Révolution.* Paris, 1891.
Ricord *âiné. Les Fastes de la Comédie Française.* 2 vols. Paris, 1821–1822.
Rigby, Edward. *Letters from France in 1789.* London, 1880.
Rivoire, Jean-Alexis. *Le Patriotisme dans le théâtre sèrieux de la Révolution.* Paris, 1950.
Ruggiéri, Claude. *Précis historique sur les fêtes, les spectacles, et les réjouissances publiques.* Paris, 1830.
Skinner, Laurence Hervey. *Collin d'Harleville, Dramatist.* New York, 1933.
Thiers, M. A. *The History of the French Revolution.* Trans. Frederick Shoberl. 4 vols. Philadelphia, 1844.
Tiersot, Julien. *Les Fêtes et les chants de la Révolution française.* Paris, 1908.
Touchard-Lafosse, Georges. *La Révolution, l'Empire, et la Restauration.* Paris, 1828.
Tuetey, Alexandre. *Répertoire général des sources manuscrites de l'histoire de Paris pendant la Révolution française.* II vols. Paris, 1890–1914.
Vibert, Léon. *Au Temps de la Carmagnole.* 3 vols. Paris, 1942–1945.
Welschinger, Henri. *Le Théâtre de la Révolution.* Paris, 1880.

Index

A bas la calotte (Rousseau), 194
Abancourt, Charles d', 97
Abbé vert, L' (anon.), 216
Abdélazis et Zuléima (Murville), 101
Abufar (Ducis), 214
Académie Royale de Musique, see Opéra
Adèle de Sacy (anon.), 171
Adeline (actress), 135
Adolphe et Clara (Marsollier), 274
Adrien (Hoffman and Méhul), 116, 122, 145, 261
Aeschylus, 247
Agamemnon (Lemercier), 102, 247
Agricole Viala (Philippau), 205
Albitte, Antoine-Louis, 175, 176
Alcalde de Zalomea (Calderon), 30
Alexis (Marsollier), 269
Allons ça va (Cousin Jacques), 178
Almanach des spectacles, 64, 115, 132, 173, 265
Almanach général, 58, 87
Alphonse et Léonore (Leprévot d'Iray), 251
Alzire (Voltaire), 47, 99
Amant jaloux, L' (anon.), 114
Amante au tombeau, L' (anon.), 195
Amazone de Grenade, L' (anon.), 265
Ambigu-Comique, 10, 57, 65, 86, 92, 112, 165, 195, 219, 225–28, 261, 264, 267, 281, 284, 287; *see also* Audinot, Nicolas-Médard
Amélie (Voltaire), 274
Ami des lois, L' (Laya), 143–47, 150, 151, 153, 170, 212, 214
Ami du peuple, L', 137
Ami du peuple, L' (Saint-Armand), 166
Ami du peuple, L' (Saint-Aubin), 158, 175
Amis de collège, Les (Picard), 215
Amis de la Patrie, Théâtre des, 126, 205, 210; *see also* Louvois, Théâtre
Amis des Arts et Elèves de l'Opéra, Théâtre des, 267
Amour et la raison, L' (Pigault-Lebrun), 252
Amour et l'interêt, L' (d'Eglantine), 107
Amour puni par Vénus, L' (Lazzari), 112
Amphitryon (Molière), 102
Anacréon (Mendouze), 247
Anacréon chez Polycrate (Gréty), 261
Andromaque (Racine), 163, 209, 271
Andros et Almora (Picard and Duval), 184
Anniversaire, L' (Mittié), 264
anticlerical drama, 21, 22, 35, 38, 55, 76–78, 189, 190
Antilly, Berton d', 76, 184
Apelle et Campase (Demoustier), 261
Apothéose de Beaurepaire, L' (Lesur), 132
Apothéose du jeune Barra, L' (Léger), 183
Apparences trompeuses, Les (Hauteroche), 245
Arabelle et Vascos (Lebrun-Tossa), 223
architecture, 85, 113, 124, 172–74, 191, 199, 200, 241, 272
Arétaphile (Ronsin), 125
Argy, Lemierre d', 55
Arlequin cherchant un logement (Cousin Jacques), 71
Arlequin friand (Picard), 168
Arlequin gardien des femmes (anon.), 168
Arlequin imprimeur (Lépitre), 198
Arlequin journaliste (Chazet, Dupaty, and de Lamardelle), 168

Arlequin machiniste (anon.), 168
Arlequin marchand d'almanachs (anon.), 168
Arlequin marchand d'esprit (anon.), 168
Arlequin perruquier (Roland and Clairville), 230
Arlequin qui file (anon.), 266
Arlequin sculpteur (Gouffé), 229
Arlequin tailleur (Thierry and Lambert), 168
Armand, Benoît-Roussel, 279
Arnauld, François-Thomas-Baculard d', 21, 41, 77
Arnault, Antoine Vincent, 81, 107, 136, 206, 210, 273
Arné (guard), 74
Artistes (d'Harleville), 242
Artois, Comte d', 2, 5
Arts, Théâtre des, *see* Opéra
Assemblés primaires, Les (Martainville), 253, 254
Associés, Théâtre des, 10, 16–18, 30, 57, 65, 66; *see also* Sans Prétention, Théâtre
Astley, Philip, 88
Athalie (Racine), 53, 131, 251
Au retour (Radet and Desfontaines), 186
Aude, Joseph, 20, 46, 164, 254, 255, 260, 266
Audinot, Nicolas-Médard, 9, 10, 16, 30, 44, 62, 64, 66, 86, 112, 195, 225, 267
Auter d'un moment, L' (Léger), 117, 119–22, 144
Autié, Léonard, 12, 13, 31, 32, 58, 59, 84, 95
Avare, L' (Molière), 147, 271
Azémire (Chénier), 22

Bailly, Jean-Sylvain, 14, 15, 23, 38, 48, 52–54, 58, 64, 67, 100, 136
Baptiste the Elder, Nicolas Anselme, 113, 124, 154, 181, 214, 244, 271, 279
Baptiste the Younger, Eustache Anselme, 64, 107, 113, 139, 241, 279
Barbier de Séville, Le (Beaumarchais), 1, 224, 240, 250
Barbieri di Siviglia, Il (Paisiello), 57
Barneveldt (Lemierre), 43
Barra, Joseph, 181–184, 205, 209, 220
Barras, Paul-François, 125, 235, 250
Barré, Pierre-Yves, 116, 117, 120, 150, 161, 165, 185, 186, 219
Barrère, Bertrand, 160, 214, 223
Barthélemy, François, 250
Bataille de Jemmapes, La (Devienne), 139
Bathilde (Candeille), 175
Beaujolais, Comte de, 10
Beaujolais, Théâtre du, 10, 11, 14, 16, 31, 32, 66–69, 87, 88, 90 112, 124, 125, 172
Beaumarchais, Pierre-Augustin Caron de, 1–6, 22, 45, 50, 97, 113, 114, 193 224, 248, 250, 278
Beaurepaire, Nicolas, 140, 179
Beauvisage, *see* Vienne
Beffroy (actress), 249
Beggar's Opera, The (Gay), 254
Bellamy, Mrs. George Anne, 27
Belle au bois dormant, La (Bouilly and Dumersan), 225
Bellecour, Rose-Pétronille, 16, 276
Bellemont, Jean-Baptiste, 4, 52, 161, 180
Belloy, Pierre-Laurent, 19, 72
Bergasse, Nicolas, 248
Berton, Henri-Montan, 56, 185, 263
Bienfait de la loi, Le (Forgeot), 208
Blaise et Babet (Monvel), 224, 225
Blanche de Montcassin (Arnault), 273
Blasius, Mathieu-Frédéric, 185
Bleuettes-Comiques, 12, 62
Boieldieu, Marie-Jacques-Armand, 260
Boirie, Cantiran de, 267
Boissy, Louis-Laus de, 150, 151, 159
Boîte enchantée, La (anon.), 194
Boîtes, Les (Bizet), 253
Bon Fermier, Le (Ségur the Younger), 221
Bonaparte, Napoléon, 196, 220, 235, 238, 239, 250, 259, 260, 264, 269, 280–87
Bordeaux, Grand Théâtre de, 17, 234
Boucher, Jules-Armand, 81
Bouilly, Jean-Nicolas, 57, 225, 242
Boulevard theatres, 9–12, 64–66; *see also names of individual theatres*
Boullé (machinist), 217
Bouquier, Gabriel, 191
Bourgeois, Auguste-Anicet, 216
Bourgeois Gentilhomme, Le (Molière), 268, 276
Bourru bienfaisant, Le (Goldoni), 151, 190, 200, 208
Boursault-Malherbe, Jean-François, 90–93, 126, 130, 229, 230, 267
Bouthellier, Maxmilien-Jean, 19, 46
Bouyon, Abbé de, 64, 206

Boyer, Pascal, 206
Brienne (author), 157
Brigand (Hoffman), 116
Brigands de la Vendée, Les (Boullault), 194
Briois (author), 87, 88, 181, 226
Brissi (aerialist), 257
Britannicus (Racine), 163, 271
Brongniart, Alexandre-Théodore, 124
Brumoy, Pierre, 96
Brunet, Marguerite, *see* Montansier, Marguerite Brunet
Brunswick, Duke of, 128
Brutus, 90, 197, 204
Brutus (Voltaire), 27, 30, 54, 55, 81, 82, 84, 96, 99, 146, 165

Ça ira, 59, 69, 73, 104, 107, 110, 115, 120, 122, 135, 149, 238
Cadet Roussel au Café des Aveugles (Aude and Tissot), 164
Cadet Roussel misanthrope (Aude), 255
Cailhava, Jean-François, 50, 61
Cailleau, André-Charles, 267
Caïn (Chénier), 209
Caïus Gracchus (Chénier), 104, 119, 131, 165, 176, 181
Calais (aerialist), 257
Calas (d'Argy), 55
Calas (Chénier), 95, 97, 199
Callias (Hoffman), 116, 217
Camp de Grandpré, Le (Chénier and Gossec), 131
Campan, Jeanne-Louise-Henriette de, 2, 3
Candeille, Amélie-Julie, 103, 136, 149, 175, 210
Cange (commissioner of Saint-Lazare), 209, 210, 221
Cange (Gamas), 210
Cange (Villiers and Gouffé), 210
Cannonier convalescent, Le (Radet), 188
Capucin qui se marie, Le (anon.), 226
Capucins, Les (anon.,) 77
Capucins à la frontière, Les (anon.), 161
Careau, Louise-Julie, 41, 49, 80, 89, 136
Carentan, Jullien de, 160
Carmagnole, 135, 149, 157
Carmagnole à Chambéry, La (Dorvigny), 139
Carnot, Lazare, 250
Carolin, actress, 139, 265
Castle of Otranto, The (Walpole), 265
Castor et Pollux (Bernard), 101
Catilinas modernes, Les (Feru the Younger), 190
Caton d'Utique (Saint-Marcel), 240
Caumont, Thomas, 279
Cavanagh (bookseller), 229
Cécile (Souriguières), 244
Cellerier, Jacques, 131, 164, 171, 261
censorship, 1–3, 9–12, 17, 18, 21–23, 35, 38, 40–43, 72, 103, 120, 123, 179, 250, 251, 260, 269, 273, 274, 285
Chagot-Defays, M. B., 212
Chambon, Nicolas, 146
Champagny, Jean-Baptiste, 285
Championnet, Jean-Etienne, 262
Champville, Gabriel-Léonard-Hérve Dubus de, 161
Chanoine de Milan, Le (Duval), 241 242
Chant des vegeneances (de Lisle), 261
Chapelier (delegate), 74, 75
Chaptal, Jean-Antoine, 283
Charlemagne, Armand, 215, 230, 253
Charles IX (Chénier), 21–30, 36–39, 41, 44, 46–49, 51, 53, 76, 99, 104, 119, 121, 276
Charles et Caroline (Pigault-Lebrun), 181
Charlot ou La Nuit des fiançailles (anon.), 121
Chaste Suzanne, La (Radet and Defontaines), 144, 149, 161, 186
Chastenet, Armand-Marie-Jacques, 184
Château de Belle-Vue, 256
Château d' Udolphe, Le (Duval), 265
Châteaux en Espagne, Les (d'Harleville), 42, 43, 106
Chaumette, Pierre-Gaspard, 174, 187
Chaussard, Pierre, 126
Chaussier, Hector, 225, 227, 231
Chazet, Réné de, 168, 281
Chêne patriotique, Le (anon.), 46
Chénier, André, 209
Chénier, Marie-Joseph: early works, 21–22; *Charles IX* performed, 21–30; *Charles IX* withdrawn, 36; *Charles IX* revived, 36–39; Théâtre de la Rue de Richelieu, 79, 80, 83; Mirabeau's epitaph, 89; Voltaire's obsequies, 96, 97; *Caïus Gracchus*, 104; satires at minor houses, 117, 119, 121; Julie Talma's *salon*, 136; plea on behalf of Goldoni, 151, 152; denounced, 176, 203; André's death, 209; duel with

Chénier (*cont.*)
Kerboux, 246; ceremony honoring Napoléon, 260; report on decline of theatre, 271; *see also titles of individual works*
Chéron, Augustin-Athanase, 218
Cherubini, Maria-Luigi-Carolo-Zenobi, 185, 217
Chévalier (actress), 164
Chimène (Guillard), 132
Chronique de Paris, 52, 67
Cicero, 90
Cid, Le (Corneille), 84, 145, 279, 283
Cirque du Palais-Royal, 111
Cirque Olympique, 283
Cité-Variétés, 134, 162, 164, 188, 195–97, 205, 206, 210, 230–33, 239, 252, 264, 265, 282, 287
Clairon de Latude, Claire-Josèphe Hippolyte, 102
Clairville, Nicolaïe, 194
Cléry, Jean-Baptiste, 150
Club des bonnes gens, Le (Cousin Jacques), 122, 123
Coffin-Rosny, André-Jacques, 225
Collé, Charles, 19, 99, 102, 131
Combat de Nancy, Le (anon.), 84
Combat de taureaux, Le (anon.), 274
Comédie Française, 1–5, 8, 11–30, 33–55, 64, 68, 70–84, 87, 90, 94–96, 100–04, 150, 198, 202, 206, 243, 251, 259, 266, 267, 272, 278, 279, 282–85; *see also* Egalité, Théâtre de l'; Nation, Théâtre de la; République, Théâtre de la; *and* Richelieu, Théâtre-Français, Rue de
Comédie Italienne, 8, 24, 31, 38, 44, 51, 56, 57, 68, 76, 84, 88, 93, 103, 112–16, 121, 151, 283, see also Opéra-Comique, Favart, Salle
Comédiens du Bois, *see* Ambigu-Comique
Comédiens sans Titre, *see* Beaujolais, Théâtre du
Commissionnaire, Le (Villeneuve), 210
Commissionnaire de Saint-Lazare, Le (Hapdé), 210
Communauté de Copenhague, La (d'Antilly), 76, 77
Compiègne, theatre at, 32
Comte de Comminges, Le (d'Arnauld), 41, 77
Comte Oxtiern (de Sade), 126
Concert de la rue Feydeau, Le (anon.), 227
Concert de la rue Feydeau, Le (Martainville and Chaussée), 227, 229
Concert Spirituel, 111
Conciliateur, Le (Demoustier), 100, 122
Concorde, Théâtre de la, 86
Condorcet, Marie-Jean-Nicholas de Caritat, 136
Congrès des rois, Le (de Maillot), 185
Conjectures, Les (Picard), 215
Conservateur des principes républicains, 197
Contat, Emilie, 161, 180, 213, 279
Contat, Louise, 4, 19, 27, 35, 53, 74, 78, 83, 105, 161, 180, 208, 213, 248, 258, 275, 279
Conteur, Le (Picard), 150
Contre-révolutionnaires jugés par eux-mêmes, Les (Dorvo), 180
Convalescent de qualité, Le (d'Eglantine), 88
Convitato di pietra, Il (anon.), 266
Corday, Charlotte, 158, 167
Cordelier society, 28
Coriolan (Laharpe), 50
Corneille, Pierre, 16, 74, 83, 84, 145, 163, 199, 244, 246, 279, 283
Corsange, Jean-François-Jacques, 254
Corsse, Labanette, 254, 267
costume, 27, 28, 81, 82, 101, 102, 107, 224, 239, 247, 248, 258
Coulon (entrepreneur), 66
Courcelles (director of Marias), 113
Couronne des fleurs, La (Cousin Jacques), 68
Courrier français, Le, 134
Courtisans, Les (Palissot), 106
Cousin Jacques (Beffroy de Reigny), 62, 67–71, 84, 87, 116, 122, 123, 178, 226
Couvent, Le (Laujon), 40, 41, 77, 179
Crébillon, Prosper-Jolyot de, 74
Cri de la patrie, Le (anon.), 184
Crispin rival de son maître (Lesage), 210
Crumpipen (Dumouriez' mistress), 164
Cubière, Palmézeaux-Dorat, 30
Curtius, Salon de, 14
Cuvelier, J. G. A., 205, 226, 265

Dalayrac, Nicolas, 185, 210, 224
Damas, Auguste-Alexandre-Martial, 244, 279
Danger des conseils, Le (Léger), 62
Dangers de l'ivresse, Les (Pujoulx), 182
Dangers de l'opinion, Les (Laya), 36

Danton, Georges-Jacques, 22, 23, 28, 48, 119, 125, 130, 131, 181, 191, 192
David, Jacques-Louis, 27, 79, 81, 96, 97, 102, 107, 116, 136, 191, 203, 216, 236, 250, 258
Dazincourt, Joseph-Jean-Baptiste Albouy, 4, 30, 38, 39, 44, 78, 100, 144, 147, 150, 160, 161, 180, 212, 243, 271, 275, 278, 279, 282
Débarquement de Madame Angot, Le (anon.), 255
Déchosal (patriot), 52
Dejaure, Jean-Claude Bédéno, 55, 90, 115
Delacroix, Charles, 165
Délassements-Comiques, 12, 15, 57, 65, 86, 111, 112, 165, 170, 260, 267
Delomel (entrepreneur), 10, 11, 31, 32, 66–69, 87, 88, 124–26, 205, 243
Delpeche (actor), 149, 150
Demosthenes, 90
Demoustier, Charles-Albert, 100, 122, 221, 245, 261, 278
Dénouement inattendu, Le (Joigny and Berton), 260
Dentiste, Le (Martainville), 225
Départ des volontaires, Le (Levallée), 139
Depaure (dramatist), 263
Dernier Couvent de France, Le (Corsange and Hapdé), 254
Derniers Folies de Madame Angot, Les (anon.), 255
Desaudrais (entrepreneur), 170
Desaugiers, Marc-Antoine, 44
Descartes, René, 96
Descartes (Bouilly), 242
Descente d'Orphée aux enfers, La (anon.), 257
Descente en Angleterre, La (Mittié), 264
Deschamp, Jacques, 188
Deschanel, Emile, 101
Déserteur, Le (Gardel), 239
Désespoir de Jocrisse, Le (Dorvigny), 139
Desessarts, Denis, 4, 161
Desfontaines, George-François, 38, 55, 73, 144, 149, 157, 161, 186, 188, 260, 281
Desforges (actor), 113
Desforges, P. J. B. Choudard, 64, 88, 245
Desgarcins, Magdeleine-Marie, 42, 53, 79, 83, 101, 105, 214, 247
Deshayes, Prosper-Didier, 185
Desmoulins, Camille, 13, 14, 28, 49, 60, 127, 128
Desnoyer, Charles-Louis-François, 62, 85
Desorgues, Joseph-Théodore, 203
Despotisme renversé, Le (anon.), 131
Desprez-Valmont, Maximilien-Jean, 20, 46, 175, 260
Desrozières, Angélique, 130
Destouches, Philippe-Néricault, 7, 245, 247, 270, 271
Desverois (soldier), 126, 127
Détenus, Les (Dalayrac and Marsollier), 210
Deux Angot, Les (anon.), 225
Deux Nicodèmes, Les (Cousin Jacques), 112
Deux Soeurs, Les (Laya), 243
Deux Voisins, Les (d'Harleville), 242
Deux Voisins, Les (Laroche), 88
Devienne, François, 139, 185
Devienne, Jeanne-Françoise Thévenin, 16, 161, 190, 212, 244, 279
Devigny, Augustin-Gervais Le Chauve, 130
Diderot, Denis, 18
Didon, Le (Pompignan), 131
Directeur dans l'embarras, Le (Dubuisson), 31
Dissipateur, Le (Destouches), 270
District de village, Le (Desfontaines), 38
Dognon, Jean-François, 269
Dorfeuille, Poupart, 10, 18, 61, 62, 78, 131, 234, 241, 243, 245, 277
Dorvigny, Louis-Archambault, 139, 188, 200, 225, 238, 239
Dorvo, Hyacinthe, 140, 180, 230, 277
Dubreuil, Alphonse-Ducongé, 183
Dubuisson, Paul-Ulric, 31, 64
Ducancel, Charles-Pierre, 190, 232, 233, 240, 251
Ducis, Jean-François, 50, 82, 83, 97, 140–42, 178, 179, 199, 213, 248, 271, 278, 284
Ducos, Pierre-Roger, 281
Duel d'Arlequin, Le (anon.), 168
Dufresse (actor), 64
Dugazon, Jeas-Henri Gourgaud, 4, 15, 30, 51–53, 74, 79, 80, 82, 125, 130, 137, 139, 158, 177–79, 210, 211, 222, 241, 243, 269, 271, 279
Dugazon, Louise-Rosalie, 115, 135, 224
Dumily (actor), 69

Dumouriez, Charles-François Duperrier, 130, 135–38, 153, 154, 156, 164, 174, 192, 241
Dunant (actor), 161, 180, 251
Dupaty, Emmanuel, 281
Duplessis, Pierre, 197
Dupont (actor), 81, 106, 161, 180, 243, 251, 275
Durand, Charles, 139
Dusaulchoy, Joseph-François-Nicolas, 260
Duval, Alexandre, 161, 180, 241, 242, 244, 252, 265, 279

Easter closing, 37, 56, 78, 90, 107, 155
Ecole des bourgeois, L' (d'Allainval), 160
Ecole des femmes, L' (Molière), 50
Ecole des maris, L' (Molière), 21, 51, 81, 279
Edgar (Chénier), 22
Egalité, Théâtre de l', 198–200, 207, 208, 210, 233, 234, 241; *see also* Comédie Française *and* Nation, Théâtre de la
Eglantine, Fabre d', 22, 37, 42, 43, 50, 65, 82, 88, 102, 106, 107, 125, 192, 206
Elèves de l'Opéra, Théâtre des, *see* Beaujolais, Théâtre du
Elisca (Gréty), 262
Elizabeth, Philippine-Marie-Hélène, 115
Elleviou, Pierre-Jean-Baptiste-François, 138, 222
Elysée-Bourbon, 256, 266
Emigrant, L' (Dugazon), 139, 140
Emigrés aux terres australes, Les (Gamas), 126
Empereur, Théâtre, de l', 285; *see also* Comédie Française
Emulation, Théâtre d', 225, 239, 254, 265; *see also* Gaîté, Théâtre de la
Encore un curé (Radet and Desfontaines), 186
Enlèvement, L' (anon.), 225
Enrôlement d'Arlequin, L' (anon.), 110
Enrôlement de bûcheron, L' (anon.), 110
Entrée de Dumouriez à Bruxelles, L' (de Gouges), 148, 149
Envieux, L' (Dorvo), 277
Epicharis et Néron (Legouvé), 181, 206
Epiménide français, L' (de Riouf), 46, 57, 58
Epoux mécontents, Les (Dubuisson and Storace), 64
Epoux républicain, L' (Pompigny), 196, 197
Epreuve délicate, L' (Roger), 270
Epreuve nouvelle, L' (anon.), 79
Ericie (Fontanelle), 21, 38
Esclavage des nègres, L' (de Gouges), 148
Espoir de faveur, L' (Etienne and Nanteuil), 192
Esprit des prêtres, L' (Prévost-Montfort), 223
Estrapade, 111
Eve, Antoine-François, 254, 266
Evénéments imprévus, Les (d'Hèle), 115

Fabius (Martin), 132, 165
Faciolle, A., 196
fair theatres, 9, 58, 60, 84
Falbaire, Fenouillet de, 35
Falkland (Laya), 271
Famille patriote, La (d'Herbois), 58–60, 68
Farfar et Colas (anon.), 260
Faro, Jean-Léonard, 192
Fausse Dénunciation, La (Clairville), 194
Fausses Confidences, Les (Marivaux), 84, 208, 211, 271
Fausses Présomptions, Les (Robert), 20
Faux Député, Le (Dorvo), 230
Favart, Charles-Nicolas, 8, 32, 116
Favart, Salle, 114–16, 139, 163, 164, 168, 179, 184, 185, 191, 195, 215, 218–20, 222–25, 237, 239, 260, 262, 271, 277, 283; *see also* Comédie Italienne
Favart the Younger, 73, 254
Favières, Edmond-Guillaume de, 88
Fédération du Parnasse, La (Cousin Jacques), 68
Fénélon (Chénier), 151, 154, 157, 170, 199
Féraud, Jean, 222, 224
Feru the Younger, 190
Festin de Pierre, Le (Molière), 244, 266
festivals, Revolutionary: Festival of Federation, 34, 43–46, 58, 59, 96, 100, 105; July, 1792, festival, 109; Festival of Law, 107; Festival of Liberty, 106; Festival of the Supreme Being, 204–06; *see also* obsequies
Fête americaine, La (anon.), 217
Fête de la Fédération, La (Cousin Jacques), 68

Fête de la Liberté, La (Ronsin), 46
Fête de la Raison, La (Maréchal), 189
Fête de l'Egalité, La (Radet and Desfontaines), 188
Fête de l'Etre Suprême, La (Cuvelier), 205
Feuille de la République, 178
Feuille du jour, 120
Feuille du salut public, 159, 160, 169, 177, 179
Feux Physiques, *see* Beaujolais, Théâtre du
Feydeau, Théâtre, 95, 121–23, 135, 178, 183, 184, 195, 212, 214, 217–23, 225, 227, 229, 235–45, 248, 260, 262, 268, 270–73, 277, 279, 283; *see also* Monsieur, Théâtre de
Fiat (actress), 61
Fiévée, Joseph, 56
Fille de Madame Angot, La (Siraudin and Koning), 255
Fille hussard, La (Cuvelier), 265
Fille sauvage, La (Cuvelier), 265
Fleury, Abraham-Joseph Bénard, 3, 4, 16, 23, 28, 30, 39, 51, 54, 65, 77, 100, 102, 144, 156, 157, 160, 180, 207, 243, 279
Fleury, Jules, 161
Fleury, Marie-Florence Nones, 161, 243, 251, 279
Flins des Oliviers, Carbon de, 34, 35, 58, 70, 76, 103, 141, 287
Florence, Joseph-Florence Laferrière, 161, 251, 279
Folie de Georges, La (Lebrun-Tossa), 195
Fontainbleau, theatre at, 32
Fontanelle, Jean-Gaspard de, 21, 38
Forgeot, Nicolas-Julien, 208
Fouché, Joseph, 281
Fouquier-Tinville, Antoine-Quentin, 180, 200, 222
Framery, Nicolas-Etienne, 76
France régénérée, La (Chaussard), 126
Francoeur, Louis-Joseph, 131, 164, 171, 261
Franklin, Benjamin, 46, 90, 229
Fusil (actor), 210, 211, 218
Fusil, Louise, 42, 137

Gaillard, Antoine, 10, 18, 61, 62, 78, 131, 165, 211
Gainsborough, Thomas, 247
Gaîté, Théâtre de la, 112, 165, 168, 195, 225, 265, 267, 280, 282, 286, 287; *see also* Grands Danseurs du Roi; Emulation, Théâtre d'; *and* Nicolet, Jean-Baptiste
Galant Savetier, Le (Saint-Firmin), 225
Galathée (Poultier), 220
Gallet, Sébastien, 138
Gamas (dramatist), 126, 210, 260
Garat, Pierre-Jean, 217
Garnerin, André-Jacques, 70, 257, 259
Gaston et Bayard (Belloy), 19, 72
Gaudet, Victor-Maurice, 136
Gavaudan, Jean-Baptiste Sauveur, 138
Gennevilliers, Château de, 3
Gensonné, Armand, 136
Georges Dandin (Molière), 51, 84
Gérard (actor), 161
Gervais (director), 170
Géta (Petitot), 247
Gilbert (actor), 139
gilded youth, 216–20, 222, 223, 227–29, 233, 235, 258, 264
Gilles Lovelace (Léger), 121
Girondist Club, 120, 127, 135, 156, 158, 168, 177, 190
Girouette de Saint-Cloud, La (Barré, Radet, Desfontaines, Maurice, Dupaty, and Bourgueil), 281
Glorieux, Le (Destouches), 170, 247, 271
Gluck, Christoph-Willibald, 8
Gobel, J. B., 186, 187
Goldoni, Carlo, 103, 151, 159, 190, 200, 208
Gossec, François-Joseph, 96–98, 100, 106, 131, 203
Gouffé, Armand, 210, 229, 281
Gouges, Olympe de, 55, 89, 90, 148, 149, 154
Gourion, de (major general), 67
Goûter, Le (de Senlis), 168
Gouthier (actress), 260
Gouttes, Jean Louis, 41
Gouvernante, La (La Chaussée), 100
Gozzi, Carlo, 151
Grammont, Jean-Baptiste-Jacques Nourry, 48, 64, 206
Grandménil, Jean-Baptiste Fauchard de, 50, 79, 177, 271, 277, 279
Grands Danseurs du Roi, 64, 84, 112; *see also* Gaîté, Théâtre de la, *and* Nicolet, Jean-Baptiste
Gréty, André-Ernest-Modeste, 168, 185, 261, 262
Griselidis (Desforges), 88

Guerville, Harny de, 73, 74
Guillaume Tell (Lemierre), 131, 146, 165, 247

Hamlet (Ducis), 82, 284
Hapdé, Augustin, 210, 254, 265
Harcourt, George Simon, Earl of, 27
Harleville, Colin d', 42, 105, 106, 182, 242, 278, 283
Hébert, Jacques-René, 149, 174, 191
Hénault, Charles-Jean-François, 35
Henri IV, Théâtre d', 111
Henri IV et la jeune Desilles (de Gouges), 55
Henry VIII (Chénier), 79, 80, 83, 95, 199
Herbois, Collot d', 22, 58–60, 68, 150, 180, 200, 214, 230
Héritière, L' (d'Eglantine), 102
Héritiers (Duval), 242
Hermitage, 256
Héros de retour d'Egypte, Le (anon.), 280
Heureuse Décade, L' (Léger, Barré, and Rosières), 186
Heureuse Nouvelle, L' (d'Olivet), 195
Heureuse Nouvelle, L' (Saint-Just, Longchamps, and Boieldieu), 259
Hoffman, François-Benoît, 116, 145, 217, 241, 274
Homme sans façon, L' (Léger), 272
Honnête Criminel, L' (de Falbaire), 35
Horace (Corneille), 84, 199
Horatius Coclès (Arnault), 132
Hôtel de Bourgogne, 285
Hôtel de Richelieu, 256
Hôtellerie de Worms, L' (anon.), 99
Houdon, Antoine, 97
Hugot (actor), 88, 125

Imbert, Barthélemy, 23, 246, 268
Impératrice, Théâtre de l', *see* Odéon
Impromptu de campagne, L' (Poisson), 42
Inauguration du Temple de la Vérité, L' (anon.), 189
Incas, Les (anon.), 265
Intérieur des comités révolutionnaires, L' (Ducancel), 232, 233, 240, 251
Intérieur d'une ménage républicaine, L' (Chastenet), 184
Intrigue épistolaire, L' (d'Eglantine), 82
Iphigénie en Aulide (Durollet), 81, 132, 171
Italian, The (Radcliffe), 265

Jacobin Club, 28, 71, 115, 119–24, 127–30, 135, 136, 143, 144, 150, 155, 158–60, 170, 177, 180, 182, 192, 203, 204, 206–08, 210, 211, 213, 214, 216, 219, 221, 223–25, 227–34, 252, 264, 281
Jacobins aux enfers, Les (Chaussier), 231
Jadin, Adolphe, 185
Jaloux malgré lui, Le (Imbert), 246
Jaloux sans amour, Le (Imbert), 268
Jardin Biron, 256, 257
Jardin Idalie, 256
Jean Calas (Laya), 55
Jean Jacques Rousseau à ses derniers moments (Bouilly), 57
Jean Jacques Rousseau dans l'Ile de Saint-Pierre (anon.), 103
Jean Sans-Terre (Ducis), 82, 83
Jeanne d'Arc (anon.), 84
Jeanne de Naples (Laharpe), 50
Jenny (actress), 164
Jeune Hôtesse, La (Flins des Oliviers), 103
Jeunes-Artistes, Théâtre des, 253, 254, 267, 281, 287
Jeunes-Comédiens, 287
Jeunes-Elèves, 287
Joigny (actor), 139, 260, 267
Joly (censor), 76
Joly, Marie-Elisabeth, 53, 161, 180, 243, 251, 270, 272
Joseph (Favart the Younger), 254
Jouan (director), 170
Journal de la montagne, 170
Journal de Paris, 5, 23, 213, 224, 261
Journal des débats, 170
Journal des spectacles, 158, 161, 171, 206
Journal des théâtres, 211
Journal général de la cour et de la ville, 120
Journaliste (de Langre), 248
Journaliste des Ombres, Le (Aude), 46
Journée de Saint-Cloud, La (anon.), 281
Journée de Saint-Cloud, La (Léger, Chazet, and Gouffé), 281
Journée de Varennes, La (anon.), 92
Journée difficile, La (Dumaniant), 241

Journée du dix août, 1792, La (Saulnier and Darrieux), 132
Journée du jeune Néron, Une (Laya), 277
Journée du Vatican, La (Giennaro-Chiavacchi), 166
Jugement dernier des rois, Le (Maréchal), 176, 177, 189
Juliette (actress), 195
Julius Caesar (Shakespeare), 204
Junius (Monvel), 246

Kemble, John Philip, 27
Kolly (aristocrat), 135
Koning, Victor, 255
Kotzebue, Augustus von, 60, 225, 276, 277
Kreutzer, Rodolphe, 88, 185, 200

La Chapelle, Solomon de, 230
La Chassaigne, Marie-Anne-Hélène Broquain, 161, 279
La Chaussée, Pierre-Claude, 100, 159
La Grange, Charles-Varlet de, 8
La Martelière, J.-Henri-Ferdinand, 84, 123, 124, 154, 183
Labussière, Charles-Hippolyte, 200–02, 206, 284
Lacane (actor), 64
Lafayette, Marie-Joseph-Paul-Yves, Marquis de, 14, 20, 53, 130, 136, 192
Lafon, Pierre-Rapenouille, 279
Lafont, Joseph de, 249
Laharpe, Jean-François, 21, 50, 71, 72, 74, 96, 103, 107, 113
Lamarque, François, 271
Lambert, L.-T., 168, 187
Lancival, Luce de, 157
Lange, Anne-Françoise-Elisabeth, 47, 79, 180
Langre, Lombard de, 248
Larive, Jean Mauduit de, 4, 41, 49, 87, 213, 243, 251
Larivière, Henri-P.-F.-J., 120
Larnac, François, 272
Laroche (dramatist), 88
Larochelle, Barthélémy, 78, 144, 161, 215, 244, 251, 279
Lartique (singer), 138
Laujon, Pierre, 40, 41, 77, 179
Laurence (Legouvé), 245
Lavallée, Joseph de, 139
Laveaux, Jean-Charles-Thiébault de, 170
Lawrence, Sir Thomas, 247
Laya, Jean-Louis, 36, 55, 61, 95, 143–47, 150, 151, 153, 170, 212, 214, 243, 271, 277
Lays, François, 213
Lazzari, Ange, 112, 194, 260, 266, 275
Lazzari, Théâtre, *see* Variétés Amusantes (second)
Le Clerc (architect), 241, 245, 252, 270, 273, 277
Le Page (director), 245, 252, 273, 277
Le Pelletier de Saint-Fargeau, Louis-Michel, 148, 157, 179, 181, 187, 197, 219, 241
Léar (Ducis), 82
Leblanc (composer), 254
Lebrun-Tossa, Jean-Antoine, 195, 223
Léger, François-Pierre-Auguste, 62, 117, 119–22, 144, 183, 186, 188, 267, 272, 281
Legouvé, Gabriel-Marie-Jean-Baptiste, 106, 121, 181, 206, 214, 245, 278, 283
Legrand, Jacques-Guillaume, 31, 85
Lejeune, Silvain-Phalier, 165
Lekain, Henri-Louis Cain, 61, 102
Lemercier, Népomucène-Louis, 102, 107, 121, 214, 240, 246, 276
Lemierre, Antoine-Marin, 43, 131, 146, 165, 247
Lemoyne (architect), 5
Lendemain des noces d'Arlequin, Le (anon.), 168
Lenoir, Jean-Pierre, 1, 2
Lenoir, Nicolas, 117, 162, 190
Léon (Hoffman), 274
Lepipe (vicar), 80
Leroy (actress), 206
Lesage, Alain-René, 1, 210
Lesage, Nicolas-Léonard, 61, 260
Lesueur, Jean-François, 183
Lévêque, Marie-Jacqueline, 167
Lévite d'Ephrain (Lemercier), 240
Lewis, Matthew Gregory, 265
Liberté, Théâtre de la, 86, 111
Liberté conquise (de Guerville and Favart), 73, 74
Liberté des femmes, La (Brienne), 157
Liberté et l'Egalité, Théâtre de la, *see* Richelieu, Théâtre-François, Rue de
Ligue des fanatiques et des tyrans, La (Ronsin), 91, 126
Limodin (police chief), 253
Loaisel de Tréogate, Joseph-Marie, 265
Lodoïska (Dejaure), 115
Longchamps, Charles de, 259
Lornaison, Clément de, 62

Louis, Victor, 17, 90, 172
Louis XII (Ronsin), 37, 61, 77, 92
Louis XIV, 7, 35, 84, 92, 141
Louis XIV ou Le Masque de fer (Legrand), 126
Louis XIV, 1–5, 12–20, 29, 30, 33–35, 37, 45, 46, 56, 59, 68, 73, 78, 89, 92–94, 103, 107–10, 114, 120–22, 140, 142–44, 146–50, 164, 176, 249, 263
Louvois, Théâtre, 87, 124, 126, 165, 172, 239, 243–47, 249–52, 266, 268–70, 278, 284; *see also* Amis de la Patrie, Théâtre des
Lovelace (Lemercier), 107, 121
Lovelace des Halles, Le (Camel), 255
Lovelace français, Le (Duval and Monvel), 244
Lucrétia (Arnault), 107
Lulier, Louis-Marie, 175
Lully, Jean-Baptiste, 7
Lunes, Les, 68
Lycée des Arts, 151, 161, 168, 170

Macbeth (Ducis), 82, 199, 271
Macklin, Charles, 27
Madame Angot (Eve), 254, 266
Madame Angot au Malabar (Aude and Lion), 255
Madame Angot au muséum (anon.), 255
Madam Angot au Sérail de Constantinople (Aude), 255
Madame Angot dans son ballon (Aude), 255
Madame Angot dans son grénier (anon.), 255
Mahérut (assistant to Neufchâteau), 278
Mahomet (Voltaire), 27, 87, 163
Maire du village (Boissy), 150, 151
Manuel (procurator), 155
Marais, Théâtre de, 8, 113, 114, 131, 154, 193, 194, 248, 287
Marat, Jean-Paul, 125, 127, 133, 136–39, 143, 154, 158, 166, 174, 175, 178, 179, 181, 184, 185, 187, 197, 200, 207, 208, 211, 219, 220, 241
Marat dans le souterrain des Cordeliers (Mathelin), 184
Marbeuf, 256
Maréchal, Pierre-Sylvain, 176, 177, 189
Maret (dramatist), 14
Marguerit, Jacques, 88
Marguerite (Ribié and Saint-Aubin), 225
Mari directeur, Le (Flins des Oliviers), 76
Mari jaloux, Le (Desforges), 245
Mariage à la paix, Le (Gamas), 260
Mariage de Figaro, Le (Beaumarchais), 1–5, 22, 27, 29, 45, 51, 114
Marie Antoinette, 2, 30, 32, 67, 92, 104, 115, 117, 168, 170, 174, 177
Marie de Brabant (Imbert), 23
Mariniers de Saint-Cloud, Les (Sewrin), 281
Marius à Minturnes (Arnault), 81, 107, 206
Marivaux, Pierre Carlet de, 8, 84, 103, 208, 211, 252, 258, 271
Marmontel, Jean-François, 128
Mars, Anne-Françoise-Hippolyte, 64, 275, 279
Marseillaise, 110, 132, 135, 149, 162, 183, 200, 211, 238
Marsollier de Vivetières, 210, 224, 260, 269, 270, 274
Marsy (actor), 161, 251
Martainville, Alphonse-L.-D., 125, 227, 229, 253, 254, 267
Martin, Marie-Joseph-Désiré, 132, 165
Martini (musician), 257
Mathilde (Monvel), 274
Matinée d'une jolie femme, La (Vigée), 146
Maury, Jean-Siffrein Abbé, 33, 155, 166
Médecin malgré lui, Le (Molière), 147
Méhul, Etienne-Nicolas, 116, 122, 136, 145, 185, 208, 260, 261
Mélanie (Laharpe), 103
Ménage truc d'Arlequin, Le (anon.), 168
Menou, Jacques-François, 225
Menteur, Le (Corneille), 163, 244
Menuisier de Bagdad, Le (Guillemain), 33
Menus-Plaisirs, 2
Mercier, Louis-Sébastien, 8, 50
Mercure galant, Le (Boursault), 103
Mère coupable, Le (Beaumarchais), 113, 114, 248
Merlin of Douai, Philippe-Antoine, 238–40, 249, 250
Merlin of Thionville, Antoine-Christophe, 223
Mérope (Voltaire), 163
Métromanie (Piron), 208
Mézeray, Marie-Antoinette-Josephine, 96, 100, 161, 180, 243, 251, 271, 279
Michel Montaigne (anon.), 275
Michot, Antoine, 61, 177, 206, 212, 241, 244, 271, 279

Mieux fait douceur que violence (Pompigny), 168
Mille et un théâtres, Les (Barré), 117
Miltiade à Marathon (Guillard), 132
Minuit (Desaurdras), 243, 269
Minuit ou L'Heure propice (anon.), 103
Mirabeau, Honoré-Gabriel Riguetti, Comte de, 28, 33, 44, 46, 49, 54, 75, 78, 89, 90, 208
Mirabeau à son lit (anon.), 90
Mirabeau aux Champs-Elysées (de Gouges), 90
Misanthrope, Le (Molière), 37, 49, 272
Misanthrope et Repentir (Molé), 276, 277
Misanthropy and Repentance (Kotzebue), 276
Mistress of the Inn, The (Goldoni), 103
Mittié, J.-Corisandre, 260, 264
Modéré, Le (Dugazon), 178
Modernes Enrichis, Les (Pujoulx), 268, 269
Moine, Le (Ribié and Saint-Aubin), 265
Moissoneurs, Les (Favart), 32
Molé (actress), 276
Molé, François-René, 4, 19, 27, 30, 35, 61, 105, 190, 212, 244, 247, 249, 251, 268, 271, 275, 279
Molière (actress), 243
Molière, Jean-Baptiste Poquelin, 1, 7, 8, 17, 41, 49–51, 81, 84, 91, 102, 106, 145, 147, 152, 180, 194, 199, 214, 244, 266, 268, 271, 276, 279, 285
Molière, Théâtre National, 91–93, 97, 126, 127, 130, 131, 133, 229, 230, 253, 267, 280; *see also* Sans-Culottes, Théâtre des, *and* Troubadours, Théâtre des
Molinos, Jacques, 31, 85
Mongol, Le (anon.), 265
Moniteur, Le, 140
Monk, The (Lewis), 265
Monsieur, Louis Stanislaus Xavier, 12, 92
Monsieur, Théâtre de, 12, 13, 20, 30, 31, 34, 44, 57–61, 68, 77, 84, 85, 95, 183; *see also* Feydeau, Théâtre
Monsieur de Crac dans son petit castel (d'Harleville), 105
Montagnards (Pujoulx), 217
Montagne, La (Desriaux), 132
Montagne, Théâtre de la, 175, 190, 228; *see also* Variétés Montansier
Montaigne, Michel-Eyquem de, 233
Montano et Stéphanie (Depaure and Berton), 263
Montansier, Marguerite Brunet, La, 12, 13, 31, 32, 64, 90, 124, 125, 134, 138, 139, 164, 172, 174, 190, 206, 228, 229, 283; *see also* Neuf Millions, Théâtre des, *and* Variétés Montansier
Montansier, Théâtre, *see* Neuf Millions, Théâtre des, *and* Opéra
Montesquieu, Charles de Secondat, Baron de, 90
Montgautier (actress), 161
Montgolfier, Joseph-Michel, 70
Montparnasse, Théâtre, 111
Monvel, Jacques-Marie Boutet, 61, 77, 79, 82, 95, 101, 105, 108, 130, 140, 179, 242, 244, 247, 248, 271, 279
Moreau, Jean-Charles-Alexandre, 272
Mort d'Abel, La (Legouvé), 106, 121, 283
Mort de César, La (Voltaire), 41, 55, 131, 146, 181, 212, 283
Mort de Madame Angot, La (Saint-Armand), 255
Mort de Marat, La (Barrau), 194
Mort de Molière, La (Cubière), 30
Mort de Turennes, La (Cuvelier and Bouilly), 265
Mort du jeune Barra, La (Briois), 181
Morte vivante, La (Caignez), 265
Moulin brulé, Le (anon.), 194
Mousseaux, 256
Murville, Pierre-Nicolas, 37, 101
Muses, Théâtre des, 111
Mutius Scévola (Lancival), 157
Myrrha (Souriguières), 237, 238, 244
Mysteries of Udolpho, The (Radcliffe), 265

Nanine (actress), 247
Nanine (Voltaire), 99, 159, 283
Nanteuil, Charles-Gaugiran, 192
Nation, Théâtre de la, 19, 81, 83, 94, 95, 98, 100, 102, 103, 105, 106, 108, 110, 114, 121, 129, 131, 143–47, 150, 151, 154–61, 164, 169, 170, 175, 180, 181, 183, 190, 198–202, 207, 208, 212, 214, 215, 221, 233, 243, 270; *see also* Comédie Française, Egalité, Théâtre de l', *and* Odéon
Naudet, Jean-Baptiste-Julien-Marcel, 15, 26, 47, 48, 53, 74, 81, 161, 243, 251
Necker, Jacques, 13, 14, 19

Neuf Millions, Théâtre des, 172–74, 190, 191, 212, 228, 261; *see also* Montansier, Théâtre, *and* Opéra
Neufchâteau, François-Nicolas de, 159, 160, 170, 176, 180, 212, 214, 250, 278
Neuville, Bourdon de, 64, 174, 190, 228
Nicodème dans la lune (Cousin Jacques), 62, 69–71, 122
Nicolet, Jean-Baptiste, 9, 16, 57, 64, 66, 84, 112, 168, 195, 225, 265; *see also* Gaîté, Théâtre de la, *and* Grands Danseurs du Roi
Nozzi di Dorina (Sarti), 85

obsequies: of Marat, 208; of Mirabeau, 89; of Voltaire, 96–99
Odéon, 241, 245, 252, 260, 270–78, 285; *see also* Nation, Thèâtre de la
Oedipe (Voltaire), 247, 272
Oedipe à Colone (Ducis), 248
Oedipe à Colone (Guillard), 132, 171, 213
Oedipe à Thèbes (Duprat), 101
Oedipe chez Admète (Ducis), 140
Oedipus (Sophocles), 41
Officier de fortune, L' (Patrat), 183
Old English Baron, The (Reeve), 265
Olivet, Fabre d', 65, 132, 195
Olivier, Jeanne-Adelaide, 4
Olympie (Voltaire), 261
Ombres Chinoises, Les, 16
On respire (Tissot), 223
Opéra, 7, 8, 10, 17, 56, 61, 67, 95, 98, 101, 114–16, 128, 131–35, 140, 164, 171, 172, 182, 188–91, 203, 206, 218, 220, 222, 223, 227, 238, 261, 266, 271, 278, 283, 284
Opéra-Buffa, 283
Opéra-Comique, 184, 281–86; *see also* Comédie Italienne, *and* Favart, Salle
Ophis (Lemercier), 276
Optimiste, L' (d'Harleville), 182
Orange de Malte, L' (d'Eglantine), 192
Original, L' (Hoffman), 241
Orléans, duc d', 10, 14, 17, 22, 61, 125
Orosome (Voltaire), 99
Orpheline de Chine, L' (Voltaire), 145, 283
Oscar (d'Arnauld), 21
Othello (Ducis), 140–42, 179

Paché (Montansier apprentice), 190
Paillardelle (actor), 60
Paisiello, Giovanni, 57
Paix, La (Aude), 260
Paix, La (Mittié), 260
Palais-Royal, *see* Variétés-Palais-Royal
Palais-Variétés, *see* Cité-Variétés
Palissot, Charles, 28, 44, 47, 50, 55, 79, 83, 106, 121
Paméla (Neufchâteau), 159, 160, 170, 176, 212
Paméla nubile (Goldoni), 159
Panard, Charles, 116
Paphos, 256
Papillon de Bourneuf, Jean-François, 206
Parc de Monceaux, 257, 259
Parc Saint-Cloud, 256
Parcin, Pierre-Mathieu, 99
Parfaite Egalité, La (Dorvigny), 200
Pari, Le (Desfontaines, Barré, Radet, Desprez, and Deschamps), 260
Pariseau, Nicolas, 58
Partie de Chasse de Henri IV, La (Collé), 19, 99, 102, 131
Passé, le présent, et l'avenir, Le (Picard), 96
Patrie reconnaissante, La (Leboeuf), 140
Patriote du dix août, Le (Dorvo), 140
Patriotique, Théâtre, *see* Associés, Théâtre des
Paul et Virginie (Favières and Kreutzer), 88
Paulin et Clairette (anon.), 84, 103
Paulin et Virginie (Dubreuil and Lesuer), 183
Pausanias (Trouvé), 221
Pauvre Femme, La (Marsollier and Dalayrac), 224
Payan, Claude-François de, 193
Paysan Magistrat, Le (d'Herbois), 30
Père de famille, Le (Diderot), 18
Père Duchesne, Le, 177
Péristyle du Jardin Egalité, Théâtre du, *see* Variétés Montansier
Perrière (observer), 182
Perrin (magician), 86, 112
Perrin, René, 7
Perruque blonde, La (Picard), 216
Pessimiste, Le (Pigault-Lebrun), 61
Pétion, Jerôme, 108, 119, 127, 128, 146, 147
Petit Théâtre du Lycée, 236, 237
Petitot, Claude-Bernard, 247
Petits Affiches, Les, 88, 115
Petits Comédiens du Palais-Royal, Les, 86
Petits Comédiens Français, Théâtre des, 111

Petit-Vanhove, Cécile-Caroline-Charlotte, 36, 37, 161, 180, 214, 244–46, 271, 275, 279
Peuple, Théâtre du, *see* Egalité, Théâtre de l'
Peuples et les rois, Les (Duplessis), 197
Peyre, Marie-Joseph, 1
Phèdre (Racine), 163, 270
Philinte de Molière, Le (d'Eglantine), 37, 42
Philosophe sans le savoir, Le (Sédaine), 102
Philosophes amoureux, Les (Destouches), 245
Picard, Louis-Benoît, 96, 150, 183, 184, 215, 216, 243, 249, 276, 285
Picardeaux (director), 112, 195, 225
Pied de nez, Le (Dusaulchoy), 260
Pierre le Grand (anon.), 84
Pigault-Lebrun, Guillaume-Charles-Antoine, 61, 181, 252
Piis, Augustus, Chevalier de, 116, 117, 161, 165, 186, 267
Pixérécourt, R.-C. Guilbert de, 123, 227, 265, 267
Plaisir et la gloire, Le (Sewrin), 184
Plaque retournée, La (Thierry and Lambert), 187
Plutarch, 125
Point du jour, Le, 169
Poisson, Philippe, 42
Pomme, La (anon.), 195
Pompe funèbre de général Hoche, La (anon.), 261
Pompigny, Maurin de, 131, 168, 196, 197
Ponceau, Doigny de, 99
Porte-Saint-Martin, Théâtre de la, 17, 266, 286, 287
Portrait d'un magistrat verteux, Le (anon.), 221
Poste évacué, Le (Deschamp), 188
Poultier d'Elmotte, François-Martin, 220
Premier Rayon du soleil, Le (Saint-Victor), 281
Premier rossé, Le (anon.), 121
Présomptueux, Le (d'Eglantine), 42, 43, 106
Prestat (police officer), 119, 120
Préville, Pierre-Louis Dubus, 5, 102, 208
Prise de la Bastille, La (Desaugiers), 44
Prise de la Bastille, La (Parcin), 99
Prise de la Bastille, La (Ruggieri), 46
Prise de Toulon, La (Faciolle and Bizet), 196
Prise de Toulon, La (Picard), 183
Prise de Toulon par les français, La (d'Antilly), 184
Prisonniers français en Angleterre, Les (Dognon and Rebory), 269
Procès de Socrate, Le (d'Herbois), 59, 60
Pujoulx, Jean-Baptiste, 182, 217, 268, 269

Quintus Cincinnatus (Arnault), 210
Quintus Fabius (Legouvé), 214
Quotidienne, La, 209, 251

Racine, Jean, 53, 74, 131, 163, 192, 209, 251, 258, 271
Racoleurs, Les (anon.), 110
Radcliffe, Ann, 265
Radet, Jean-Baptiste, 144, 149, 161, 186, 188, 260, 281
Rafford-Brienne, J.-S., 188
Rameau, Jean-Philippe, 8, 98
Raucourt, Françoise-Marie-Antoinette, 16, 53, 74, 107, 161, 180, 243–47, 249–51, 258, 270, 272, 275, 279
Raymond V (Sédaine), 24
Rebory (dramatist), 269
Réclamations contre l'emprunt forcée, Les (Dorvigny), 225, 238, 239
Regnard, Jean-François, 172
Religieuses, Les (anon.), 57
Religieuses délivrées, Les (anon.), 57
République, Théâtre de la, 175–83, 189, 190, 195, 206, 208, 210, 213–15, 222, 234, 237, 239–48, 251, 252, 260, 268–73, 276, 278; *see also* Richelieu, Théâtre-Français, Rue de
République et des Arts, Théâtre de la, *see* Opéra
Retour à l'esperance, Le (anon.), 280
Retour de Camille à Rome, Le (Aude), 20
Retour du Champ-du-Mars, Le (Cousin Jacques), 68, 69
Réunion du dix août, La (Bouquier), 191
Revanche, La (Barré), 116, 117
Réveil d'Epiménide à Paris, Le (Flins des Oliviers), 34, 35, 58, 70, 103, 141, 287
Réveil du peuple, Le, 210, 211, 213, 222, 238

Révolte des nègres, La (anon.), 161
Révolutions de France et de Brabant, Les, 49
Rhamin (actor), 195
Ribaut (actress), 161
Ribié, César, 225, 254, 265, 266, 271, 278
Richard (anon.), 114
Richardson, Samuel, 159
Richelieu, Théâtre-Français, Rue de, 78–79, 81–83, 95, 99, 101–04, 106–08, 110, 131, 133, 134, 136, 138–40, 143, 145, 148, 151, 154, 156–58, 161, 175; *see also* République, Théâtre de la, *and* Variétés-Palais-Royal
Rigby, Edward, 14
Rigueurs du cloître, Les (Fiévée and Berton), 56
Riouf, de (dramatist), 46, 57, 58
Rivière (actress), 139
Robbers, The (Schiller), 123
Robert (dramatist), 20
Robert, chef de brigands (La Martelière), 84, 123, 124, 154, 183
Robespierre, Maximilian-Isidore, 33, 116, 125, 127, 143, 154, 160, 169, 170, 181, 182, 184, 187, 190, 192, 193, 200, 202–10, 218, 221, 223, 224, 228, 231, 250
Roederer, Pierre-Louis, comte de, 33
Roger, Jean-François, 270
Roland, Jean-Marie, 136
Roland (Quinault), 128, 132
Roland de Montglare (Loaisel de Tréogate), 265
Roméo (Ducis), 82
Ronsin, Charles-Philippe, 37, 46, 61, 77, 92, 125
Rosalie (Pariseau), 58
Rose et Picard (d'Harleville), 182
Roselly (actor), 206
Rosières, Lecouppey de la, 186
Roucher, Jean, 209
Rouget de Lisle, Claude-Joseph, 110, 261
Rousseau, Jean-Jacques, 26, 46, 57, 90, 103, 140, 179, 188, 197, 200, 220, 229
Rousseau, Pierre, 194
Rousselin de Corbeau, Alexandre-Charles-Omer, 177, 179
Rue Martin, Théâtre de la, 230; *see also* Molière, Théâtre National, *and* Sans-Culottes, Théâtre des
Rue Renard Saint-Méry, Théâtre de la, 110
Rue Saint-Antoine, Théâtre de la, 86, 110
Ruggieri, Claude, 46, 256

Sade, Donatien-Alphonse-François, Marquis de, 126
Sageret (entrepreneur), 221, 248, 262, 268, 270, 272–77
Saint-Armand, Gaussier, 166, 255
Saint-Aubin (actress), 262
Saint-Aubin, M.-C.-Cammaile, 158, 175, 225, 265
Saint-Clair (actor), 61
Saint-Cloud, theatre at, 32
Saint-Edme (director), 196
Saint-Fal, Etienne-Maynier, 26, 35, 42, 78, 81, 107, 161, 243, 251, 275, 279
Saint-Just, C.-Godard d'Aucourt de, 259
Saint-Marcel, A.-Philippe Tardieu de, 240
Saint-Pierre (entrepreneur), 111
Saint-Prix, Jean-Amable Foucault, 15, 26, 40, 47, 48, 81, 106, 107, 144, 161, 164, 212, 243, 251, 275, 279
Saint-Victor, M.-J.-B. de, 281
Sainte-Amaranthe, Jeanne-Françoise-Louise Demier, 160, 207
Sainte Omlette (Ducancel), 190, 232
Sainval the Elder, Marie-Pauline, 64
Sainval the Younger, Marie-Blanche, 4, 53, 64, 74, 102
Sallé, Jean-Baptiste, 10, 18, 65
Salliort (police officer), 122, 123
Salpêtres républicains, Les (Tissot), 197, 198
Samson (Voltaire), 98
Sans Adieux (Cousin Jacques), 68
Sans-Culottes, Théâtre des, 191, 195, 206, 229; *see also* Molière, Théâtre National
Sans-Prétention, Théâtre, 267, 287; *see also* Associés, Théâtre des
Santerre, Antoine-Joseph, 136, 137, 146, 147
Sarrazin (deputy), 47
Sarti, Guiseppi, 85
Sauvigny, Billardon de, 95, 269
scenery, 70, 81, 217, 225–27, 231–32, 257, 266
Schiller, Friedrich von, 123
Scipion l'Africain (Sauvigny), 269
Séchilles, Herault de, 179
Sédaine, Jean-Michel, 24, 50, 102, 178, 209

Ségur the Younger, Alexandre-Joseph Pierre, 221, 245
Sémiramis (Voltaire), 146
Sermet civique de Marathon, Le (Kreutzer), 200
Seveste (actor), 139
Sewrin, Charles-Augustus de Bassompierre, 184, 281
Shakespeare, William, 82, 140–42, 156, 204
Siège de Lille, Le (Joigny), 139
Siège de Thionville, Le (Saulnier and Dutheil), 132, 182
Sieur Doyen, Théâtre du, 110
Sieyès, Emmanuel-Joseph, 281
Simon (actress), 79, 83, 140, 243, 251
Simoneau, Jacques, 107
Siraudin, Paul, 255
Socrates, 60, 258
Soeurs du pot, Les (Prévost-Montfort), 57
Soirée de Vaugiraud, La (Charlemagne), 253
Solié (composer), 185
Sortie du couvent, La (anon.), 57
Sot intrigant, Le (Duval), 252
Souper de Henri IV, Le (Bouthellier and Desprez-Valmont), 19, 46
Souper des Jacobins, Le (Charlemagne), 230
Souper magique, Le (Murville), 37
Sourd, Le (Desforges), 64
Sourd guéri, Le (Léger and Barré), 188
Souriguières, J.-M., 237, 238, 244
Spartacus (Saurin), 51
Spectacles de Paris, Les, 205
Suard, J.-B.-Antoine, 22, 23, 76, 79
Suin, Marie-Denise Vriot, 144, 148, 161, 279
Surprise de l'amour, La (Marivaux), 103, 212

Talma, Mme., *see* Careau, Louise-Julie
Talma, François-Joseph: early years, 26, 27; in *Charles IX*, 28; other early roles, 30, 34, 42; quarrel with the "blacks," 38–40; marriage, 41; revival of *Charles IX*, 47–49; expelled from Comédie, 49; readmitted, 52–54; joins the Richelieu, 79–81; in *Jean Sans-Terre*, 82, 83; *Calas*, 95; *Charles IX* at Richelieu, 99; *Abdélazis et Zuléima*, 101; *Caïus Gracchus*, 105; *Virginie*, 108; at Montansier's *salon*, 125; appeal for subsidy, 130; host to Dumouriez, 136–38; in *Othello*, 140–42, 179; *Fénélon*, 151; threatened under the Terror, 172, 177; in *Epicharis et Néron*, 181; Festival of the Supreme Being, 204; reopening of the Nation, 208; attacked during the Thermidorian reaction, 210–12; in *Quintus Fabius*, 214; offered position at the Louvois, 243; in *Junius*, 246; *Agamemnon*, 246; *Guillaume Tell*, 247; at Feydeau, 271, 275; Comédie reunited, 279; Labussière benefit, 284
Tancrède (Voltaire), 163
Tartuffe (Molière), 41, 145, 163, 180, 194, 214
Tartuffe révolutionnaire, Le (Lemercier), 214
Temple de la gloire, Le (Voltaire), 98
Tentation de Saint Antoine, La (anon.), 231, 265
Tête de bronze, La (Hapdé), 265
Thé à la mode, Le (Ducancel), 240
Théâtre-Français Comique et Lyrique, 62, 69–71, 85, 112
Théâtre-Français de la Liberté et de l'Egalité, *see* République, Théâtre de la, *and* Richelieu, Théâtre-Français, Rue de
Théâtre-Français, Rue de Richelieu, *see* Richelieu, Théâtre-Français, Rue de
Théâtre-Lyrique de la Rue Feydeau, *see* Feydeau, Théâtre
Thémistocle (Larnac), 272
Thénard, Magdeleine-Claudine Perrin, 161, 243, 251, 279
Théodore (anon.), 284
Thierry (dramatist), 168, 187
Tiercelin, actor, 265
Timoléon (Chénier), 175, 199, 203, 208
Tissot, Charles-Louis, 162, 198, 199, 223
Tivoli, 257, 266
Tolérant, Le (Demoustier), 221
Tombeau de Desilles, Le (Desfontaines), 55, 73
Tonnerre, Clermont, 33
Toulon soumis (d'Olivet), 132
Tout par l'opium (anon.), 115
Tout pour la liberté (Tissot), 162, 198
Tout pour l'amour (Monvel), 115
Toute la famille (Cousin Jacques), 87
Traité nul, Le (Marsollier), 270

Treilhard, Jean-Baptiste, 273
Trial, Antoine, 218
Trial the Younger, 185
Tribunal révolutionnaire, Le (Ducancel), 240
Trois Fils, Les (Demoustier), 245
Trois Frères rivaux, Les (Lafont), 249
Trois Mages, Les (anon.), 62
Trois Noces, Les (anon.), 37
Trois Voyageurs, Les (Cousin Jacques), 68
Trop de délicatesse (Marsollier), 270
Troubadours, Théâtre des, 280, 281, 287; *see also* Molière, Théâtre National
Trouvé, Charles-Joseph, 221
Tuileries, theatre at, 14, 30, 57

Urgande et Merlin (Monvel), 168, 179

Valcour, Plancher de, 16, 65, 170, 188
Vallière (actor), 218
Valois (actor), 105
Vanhove, Cécile-Caroline Petit; *see* Petit-Vanhove, Cécile-Caroline-Charlotte
Vanhove, Charles-Joseph, 4, 26, 52, 81, 102, 144, 161, 251, 279
Vanhove, Ernest, 161
Variétés Amusantes (first), 10, 12, 16, 17, 30; *see also* Variétes-Palais-Royal
Variétés Amusantes (second), 168, 194, 206, 210, 219, 231, 253, 266; *see also* Variétés Comiques et Lyriques, *and* Lazzari, Ange
Variétés Comiques et Lyriques, 85, 112, 121; *see also* Lazzari, Ange, *and* Variétés Amusantes (second)
Variétés Etrangères, 286, 287
Variétés Montansier, 32, 44, 46, 64, 81, 90, 124, 128, 139, 174, 190, 220, 228, 229, 231, 233, 236, 237, 260, 265, 266, 279; *see also* Montagne, Théâtre de la
Variétés-Palais-Royal, 55, 61, 62, 78–80, 84, 90; *see also* République, Théâtre de la; Richelieu, Théâtre-Français, Rue de; *and* Variétés Amusantes (first)
Variétés Saint-Germain, 111
Vaudeville, 116–22, 144, 149, 150, 157, 161, 165, 185–88, 216, 219, 220, 236, 237, 240, 260, 267, 281, 286, 287
Vaudreuil, Joseph-Hyacinthe-François, Comte de, 3
Vauxhall d'Eté, 86, 111
Vauxhall d'Hiver, 117
Vengeance, Le (Bourlain-Dumaniant), 102
Vénitiens, Les (anon.), 274
Véritables honnêtes gens, Les (anon.), 252
Versailles, theatre at, 24, 31, 32, 42, 64, 191
Verseuil et Saint-Elmont (Ségur the Younger), 245
Vert Vert (Bernard-Valville), 57
Vestale, La (de Jouy), 163
Vestris, Marie-Rose-Gourgaud, 21, 26, 27, 47, 48, 53, 79, 95, 101, 102, 105, 130, 271
Veuve du républicain, La (Lesur and Loraux), 184
Viala, Agricole, 205, 209, 220
Victimes cloîtrées, Les (Monvel), 77, 78
Victor (Pixérécourt), 265
Vienne (actor), 10, 18, 66
Vieux Célibataire, Le (d'Harleville), 42, 283
Vigée, Louis-Guillaume-Bern-Etienne, 146, 157
Vignée-Lebrun, Elisabeth-Louise, 3
Villeneuve, Jean, 210
Villette, Charles-Michel, Marquis de, 96, 98
Villiers, Pierre-Antoine-Baptiste, 210
Vincent, François-André, 102, 107
Viotti, Giovanni-Battista, 13, 31, 58, 59, 84, 85, 95, 123
Virginie (Laharpe), 107, 108
Virginie (Ponceau), 99
Vivacité à l'épreuve, La (Vigée), 157
Volnais, Claudine-Placide Croizet, 279
Volontaires en route, Les (Rafford-Brienne), 188
Voltaire, François-Marie Arout de, 18, 26, 27, 29, 30, 41, 46, 47, 54, 55, 66, 68, 81, 82, 87, 90, 96–101, 103, 107, 131, 140, 146, 152, 155, 163, 165, 179, 181, 212, 229, 247, 261, 272, 274, 283
Voltaire à Romilly (d'Abancourt), 97
Voyage au Mont Saint-Bernard (Cherubini), 217
Voyage interrompu, Le (Picard), 276
Vraie Républicaine, La (Boissy), 150, 151

Wailly, Charles de, 1
Walpole, Horace, 265
Warwick (Laharpe), 50
Washington (Sauvigny), 95

Zaïre (Voltaire), 18, 66, 163, 274